The World Under Capitalism

The World Under Capitalism

Observations on Economics, Politics, History, and Culture

Branko Milanovic

polity

Copyright © Branko Milanovic 2025

The right of Branko Milanovic to be identified as Author of this Work has been asserted in accordance with the UK Copyright, Designs and Patents Act 1988.

First published in 2025 by Polity Press

Polity Press
65 Bridge Street
Cambridge CB2 1UR, UK

Polity Press
111 River Street
Hoboken, NJ 07030, USA

All rights reserved. Except for the quotation of short passages for the purpose of criticism and review, no part of this publication may be reproduced, stored in a retrieval system or transmitted, in any form or by any means, electronic, mechanical, photocopying, recording or otherwise, without the prior permission of the publisher.

ISBN-13: 978-1-5095-6776-8

A catalogue record for this book is available from the British Library.

Library of Congress Control Number: 2024944948

Typeset in 10.5 on 12pt Sabon
by Fakenham Prepress Solutions, Fakenham, Norfolk NR21 8NL
Printed and bound in Great Britain by TJ Books Limited, Padstow, Cornwall

The publisher has used its best endeavors to ensure that the URLs for external websites referred to in this book are correct and active at the time of going to press. However, the publisher has no responsibility for the websites and can make no guarantee that a site will remain live or that the content is or will remain appropriate.

Every effort has been made to trace all copyright holders, but if any have been overlooked the publisher will be pleased to include any necessary credits in any subsequent reprint or edition.

For further information on Polity, visit our website:
politybooks.com

CONTENTS

Detailed Contents	vii
Preface	xiii
Acknowledgments	xv
Part I The World Under Capitalism	**1**
1 Growth and Climate Change	3
2 Migration	25
3 Politics	43
Part II Inequality	**77**
4 Inequality Within Nations	79
5 Global Inequality	119
6 Wealth Inequality	141
7 Inequality and Literature	166
Part III Globalization and Multi-Polar World	**177**
8 Globalization	179
9 China	199
10 Russia	222

v

CONTENTS

Part IV   History   **243**

11 Economic History   245

12 Adam Smith   270

13 Ricardo and Marx   299

14 Communism   338

15 Transition to Capitalism   381

Part V   Reflections   **393**

16 Reflections   395

References   438

Index   461

DETAILED CONTENTS

Preface   xiii

Acknowledgments   xv

Part I   The World Under Capitalism   1

1 Growth and Climate Change   3

   1.1   The illusion of "degrowth" in a poor and unequal
world   3
   1.2   Degrowth: Solving the impasse by magical thinking   6
   1.3   Climate change, covid, and global inequality   10
   1.4   Is Norway the new East India Company?   13
   1.5   And does growth in the North by itself make
Africa poorer?   16
   1.6   Kate Raworth's economics of miracles   19
   1.7   Abundance, capitalism, and climate change   22

2 Migration   25

   2.1   Should some countries cease to exist?   25
   2.2   Migration into Europe: A problem with no solution   28
   2.3   Migration's economic positives and negatives   31
   2.4   Trade and migration: Substitutes or complements?   34
   2.5   Habermas and pimps: The world of the day and
the world of the night   37
   2.6   The simplicity of views regarding civil conflicts   40

vii

DETAILED CONTENTS

3	Politics		43
	3.1	What is a paleo-left agenda?	43
	3.2	Toward global progressiveness	47
	3.3	Democracy or dictatorship: Which works better?	51
	3.4	How is the world ruled?	54
	3.5	Multi-party kleptocracies rather than illiberal democracies	57
	3.6	Thinkin' 'bout a revolution	60
	3.7	There is no exit for dictators	64
	3.8	Trump as the ultimate triumph of neoliberalism	68
	3.9	What we owe to Donald Trump: A different angle	70
	3.10	The comprador intelligentsia	73

Part II Inequality **77**

4	Inequality Within Nations		79
	4.1	Why inequality matters	79
	4.2	In defence of equality (without welfare economics)	82
	4.3	Why twentieth-century tools cannot be used to address twenty-first-century income inequality	86
	4.4	The welfare state in the age of globalization	89
	4.5	All our needs are social	92
	4.6	Why the focus on horizontal inequality undermines efforts to reduce overall inequality	95
	4.7	Basic difference between wage inequality and income inequality studies	98
	4.8	Distinguishing incomes from capital and labor	101
	4.9	Why "Make America Denmark Again" will not happen	104
	4.10	À *la recherche* of the roots of US inequality "exceptionalism"	108
	4.11	What are the limits of Europe?	112
	4.12	The role of economics	115

5	Global Inequality		119
	5.1	The history of global inequality studies	119
	5.2	Athenian dialogues on global income inequality	123
	5.3	How much of your income is due to your citizenship?	127
	5.4	Is citizenship just a rent?	131

viii

DETAILED CONTENTS

| 5.5 | Why foreign aid cannot be regressive | 134 |
| 5.6 | Formal and actual similarities between climate change and global inequality, and suboptimality of the nation-state | 138 |

6 Wealth inequality — 141

6.1	What is wealth?	141
6.2	Historical wealth: How to compare Croesus and Bezos	145
6.3	My wealth and the lives of others	147
6.4	Dutiful dirges of Davos	151
6.5	On luxury	153
6.6	Absurdity of World Bank wealth accounting	156
6.7	Repeat after me: Wealth is not income and income is not consumption	158
6.8	Was everybody under socialism a millionaire?	163

7 Inequality and Literature — 166

7.1	Literature and inequality	166
7.2	Was the novel born and did it die with bourgeois society?	171
7.3	Inheritance, marriage, and swindle: The three ways to the top	174

Part III Globalization and Multi-Polar World — 177

8 Globalization — 179

8.1	Eleven theses on globalization	179
8.2	Disarticulation goes North	183
8.3	Let's go back to mercantilism and trade blocs!	187
8.4	The hidden dangers of Fukuyama-like triumphalism	190
8.5	How to dine alone ... in a hyper-competitive world	193
8.6	No one would be unemployed and no one would hold a job	196

9 China — 199

9.1	Socialism with Chinese characteristics for the young person: A review of the book of Xi Jinping's sayings	199
9.2	The long NEP, China, and Xi	203
9.3	Hayekian communism	207

DETAILED CONTENTS

9.4	*The World Turned Upside Down*: A critical review	210
9.5	License to kill: *The World Turned Upside Down*: A laudatory review	213
9.6	Interpreting or misinterpreting China's success	217

10 Russia — 222

10.1	Russia's circular economic history	222
10.2	The lessons and implications of seizing Russian oligarchs' assets	225
10.3	The novelty of technologically regressive import substitution	228
10.4	Russia's economic prospects: The short-run	231
10.5	Long term: Difficulties of import substitution and delocalization	235
10.6	What if Putin's true goals are different?	239

Part IV History — 243

11 Economic History — 245

11.1	Byzantium: Economic reflections on the Fall of Constantinople	245
11.2	Global poverty over the long term: Legitimate issues	249
11.3	On Eurocentrism in economics	252
11.4	Net economic output in history: Why we work	255
11.5	Capital as a historical concept	258
11.6	The plight of late industrializers: What if peasants do not want to move to cities?	261
11.7	Can Black Death explain the Industrial Revolution?	264
11.8	Why were the Balkans underdeveloped? A geographical hypothesis	266

12 Adam Smith — 270

12.1	Through the glass, darkly: Trying to figure out Adam Smith, the person	270
12.2	America's Adam Smith: A review of Glory M. Liu's *Adam Smith's America*	274
12.3	People, associations, and government policy in Adam Smith	278
12.4	Is democracy always better for the poor?	288

x

DETAILED CONTENTS

12.5	Why slave-owners never willingly emancipated their slaves	291
12.6	How Adam Smith proposed to have his cake and eat it too	296

13 Ricardo and Marx — 299

13.1	Ricardo, Marx, and interpersonal inequality	299
13.2	Reading David Ricardo's letters	303
13.3	The Ricardian windfall: David Ricardo and the absence of the equity-efficiency trade-off	308
13.4	The influence of Karl Marx—a counterfactual	311
13.5	Marx for me (and hopefully for others too)	315
13.6	Marx on income inequality under capitalism	318
13.7	Transcending capitalism: Three different ways?	321
13.8	On unproductive labor	325
13.9	When Tocqueville and Marx agreed	328
13.10	A short essay on the differences between Marx and Keynes	332
13.11	Marx in Amerika	335

14 Communism — 338

14.1	A secular religion that lasted one century	338
14.2	State capitalism one hundred years ago and today	341
14.3	Milton Friedman and labor-managed enterprises	344
14.4	Socialist enterprise power structure and the soft-budget constraint	347
14.5	Disciplining workers in a workers' state	351
14.6	How I lost my past	354
14.7	The red bourgeoisie	357
14.8	On charisma and greyness under communism	360
14.9	Trotsky after Kolakowski	363
14.10	Notes on Fanon	366
14.11	The book of the dead: Victor Serge's *Notebooks 1936–1947*	369
14.12	Did socialism keep capitalism equal?	373
14.13	Gorbachev: A politician who did not want to rule	376
14.14	Did post-Marxist theories destroy communist regimes?	378

15 Transition to Capitalism — 381

15.1	Democracy of convenience, not of choice: Why is Eastern Europe different?	381

xi

DETAILED CONTENTS

15.2	Secessionism and the collapse of communist federations	384
15.3	Coase theorem and methodological nationalism	388
15.4	Trump and Gorbachev	390

Part V Reflections — 393

16 Reflections — 395

16.1	Non-exemplary lives	395
16.2	The perverse seductiveness of Fernando Pessoa	397
16.3	Henry and Kant: Outsourcing morality	400
16.4	The mistake of using the Kantian criterion in ordinary economic life	402
16.5	Is liberal democracy part of human development?	406
16.6	Living in own ideology ... until it falls apart	409
16.7	Freedom to be "wrong": The greatest advantage of democracy	412
16.8	99 percent Utopia and money	415
16.9	On the general futility of political discussions with people	419
16.10	The many in one: A review of Amartya Sen's *Home in the World: A Memoir*	422
16.11	*Du passé faisons table rase*	426
16.12	English language and American solipsism	428
16.13	The problems of authenticity under capitalism	431
16.14	The abolition of paper and the pompous rule of the present	433
16.15	Who are we?	436

References	438
Index	461

xii

PREFACE

This book contains selected short essays written between 2014 and 2024 and published on my blogs and Substack. Only a couple of them were written for specific occasions (The Adam Smith lecture in Edinburgh) or published as op-eds. The subjects are those that, for most of my life, I was interested in: income and wealth inequality, economic growth, migration, history of economic thought, globalization, Russia, and China. They are relatively short pieces, containing between 1,000 and 1,500 words.

Of all my writings, including academic articles and books, I found the writing of short essays the most pleasurable. They were written on the spur of the moment, on a given topic, and at a single go. I would have an idea, which would come to me while strolling or reading, and I would then be seized by a burst of impatience to write about it and share it with others. Writing a blog would take me between an hour and two, almost never longer. In some cases, I would interrupt my walk, hurry home trying to remember all the clever phrases that seemingly so easily and so naturally came to me when walking, and write them down before I forgot them. I would write quickly, perhaps even impatiently. I would then read the text just once or twice, and publish it on the Web. The pleasure of the exercise came both from writing on something very specific (for the form would not allow addressing numerous topics in one piece), ability to express what was on my mind immediately, and to spread it, equally immediately, to "the rest of the world." The latter was very important to me. It allowed me to avoid the editing, including self-editing, which often improves the text but leads to the loss of freshness, and of that burning desire – recognized by the readers – to write what is on one's mind. Now, almost instantly too, the writer gets a response from the

PREFACE

readers and can gauge what they are thinking or feeling. Are we on the same wavelength or not?

These advantages have their reverse side too. The topics that interest me today may become indifferent to me after some time. And, more importantly, they can lose all interest for the audience. Thus, the genre of short texts, often journalistic articles, which are published *ex post* as a collection, is a very specific genre: it gains from the directness and immediacy, but loses with the passage of time. I believe, however, that I do not have to fear too much from the latter. It may not apply with the usual strength to most of the short essays published here. The reason is that, while the essays were often triggered by events, accidents, or thoughts that came suddenly, they address issues that are not affected easily by the passage of time. When I write about what drives global inequality down, what it means to be rich in different societies, or how that wealth may be measured, or what type of citizenship rights migrants should have, or whether one can be a good social scientist while never politically active, or what is the "correct" way to interpret Adam Smith's *Theory of Moral Sentiments*, these are not the topics likely to disappear from our purview within any conceivable period of time. So, I please myself to believe that the pieces published here retain the immediacy and freshness with which they were drafted, while suffering relatively little from obsolescence. They can indeed suffer from the difference in interests between the writer and the public. What I find interesting and worth writing about may not be what others may find worth reading. But this is a general problem of the relationship between the writer and their audience, not the problem of the literary genre.

The original blogs or essays have been corrected only for typos or English language mistakes. There are practically no other editing interventions. This was a prior decision, before I even selected the pieces to be published; although, when I reread the texts, even had I not so decided at the outset, I would not have made any changes. Neither my thinking on these topics, nor my way of expressing it have changed in the meantime. They are thus here in the way they were originally written, and, I am delighted, in paper form, which ultimately might prove more durable than the scintillating effervescence of electronic publishing.

New York, July 5, 2024

ACKNOWLEDGMENTS

This book would not have existed were it not for the idea and encouragement that my editor Ian Malcolm, with whom I have, with great pleasure, worked before, gave me to collect my blogs, short essays, and Substacks in one place, select those that I thought worth publishing, and thus have them move from the ephemeral world of electronic self-publishing to the old-fashioned but ultimately more sturdy and durable world of paper print. I always thought that it would be a good idea to see my blogs in a paper edition but without Ian it would have never happened. It was not easy to decide which, from among some 500 posts that I wrote over a decade, would be granted this new life. As mentioned in the Introduction, we decided to drop almost all book reviews. It was not an always easy decision because I really liked some books and some reviews. So we decided to keep a few to the extent that they could be easily "allocated" into different thematic sections.

The decision to leave the writing exactly the same as it was when the articles were originally published meant that the copy-editing job was relatively light. However. English mistakes, typos and only in a few cases unclear sentences had to be corrected. Susan Beer and David Watson did an excellent job in catching all English-language mistakes, wrongly-placed upper case letters or commas, and mixed-up metaphors. I am very grateful to them for that work. Ellen McDonald-Kramer worked on the promotion of the book and translations. The index was expertly done by Elizabeth Ball.

It is hard for me to decide whom else to thank. This is because the pieces that the reader will find in the book were written under the great variety of circumstances: mostly when I was lying on my bed in the apartment in New York, or sitting at my desk at the Graduate

xv

ACKNOWLEDGMENTS

Center of City University in New York. But some were written in cafes around the world, a couple in restaurants while discussing finer points with bar-tenders, a couple even on a beach in Puerto Rico, and one in a museum in Shanghai. All these people who were around, helping with coffee, food and often the wine, should be thanked. But they are many and I do not remember their names. Perhaps some of them might, by accident, see this book and then remember ... To all of them my heart-felt thanks.

Branko Milanovic
Washington, 26 December 2024

— PART I —

THE WORLD UNDER CAPITALISM

— 1 —

GROWTH AND CLIMATE CHANGE

1.1 The illusion of "degrowth" in a poor and unequal world

I recently had Twitter [now X] and email discussions with a couple of people who are strong proponents of "degrowth." From these exchanges I got the impression that they were unaware of just how unequal and poor (yes, poor) the world is today and what the trade-offs would be if we really were to decide to fix the volume of goods and services produced and consumed in the world at the current level.

This is just an attempt to present some back-of the-envelope calculations, which should be very much improved in a serious attempt to examine the alternatives.

Let us suppose, for the sake of argument, that we interpret "degrowth" as the decision to fix global GDP at its current level (assuming for the time being that the amount of emissions is also fixed at the current level). Then, unless we change the distribution of income, we are condemning to permanent abject poverty some 15 percent of the world's population, who currently earn less than $1.90 per day, and some quarter of humankind, who earn less than $2.50 per day. (All dollar amounts here are in PPP terms; that is, in dollars of equal purchasing power across the world, based on the 2011 International Comparison Project.)

Keeping so many people in abject poverty so that the rich can continue to enjoy their current standard of living is obviously something that the proponents of degrowth would not agree with. One of my correspondents explicitly rejected that scenario. So, what are we to do then? We can, of course, they say, increase the incomes of the poor and reduce the incomes of the rich, so that we stay within the envelope of the current global GDP. So, let's suppose that we decide to "allow" everybody to reach the level of median income currently existing in Western countries, and, as people who are below that level move toward the target, we gradually reduce incomes of the rich (for simplicity I shall assume all to be living in the West).

The "problem" is that the median after-tax income in the West (about $14,600 per person per year) is at the 91st percentile of the global income distribution. Clearly, if we let 90 percent of people increase their incomes to that level, this would "burst" our GDP envelope several times over (2.7 times to be exact). We cannot be this "generous." Let us suppose next that we let everybody reach only the income level that is slightly higher than the Western tenth percentile, exactly that of the thirteenth Western percentile ($5,500 per person per year). Now, by a "lucky accident," the Western thirteenth percentile coincides with the global mean income, which is at the 73rd global percentile. We could bring up all the bottom 72 percent of the world population to that level, but we should obviously also have to reduce incomes of everybody above so that the entire world lives at the global mean.

How much of a reduction would this imply for the global top 27 percent (those with incomes above the global mean)? Their incomes would have to be cut by almost two-thirds. Most of them, as we have said, live in the West. The immiseration of the West would not take place through transfers to the poor: we have "allowed" them to produce and earn more. The immiseration of the West would take place through gradual and sustained reduction of production and income until everybody who is "rich" loses sufficiently so that they drop to the level of the global mean. On average, as have seen, the drop would be about two-thirds, but the very rich would have to lose more: the global top decile would have to lose 80 percent of their income; the global top ventile (the richest 5%) would have to lose 84 percent: and so on. Factories, trains, airports, schools, should work one-third of their normal time; electricity, heating, and hot water would be available for eight hours a day; cars may be driven one day out of three; we would work only thirteen hours per week (Keynes would be happy to know he had guessed correctly about reduced hours in his *Economic Possibilities for our Grandchildren*), etc.—all in order to produce only a third as many goods and services that the West is producing now.

Stop for a moment to consider the enormity of what is being proposed here. The global Gini would go to zero, from the current value of 65. The world would have to move from an inequality level that is higher than that of South Africa to a complete equality that

GROWTH AND CLIMATE CHANGE

has never existed in any recorded society. Countries have difficulties implementing policies that reduce Gini by 2 to 3 points, and we are proposing here to shave off 65 Gini points.

On top of this, the world population is projected to increase by several billion. Our envelope, which is fixed in the absolute amount, will have to sustain more people; in other words, the mean income will have to drop further.

On the positive side, however, such a dramatic squeeze of the income distribution will change consumption patterns. We know that the rich create more emissions per dollar spent than the poor. This is because they consume emission-intensive services and goods, like airplane trips and meat, much more than the poor do. Squeezing everybody to the same level would mean that the total emissions produced by the new GDP (that would remain the same in value but whose composition would change) would be less. There would be thus some "slack" in our envelope, which might allow us either to allow some people be a bit better off than the rest, or to move everybody to a mean income slightly above that of the Western thirteenth percentile.

Say that the increase in population and the decline in average emissions per dollar spent just offset each other: we are then back to the original scenario described before, when everybody will have to live at the point of the current Western thirteenth percentile and the rich world would have to lose about 2/3 of their income.

It does not seem to me that this outcome, however much we may tweak the assumptions, is something that is even vaguely likely to find any political support anywhere, including from the proponents of degrowth themselves, many of whom would have to cut their consumption by perhaps 80 to 90 percent. It would make more sense, if we want to think seriously about how to reduce emissions, not to engage in the illusions of degrowth in a very poor and unequal world but to think how the most emission-intensive goods and services could be taxed in order to reduce their consumption. The increase in their relative prices would cut real income of the rich (who consume them) and would reduce, even if slightly, global inequality. Obviously, we need to think about how new technologies can be harnessed to make the world more environment-friendly. But degrowing is not the way to go.

(Published November 18, 2017)

1.2 Degrowth: Solving the impasse by magical thinking

The difficulty of discussion with degrowers comes from the fact that they, and the rest of us, live in two different ideological worlds. Degrowers live in a world of magic, where merely by listing the names of desirable ends somehow makes them happen. In that world, one does not need to bother with numbers or facts, trade-offs, first or second bests; one merely needs to conjure up what he/she desires and it will be there.

Now, degrowers are not irrational people. The reason why they are pushed into this magical corner is because when they try to "do the numbers" they are led to an impasse. They do not want to allow for a significant increase in world GDP because it will, even if decoupling (of which they are skeptical) happens, drive energy emissions too high. If one wants to keep world GDP more-or-less as it is there are two choices. One can (A) "freeze" today's global income distributions so that some 10 to 15 percent of the world population continue to live below the absolute poverty line, and one-half of the world population continues to live below $PPP7 dollars per day (which is, by the way, much less than the Western poverty line). But this is unacceptable to the poor people, to the poor countries, and even to degrowers themselves.

Thus, they must try something else: introduce a different distribution (B) where everybody who is above the current mean world income ($PPP16 per day) is driven down to this mean, and the poor countries and people are, at least for a while, allowed to continue growing until they too achieve the level of $PPP16 per day. But, the problem with that approach is that one would have to engage in a massive reduction of incomes for all those who make more than $PPP16, which is practically all of the Western population. Only 14 percent of the population in Western countries live at a level of income lower than the global mean. This is probably the most important statistic that one should keep in mind. Degrowers need to convince 86 percent of the population living in rich countries that their incomes are too high and need to be reduced. They would have to preside over economic depressions for about a decade, and then let the new real income stay at that level indefinitely. (Even that would not quite solve the problem because in the meantime, many poor countries would have reached the level of $PPP16 per day and they too would have to be prevented from growing further.) It is quite obvious that such a proposition is a political suicide. Thus, degrowers do not wish to spell it out.

They are brought to an impasse. They cannot condemn to perpetual poverty people in developing countries who are just seeing the glimpses of a better life, nor can they reasonably argue that incomes of nine out of ten Westerners ought to be reduced.

The way out of the impasse is to engage in semi-magical and then outright magical thinking.

Semi-magical thinking (that is, thinking where the objective—however laudable—is not linked to any tools of achieving it) is to argue that GDP is not a correct measure of welfare, or that better outcomes in certain dimensions can be achieved by countries or peoples with a lower GDP (or lower incomes). Both propositions are correct.

GDP does leave out non-commercialized activities that are welfare-enhancing. It is, like every other measure, imperfect and one-dimensional. But it is imperfect at the edges, while fairly accurate overall. Richer countries are generally better-off in almost all metrics, from education, life expectancy, child mortality to women's employment, etc. Not only that: richer people are also on average healthier, better educated, and happier. Income indeed buys you health and happiness. (It does not guarantee that you are a better person; but that's a different topic.) The metric of income or GDP is strongly associated with positive outcomes, whether we compare countries to each other, or people (within a country) to each other. This is something so obvious that it is bizarre that one needs to restate it: people migrate from Morocco to France because France is a richer country and they will be better-off there. American Blacks are worse off than American Whites in all dimensions, not least in terms of their income. This is the background to the Black Lives Matter movement that wants to make Blacks better off and equal in income and health to Whites.

Since this fails, the next approach taken by degrowers consists in pulling out individual cases of countries that have performed exceptionally well on some metrics (like Cuba on health) and those that have performed exceptionally badly (like the US on life expectancy) and to argue that a certain desirable outcome can be achieved with much less money. It is indeed true that some countries or some people, despite their lack of income, have achieved excellent things, while others have used their income inefficiently or wastefully. But, such individual examples do not overturn the regularities described in the previous paragraph. What degrowers do is to first metaphorically run a regression of a desirable outcome on GDP or income, and, when they observe that

THE WORLD UNDER CAPITALISM

the two are closely correlated, forget about the regression, pull out an outlier, and claim that the outlier shows that the relationship does not exist.

That is clearly wrong too. So, the next stage in semi-magical thinking consists in trying to convince people that they are wrongly pursing the Golden Calf of wealth and that much more modest lives would be better, or at least are feasible. To that effect they use baskets of goods and services that allow a "modest" standard of living and satisfy all basic needs. But they fail to show us how such "modest needs" are to be implemented: how will people be obliged to consume only so much and not more? In war situations, this is done through rationing. Indeed, one could ration the number of square meters of textile that each household may be able to buy, introduce meat and gasoline coupons, and so forth. It has been done many times. But degrowers know that a wartime economy in peacetime would not be politically acceptable, so they just do the basket calculation, show that it is compatible with "planetary boundaries," and leave it at that. How we are going to have that basket accepted by people, or implemented against their will, is not something they desire to be disturbed with.

After this comes direct magical or religious thinking. Its first component, in an asceticism reminiscent of early Christendom, is to point out the vanity of all material acquisitions. People indeed can live happy lives with much less "stuff." That is true for some special people like Christian or Buddhist monks. For example, Simeon the Stylite, an early Christian monk, is reputed to have lived several decades on top of a pillar in a desert. But this is not true for the remaining 99.99 percent of the people, who are not attracted by monastic lives. And it certainly is not true today, when capitalism, and thus both the relentless search for profit and the value system that places wealth on the pedestal, is more dominant than ever. Had degrowers preached material abstinence in thirteenth-century Europe, or tenth-century Byzantium, it might have had more appeal. Commercial society, capitalism, and numerical abilities were less developed than today. But now, the relevance of moral preaching of abstinence is close to zero.

When all arguments and quasi-arguments are exhausted, the magical thinking moves into the realm of rhetoric. Thinking is now replaced by phrase-mongering: "thriving," "flourishing," and "self-fulfilling" lives are possible and they are just around the corner. Everybody can be happier with much less. We can just cultivate our own gardens. If you string all the desirable words

8

together, "no exploitation," "living wage," "ethical business," "self-sufficiency," "fair price," they will somehow take on a life of their own and the Elysian fields will open up in front of us. For all and forever.

(Published April 28, 2021)

1.3 Climate change, covid, and global inequality

I recently criticized what I regard as "magical" or quasi-religious thinking among degrowers. It was not the first time. I have criticized Kate Raworth's interesting, but thoroughly "magical," book (Section 1.6 below) and have had a debate with Jason Hickel (Section 1.1 above). So, the question can rightly be asked: what is non-magical thinking in dealing with climate change?

I am not original in asking this. This is an area that many (hundreds or thousands) have studied and know much better than I. But it is an area where I think that the knowledge of global inequality can be usefully combined to produce some tentative answers.

High global inequality, otherwise a scourge, can here be used to our advantage. We know that the top decile of world population (call them "the rich") receives about 45–47 percent of global income. We also know that the elasticity of carbon emissions with respect to income is one, which is a fancy way of saying that as real income goes up by 10 percent, we generate 10 percent more emissions. This then implies that the top global decile is responsible for 45–47 percent of all emissions. That percentage can be calculated with even more precision because we have detailed consumption data (by a number of categories, running into hundreds) and we can assign to each consumption category its precise carbon footprint. It is not unlikely that we could find that the carbon emissions of the top decile are even over one-half of the total.

The question thus gets simplified. Suppose that we draw up a list of goods and services that are (a) carbon intensive and (b) consumed predominantly by the rich. We could then in a concerted international action try to curb significantly the consumption of such goods and services, while leaving *entirely free* other decisions: there would be no limits to growth, no degrowth in either poor or rich countries.

The entire onus of the adjustment falls on the rich. Who are the rich, *viz.* the global top decile? About 450 million people from the Western countries, or the entire upper half of Western countries' income distributions; some 30–35 million people from both Eastern Europe and Latin America, that is respectively about 10 percent and 5 percent of their total populations; about 160 million people from Asia or 5 percent of its population; and a very small number of people from Africa.

Curbing consumption can be done either through rationing or draconian taxation. Both are feasible technically, although their political acceptability may be another matter.

If one were to use rationing, one could introduce physical targets: there will be only x liters of gas per car annually and no family will be allowed to have more than two cars; or y kilograms of meat per person per month. Clearly, there may be a black market for gas or meat, but the overall limits will be observed simply because they are given by the total availability of coupons. Some people might think that rationing is extraordinary, and I agree with them. But it has been done in a number of countries under wartime, and at times even during peacetime conditions, and it has worked. If indeed we face an emergency of such "terminal" proportions as the advocates of climate change claim, I do not see any reason why we should not resort to extreme measures.

But another approach (draconian taxation) is possible too. Instead of limiting physical quantities of goods and services that fulfil criteria (a) and (b) we could impose extremely heavy taxes on them. There is always a tax rate that would drive consumption of a good down to the level that we have in mind. It is here that I think we can use—again if we believe that the climate emergency is so dire—the lessons of covid.

Let me illustrate that by using air transport, one of the important sources of emissions. No one in the world could have imagined that air traffic could be cut by 60 percent in one year. This is what happened in 2020. What is our experience? That it is indeed an inconvenience but did the world survive? Yes. Did we reorganize our lives so as not to travel, and especially not to travel far because most countries closed their borders, which further dampened travel? Yes. So, is a permanent decrease of 60 percent in air travel possible to envisage? Yes.

If we were serious, we could, in this case, as in the others, argue for such a tax that would keep air travel at its 2020 level indefinitely. The tax might mean that a ticket between New York and London would not cost $400, but $4,000, that people in rich Western countries might travel to foreign countries once in a decade rather than once per year, but, as we learned from the experience of 2020, we can do it and we can live with it.

Economic dislocations, it is true, would be huge. It is not only the question of the entire upper middle class and the rich in advanced countries (and, as we have seen, elsewhere) losing significant parts of their real income as prices of most "staple" commodities (for them) increase by two, three, or ten times; the dislocation would affect large sectors of the economy. Go back to the example of travel. A permanent 60 percent decrease would more than halve the number of airline employees, would practically leave Boeing and Airbus with no new orders for airplanes for years, and possibly lead to a liquidation of one of them, would decimate hotel industry, close even more restaurants than were closed by the pandemic, and make parts of most touristy cities that currently complain of excess of tourists (Barcelona, Venice, Florence, probably even London and New York) look like ghost towns. The effects would trickle down: unemployment will increase, incomes will plummet, the West will record the largest real income decline since the Great Depression.

However, if such policies were steadfastly pursued for a decade or two, not only would emissions plummet too (as they did in 2020), but our behavior, and ultimately the economy, would adjust. People will find jobs in different activities that will remain untaxed and thus relatively cheaper and the demand for them will go up. Revenues collected from taxing "bad" activities may be used to subsidize "good" activities or retrain people who have lost their jobs. We may not be able to drive to visit friends and family every week, but we shall be able, using our covid experience, to see them on screen. Secondary homes could be taxed in such a confiscatory manner that most people will be eager to sell them. Governments could then buy them, create a kind of Paradores (Spanish state-owned hotel chain that uses vacated monasteries), and people in (say) England, rather than jetting off on vacation to Thailand, would spend their annual holidays nearby in some of the formerly privately owned mansions.

This is not magical thinking. These are policies that, with intergovernmental cooperation, knowledge of economics, data on global inequality, and the experience of covid, could be implemented. Is there appetite for such policies? I do not know. I think that most of the population of rich countries would not be excited if told that a quasi lock-down would have to continue for an indefinite future. But, if conditions become so dire that the public mood shifts, if climate change is but a long-term covid, if we have learned to live with covid and to survive, could we not adjust to this "new normal" too? I do not know—but I think it would be fair and candid of the partisans of radical change to put these questions squarely in front of the public and not to try to hoodwink them with the sweet talk of "thriving" monastic lives.

(Published February 21, 2021)

1.4 Is Norway the new East India Company?

In the eighteenth century, the English-led East India Company gradually came to control most of India. Its rule was a disaster for India, but made many directors and stockholders of the company exceedingly rich. The wealth enabled many of them to play important roles in English political, intellectual, and business life. As Adam Smith, an uncompromising critic of the Company, wrote: "The government of an exclusive company of merchants is, perhaps, the worst of all governments for any country whatever" (*Wealth of Nations*, bk. IV, ch. 7). Faced with so many depredations, the British government finally took away the monopoly of Indian trade from the company in the midst of the Napoleonic wars.

This led the Company to redouble its efforts elsewhere: to trade with China. The problem with China was that nothing that company could sell to the Chinese was of interest to them. There was a lot that the company wanted to buy from China (porcelain, tea) but nothing to sell. Until it came to the idea of using opium produced in India to sell to China. Despite the ban that the Chinese government had put on opium imports there was domestic demand for it. To overcome the ban, and in order to sell a widely addictive substance that for ethical reasons it could not sell anywhere else, the company decided to engage in a war to open Chinese ports. This was the origin of the infamous Opium War whose final outcome in 1842 was the opening of five Chinese "treaty ports," the cession of Hong Kong, and extraterritoriality for foreigners living in China. The "century of humiliations" had begun. And the company could finally sell to far-away foreigners a product of whose consumption they themselves disapproved.

The Norwegian government is one of the most active governments in highlighting the threat of climate change. It tries to replace almost entirely the country's use of gas-fueled cars by electric. It is proud of the decrease of the footprint of its consumption. It funds international activities that are supposed to limit and reverse deforestation in the world. Yet, at the same time, for half a century, Norway has been one of significant world producers, and even more important, exporters, of oil and gas (for gas, the third largest in the world), and some 50 percent of its goods exports consist of gas and oil. Moreover, the government has recently decided to expand the exploration and production of gas and oil in one of the areas that the very same government acknowledges are most sensitive to climate change—the Arctic Circle.

Norway thus increases the production and sales of a commodity that it deems noxious itself, and sells it, like the East India Company did with opium, to faraway foreigners, while staying domestically clean. "Money has no smell."

Norway's behavior is not only surprising because it is hypocritical: the virtue-signaling stands in a manifest contrast with what the government does. It is even more striking when so many climate-change activists, in their struggle to reduce emissions, try to convince poorer and middle-income countries of the benefits of lower production and consumption.

The question can then be asked: if they are so clearly unable to convince the population and the government of the richest country in the world of the benefits of climate control, what type of arguments do they plan to use to convince Mexico, Gabon, Nigeria, or Russia to reduce the production of gas and oil? These are countries whose incomes are a fraction of Norway's: for example, the median-income person in Nigeria has one-twentieth (not a typo: 1/20) of the real income of the median-income person in Norway.

I can fully understand why Mexico or Nigeria would refuse to reduce production of gas and oil. Without it, there would be a significant impoverishment of their population. But there will be no impoverishment of the Norwegian population—by any reasonable metric. Norway, a country with a very high level of income (GDP per capita of 66,000 international dollars, 20 percent higher than that of the United States) and with this income fairly equally distributed among its citizens (Gini coefficient of 26), should be able to give up the production of its "opium-equivalent." But there is apparently no political support for such a measure. The current government, in its new decision about a more extensive exploration and production, seems fully assured of majority support.

There is here a very important lesson for all climate-change activists. They need, as I have many times insisted, to think much more seriously about the trade-off between economic growth and climate-change control. While in their models, the advantages of controlling climate change are incontrovertible, when they come to policies that need to be implemented, from taxes on airplane fuel, to taxes on gas (which provoked the Gilets Jaunes movement in France), they face popular resistance. The popular resistance is due to the unwillingness of almost anyone in the world to accept lower income. Climate-change activists might talk in their conferences about people "thriving" on lower incomes, but when offered that alternative, even the citizens of the richest country in the world decline it.

GROWTH AND CLIMATE CHANGE

If we want really to confront—as opposed to just talking about—climate change we should first be rid of extreme hypocrisy (like this), and second, design policies that would be acceptable to the population. And we should start with rich countries, not only because historically they have been the most important contributors to climate change (through historical accumulation of emissions) but because they should be able to bear costs more easily than the rest.

(Published July 23, 2023)

1.5 And does growth in the North by itself make Africa poorer?

In a recently published paper on the effects of climate change on growth, Noah Diffenbaugh and Marshall Burke argue, using a complex model, that the temperature change driven by CO_2 emissions has affected poor counties the most, and reduced their growth by a cumulative 17 to 31 percent between 1961 and 2010. Population-weighted between-country inequality has therefore increased because of climate change. The key result of their study, published in the American journal *Proceedings of the National Academy of Sciences,* is in a graph (panel B) shown in Figure 1.1.

It shows that, compared to the situation without climate change, the poorest 10 percent of the population in the world (more exactly, the poorest decile of world population, if people are ranked by their countries' GDPs per capita) have lost a quarter of their output, while the rich countries have gained approximately 25 percent.

Now, the full model is impossible to figure out from the accompanying text of just five pages, but, so far as I can tell, it is based on three key links. First, that increased carbon emissions caused an increase in worldwide temperature. Second, that the increase in temperature is uneven across the world. Third, that the increase in temperature is

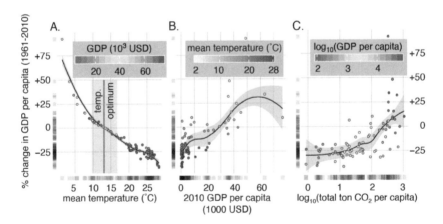

Figure 1.1 Relationship between the economic impact of historical global warming and temperature, wealth, and cumulative carbon emissions

Source: Noah S. Diffenbaugh and Michael Burke, "Global warming has increased global economic inequality," *Proceedings of the National Academy of Sciences,* 2019. Available at https://www.pnas.org/doi/epdf/10.1073/pnas.1816020116.

GROWTH AND CLIMATE CHANGE

particularly bad for the countries in the tropics which already suffer from a hot climate, and from extreme climate events like droughts, storms, etc. As the authors write: "historical warming has reduced economic growth and lowered per capita GDP" of poor countries because "the mean temperature of … many poor countries lies in the extreme warm tail," which is too high for economic activity.

Of the three links the most difficult to prove is, I think, the third: that climate change (more exactly, higher temperature) is responsible for the slowdown in poor countries' growth (mostly in Africa). Notice that if true, the claim would imply a theory of growth largely driven by geography and climate. For, if the recent increase in temperature in Africa pushed the continent further away from the optimal temperature for economic activity (which, according to the authors' model, is around 13 degrees Celsius), then the fact that Africa was, even before anyone heard of climate change, warmer than this optimal temperature, must have historically had a negative effect on Africa's growth.

We are thus facing here a variant of economic growth theories that put the emphasis not only on exogenous factors, not only on geography (like navigable rivers, impassable mountains), but on specific exogenous geographic factors like climate. The growth regression (the step No. 3) reported in the paper is breathtaking in its simplicity. It is a country fixed effect panel regression where a country's growth rate depends on contemporaneous temperature and precipitation (both linearly and squared), country and time fixed effects … and nothing else! No employment, no capital, no saving rates, no institutions, no civil wars …

I will leave it at that: climatological explanations have been used for many things over the centuries: from Montesquieu, who thought that climate explained differences in political systems, to Paul Bairoch's argument regarding the non-transmission of the agricultural revolution.

But let's suppose that this explanation is true and that indeed, as the authors claim, climate change was responsible for slowing the growth of poor countries. That would have enormous consequences (which, by the way, they, at least in this paper, fail to mention).

Since the change in climate is brought about by the historical emissions of the currently rich counties (the stock effect), and by their current emissions, plus those of China (the flow effect), this means that the very growth in the North is directly responsible for the lack of growth in the South. The implication is quite extraordinary. In the past, *dependencia* theorists proposed that the "center," the Global North, deepened the underdevelopment of the Global South through

17

THE WORLD UNDER CAPITALISM

a division of labor that let the South produce only agricultural goods; or that the Global North helped develop only some parts of Southern economies, while leaving the rest underdeveloped. Such theories saw delinking from the North as a solution.

But the important point is to notice that in those theories the integration of the Global North and the Global South was bad for the South; in the new "climate theories" it is simply the fact that the North *grows* that is bad. It need not interact with the South at all. Northern growth alone makes the South poorer. This is quite extraordinary. It is not that my exploiting or cheating somebody is a condition for my wealth; it is that my wealth as such (acquiring it with no interaction with the injured party) is bad news for somebody else (Africa in this particular case).

Moreover, it means that the very growth of the Global North makes the reduction or the eventual elimination of African poverty difficult, if not impossible. If we are to believe the authors, then every percentage point of additional GDP in the North makes conditions in Africa worse and the reduction of poverty there more difficult.

Thus, for the elimination of global poverty, we need a drastic reduction in emissions, which means an absolute reduction of Northern incomes, namely, a steady negative rate of growth of rich countries.

I will leave it to the reader to reflect on how politically feasible such a solution is (I wrote about that before in Section 1.1 and will again in Section 1.6)—but I think that the enormity of the implications of these results should be realized. Now, whether the results really make sense or not: whether the level of temperature by itself is a significant explanatory factor of economic development is a thing that needs to be proved. More panel regressions of economic growth? I thought we had left them in the 1990s but perhaps I was wrong.

(Published April 22, 2019)

1.6 Kate Raworth's economics of miracles

My first summer book to read and review is Kate Raworth's very successful *Doughnut Economics: Seven Ways to Think Like the 21st-Century Economist*. It is an ambitious book, whose objective is to change the ways economists think, and the economics is framed in order to respond to calls for "limits to growth." It thus reconsiders the organization of the economy, from the financial sector, money creation, ownership structure of companies to the distribution of assets. It also wrestles with the "addiction" to economic growth, not only among policy-makers but among most of the population (who understandably want more things) and it finally envisages a rich society with "zero growth." The last term is avoided by Raworth by saying she is agnostic about growth and by presenting future growth as undulating around a stable level, with the economy at times going down and at times up ("[we] embrace growth without exacting it," p. 270: whatever that means).

The book is probably better than its competitors in the area. For example, Raworth's discussion of inequality, where she argues for the equalization of endowments rather than expansion of policies that redistribute current income, makes lots of sense. Suggestions for the use of various incentives to make companies more environment-friendly are also plausible. Perhaps even the imaginative use of electronic currencies may help.

Yet the book fails to convince for three reasons.

First, it never faces squarely (or even indirectly) the fact that if everybody in the world is to be "allowed" to have income level equal to the current median in the rich countries, world GDP would have to increase three times—not accounting for the rise in the world population. This is a fact for which Raworth has no answer and thus prefers not to mention. (For, obviously, if one is against trebling world GDP, one needs either to accept that half of the world population will continue living in poverty, or to produce some evidence that carbon intensity of production will suddenly plummet.)

Second, numerous examples of companies and people who do innovative "green" things are listed (which is quite useful) but their importance is never assessed. The reader is right, I think, to feel that their importance is marginal and, while they represent progress, this is minimal compared to what needs to happen.

Third, the interpretation of the current phase of globalized capitalism is, in my opinion, wrong. Rather than seeing it, as Raworth does, as becoming more cooperative and "gentler," it is more correct to see the inroads of commodification into our personal lives (which we not only willingly accept but promote) as moving us further toward a self-centered, money- and success-oriented society—that is, going exactly in the opposite direction from that which Raworth favors.

I will illustrate this final point with Raworth's discussion of intrinsic vs. extrinsic motivation. This last point (chapter 3), where Raworth shows, based on empirical studies, that extrinsic (money-driven) motivations may at times produce worse outcomes than the use of non-cash motivation (emulation, social pressure, etc.) is, in my opinion, the best part of the book, but it is also one where I disagree, not with the arguments, but with Raworth's interpretation of the current state of the world and tacit forecasts for the future.

Raworth very persuasively shows that working on intrinsic motivations may often be preferable (measured in terms of hard-nosed efficiency) to using cash grants. I agree with that (actually, I just follow the studies that show that) but I think that contemporary hyper-commercialized capitalism leads us more and more to value only monetary incentives and to disregard others—even if the latter can produce better outcomes. But to do so they ("intrinsic incentives") have to be grounded in traditional social norms, traditional hierarchy, social capital, and the like, the very things that globalized capitalism erodes daily. Thus, I conclude that non-cash incentives, despite their advantages in many situations, are doomed to extinction. Kate implicitly argues the opposite: if they are better they should be used more. But by whom? What are the social forces to promote them? Who has the incentive to do so? Is today's societies' ethos compatible with them?

And here appears the major weakness of the book. The world Kate has in mind is a world essentially devoid of major *social* contradictions. It often comes close to the world of Bastiat's "universal harmonies." In many instances, Kate writes in the first-person plural, as if the entire world had the same "objective": so "we" have to make sure the economy does not exceed the natural bounds of the Earth's "carrying capacity," "we" have to keep inequality within the acceptable limits, "we" have an interest in a stable climate, "we" need the commons sector. But in most of real-world economics and politics, there is no "we" that includes 7.5 billion people. Different class and national interests are fighting each other.

The same "we-ism" is apparent when Raworth calls for deemphasis of (or "agnosticism" about) economic growth. I have already mentioned that the world's poor get short shrift, but the argument about why growth in the rich countries should cease, and how to go about curbing it, is also presented in a most confused fashion (and perhaps there is no way to present it better). Raworth acknowledges that economic growth is needed to soften distributional conflicts, to maintain democracy, as well as for people's subjective happiness but she fails to provide any persuasive arguments about how a new "no-growth" regime will come about, nor how it would solve these real issues. "We" should somehow be magically transformed from acquisitive and money-grubbing beings, which the system itself encourages us to be, to people who, under the same system, are rather indifferent to how well we do compared to others, and do not really care about wealth and income.

Short of magic, this is not going to happen. It then becomes apparent that Raworth's book is a book of miracles, as well as why in such a world of miracles, the real "miracle"—that Chinese growth has pulled some 700 million people out of abject poverty—goes all but unmentioned. The reason is that poverty was eliminated by "dirty" growth, which has polluted Chinese cities and the countryside, disrupted the Arcadian idyll between man/woman and nature—and yet made the lives of millions incomparably better.

Raworth's ideal world seems to be the one that we find in Giotto's paintings of St. Francis, but it is not the world we inhabit. In an attempt to convince us that "other worlds are possible" Raworth uses the example of an Indian tribe in northern Manitoba, which a couple of centuries ago responded to an increase in price by providing fewer goods. Yes—this clinches it.

Rather than proposing economics for the twenty-first century, Raworth's book brings us back to the imaginary world of the early Christendom. Perhaps such imaginary people were then "thriving" (a term Raworth uses at least fifty times in the book), but the real world, even in those times, was different: it was the world of Caesar and Spartacus, burned temples and fortunes made through violence. Exactly like ours. Except that we are richer. Which is a good thing.

(Published June 8, 2018)

THE WORLD UNDER CAPITALISM

1.7 Abundance, capitalism, and climate change

In classical Marxism, communism is defined as a society of material abundance. It is a society where goods flow in abundance ("after the productive forces have ... increased ... all the springs of co-operative wealth flow more abundantly," Marx, *Critique of the Gotha Program*). It is also a society that, having overcome the division of labor, allows for full self-realization and flowering of individual abilities:

> He is a hunter, a fisherman, a herdsman, or a critic, and must remain so [under capitalism] if he does not want to lose his means of livelihood; while in communist society, where nobody has one exclusive sphere of activity but each can become accomplished in any branch he wishes, society regulates the general production and thus makes it possible for me to do one thing today and another tomorrow, to hunt in the morning, fish in the afternoon, rear cattle in the evening, criticize after dinner ... without ever becoming hunter, fisherman, herdsman or critic. (*The German Ideology*)

When we define abundance in communist society it is important to keep in mind that it is material abundance, *viz.*, abundance of physical goods and some services. This cannot be abundance in everything. We can each have as many cars as we wish but the number of desirable parking places near the good restaurant, where we get a free dinner, or near a good theater will always be limited.

One could even argue that the abundance of material goods cannot be absolute. For example, if cars are abundant and one can have as many as he or she wishes, they can indulge in anti-social behavior by destroying a car each day. Thus eventually, society must step in and impose a limit on the number of cars. It can be countered, however, that this is not a likely behavior because a socially destructive behavior is generally indulged in order to show power and wealth. One could expect this kind of behavior to be minimized in communist societies because wanton destruction of goods that are accessible to all does not convey status. A useful comparator may be the wastefulness with which the things that are relatively cheap today like water or electricity are used. Neither of them is, for most households in rich countries, very expensive. Thus, one gets no particular status by being ostentatiously wasteful with them. The same might apply for most goods under communism:

since they are accessible to all, intentional wastefulness is not signaling power.

This summary of the standard Marxist view faces one significant problem. The definition of abundance implies full satisfaction of all needs. However, Marx very clearly defines needs as a social category, something that evolves with the development of society. What it means is that what we perceive as a need today is a function of what currently exists in the world and, consequently, what is the current level of development. In Roman times nobody felt the need for a smartphone, nor a frustration if they did not have one. Likewise, we do not experience the need to spend a weekend on Mars simply because such a good is unavailable.

If needs are a historical category, then new needs arise with technological progress. If new needs are constantly born, the abundance that was presumed in the opening paragraphs cannot be achieved because sufficient material means to satisfy these new needs will always be deficient. When the first laptop was invented, no matter how efficient the production, society could not create billions of laptops almost instantly. Some people's needs for a new laptop had to go unsatisfied. The access to new goods must always be unequal, and this inequality will produce frustration and imply absence of abundance.

To summarize: Our needs increase in step with technological progress but the technological progress cannot at all points in time satisfy the needs of everybody. Abundance defined as full satisfaction of all material needs cannot be achieved in technologically advancing societies.

When can all needs be covered by societal production? Only in a society that does *not* experience technological progress and where no new needs can arise. In such a society it is possible to imagine an almost unlimited production of things that already exist. That society can be related to today's society by realizing that in the rich part of the world most of our current material needs, defined in terms of goods that *already exist*, can be fully satisfied. Given the productive capacity of rich countries, everyone could have a decent home, refrigerator, laptop, dishwasher, car, etc.

To reach a society of abundance requires that we accept absence of technological change or economic stationarity. The question then becomes whether capitalist society can ever be stationary. Schumpeter thought that imagining capitalism as a stationary society is a contradiction in terms. Capitalism can exist only if profits, on average, are positive. No capitalist or entrepreneur would invest if they cannot expect a net return, no more than a worker would work for a zero

THE WORLD UNDER CAPITALISM

wage. If profits are positive, they will be used for investment; investments will generate growth, and that very growth will create new products, which in turn will create new needs and make the society of abundance impossible.

This, then, means that the stationary society that is compatible with full satisfaction of all human needs cannot be capitalist. Capitalism, by definition, means limitless change and limitless progress. With the society of limitless change and limitless progress we cannot have abundance.

Degrowth advocates therefore might have a valid point when they argue for an end to capitalism if they believe that climate change can be stopped only if society is stationary. Stationary society, end of capitalism, and abundance are logically consistent.

P.S. The last point is an implication based (I hope correctly) on Kohei Saito's arguments from *Slow Down: The Degrowth Manifesto*. I had the privilege of participating in a panel with Kohei and my interpretation is based on that discussion.

(Published April 25, 2024)

— 2 —

MIGRATION

2.1 Should some countries cease to exist?

Working on global inequality makes you ask questions you would never ask otherwise, simply because they would not occur to you. It is like going from a two-dimensional world to a three-dimensional: even the familiar suddenly appears unusual.

Take the convergence economics. In theory of growth, convergence indicates the (hopeful) regularity that poorer countries tend to grow faster than richer countries because they can use all the knowledge and innovations that the richer have already produced. Simply put, when you are at the technological frontier, you need to invent something new all the time and you may grow at say, 1 or 1.5 percent per year. When you are below the frontier, you can copy and grow at the higher rate. (Of course, economists talk of "conditional convergence" because the theory assumes that all other factors, which in reality differ between the rich and poor countries, are the same.) Nevertheless, there is some evidence for conditional convergence in empirical studies and it is, for obvious reasons, considered a good thing.

Now, when you look more closely you realize that convergence is studied in terms of countries but, in reality, it deals with the convergence in living standards among *individuals*. We express it in terms of a poorer country catching up with the richer because we are used to doing our economics in terms of nation-states; and we implicitly assume that there is no movement of people between countries. In reality, however, convergence is nothing else but the diminution of income inequality between all individuals in the world.

So, how best to achieve such a decrease in inequality between people? Economic theory, common sense, and simulation exercises clearly show that it can best be done by allowing free movement of people. Such a policy would increase global income (as any free movement of factors of production in principle should), reduce global poverty and global inequality. It is immaterial, from a global perspective, that it might slow between-country convergence (as some recent results for the EU indicate) because contries are, as we have just seen, not the relevant entities in global economics: the relevant entities are individuals and their welfare levels. If people's incomes are more equal, it is wholly immaterial if the gap between the average incomes in A and B increases. To see this point, think in the familiar terms of the nation-state: no one in his or her right mind would argue that people from the Appalachia in the US should not be allowed to move to California because the average income in the Appalachia might go down. In fact, both the average income in California and in Appalachia might go down, and both inequalities in the Appalachia and California might go up, and yet the overall US income would rise and US inequality would be less.

The argument is identical for the world as a whole: a highly skilled Nigerian who moves to the United States might lower the mean income of Nigeria (and might also lower the mean income of the US), and might, in addition, cause both inequalities to go up, and yet the global GDP would be greater and global inequality would be less. In short, the world would be a better place. The objections to migration raised by Paul Collier in his book *Exodus*, namely that it might reduce the average income in recipient countries, are immaterial because the real subject of our analysis is not the nation-state but the individual.

Thus far the argument seems to me entirely incontestable. But, then, things get a bit messier. Pushing this logic further, and using the results of the Gallup poll that show the percentage of people who desire to move out of their countries, we find that in the case of unimpeded global migration some countries could lose up to 90 percent of their populations. They may cease to exist: everybody but a few thousand people might move out. Even the few who might at first remain, could soon find their lives there intolerable, not least because providing public goods for a very small population may be exceedingly expensive.

So, what?—it could be asked. If Chad, Liberia, and Mauritania cease to exist because everybody wants to move to Italy and France, why should one be concerned: people have freely chosen to be better off in Italy and France, and that's all there is to that. But then, it could be asked, would not disappearance of countries also mean disappearance of distinct cultures, languages, and religions? Yes, but if people do not care about these cultures, languages, and religions, why should they be maintained?

Destroying the variety of human traditions is not costless, and I can see that one might believe that maintaining the variety of languages and cultures is not less important than maintaining a variety of flora and fauna in the world, but I wonder who needs to bear the cost of that. Should people in Mali be forced to live in Mali because somebody in London thinks that some variety of human existence would be lost if they all came to England? I am not wholly insensitive to this argument, but I think that it would be more honest to say openly that the cost of maintaining this "worldwide heritage" is borne not by those who defend it in theory but by those in Mali who are not allowed to move out.

There is a clear trade-off between the maintenance of diversity of cultural traditions and freedom of individuals to do as they please. I would be happier if the trade-off did not exist, but it does. And, if I have to choose between the two, I would choose human freedom, even if it means loss of tradition. After all, are traditions that no one cares about worth preserving? The world has lost Macromanni, Quadi, Sarmatians, Visigoths, Alans, Vandals, Avars, and thousands of others. They have disappeared together with their languages, cultures, and traditions. Do we really miss them today?

(Published December 13, 2016)

2.2 Migration into Europe: A problem with no solution

Sometimes seeing things, even when you are prepared for them, is helpful in focusing your mind. A couple of nights ago, as I got out of a bus that takes passengers from the Malpensa airport in Milan to the Central Railroad Station, I was struck by the number of people, obviously African migrants, camping in the piazza in front of the railroad station. It is not the first time that I have seen migrants en masse in Italy, but never have I seen entire families cooking and eating meals, while sitting on the lawn (or what remains of the lawn), in a large city park.

One needs just to look at the newspaper headlines to see that the problem of migrants is growing daily in Europe and that its gravity is greater than before. The number of migrants in the year 2015 has already exceeded 100,000 (about 15% higher than the last, record, year); the number of the dead has reached at least several thousand, although the statistics are murky, since no one has the incentive to compile them. People just die in desert or sea and no one cares. Practically every European country thinks about either deporting the migrants, making the asylum laws more difficult, or simply shutting the borders: from France, which under Sarkozy deported European Roma, to Hungary, which threatens to shut its southern border to Serbia, and to Bulgaria, which, at the EU urging, has built a wall against Turkey.

For now, Italian border police, together with the Austrian police, patrol its Northern border so as not to allow migrants to cross into Austria. This may not last, however. According to the EU internal rules, the country where migrants first arrive is supposed to deal with them, giving them a temporary authorization to stay or political asylum. But many migrants wish to go North, to Germany and Scandinavia, where they have relatives and better prospects of finding a job. So, the Italian PM Matteo Renzi has threatened simply to issue them with Schengen visas, so that they can go wherever in Europe they wish. Italy wants to be rid of them and is tired of having to deal with the problem (as they see it) alone, with little help from the North. Every country in Europe is willing, at most, to be the transit point for the migrants; none is willing to be the point of settlement. Thus, everybody tries to pass the hot potato of migrants to its neighbor. The only way to make sure you will not have to accept the hot potato is to build a wall, as Bulgaria has done, and Hungary plans to. No walls have yet been planned or erected within EU member states; but that too cannot be excluded.

And it is, in fact, a delicious irony of history that the countries who complained the most about the existence of border fences and walls, and vowed to bring them down forever, are now busily constructing them.

Perhaps it might seem odd to an impartial observer that rich Europe is unable to cope with one hundred thousand migrants and refugees, while much poorer Turkey has accepted 1.7 million refugees from Syria and Pakistan, and Iran has accepted several hundred thousand from Afghanistan and Iraq respectively. The difference is that the African and Middle Eastern migrants who come to Europe have often no relatives, friends, or even the vague possibility of a job. They are left to fend for themselves, living on public or private charity, and small, often illegal, trade. They are culturally, religiously, and linguistically more different from the average Italian or Spaniard than are Syrian refugees from the Turks (or, more to the point, Syrian Kurds from the Turkish Kurds). Thus, the refugees and migrants often remain totally unintegrated.

Now, several things are clear. First, the migration wave, even if the Europeans manage to control it this summer, reflects more deeply seated and permanent factors, which are unlikely to abate any time soon. These factors are political chaos in the Middle East, and, more importantly, the extraordinarily huge income gaps between Europe and Africa. With globalization, the knowledge of these gaps as well as the practical means to bridge them by migrating to a rich country, are more known and affordable than ever. These trends look even more unmanageable for Europe when one takes a longer-term view and realizes that the sub-Saharan African population, which is currently equal to that of the EU, is expected to be three times greater by 2100. Thus, economic migration will, if anything, increase.

Second, European difficulty in absorbing the migrants is not only due to cultural or religious differences but also (unlike the US, Canada, Australia) to the lack of history of being a land of immigration. Although some countries have received political refugees in large numbers (examples of France receiving refugees from the Spanish civil war, or, more recently, many EU countries accepting refugees from Bosnia, come to mind), Europe has generally been an emigrant continent, from the Hebrides and Ireland in the North to Sicily and Greece in the South. Furthermore, lack of economic growth, sluggish domestic employment numbers, and high unemployment rates in Southern Europe, make the availability of real, however modest, jobs for the migrants low.

Third, the European Union has in the past several years committed a number of political blunders that have aggravated the crisis and created instability on its borders. The mistakes include the mindless overthrow of Gaddafi, whose regime was replaced by feuding tribes and Hobbesian chaos, leading to the absence of any control over Libyan borders, both in the South and the North. Then, the equally mindless ultimatum to the previous Ukrainian government (namely, German insistence that the condition for the signing of the trade agreement be the release of Yulia Tymoshenko from prison and her medical treatment in Germany); this has led to the overthrow of the Yanukovych government, the civil war, and Russian intervention in Ukraine. And, finally, the current impasse over Greece, which threatens to create chaos not only on the borders of the Union but within itself. The EU thus needs to think long and hard about whether it is in the process of transforming itself, through a combination of arrogance and incompetence, from a source of stability to an exporter of political and economic chaos.

Fourth, it is I think obvious that the EU has absolutely no solution to this latest migration crisis. It is simply lost: with no strategy, no policy, and no ideas. Not that the problem is easy. But the only approach that might begin to produce something that resembles a solution would be multilateral, not solely among EU members (as in the current, strongly contested, idea of allocating migrants among EU member-countries), but in including also the emitting countries from Africa. A general system of both emitting and receiving country quotas seems the only way of imposing some order and stability. The quota system may not be able to deal with random events like the Syrian civil war, but it should be able to deal with economic migration. With an orderly quota system, a person from Mali who is considering migrating to France may prefer to wait several years and get an official permission to settle there, rather than pay a smuggler for an uncertain entry into France, or possible death.

But, such a multilateral approach would require (i) a huge amount of coordination and goodwill among both European countries themselves and between them and African countries, and (ii) European recognition that in the next 50 to 100 years they will have to accept a strong influx of African population, simply because demography and economic gaps are dictating it. Unfortunately, neither of these two conditions is close to being satisfied. So, the problem, among permanent political improvisation, will continue to worsen.

(Published July 1, 2015)

2.3 Migration's economic positives and negatives

I was always a strong believer that geography determines one's worldview. (I think it was de Gaulle who is credited for saying that "history is applied geography.") When you spend one month in Europe traveling to various places, you just cannot avoid the biggest issue in Europe today: migration.

So, let me go briefly over some key issues (again). I discuss them at much greater length in the third chapter of my book *Global Inequality: A New Approach for the Age of Globalization*.

To an economist, it is clear that most (not all; I will come to that later) economic arguments are strongly in favor of migration. If comparative advantage and division of labor have any meaning they must hold worldwide; they are surely not valid only within the confines of the arbitrarily drawn national borders. It was very well, and presciently, asked by Edwin Cannan a century ago: "if ... indeed, it [is] true that there is a natural coincidence between self-interest and the general good, why ... does not this coincidence extend, as economic processes do, across national borders [?]" (quoted from Frankel's 1942 Presidential Address to the South African Economic Society; Tony Atkinson brought to my attention this undeservedly obscure reference). If this were not the case, we could equally plausibly argue that there should be limits to the movement of labor between the regions of a single country. Since almost nobody would argue for that, it logically follows that the same principle of free movement must hold internationally. In other words, free movement of labor leads to the maximization of global output. We also know that migration, by raising incomes of the migrants (who are generally poor), is the most potent force for the reduction of global poverty, as well as for the reduction of global inequality.

So far so good. But, it could be argued, would not migration reduce wages of native workers with whom migrants compete? Although empirical studies find the negative effect on comparable native workers to be small (and we shouldn't forget that there are also native workers who benefit from migrations, if their skills are complementary with those of migrants), the effects may not be zero. But there Lant Pritchett's point comes to the rescue: to migration, Pritchett argues, we should apply the same principles as we apply to trade. We are not against free trade, even if it has negative effects on some domestic producers. The first-order effects of free trade are positive, and we deal with the second-order negative effects by compensating the losers (paying unemployment benefits or retraining workers). The same principles should apply to migration.

Thus, we have seemingly solved, from an economic point of view, the problem of migration. It must be a force for the good and, if there are problems or objections to it, they must stem from extra-economic reasons like social cohesion, preference for a given cultural homogeneity, xenophobia, and the like.

However, I think that this is not so simple. There may be also some negative economic effects to consider. I see three of them.

First, the effect of cultural or religion heterogeneity on economic policy formulation. In the 1990s, Bill Easterly and Ross Levine had started a veritable cottage industry of studies, arguing that religious or ethnic heterogeneity makes economic policy less efficient, subject to constant conflict and horse-trading: I let you devalue if you let me impose price controls. The literature was concerned mostly with Africa (trying to explain its dismal growth performance), but there is no reason not to have it apply to Europe too. The rationale of Easterly's effect is that groups jockey for the projects or policies that benefit their members, in conditions where the trust between the groups, because of religious or ethnic differences, is low. Thus, one group would like currency devaluation if its members are engaged in export activities or import substitution, and another would prefer protection for the goods their members are mostly producing. It is true that the minorities' economic roles in Europe are not as clear-cut as they are in Africa: Muslims in the UK do not have a preference for low or high exchange rate of the sterling, since they are not concentrated in specific industries in the same way that the ethnic groups in Nigeria who live in the Delta have an incentive to ask for a high share of oil revenues. Nevertheless, this problem of difficulty of policy coordination in the presence of religious or ethnic diversity should be kept in mind. It may become more important in the future, as Europe becomes more diverse.

Second, cultural differences may lead to the erosion of the welfare state. This was the point brought up twenty years ago by Assar Lindbeck. The roots of the European welfare state (most clearly seen in the Swedish "Our Home" beginnings in the 1930s) were always strongly nationalistic, based on a homogenous community and mutual help between its members. It relied on commonality of norms or affinities between the members. But, if that commonality no longer exists, the observance of certain norms upon which the welfare state is built (e.g. not to call in sick when one is not, or not to drink at work) is shaken, then the welfare state begins to be eroded. If you do not observe the same norms as I, and benefit at my expense, I lose interest in funding such an arrangement. Migration thus poses an important threat to the integrity of the welfare state in Europe. It is not by accident that the current moves in the Nordic countries can be, without giving it a pejorative meaning, described as a welfare state for the native-born population, or differently as national socialism.

Third, migration might have important negative effects on the emitting countries. The point was made a couple years ago by Paul Collier in his book *Exodus: How Migration is Changing our World*. I was inclined to dismiss it as a veiled xenophobia, which does not dare express its opinions openly, until I read last summer several articles on the effects of large emigration from smaller East European countries. These countries have been losing a significant number of their doctors, nurses, and engineers to the richer countries in the West and North of Europe. Now, one could say that eventually higher salaries for doctors in the East will be sufficient to keep them at home, or perhaps bring doctors from elsewhere, say from Nigeria to Hungary. But that approach ignores the length of time that it takes, not only to train doctors but for the markets to send the correct signals and for the people to act upon them. As Paul Krugman has nicely said: "if there were no adjustment costs, the history would not matter." But, while an economic model might assume such an instantaneous adjustment, the real life does not evince it. In between, thousands of people may die because of poor health care. Similarly, loss of some specialists may be, especially in small countries, very hard to compensate. If your country trains ten water sanitation engineers annually, and if they all move to richer countries, soon you will find yourself without anybody being able to control water quality.

We have, I think, also to take into account the negative economic effects of migration. I do not think that the three effects I listed here (and perhaps there could be others) are sufficiently strong to negate the positive economic effects. But neither can they be entirely disregarded or ignored.

(Published January 28, 2016)

THE WORLD UNDER CAPITALISM

2.4 Trade and migration: Substitutes or complements?

A friend sent me an interesting but also slightly odd (I have to say so at the outset) article by Robert Shiller published in the *Guardian*. Shiller begins by predicting, somewhat against the grain of what we see today, an "anti-nationalist" intellectual revolution that would address injustice of birth, that is, of having what I call in my *Global Inequality* the "citizenship premium" or "citizenship penalty," depending on whether a person is born in a rich or poor country.

At the beginning of the article the reader thinks that Shiller, quoting the precedents of the Glorious Revolution, the movement for the abolition of slavery and the suffragette movement, has in mind some kind of cosmopolitan movement that would tend to do away with national borders and allow free migration. While he perhaps might not mind that, his argument is different: he sees that forthcoming intellectual revolution arguing in favor of free trade that would through "factor-price equalization" (that is, equalization of wages and incomes across nations) bring about a world where the injustice of birth—at least as far as location is concerned—will be eliminated. It would be brought about without huge migrations (that may be seen as politically unsustainable) because trade would equalize income levels between the countries.

Clearly, if the world were to become a EU15, yes, you could have both a borderless world and preservation of national cultures since there would not be structural incentives to migration. (By "structural" I mean that there are significant monetary incentives that let workers from poorer countries increase their incomes by five or ten times by migrating to a richer country. "Non-structural" incentives for migration would remain; but they are due to idiosyncratic preferences for, say, warm weather, golf courses, espressos, or whatever else—such that they do not produce massive flows of people moving in search of higher pay.) But is it really possible to envisage a world of approximately equal country incomes coming about any time soon?

First, even assuming that such a world is feasible and that free trade will bring it about (the latter by itself is very dubious), we have to allow for the fact that wage equalization would imply a decrease, or a very slow growth, of wages for many people in the rich world. This is precisely the problem with which one grapples today. While trade was an overall "good," it has hurt many people in rich countries. The transition to a world of equal country incomes would necessarily

34

involve many bumps along the road and would require finding in rich countries much better ways to compensate losers (a point also made by Shiller). This, however, does not seem to be happening right now—nor is an intellectual revolution in favor of free trade on the horizon. At least, I cannot see it. Moreover, trade is today almost certainly freer than at any point in the past one hundred years, which makes the objective of such a "revolution" even more vague.

And there is another problem. Income gaps in the world are enormous and it is impossible, under the best of scenarios, that they should be done away with within this century. Consider the most extraordinary, and probably unrepeatable, feat of Chinese convergence. In 1977, the US–China gap in GDP per capita (and probably very similarly in wages) was almost 50 to 1, adjusted for the difference in price levels between the two counties. It is now 4 to 1. And this is the result of an average growth rate of Chinese GDP per capita of 8.5 percent per year over four decades.

The gap between German GDP per capita (proxy for that of Western Europe) and sub-Saharan Africa's today is 13 to 1. (German's GDP per capita is about $45,000 vs. population-weighted sub-Saharan GDP per capita of $3,500; all in purchasing power parity dollars.) With Africa's population expected to more than double by 2050, do we really see Africa able in the next three or four decades to repeat Chinese growth experience? Note that replicating Chinese per capita growth, and given the projected population growth in sub-Saharan Africa of 2.4 percent per annum, would require African countries to grow on average by almost 11 percent per year for approximately half a century. And, how did sub-Saharan Africa fare during the last, relatively good, decade? Its overall GDP grew by 4.5 percent per annum.

Thus, even under the most favorable assumptions of convergence, income gaps are unlikely to be eliminated. Which, in turn, shows the importance of migration. If a borderless cosmopolitan world is to be achieved (an objective with which I agree but see enormous political difficulties in reaching it), migration is absolutely essential. But, as economic migration faces increasing obstacles in rich countries (and, it has to be added, not solely because of xenophobia but for economic reasons as well), the ideal of a world "without injustice of birth" recedes.

To make my point clear. I am very sympathetic to the borderless world but to believe that it can be achieved through trade alone, and without significant migration, is unrealistic. And, once we say "migration," we immediately open the Pandora's box that the most recent elections in Europe and the United States have shown is a reality, not an imagination. Thus, our new "intellectual revolution" should be rather to address the issue of migration and citizenship than free trade. Free trade alone cannot solve the world's problems.

(Published October 7, 2017)

MIGRATION

2.5 Habermas and pimps: The world of the day and the world of the night

The Serbian Prime Minister Zoran Djindjić was assassinated in 2003, after being in power for less than three years (the first PM after the fall of Slobodan Milošević). Because of his relative youth (50 years) when he was killed, exceptional intelligence, and most unusual life, he became, and is increasingly seen as, a hero, an icon to many in Serbia. Not unlike Kennedy, having been killed early in his political life, his interrupted life allows everyone to build a plausible story of how things would have been much better had he stayed alive. Djindjić's friend from high school (gymnasium) and university Dragan Lakićević has just written an excellent memoir on their friendship, entitled (with an obvious nod to Joyce) *Portrait of a Politician as a Young Man*.

The book is very good and I would recommend to all Serbian (Croatian) readers. But my intention here is not to discuss Djindjic's life, but to highlight one small, incidental, feature of the book. Both Djindjić and Lakićević studied philosophy at the graduate school in Frankfurt (in the early 1980s). They listened to many famous professors, Habermas being one of them. Djindjić succeeded, after being rudely turned down by Habermas' secretary, to talk to Habermas himself by climbing and jumping through the window of his office (and, in the process, seriously scaring Habermas). That's how he managed to become a graduate student.

The author's (Lakićević's) path to graduate education was somewhat less flamboyant, but it is his story that I find most interesting. Both Djindjić and Lakićević were almost totally penniless, living on irregular and minute stipends, and surviving by doing odd jobs (from construction to night clubs and smuggling), mixing with Yugoslav and Turkish Gastarbeiters, and being treated by them, or by accidental women they seduced, to dinners and drinks.

It is the contrast between the day life composed of philosophy lectures at a prestigious and orderly university, where professors appear exactly in time, give appointments one month in advance, deliver lectures on social contract, alienation, ontology, epistemology … where libraries are immense and quiet, books arrive quickly, carried by the silent helpers, and the world of the night—when our heroes return to their lair—that is striking.

The large rental building where they live is divided into tiny rooms that have only sinks with shared bathrooms, where practically no tenant owns any furniture, and where in many rooms live five, six, or seven illegal or legal workers (with their families) from Yugoslavia, Turkey, Morocco, Bangladesh, Nigeria. The tenants, Lakićević writes, almost never greet each other: ashamed of their poverty they silently cross each other "like phantoms" if they happen to meet in front of the building.

But some apartments are an exception to this surly, beaten-up, docile, and bitter crowd. These are the apartments where pimps arrange fake marriages between Gastarbeiters and German prostitutes—marriages that, as in the US, allow illegal workers to become legal. Serious, middle-aged men, dressed in their best checker-patterned suits, and with white socks and shoes on their feet, come to the pimps' apartments, where they choose from among the prospective wives and agree on the price and duration of the marriage.

When the night is over, Lakićević goes back to the world of learning, where the discussion is about the best ways to organize a community, citizens' rights and duties, working class and bourgeoisie, *l'être et le néant*. But the world of the day and the world of the night have nothing in common. It is not solely that the people of the day and the people of the night have different interests and backgrounds. The two cannot be said, in any meaningful way, to belong to the same community. They are two worlds.

Naipaul saw the same duality between the Whites and the enslaved and miserable African populations, between day and night lives. In a beautiful passage he writes:

> There was the world of the day; that was the white world. There was the world of the night; that was the African world, of spirits and magic and the true gods. And in that world, ragged men, humiliated by day, were transformed—in their own eyes, and in the eyes of their fellows—into kings, sorcerers, herbalists, men in touch with the true forces of the earth and possessed of complete power ... To the outsider, to the slave-owner, the African night world might appear a mimic world, a child's world, a carnival. But to the African ... it was the true world: it turned white men to phantoms and plantation life to an illusion. ("The Crocodiles of Yamoussoukro," p. 280)

I saw myself too, although in much less dramatic ways, the gaping distance between the two worlds during the *Indignados'* demonstrations in Spain. The demonstrations started in 2011 at Plaza del Sol, one evening in March, not more than 100 meters from the apartment where I lived. The demonstrations continued for days, spreading to the rest of Spain. Many have commented on how passionate and well-behaved were the young people who took over the streets of Spanish cities. And, indeed, I have frequently seen them in the evenings and even late on warm Spanish nights, sitting in small circles as in agoras, discussing, raising their hands, voting on different proposals.

But what was never commented upon were the people at the edges of these exercises in direct democracy. They were not the police, or Guardia Civil. They were hundreds of Africans to whom the assemblies of so many people in one place provided new business opportunities: selling bottled water, chewing gums, fruits, fake Vuitton bags, and Rolex watches. Their activity, always present at Plaza del Sol and in the neighboring streets, now skyrocketed. There were more and more of them and they were selling more stuff. The police, who refrained from intervening against the Spanish youth, could not move in force against the Africans. So, the business flourished.

But the striking thing was the enormous chasm between these two worlds of the young—people of the same age. (I think that the young Spaniards, by and large, did not even notice the young Africans; they must have looked to them like the stage extras.) While one group discussed Habermas and Bauman, the other group, probably unaware even of what the whole fuss was about, saw this human agglomeration as an opportunity to add a few more euros to their miserable incomes.

Were they part of the same community? Not at all. As in the German case from the 1980s, the Spanish case of 2011 illustrates the immense distance between those who are members of a community and those who are not.

The (difficult) task of Europe will be to integrate these two groups. But, as the examples also show, little has changed in thirty years, and it is not easy to expect that things will get better in the next thirty years. Can two different communities, composed of citizens and meteques, coexist forever?

(Published May 30, 2021)

2.6 The simplicity of views regarding civil conflicts

Twenty years ago, Alberto Alesina and Enrico Spolaore published a much-quoted article entitled "On the Number and Size of Nations." It was the time of the break-up of communist-ruled "ethnically based" federations and, on the other end of the continent, of European integration. The view underlying the Alesina–Spolaore (A–S) paper was both simple and seemingly very persuasive. There are manifest advantages of sharing public goods (as per capita costs of provision decrease with larger population size). Short of any countervailing costs, the optimal size of political organization would be a unified world. However, as people live further apart from each other and have different preferences, sharing public goods makes less sense: some prefer to invest more in defense, others in education, the third group in religious schools, etc. So, the optimal size of a state is where the two tendencies just offset each other: similar peoples will share a state, federation, or confederation up to a point where dissimilarities in preferences take over.

People who looked at the world in the 1990s and did not concern themselves much with history thought that this approach made lots of sense: does not the EU bring together people who are similar, from Sweden to Greece? And did not the Soviet Union fall apart because little was shared between Estonians and Tajiks?

I thought that the Alesina–Spolaore model was simplistic to the point of naiveté. (My own view, unfortunately published in a collected volume that no one reads, was different: that the optimal size of a state is determined by the trade-off between sovereignty and income. You give up sovereignty to enter into WTO or the European Union: this, in turn, gives you higher income, but diminishes your power autonomously [or independently] to decide on economic policies. I will not discuss my paper "Nations, Conglomerates and Empires: The Trade-off between Sovereignty and Income"; for those interested, the reference is given below.)

Why was the A–S view simplistic? Because of the fundamental (and I think faulty) assumption that people who live close to each other are "similar," have similar preferences and want to live together in a country or a union. A simple reflection about the past or the 1990s should have sufficed to show that this is often not the case. Germany and France did want to live in a European Union in the 1990s, but for two centuries before they had been in an almost incessant war. Yet Germans and French were not less "similar" in 1914 or 1940 than they were in 1997

MIGRATION

(or today). The 1990s were also the time of the war in Yugoslavia: yet to any external observer, there was not that much dissimilarity between the Serbs and Croats, and certainly not more in the 1990s than in 1918, when they unified. Turks and Kurds, entangled in a decades-old war, are not dissimilar in their preferences or way of life.

This point is even more obviously true today and should, I think, invalidate the A–S fundamental assumption. As we read about the endless conflict between Catalonia and Spain (see July 1–2, 2017, *Financial Times*, "Catalonia's referendum exposes a divided Spain"), or about the Scottish referendum, or Brexit, or the bloody war between the Shia and the Sunni in Iraq and Syria, we are not struck by some "objective" and huge differences that exist between Catalans and Spaniards, nor between the English and the Scots, nor between the Iraqi Shia and the Sunnis. The preferences of each duo can be thought to be very similar; yet they are at loggerheads, and at times in violent wars, about the type of country, union—or "disunion"—in which they wish to live.

The liberal nostrum reflected in the A–S assumption (that similar people want to live together) had its corollary in the common misconception that one often hears even today, namely that ethnic or religious conflicts are somehow the product of lack of knowledge of the two communities about each other and that if people only spent more time with each other, the conflict would lose its *raison d'être* and dissipate.

Only a few days ago, a development economist circulated on Twitter [X] a poll asking people whether they shared a meal with a person of a different religion (implying that, were such meals more widespread, likelihood of conflict or misunderstanding would be lessened). But this is based on a misconception: Shia and Sunni in Iraq are warring not because they do not know each other well enough: they have lived together as neighbors for centuries. Does anybody think the Spaniards and Catalans do not sufficiently know each other? Or Serbs and Croats and Bosniaks who speak the same language and who have intermarried prior to the Civil War in the 1990s *more* than if the marriage pairing was random? The same is true for ethnic and religious wars in other places: Catholic and Protestant Irish, Ethiopians and Eritreans, Greek and Turkish Cypriots. Even the worst civil conflict of all, the Holocaust, did not happen because ethnic-German Germans and Jewish Germans did not know each other well or did not intermarry sufficiently. On the contrary, it is often argued that of all countries in Europe, Jews were most integrated in Germany.

41

THE WORLD UNDER CAPITALISM

I do not know what causes civil wars. I could write down a laundry list of things that seem to me to make its likelihood greater: economic hardship, youth unemployment, desire to find a scapegoat, inability to resist demagogues, interested minorities who have much to gain from war, etc. Moreover, once a determined and violent minority within one group is able to create bloodshed, there is a natural tendency of the other side to react and then, very soon, the lines between the groups are drawn and those who refuse to join either side are the prime target for elimination by both groups. War thus feeds on itself.

I know that this is not an elegant theory that can be set out in a model, but I think—and I trust that this is something increasingly confirmed—that similar people are as likely to want to share a state as to be willing to split up or to go to war, and that believing that conflict can be prevented by people knowing each other better is merely an illusion.

(Published July 2, 2017)

[June 2024. Note: I think that all of this, written in 2017, was amply confirmed by the ongoing war between Russia and Ukraine.]

— 3 —

POLITICS

3.1 What is a paleo-left agenda?

When I had a discussion with Alex Hochuli and Philip Cunliffe at their podcast (see the link below), they mentioned one of my pieces on what I called the paleo-left. In the podcast, I went over the main features of the paleo-left, and I think that it may be useful to put them down again in writing. And, hopefully, show that they can be readily made into actionable policies and are not just a set of nice words strung together.

The paleo-left, in my opinion, has four key planks: it is pro-growth, pro-equality, for freedom of speech and association, and for international equality. Let me explain each.

Being in favor of growth means that the paleo-left acknowledges that income and wealth are indispensable conditions for human self-realization and freedom. We cannot achieve our potential, nor enjoy other non-pecuniary activities unless we have enough income not to worry where the next meal comes from, or where we are going to sleep the next night. The paleo-left is against the constant denigration of growth because it recognizes that for an ordinary person improved material conditions of living open the "realm of freedom": we do not want households where mothers have to wash clothes in the nearby creek or in the bathtub; we want households with washing machines. (Of course, for people who already own washing machines this might seem like a trivial demand. But, for half the world that does not, it is not trivial at all.)

Growth as such, without taking into account who benefits from it, is neither ethically acceptable, nor politically sustainable. That's where the second plank comes in: economic equality. Growth cannot be blind, nor can it be such that most of it, like in the US in the period from 1986 to 2007 (see Figure 3.1) is collected by the rich. It must be pro-poor which means that incomes of the lower groups should rise, in percentage terms, at least as much as incomes of the richer groups. How to achieve this? Not only through direct taxation or indirect taxation of activities and goods consumed by the rich (the latter is an area which is, in my opinion, under-utilized). It can be achieved through high inheritance taxes, which would ensure a reasonably equal starting position, regardless of parental wealth, by almost free or fully free public education and health, and by special support for the young, around the time of their first jobs. The young are now in the developed Western societies as a group in need of as much support as that which people who are currently old managed to achieve politically in the 1960s and 1970s.

Reduced income and wealth inequalities are both an objective in themselves and a tool for achieving something else: relative political

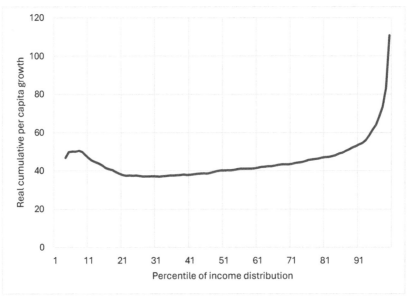

Figure 3.1 Cumulative growth of real per capita income across income distribution (in percent), US 1986–2007

Note: The graph shows real (inflation-adjusted) growth of per capita income in the United States between 1986 and 2007, across all percentiles of income distribution. The graph shows that the top one percent real income more than doubled, whereas income at the median increased by only 40 percent.

equality. That equality is undermined in today's advanced societies not, as it is claimed, by an ill-defined "populism," but by a very opposite danger: that of plutocracy. The fact that rich people fund the campaigns, pay politicians (which is just a more subtle form of bribery), and control most of the mainstream media, makes mockery of political equality.

The paleo-left should, in my view, eschew such terms that the neoliberal discourse has captured and made meaningless, like democracy. We have to acknowledge that the term "democracy" has been hijacked by the neoliberal plutocracy in the same way that the term "people" was hijacked by the communist authorities in Eastern Europe. Both terms are used to cover up the reality.

Instead, the paleo-left should focus on something much more real and measurable: approximate political equality. The latter implies public financing of political campaigns, limits (or bans) on rich people's control of the mass media (no *Washington Post* ownership for Jeff Bezos), and equal participation in the electoral process, which in turn means making participation in the elections easier for hard-working people. Current elections in the US are intentionally scheduled for a working day, and it is neither a surprise, nor an advertisement for "democracy," that even in the most important elections one-half of the electorate simply does not participate.

The paleo-left also recognizes that the freedoms of speech and association are largely meaningless, so long as approximate political equality does not exist. Individuals can spend hours and days complaining on Twitter [X], but it will carry zero political influence as compared to the well-paid and organized think-tanks and other institutions whose objective is to affect policy directly. It is in that area that a vague use of the term "democracy" in reality conceals vast inequality in access to political power.

The last plank is internationalism. This is, of course, an old left-wing slogan, and it should not be seen as something that is just tacked on to the rest of the domestic agenda. It is a constituent part of the overall agenda. The paleo-left accepts that different countries and cultures may have different ways in which they choose their governments or in which they define political legitimacy. The paleo-left is not ideologically hegemonic. The paleo-left might believe (and should believe) that its own approach is the best, and is right to argue for it, but the argument must be always at the level of ideas, must avoid gross interferences in the internal affairs of other countries, and must obviously never use violence. The paleo-left must get rid of the noxious idea of a "liberal world order," which is either meaningless

THE WORLD UNDER CAPITALISM

(as it changes depending on what is politically convenient for its proponents), or is an outright invitation to wage wars. The paleo-left respects the international law as defined by the United Nations, and by other institutions that are inclusive of all peoples. The paleo-left proselytism is made only by non-violent means, with respect for other cultures and states, and no coercion of any kind.

There are many other issues that cannot be directly covered by these simple rules. They concern migration, gender, and racial equality, relations between the Church and state, etc. but they can be, I believe, relatively easily deduced from these four general principles.

(Published September 7, 2022)

POLITICS

3.2 Toward global progressiveness

Is it possible to define a series of approaches to global problems for the group of people who may be called "global progressives" (GPs)? Before I try to answer this question, I need to define the terms. "Progressive" is meant to include all those who identify with broad left-wing movements, from Marxist to social democracy and even up to the fringes of liberals (in the American sense of the term). "Global" is supposed to cover issues that can, at least in principle, either be acted upon or actively pursued on the global, as opposed to national, level. "Approach" is supposed to mean activities that are between policies (since global policies are extremely rare, and most policy-making is made at the national or local level), and the rather vague "values" or "opinions." "Approach" therefore has an activist component attached to it, which moves individuals and groups beyond mere expressions of what they believe or hold dear. But it is less than policy, simply because the world has currently very few such tools at the global level.

What are the areas where such global approaches can be defined? The seven areas listed start from the final objective which is higher income (and the attendant greater "happiness") to the means to realize it, which concern capital, labor, technology, and taxes.

Economic growth. It is true by definition that economic growth is an indispensable condition for the reduction of global poverty. Reduction and ultimately elimination of global poverty (at whatever modest poverty line one can envisage today), is probably the most important task to realize in the twenty-first century. Nobody in the world should live in misery. In order for this to become reality, GPs must be in favor of economic growth, and especially so in poor and middle-income countries. Higher economic growth in poor and middle-income countries would also reduce global inequality, which may be considered as the number 2 global goal for this century. Reduction of material inequality between individuals in the world is a requirement for the existence of a, however weak, global community of interests and values because such community cannot be based on vastly different levels of material welfare.

Climate change. The focus on global poverty elimination and global inequality reduction must be considered within the framework where climate change is an important challenge to many people (not necessarily all, because some are likely to benefit from it). While some trade-off between global growth and growth-reducing policies

47

THE WORLD UNDER CAPITALISM

needed to combat climate change may be allowed, that trade-off must acknowledge that economic growth is the most important global objective. Global growth and control of climate change, however, are not lexicographically ordered (with growth coming first) because that would exclude any trade-off between the two. But the trade-off must be such as to prioritize growth-compatible methods of control of climate change: "green growth" brought about by suitable (and subsidized) technology, and changes in the consumption patterns through subsidies and taxes. Most of the tools to control climate change are national, and GPs cannot affect them much at the global level. However, since the issue of climate change has acquired worldwide importance and is subject of international cooperation by nation-states, a unified approach by GPs may make a difference.

It is obvious from the above that GPs should not be in favor of degrowth, because it would negatively affect elimination of global poverty and reduction of global inequality.

International aid. GPs should be in favor of rich countries finally achieving their pledge (made more than half-century ago) of transferring 0.7 percent of their GDPs in the form of aid to poor countries. This objective, however modest, has recently receded in importance and public interest because of sluggish growth in rich countries and the rise of Asian middle-income countries. But the objective is still crucial, given vast inequalities that exist between countries and peoples.

Global aid should not be confused with purely commercial transaction (like foreign direct investments) and loans by national or international development agencies that are only in part aid (to the extent that the interest rate charged on loans is below the market rate).

Migration. GPs must be in favor of free movement of people. This derives from the first principles of equal opportunity, which, for those who think globally, must be equal opportunity at any point in the world, and not solely within one's own country. It derives also from the support of globalization, which includes free movement of capital, goods, services, and technology. There is no reason why labor should be treated differently. But that principle must be, within each individual country, moderated (and in some cases modified) to be compatible with what is politically feasible. While various compromises and temporary solutions are possible, one should not forget that it must be done with the principle of free movement of people always in the background and not being forgotten.

Technology. GPs must be in favor of facilitating transfer of technology from rich to poor countries. It is one of the principal ways in which growth of poor countries can be accelerated. Recent exaggerated concerns about the protection of intellectual property rights are not only antithetical to the achievement of global poverty eradication but are at variance with rich countries' own stated objectives, repeated over many years, of being in favor of easing transfer of technology to poorer countries. This exaggerated concern also derives from the *de facto* control of most international bodies (in this case the World Trade Organization) by rich countries. This last issue must also be addressed (see below).

Taxation. International taxation (such as tax on financial transactions, or more ambitiously, global tax on the most polluting activities) should lead to the creation of a global tax authority. It is unrealistic that such global tax authority will, within the foreseeable future, come close to national tax authorities' power, but any move in that direction is welcome. The global tax authority, with its own source of funds, derived from global taxes, could be used for green energy subsidies across countries, to help migrants, or for financial support under extraordinary conditions such as pandemics and natural catastrophes.

Equality between countries. This is an important principle that, as in federal countries' constitutions, must be balanced with the approach mentioned above regarding global poverty elimination, which treats all persons in the world (not countries) as equal. But treatment of all countries equally implies non-interference in their internal affairs, so long as they do not have implications beyond their borders, and preference for the organizations like the United Nations that are, at least in principle, built on the assumption of equality of nations. It also means that international institutions like the World Bank, and International Monetary Fund, which are built on the principle of richer countries having greater rights, should be forced to move toward greater country-equality. (The same applies to the World Trade Organization, which is in deed even if not legally, biased in favor of rich countries.)

What cannot be dealt with globally? The issues that can be addressed only at the national level are those that belong to inequalities of opportunity (different from inequality of opportunity due to citizenship) like inequalities of parental background, gender, race, etc., and inequalities of outcome. Global equality of opportunity can be helped by being pro-growth, pro-migration, pro-technology transfer, and pro-aid, as GPs should be. But lots of inequality of opportunity is nationally based and can only be dealt with at that level. This includes inequalities linked to one's background (wealth of parents), gender, race, or sexual orientation. Inequalities of outcome in income and wealth can also be remedied mostly nationally through higher taxation of inheritance, more accessible education, higher income taxes for the rich, deconcentration of financial wealth (through worker shareholding). But these objectives, however laudable, cannot be currently addressed at the global level.

While the just discussed group of objectives cannot be dealt with globally because the means of doing so are national, another group of objectives cannot be included because global consensus on them, even among the global progressives, is impossible to reach. They are philosophical and political issues, such as alienation of labor (wage labor as opposed to labor having the entrepreneurial role), hyper-commodification of daily life, and political systems of different countries. Thus, they have to be left aside.

Historical context. Global progressiveness tries to combine elements from the New International Economic Order (NIEO) of the 1970s, which gave agency to countries (and especially so, to the formerly colonized countries) and the neoliberal or Basic Needs approach that focused on individuals only. The objectives of global poverty elimination and freedom of migration are part of the latter worldview, but the goals of international aid, transfer of technology, and equality of nation-states were formulated already in the 1970s. The defect of NIEO was that it gave too much power to nation-states so they often ignored the needs of their citizens. The defect of neoliberalism was that it circumvented the nation-state altogether and gave the power to decide what mattered to international organizations that were themselves controlled by the Global North. The new global progressiveness should avoid both of these pitfalls.

(Published July 4, 2021)

POLITICS

3.3 Democracy or dictatorship: Which works better?

Last night, in a response to something I had written on Twitter [X], a friend tweeted Oscar Wilde's quip that "the trouble with socialism is that it takes up too many evenings." And, although Wilde wrote long before socialism got established anywhere, and, although it looks like a clever comment, I think there is more in it: like many artists, Wilde captured the essence of the advantages and the problems of a political and economic system even before it became a reality.

How come?

When I arrived in the United States, coming from the worker-management world of Titoist Yugoslavia, I was somewhat surprised at how Americans took the strongly hierarchical, quasi-dictatorial relations in the business world as fully "normal." I was half expecting that workers would have a say in the choice of their "managers" (actually, for a long time, I could not even figure out who exactly is a "manager") but, of course, they did not. The promotions were made by co-option or even direct appointment of lower echelons by the higher echelons. And, of course, the management was selected by the owners themselves. So, the system was entirely top-down: the top selected the down it liked to have.

It was remarkably similar to the political system from which I came. There too the Central Committee coopted its new members; these selected their replacements and so forth down to the lowest level of Communist Party cell. Formally speaking, American companies were organized like the Communist Party. In both cases, to paraphrase Bertolt Brecht, the leadership selected their employees, or their members. In one case the dictatorship was in the sphere of work, in another in the social sphere.

Democracy that in the US existed in the social sphere (with lower levels electing their own political "managers") was replicated in Titoist Yugoslavia at the workplace, with workers electing their own workers' councils and those electing directors (except in enterprises that were seen to be of special importance, where the top-down system of Communist Party appointment held).

So, there were two societies with key spheres of human activity (work and social) organized according to the exactly opposite principles. One of them won, another lost. The one that lost, lost because organizing the work sphere according to democratic principles is not efficient. When you do so, an enormous amount

51

of time is spent on negotiating the minutest details of work, pay, holidays, sick leave, the right to take off when a family member is not well, payment of extra minutes of work, cleaning of bathrooms, supplies of papers, etc. Academic departments in the US are what come closest to labor management as it existed in the socialist Yugoslavia. And hardly anyone would argue that the academic departments are organized in an efficient way. People who in such an organizational context win and become successful are those who are not really interested in working at all, but debating every issue until everybody gets exhausted and gives up. They have the patience to outsit and outlast everybody else in interminable discussions and negotiations. No issue is small enough that they would not discuss it ad nauseum. Obviously, hardly anything ever gets done under such circumstances.

But, does not the same danger lurk in the political space? Do not citizen initiatives, referendums and counter-referendums, legal suits and counter-suits, carry the same danger that Oscar Wilde identified: that normal citizens do not have the time or do not care about them so that the decisions ultimately get taken by those with the greatest patience; by those who have nothing else to do but to get engaged into these "consultations"? In the heavily commercialized world of today, where every minute counts literally in terms of income forgone (you can write blogs for money, or study for your exam, or drive Uber, or charge your neighbor for taking his dog for a walk), social involvement is almost necessarily captured by professional NGOs. (I have noticed that many NGOs have presidents who, by the number of their mandates, approach Mugabe and Mubarak, but, unlike those illustrious leaders, can never be overthrown by their hapless constituents.)

This is where more technocratic political capitalism of the Chinese or Singaporean variety comes to mind. What it tells you is that essentially the same efficient and dictatorial way in which the production of cell phones is organized ought to be extended to the political sphere. It argues that the two spheres are essentially the same. In both, efficiency is reached by clear goal-directed activities, which are technical in nature and which should not be subject to the constant approval by workers or citizens.

If these societies continue to consistently outperform societies where the social sphere is organized in a democratic fashion, there is, I think, little doubt that their appeal will be such that, in a hundred years, it may seem to those who are around so very quaint that people thought that in a complex society social decisions should be taken by democratic vote. The same as it seems to us today so very quaint to believe that people once thought that a decision about what a company should produce was supposed to be made by the majority vote of shop-floor workers.

(Published May 3, 2019)

THE WORLD UNDER CAPITALISM

3.4 How is the world ruled?

It is Saturday evening and snowing in New York. I have nowhere to go, I do have things to do (my book!) but my memories take over
Like for example, the *simple* question of how the world is ruled. I think that lots of misunderstanding among people in the world comes from inability to visualize how organizations and countries are managed: people either overestimate their singularity of purpose and scheming, or try to convince themselves that there is a full freedom of action and that things are decided on merit. Neither is true. The truth is complex, elusive, and lies somewhere (somewhere!) in the middle: it is what Nirad Chaudhuri called in a somewhat broader context of human history "Libertas in imperio."
I can describe it, I am afraid, best using the examples that I knew best, from my life and long association with the World Bank.

Proposition 1. The world is ruled by a cabal.

Around 1989, when Yugoslavia was in its death-throes (which were not obvious to the naive types like myself), when on vacation there I wrote an article for an economics and politics weekly in Belgrade that argued that the best privatization strategy, under the last (sensible and brilliant) Yugoslav PM, Ante Marković, should be such that vouchers be distributed to all citizens of the country, and citizens be allowed to buy shares in enterprises in whatever part of the country they wished. It was an utterly quixotic proposal because the national nomenklaturas were precisely then working on the break-up of the country and the last thing they wanted was to cooperate with each other, which they would have to do if their citizens owned shares in companies in other republics. So, the proposal was dead on arrival.
But, one afternoon, in the weekly's nice board room, I explained the proposal in detail to one of weekly's main writers on social issues. The writer was a Serbian fascist (I am using the term not in a derogatory but strictly political sense) enamoured with Italian fascism. (German was, I think, a bit too heavy for his taste.) He was a painter, who studied and lived in Italy, was proud of his relationship with Movimento Sociale Italiano (MSI) leadership, admirer of Mussolini. He also looked the part: could have been on any of these bas-reliefs that adorn Euro city near Rome: tall, well-built, square-jawed, straight posture, walking always forward with the head held high.

54

A real *bell'uomo*. In Rome in 1934, he would have been Mussolini's favorite barbarian painter.

But he was, when at home, a Serbian nationalist. So, after carefully listening to me and basically nodding his head during most of the conversation, a couple of days later he came with a stinging two-page attack on my proposal titled "The World Bank sends its CIA spy to sell Serbian enterprises to foreigners."

Now, was he mad? Not at all. He was, I am convinced, a smart guy, but he saw the world and organizations in it as an immense plot, within which everything was strictly hierarchical: ordinary people had no ideas or will of their own. So, if I was then in Belgrade arguing X, it must have been not only cleared by my superiors, but ordered by them. And by superiors' superiors and so forth all the way to the US Secretary of the Treasury, and perhaps Wall Street and perhaps the Jews.

The truth was that I was even risking reprimand from the World Bank because I had no business doing anything with Yugoslavia, publishing articles or creating trouble while on vacation.

But what was the reverse of this view?

Proposition 2. The world is ruled on merit.

This is the view that many people hold about their own involvements and that of institutions they work for. (Academia is a bit different, so I will leave it out.) But this view of moral and intellectual integrity is widely shared in think-tanks (and I worked in one), international organizations and probably many others (like Oxfam, *Médecins sans frontières*, Open Society, etc.).

But is it true? Here I could ply the readers with numerous examples, but I will choose the one that, like the Belgrade story, sticks in my mind.

I was in the Research Department, and thus fairly independent of the World Bank's hierarchy, but it was desirable that I spend a given number of weeks annually working on concrete "operational" issues. It happened that the offer I got involved a study of how heating and transportation subsidies in a Central Asian country affected its income distribution. It was easy to do, and I promptly came back with the conclusion that the subsidies were pro-poor and should be kept.

But this was not the policy of the World Bank. The year was 1994 or 1995 and everybody believed in Fukuyama and Larry Summers.

So, the decision, or rather the diffuse feeling (because you do not need a formal decision on matters like these to know what the "correct" answer is), was made before the report was even begun that the subsidies should be eliminated. The leader of the group, not the most brilliant person, was smart enough to know what the desired conclusion was and that his/her career would be helped if the empirical analysis supported it.

So, when it did not, he/she totally ignored it and, after several endless meetings where I was supposed to be somehow convinced that the data must surely be wrong, that part of the report was either not included or totally ignored. (I cannot remember what happened exactly.) Because I was not brave or stubborn enough, I gave up a (hopeless) struggle after a couple of attempts and went back to my numbers and equations.

But I was outside that particular hierarchy; so I was relatively free. But I then thought: let's suppose that I was hierarchically under the project leader and that I was courageous enough to stick to my guns. What would have happened? My arguments would have been ignored; I would not have been demoted or fired. But in my next annual review, I would have been given the lowest possible grade, salary increase would be nil, my promotion prospect would be zero, and the explanation would never address the substantive issue: it would be that I was not collegial, failed to work in a team spirit, etc. It could even be that I would have been asked to attend "team building" seminars, just as the Soviet dissidents were sent to psychiatric asylums.

The problem would never even be mentioned to have consisted in a disagreement on substance. Rather, it would have been treated as some maladjustment problem on my part; perhaps I was harassed when young, or had a difficult childhood. Because, of course, the institution is not closed to different viewpoints and welcomes diverse opinions and "vibrant" or "robust" (these are the key words) discussion.

This is how the weeding out of undesirable views would have proceeded.

So, who was right: the Mussolini's admirer or the Washington consensus believer? Or nobody. Your call.

(Published February 17, 2018)

POLITICS

3.5 Multi-party kleptocracies rather than illiberal democracies

The term "illiberal democracy" was, I think, introduced by Fareed Zakaria. It was used as a badge of honor by Viktor Orbán, the Hungarian prime minister, the erstwhile poster-child of youthful East European reformers and liberals of the 1990, who then decided to turn over the new leaf. More recently, the term has gained further popularity as a way of naming and explaining the regimes such as Erdoğan's in Turkey or Putin's in Russia. Perhaps Venezuela can be placed in the same category.

The implication of "illiberal democracy" is that the system is democratic in the sense that there are free elections, more-or-less free, or at least diverse, media, freedom of assembly, etc., but that the "values" espoused by the regime are illiberal. Erdoğan believes in primacy of Islam over the Enlightenment-defined human rights, Orbán believes in "Christian civilization," Putin in "Russian spirituality," Maduro in "Bolivarian revolution." "Illiberal" also implies that the system is majoritarian in the sense that certain "inalienable" rights can be taken away through simple vote. At the extreme, a majority can decide to deny certain rights (say, to free speech) to a minority.

This definition, in my opinion, overstates the *value* component of these regimes. The core, or the desired objective, of this new breed of quasi-democratic regimes is multi-partyism in which, however, only one party can win. Russia has gone the furthest on the road of "electoral engineering" where there is seemingly a democracy, multiple parties, etc., but the rule of the game is that only one party can win, and that the others, in function of their "pliability" and closeness to the "party of power," are allowed to participate in the division of the spoils.

For it is precisely the "division of the spoils" that is a crucial feature of the regimes. They do not share, as some commentators believe, "values" antithetical to Western liberal values. Rather, I believe, these different values are simply invented to provide voters with a feeling that they are indeed voting for some distinct "national," "homey," "non-cosmopolitan" program, while the real objective of the party of power is to control the state in order to steal, either directly (from overcharged public works or state-owned enterprises), or indirectly (through private sector corruption and laws and regulations that are for sale).

Thus, the party of power is simply an organized thievery, which, in order to survive and prosper, needs to pretend to defend certain "values" and, most importantly, to keep on providing financial benefits to its supporters. The system is thus fully clientelistic. It functions very similarly to Mobutu's Zaire (as beautifully described in Michela's Wrong's *In the Footsteps of Mr. Kurtz*). The top guys (Erdoğan and his son, Putin, Rothenberg, and other oligarchs, etc.) do, like Mobutu, take the largest slice of the pie, but they are more than anything else, arbiters in the process of the division of money between various factions. When you read Wrong's book on Zaire, you realize that Mobutu was at the apex of the pyramid, but that he was not an unchecked dictator. To remain in power, he had to maintain support from various groups who were vying for money. This is precisely how Putin maintains his power: not as a Stalinesque dictator, but as an indispensable umpire, whose sudden departure would throw the system totally off-balance until, possibly after a civil war, a new, generally accepted arbiter emerges.

I realized that it is this particular nature of the rule combined with clientelism, which is crucial and not some opposition to "liberal" values, when I spent the summer in Serbia and Montenegro. Montenegro had been ruled by one man, Djukanović, for thirty years. He has in the meantime changed, like Putin, various positions from which he ruled: president of his party, prime minister, president of the country. Moreover, Djukanović's rule is broadly consonant with Western liberal "values" in the areas of gay rights, environment, lack of economic regulation, and the like. He has brought Montenegro to the threshold of the European Union and included it into NATO. But the structure of his rule is equivalent to that of Putin: control of the government in order to steal, and distribution of these gains to his supporters (and of course to himself and his clique).

In order for such a system to survive it needs to continue winning elections, ideally forever. Ben Ali and Mubarak, who headed similar systems in Tunisia and Egypt, eventually failed. But Djukanović, Erdoğan, Putin, Orbán, and Kaczyński have not failed so far. Again, Russia is at the forefront here. To win elections, all means are used: state sector employees are strongly "recommended" to vote for the "right" candidate or the "right" party, people are given cell phones with which they record their vote and, if they vote "right" are allowed to keep them (Montenegro used this technique for more than a decade), votes are directly bought, or false ballots are added to sow confusion. The outright stealing of the votes, by falsifying the totals, remains as the ultima ratio. In Russia, such falsification is difficult or impossible in big cities but quite feasible in small towns or faraway

POLITICS

areas, where the percentage of the vote for the "right" candidate reaches 90 percent or more.

I think that it would be wrong, though, to regard such regimes as a different species from the Western liberal regimes. They simply exaggerate some features that exist in "advanced" democracies: sale of regulations and laws is done in both but it is done more openly and blatantly in the "new" regimes; creation of a real second party in Russia is as difficult as the creation of a third party in the United States; voter suppression is just taken one step further. They amplify, sometimes in a grotesque way, the negative sides of democracies and suppress, almost fully, their positive sides.

(Published July 22, 2017)

3.6 Thinkin' 'bout a revolution

As I suppose many older people do, I was thinking about the most important parts of my life, not only personally, but socially: how did the social forces around me affect me and make me think what I think.

There is little doubt that for most of my generation in the West and the East the Cultural Revolutions of the 1960s–1970s were a crucial event. (I have to exclude the Third World from this generalization, since I do not know enough about how the Western Cultural Revolution affected ideology and the mores there.)

May and June this year was the 55th anniversary of *Les événements de mai*. Last week was the 55th anniversary of the Warsaw Pact's invasion of Czechoslovakia, which also saw the birth of the modern dissident movement in the USSR, when eight persons unfurled a poster on the Red Square condemning the invasion.

The Revolution caught me in the formative years of high school. All events that happen at that age, even when not revolutionary, have an impact on people's later lives. So much more if they are revolutionary. We were lucky that the events that affected us were revolutionary mostly in the cultural sense. At the same time China went through the Cultural Revolution, but it was an altogether different series of events, more serious, more ideological, and far bloodier. But no less significant was the Western Cultural Revolution.

What did it accomplish? It reduced social distance between the rich and the poor, a huge achievement; it liberated sex and improved women's social position in a way that led to the current acceptance of gender equality and all sexual preferences among the liberal elites; it ensured equal or similar civic rights for the Black population in the United States; it changed dramatically vestimentary habits, simplified them, and thus added to the apparent social leveling by making it more difficult to recognize social status from one's dress.

The revolution was similar in the West and in the communist East, but it produced very different effects. In the West, politically, it diminished class polarization and class antagonism. I lived through the Revolution in Belgium, where I went to high school. There was no doubt in my mind when I arrived there that Belgium was a class-stratified society, where only rich parents' boys could date rich parents' girls. The rules were clear. The Revolution, incrementally,

POLITICS

eroded them however: by the mid 1970s, this was no longer true. It produced a deep social change which, I think, has persisted.

In the East, where class differences were less, or were obliterated by the political revolution of the late 1940s, the new Revolution opened the vistas of freedom. It hinted that a different, much freer and diverse world existed close by and that it was possible—not a Utopia. It stimulated resistance to the authorities, and the feeling of freedom—both things that were anathema to the communist regimes that valued conformism and obedience.

Revolution's effects were long term and were seen well among the generation that came to power twenty years later. It may seem strange to unify in the same sentence Bill Clinton and Mikhail Gorbachev, but they do illustrate well what I have in mind. Clinton was the product of breaking class barriers to advancement, while Gorbachev was a product of the Ideas of 1968: socialism with the human face. That belief affected Gorbachev in his student years, as we know from Zdeněk Mlynař's memoirs and Gorbachev's own "confessions."

One of the complicating features of the Revolution was that it was leftist, not only in the social ways that I described, but also because it brought from oblivion the Young Marx (whose early works, by coincidence, were first published then, more than 100 years after he wrote them), and thus the belief in democratic socialism.

The challenge to the ossified pseudo-Marxist regimes in the East came from the left. And even better—thinking of the Young Marx— from the very founder of the political system the authorities claimed to represent. It was not a coincidence that almost all leaders of the Revolution in Eastern Europe came from the Communist Youth movement: the entire Praxis group in Yugoslavia, students of Lukács in Hungary, Jacek Kuroń, Adam Michnik, Leszek Kolakowski (coming from the hard Stalinist left) in Poland, Ota Šik and Alexander Dubček in Czechoslovakia.

The Revolution was similar to the Reformation: it refreshed and re-affirmed the original ideological beliefs, and thus highlighted the gap between them and reality. Later the leaders will, with the rest of the society, move toward the right: either in nationalist or classical liberal directions. But that was only possible because the first opposition came from the left, and was thus ideologically more valid than had it come from the discredited right. My point is that in 1968, East European regimes were well equipped to deal with the challenges from the right; but they were ill-equipped to deal with challenges from the left and with the seemingly apolitical challenges of long hair, loud music, and bell-bottom trousers.

61

In the West, however, after breaking up some of the social barriers and thus establishing apparent equality, the Revolution ended up, in many ways, like the Revolutions of 1848. In the latter case, formal political equality was proclaimed; in the case of the Revolutions of 1968, formal social equality was proclaimed. But in both cases economic gaps became wider. Moreover, the post-1968 economic gaps became regarded as more justifiable than before, when the revolutionaries argued that they were due to large class differences. Now, as the Revolution unfolded, the gaps reflected differences in ability and effort—in short, in merit. This is where the two iconic figures of the revolutionary generation and the turn to neoliberalism come: Bill Clinton and Tony Blair. It was the left that validated the traditional positions of the right, made them seem common-sensical and thus more firmly entrenched.

The left-wing attack on the regimes in the West soon morphed into the validation of the positions of the right, now even reinforced because shorn of its usual, and hard to justify, class support. The seemingly anti-capitalist Revolution of the 1968, made the world safe for capitalism. Joschka Fischer became foreign minister of Germany and oversaw the first deployment of German military might since the end of the Second World War; Bob Dylan received the Medal of Freedom; Mick Jagger was knighted. To more vividly appreciate the change, note that Jeremy Corbyn, perhaps the only significant political figure in the West who continued to hold the 1968-like beliefs, came to be seen in the 2020s like a relic from a distant past.

The political effects of the Revolution East and West were at first different, but over the long term, almost identical. In the East, as we have seen, the attack on the regime was from the left and that made the regimes clumsy in their response. But socialism with the human face, or any kind of socialism for that matter, was gradually discarded and, in an evolution that mimicked that in the West, the end-point was declared to be what Václav Klaus called "capitalism without adjectives." Liberals, united with strong forces of nationalism that grew independently in the meantime and were rather unimportant in 1968, brought communist regimes down. (I am not denying thereby the importance of American readiness to wage war on communism in every quarter of the globe; when I say that the regimes were brought down from within, I have in mind the fact that ideologically, by 1989, communist regimes had very little to offer to their populations.)

The Revolution—with the important exception of nationalism that I mentioned—fashioned the world in which many of us lived until the

Financial Crisis of 2008, or covid in 2019, or the war in Ukraine in 2022—whichever of the three possible markers dividing the eras one wishes to take. But, in any case, it is plain that we live in a different ideological world today.

(Published August 30, 2023)

3.7 There is no exit for dictators

In an interesting paper he tweeted yesterday, Kaushik Basu discusses, using a mathematical model, an old problem: how rulers, once they are in power, cannot leave it even if they wish to do so, because their road to power, and in power, is littered with corpses that will all (metaphorically) ask revenge if the ruler were to step down. Furthermore, since the number of misdeeds and of rulers' real or imagined enemies multiplies with each additional period in power, they need to resort to increasingly greater oppression to stay in power. Thus, even the originally well-meaning or tolerant rulers become, with the duration of their rule, tyrants. Basu is aware of the millennial nature of the problem; he cites Shakespeare's Macbeth. He could have also cited Tacitus' description of Tiberius' descent into murderous suspiciousness and folly.

Basu terms this issue "temporal inconsistency" because his assumption is that the ruler would like at one point to leave and spend the rest of his life in affluence and leisure. (I write "his" life because all individuals listed in Basu's paper are men, and he strangely resorts to the use of "she" and "her" in the mathematical part of the paper.) This assumption of a ruler who wants to retire is unrealistic, and I will explain why below. But before I do so, I need to note that there is no inconsistency in the ruler's or dictator's behavior in each individual period. (Basu acknowledges this in the latter part of the paper by stating that fully rational maximizing behavior in each individual period may still lead to an overall suboptimal outcome.) Assume that the ruler plays an annual game where he wonders: am I better off if I retire now, or if I commit another crime, which would make my retirement next year more difficult but my rule this year safer? The answer is simple: he is better off committing another crime in the expectation that this would make his overthrow less likely. He replays that game every year and every year he reaches the same conclusion. Thus, the ruler's decisions are not at all irrational or even inconsistent.

From Machiavelli's point of the art of statecraft it would be equally wrong to fault the ruler. According to Machiavelli, the role of the ruler is to rule, like the role of a baker is to bake. In order to rule he must unavoidably commit misdeeds or crimes because it is the nature of politics and human society. But he should not use unnecessary force; in other words, crimes must be acknowledged by the ruler intimately as such, and their use must be kept to the minimum necessary to stay in power. And, indeed, most rulers do believe that they are doing just that.

But why is the very assumption of a ruler who wants to retire generally wrong? (I know that there are some examples of rulers who have chosen the road of retirement but they are extremely rare: the reason why we speak of Sulla is precisely because he was unusual in choosing retirement and powerlessness after having committed many misdeeds.) The assumption is wrong because rulers' objective is not a comfortable life on a yacht in the Caribbean—the example Basu gives in the end of the paper—but raw power and enforcement of an ideology.

When power as such becomes the objective, as it is among all politicians, and autocratic rules especially, there is no amount of worldly goods that could substitute for power. Rulers cannot be cajoled (as Basu seems to believe) into leaving power. And this is not just because of the possible punishment that may await them in retirement, but because they crave, and they need, the exercise of power. Svetlana Alliluyeva writes in her memoirs that her father lived only for politics and was interested only in politics. And, indeed, whoever has read memoirs of Stalin's comrades or Stalin's biographies could not but be struck with the emptiness—in the normal human sense—of the life that Stalin led at the peak of his power. It was the life of interminable meetings, long hours of reading, quasi solitary dinners with a few scared companions, monotonous banquets; a dry life devoid of both humanity and affluence. There is nothing you can offer to Stalin to make him leave power, even if you can guarantee that he would live for the rest of his life safe in luxury.

The same applies to ideologues. Or, perhaps even more so, because ideologues believe that they are on a unique mission to save their nation or the world, and obviously then being in power is a necessary condition for such a salvation. Take Hitler as the easiest and strongest example. He believed from a relatively young age that the Providence has selected him to save Germany and make it powerful again. Thinking that offering him, say in 1938 or 1942, a retirement in the Austrian Alps, or an endless Wagner festival in his beloved Linz, in exchange for stepping down is so ludicrous that it can produce only derision and laughter.

Basu's concluding sentence—that giving rulers an escape route through luxurious retirement might make many "Individuals with no interest in power and tyranny … strive to become tyrants for no other reason but to get that castle in the Pacific Island"—although said probably in jest and with the intent of providing a paradox, is simply wrong. Rulers do not *want* to go to the Pacific islands.

Dictators often evolve during their rule, moving more toward the power-hungry tyrants and ideologues than they were in the beginning of their reign, even regardless of the amount of crimes they might have committed. Here, Putin comes to mind. He came to power by giving the impression of being ready to do the oligarchs' bidding, to be hard-working and meticulous, pro-Western, and in love of comfort and affluence. Gradually however he evolved: first, by dropping the oligarchs who brought him to power, and then by changing ideologically to see himself as a savior of Russia. If that is supposed to be his role, he obviously has no choice but to stay in power because everybody else, in his view, would drive the country to ruin.

We thus come to the conclusion that there is absolutely nothing that can be offered to dictators to leave power; that thinking that there is something shows a misunderstanding of what motivates people in politics. It also shows the naiveté of other economists (not Basu as he explicitly rejects it) who hold that *all* human activities are driven by the search for material profit and comfort.

Basu's suggestion that there should be globally enforced term-limits is thus not only impossible to implement but shows a lack of understanding of politics. Regarding the practical impossibility of its implementation, one need not only mention that such a rule would never pass through any international organization, but that even if that were to happen, there would be many ways of avoiding observing the rule, while formally adhering to it. Putin, at first, side-stepped the issue of term limits by taking the position of prime minister, while effectively still remaining in charge; Havel got rid of term limits because he argued that being president of Czechoslovakia was different from being president of the Czech Republic. Djukanović, the Montenegrin leader, ruled for more than three decades by switching between the positions of president and prime minister. Erdoğan did the same by changing the system from parliamentary to presidential. There is, in effect, no way technically of implementing the notion of global term-limits even if, somehow, miraculously, the world were to come to believe in them.

And, more importantly, there is nothing that can be offered to dictators to make them step down. They have to continue to rule until they either die peacefully in their beds, and after death became either vilified or celebrated (or at times, both), or until they are

POLITICS

overthrown, or meet an assassin's bullet. Once on the top, there is no exit. They have become prisoners like many others whom they have thrown into jails.

(Published October 28, 2023)

3.8 Trump as the ultimate triumph of neoliberalism

Modern capitalist societies are built on a dichotomy: in the political space decisions are (to be) made on an equal basis, with everybody having the same say and with the structure of power being flat; in the economic space the power is held by the owners of capital, the decisions are dictatorial, and the structure of power is hierarchical. The dichotomy was always a complex balancing act: at times, the political principles of nominal equality tended to intrude into the economic space and to limit the power of owners: trade unions, ability to sue companies, regulations regarding discrimination, hiring and firing. At other times, it was the economic sphere that invaded the political: the wealthy were able to buy politicians and impose the laws they liked.

The entire history of capitalism can be readily understood as the struggle between these two principles: is the democratic principle "exported" from politics to rule in economics too, or is the hierarchical principle of company organization to invade the political sphere? Social democracy was essentially the former; neoliberalism was the latter.

Neoliberalism justified and promoted the introduction of purely economic and hierarchical principles in the political life. While it maintained the pretense of equality (one-person, one-vote), it eroded it through the ability of the rich to select, fund, and make elect the politicians friendly to their interests. The number of books and articles that document the increasing political power of the rich is enormous: there is hardly any doubt that this was happening in the United States and many other countries around the world over the past forty years.

The introduction of the rules of behavior taken from the corporate sector into politics means that politicians no longer see people whom they rule as co-citizens but as hired employees. Employees can be hired and fired, humiliated and dismissed, ripped off, cheated, or ignored.

Until Trump came to power the invasion of the political space by economic rules of behavior was concealed. There was a pretense that politicians treated people as citizens. The bubble was burst by Trump who, unschooled in the subtleties of democratic dialectics, could not see how anything could be wrong with the application of business rules to politics. Coming from the private sector, and from its most piracy-oriented segment dealing with real estate, gambling, and Miss

Universe, he rightly thought—supported by the neoliberal ideology—that the political space is merely an extension of economics.

Many people accuse Trump of ignorance. But this is I think a wrong way to look at things. He may not be interested in the US constitution and complex rules that regulate politics in a democratic society because he, whether consciously or intuitively, thinks that they should not matter or even exist. The rules with which he is familiar are the rules of companies: "You are fired!": a purely hierarchical decision, based on power consecrated by wealth, and unchecked by any other consideration.

By introducing economics into politics, neoliberals have done an enormous harm to the "publicness" of decision-making and to democracy. They have brought many societies to a stage inferior to that of being ruled by self-interested despots. Mancur Olson, in his famous distinction between rulers who are roving or stationary bandits, recounts the anecdote of a Sicilian farmer who supports a one-man despotic rule by arguing that the ruler has "an all-encompassing interest": in order to maintain his rule and maximize his own tax intake, he does have an interest in prosperity of his subjects. This is different, and much superior, Olson argued, to a roving bandit who, like the Mongol invaders, has interest only in the short-term extraction from his (temporary) subjects.

Why is a neoliberal ruler worse than the "all-encompassing-interest" despot? Because he lacks the all-encompassing interest in his polity, as he does not see himself as being part of it; rather he is the owner of a giant company called, in this case, the United States of America, where he decides who should do what. People complain that Trump, in this crisis, is lacking the most elementary human compassion. But, while they are right in diagnosis, they are wrong in understanding the origin of the lack of compassion. Like any rich owner he does not see that his role is to show compassion to his hired hands, but to decide what they should do, and, even when the occasion presents itself, to squeeze them out of their pay, make them work harder, dismiss them without a benefit. In doing so to his putative countrymen he is just applying to an area called "politics" the principles that he learned and used for many years in business.

Trump is the best student of neoliberalism because he applies its key principles without concealment.

(Published April 7, 2020)

THE WORLD UNDER CAPITALISM

3.9 What we owe to Donald Trump: A different angle

Now as Trump is being made ready to enter history, many publications are reviewing his presidency, as indeed they have been doing during the past four years. Many of such assessments are trivial, turgid, and tedious. He is being reviled for his callousness, racism, xenophobia, arrogance, inefficiency, ineffectiveness, ignorance. Many who will defend him will probably do so for the same reasons: but in their view xenophobia, racism, and arrogance may be considered virtues, not deep moral flaws.

My assessment is entirely different. First, where I think Trump was right, and second, what Trump allowed us to learn.

Trump was right in the essential principles of foreign policy: America First and mild isolationism. To see that one ought to realize that there are only two possible foreign policies for the United States of America: American exceptionalism and America First. American exceptionalism is, as the name says, based on an ideology of American preeminence, held to be earned and deserved on account of the unique *virtu* of the new republic. The preeminence for the USA clearly implies a structured hierarchical system of countries where the USA is on the top and other countries play subsidiary and inferior roles. The ultimate unspoken objective of that policy is mastery of the world. The US is not the first country to have entertained such dreams: from Egypt, Rome, Christian Empire of Byzantium, Muslim Empire, Charlemagne, the Huns, Tamerlane, Napoleon, Hitler, the Communist Empire of the USSR, the list is long. While achieving such an empire is most unlikely, the road to that objective is paved with wars. This is why the ideology of "indispensable nation," almost by definition, calls for, in Gore Vidal's terms, "endless wars for endless peace." It is not by some accident that America has been at practically uninterrupted war for seventy years.

"America First" at least formally puts all countries on the same level. It argues that America will follow its own interests but it does not expect less from others. As Trump, not a scholar of international relations, nevertheless stated in his United Nations speech, he would expect the same policy as regards their own countries from Algeria to Zimbabwe. In the America First policy, the US will always, because of its size and importance, punch more than others but it will have no desire or illusion that it has to rule others or tell them how they should order their internal affairs. It will behave transactionally,

70

POLITICS

which is indeed a policy that makes war much less likely. Interests can be negotiated, ideologies cannot.

Trump basically followed this policy until his obsession with China broke through after covid-19, which he seemed to have considered as some kind of China-made express ploy to evict him from the presidency. Nevertheless, he began no new wars, and made, at times important, moves to end wars started almost twenty years ago, for which nobody in Washington could any longer proffer any rationale. They were pure imperial wars like the ones in *The Tartar Steppe*, where nobody at the seat of the empire even knows where their soldiers are fighting, and even less why.

Trump made two signal contributions to our knowledge of politics and business. To the politics he brought all the skills he had practiced for almost half-a-century in business and, as I wrote, his was the ultimate triumph of neoliberalism (see the previous piece). He considered citizens as his employees, whom he could at will push around and fire. He saw presidency as Bezos sees his own position at Amazon: he can do anything, unconstrained by any rules and laws.

Trump tore off the curtain that divides citizens, the spectators of the political game, from the rulers, and displayed the wheeling-dealing, exchange of favors, the use of public power for private gain in an open, in-your-face manner, available to all who attended the show to see. While in past administrations such illegal and semi-legal actions as receiving money from foreign potentates, moving from one to another lucrative position, cheating on taxes, were done with discretion and some decorum, with the curtain lowered so that spectators could not see and participate in the malfeasance, this was now done in the open. It was thus thanks to Trump that we could see the immense corruption lying at the heart of the political process.

But he did more. When he came with these corrupt manners to the presidency, they were the manners honed by fifty years of business dealings, which involved all sorts of semi-legal or illegal shenanigans. But this did not stop him in his business ascent. Rather they made the ascent possible, letting him enjoy a brilliant career in the New York business world, become rich, and be a valued guest at many parties, including being an esteemed contributor to political campaigns as, for example, the one run by Hillary Clinton for US Senate. The very fact that his climb to the business power was not seen in any way as exceptionable or unacceptable shows that everybody else around him used the same means to come to the top.

Thus, from knowing more about Trump we know more about the means used to succeed in the rich business milieu of New York,

THE WORLD UNDER CAPITALISM

and even of the world, as Trump and his companions made deals in Scotland, Russia, the Middle East, China, and elsewhere. His close confidants and family members, who betrayed him in order to garner multi-million dollar contracts, exhibited a behavior that Trump himself would have done (and approved of) but that showed what kind of ethical standards are prevalent in that environment. Trump thus gave us another very valuable lesson: it showed the rot, corruption, and impunity that lie at the heart of many powerful businesses.

His persona revealed the depth of corruption at the center of politics and at the center of business. These are unpardonable sins. Sins enjoyed in secret are acceptable or overlooked; sins flaunted are not. These who replace him will do their best, not to change corruption because it has become a systemic feature, but to cover it up. But, once you see the truth, it will be difficult to go back pretending nothing has happened.

(Published November 7, 2020)

POLITICS

3.10 The comprador intelligentsia

In *Orientalism*, Edward Said spoke of an orientalist as an interpreter of local custom and knowledge to the foreign intellectual. A common term in neo-Marxist literature of the 1960s–1980s, for the absence of articulation between the domestic areas that interacted with the rest of the world, and the hinterland that was cut off from it, was the comprador bourgeoisie. In the past thirty years, the world might have created a "comprador intelligentsia" too.

What I have in mind here is the following. On the global level, the West is unquestionably the creator of most of knowledge. Its only two significant competitors are China and Islam. However, it still dominates, economically as well as in its readiness to spread its knowledge and to influence what is produced elsewhere. Sometimes out of best intentions, sometimes out of ignorance, and sometimes out of ulterior motives, a number of academic, non-governmental, quasi-governmental, and fully governmental, associations have been created with that objective in mind.

These institutions tend to finance the projects that deal with the issues that are currently considered important or fashionable in the Center. They could hardly justify doing otherwise to their donors, who are not interested in whether such topics are of relevance in the "faraway countries of which we know nothing." The projects, or more exactly, the funding that comes with them, create a small local elite, the comprador intelligentsia. The elite becomes very savvy in packaging and presenting the results of the research so that it appeals to the Western funders. The problem, however, is that the comprador intelligentsia—being focused on pleasing the donors—is often cut off from the domestic intellectual life. Like the comprador bourgeoisie it has very few links with the "hinterland": it exists purely thanks to the foreign donors. Once the foreign donors move somewhere else, the comprador intelligentsia disappears. (If the donors move to another topic, the comprador intelligentsia will try to move, with them, to the new topic too.)

Intellectual activity, which is largely unrelated to the real issues in a given place and time, and responds to the epistemic desires of an entirely different place, is meaningless. It leaves hardly any trace domestically. It does permit the country to remain within some vaguely defined orbit of international knowledge-creation, but the motivating forces of this knowledge-generation are entirely external. They produce little domestically, other than allowing the

73

comparator intelligentsia a nice life of intellectual and material comfort.

Such phenomena are seen in all peripheral societies where financial resources to fund research are meager, and the intellectual class needs to survive. I have seen it, in rather technical matters, too. Until about ten years ago, statistical agencies in many African countries were very weak, both in terms of personnel and money. They could not organize household surveys that have been routine in the rest of the world. Thus, very little of such information existed. What did the foreign donors do? They each, responding to their temporary interests or whims of their bosses, funded a study of this or that area, or of this or that population. So, one got (e.g. in Tanzania) most disparate surveys, none of which could be combined in any time-series, and none of which was allowed to find out whether things were changing, improving or not. The Swedes would fund surveys of poor rural households in area X, the US AID would fund the survey of single mothers in Y, the British, not to be outdone, will discover sudden interests in youth unemployment in Z. Domestic statistical office will oblige—with indifference—because of need of money. The surveys will be done, the report written, and sent to the higher authorities in Stockholm, Washington, and London. To be promptly forgotten there. And they would be entirely ignored locally.

The same is happening with the so-called Randomized Controlled Trials (RCT), which were crowned with the Nobel prize. In order to proceed to many ethically questionable practices (on which much has been written, see Sanjay Reddy, Angus Deaton and Nancy Cartwright, Martin Ravallion), domestic support by few individuals is invented, in many cases probably in return for promises of fees or foreign travel. When the RTC project that subjected people in different parts of Nairobi to arbitrary water cuts led to the worldwide outcry, the Principal Investigator Paul Gertler and his colleagues wrote a pathetic defense of the project by arguing that it had local "purchase" through an ill-defined cooperation with local government: "through joint discussions between the World Bank and Nairobi Water teams, it was agreed to additionally test a softer less potentially harmful nudge [disconnection from water services!] as an alternative." Even if one leaves out the ethical problems of RCT (on which I am not focusing here), this is yet another example of a foreign-funded project with no links to any creation of useful domestic knowledge. Its only result—other than leaving poor people without water—and perhaps the only objective to start with, is the personal aggrandizement of the Center's researchers. (One wonders if Kenyan researchers could engage in a similar exploratory project by withholding RTC researchers' salaries for several months to study how they would react.)

Similarly to the comprador-driven domestic development, which never resulted in economic growth, the comprador-driven intellectual development is sterile. It will continue to be produced because it supports the ideological needs of the Center and the financial needs of the periphery, but it will never have much influence in either: the Center thinks it has nothing to learn from the periphery, and nobody in the periphery is much interested in the topics given to the comprador intelligentsia as a homework to study.

(Published February 18, 2023)

— PART II —

INEQUALITY

— 4 —

INEQUALITY WITHIN NATIONS

4.1 Why inequality matters

This is the question that I am often asked. So, I decided to write my answers down.

The argument about why inequality should *not* matter is almost always couched in the following way: if everybody is getting better-off, why should we care if somebody is becoming extremely rich? Perhaps he deserves to be rich—or, whatever the case, even if he does not deserve it, we need not worry about his wealth. If we do, that implies envy and other moral flaws. I have dealt with the misplaced issue of envy in "Why we all care about inequality ..." (in response to points made by Martin Feldstein) and also in response to Harry Frankfurt (see Section 4.4 below), and do not want to repeat it. So, let's leave envy out and focus on the reasons why we should be concerned about high inequality.

The reasons can be formally broken down into three groups: instrumental reasons having to do with economic growth, reasons of fairness, and reasons of politics.

The relationship between inequality and economic growth is one of the oldest relationships studied by economists. A very strong presumption was that without high profits there will be no growth, and high profits imply substantial inequality. We find this argument already in Ricardo, where profit is the engine of economic growth. We find it also in Keynes and Schumpeter, and then in standard models of economic growth. We find it even in Stalinist industrialization debates. To invest, you have to have profits (that is, surplus above subsistence); in privately owned economy it means that some people have to be wealthy enough to save and invest, and in a state-directed economy, it means that the state should take all the surplus.

But notice that, throughout, the argument is not one in favor of inequality as such. If it were, we would not be concerned about the use of the surplus. The argument is about a seemingly paradoxical behavior of the wealthy: they should be sufficiently rich but should not use that money to live well and consume but to invest. This point is quite nicely, and famously, made by Keynes in the opening paragraphs of his *Economic Consequences of the Peace*. For us, it is sufficient to note that this is an argument in favor of inequality *provided* wealth is not used for private pleasure.

The empirical work conducted in the past twenty years has failed to uncover a positive relationship between inequality and growth. The data were not sufficiently good, especially regarding inequality, where the typical measure used was the Gini coefficient, which is too aggregate and inert to capture changes in the distribution; also the relationship itself may vary in function of other variables, or the level of development. This has led economists to a cul-de-sac and discouragement; so much so that since the late 1990s and early 2000s such empirical literature has almost ceased to be produced. It is reviewed in more detail in the section 2 of the working paper by Roy van der Weide and myself.

More recently, with much better data on income distribution, the argument that inequality and growth are negatively correlated has gained ground. In a joint paper Roy van der Weide and I show this, using forty years of US micro data. With better data and somewhat more sophisticated thinking about inequality, the argument becomes much more nuanced: inequality may be good for future incomes of the rich (that is, they become even richer) but it may be bad for future incomes of the poor (that is, they fall further behind). In this dynamic framework, growth rate itself is no longer something homogenous as, indeed, it is not in real life. When we say that the American economy is growing at three percent per year, it simply means that the person with the average income is getting better off at that rate; it tells us nothing about how much better off, or worse off, others are getting.

Why would inequality have bad effect on the growth of the lower deciles of the distribution, as Roy and I found? Because it leads to low educational (and even health) achievements among the poor, who become excluded from meaningful jobs and from meaningful contributions they could make to their own and society's improvement. Excluding a certain group of people from good education, be it

80

because of their insufficient income or gender or race, can never be good for the economy, or at least it can never be preferable to their inclusion.

High inequality, which effectively debars some people from full participation, translates into an issue of fairness or justice. It does so because it affects inter-generational mobility. People who are relatively poor (which is what high inequality means) are not able, even if they are not poor in an absolute sense, to provide for their children a fraction of benefits, from education and inheritance to social capital, that the rich provide to their offspring. This implies that inequality tends to persist across generations, which in turn means that opportunities are vastly different for those at the top of the pyramid and those on the bottom. We have the two factors joining forces here: on the one hand, the negative effect of exclusion on growth that carries over generations (which is our instrumental reason for not liking high inequality), and on the other, lack of equality of opportunity (which is an issue of justice).

High inequality also has political effects. The rich have more political power and they use that political power to promote their own interests and to entrench their relative position in the society. This means that all the negative effects due to exclusion and lack of equality of opportunity are reinforced and made permanent (at least, until a big social earthquake destroys them). In order to fight off the advent of such an earthquake, the rich must make themselves safe and unassailable from "conquest." This leads to adversarial politics and destroys social cohesion. Ironically, social instability, which then results, discourages investments of the rich; that is, it undermines the very action that was at the beginning adduced as the key reason why high wealth and inequality may be socially desirable.

We therefore reach the end point, where the unfolding of actions that were at first supposed to produce beneficent outcome destroys by its own logic the original rationale. We have to go back to the beginning and, instead of seeing high wealth as promoting investments and growth, we begin to see it, over time, as producing exactly the opposite effects: reducing investments and growth.

(Published December 5, 2018)

4.2 In defence of equality (without welfare economics)

When I taught recently at the Summer School at Groningen University, I began my lecture on the measurement of inequality by distinguishing between the Italian and English schools as they were defined in 1921 by Corrado Gini:

> The methods of Italian writers ... are not ... comparable to his [Dalton's] own, inasmuch as their purpose is to estimate, not the inequality of economic welfare, but the inequality of incomes and wealth, independently of all hypotheses as to the functional relations between these quantities and economic welfare or as to the additive character of the economic welfare of individuals. (Corrado Gini, "Measurement of Inequality of Incomes," *Economic Journal*, March 1921)

I put myself squarely in the camp of the "Italians." Measurement of income inequality is like measurement of any natural or social phenomenon. We measure inequality as we measure temperature or height of people. The English (or welfarist) school believes that the measure of income inequality is only a proxy for a measure of a more fundamental phenomenon: inequality in welfare. The ultimate variable, according to them, that we want to estimate is welfare (or even happiness) and how it is distributed. Income provides only an empirically feasible short-cut to it.

I would have been sympathetic to that approach if I knew how individual utility can be measured. There is, I believe, no way of comparing utilities of different persons. We all agree that the marginal utility must be diminishing in income because it is the foundation of economic micro theory. (If marginal utility of income were not decreasing, we would not be able to explain why demand curves are sloping downward.) But, we have no idea whether, while both your and my marginal utility functions are decreasing, my level of utility may, at any point, be orders of magnitude greater than yours or the reverse.

The only way for the "welfaristas" to solve this conundrum is to assume that all individuals have the same utility function. This is such an unrealistically bold assumption that I think nobody would really care to defend it except when it is considered as a lesser evil that allows "welfaristas" to cling to their utilitarianism, to define measures like the Atkinson index and to continue believing that the real thing we want and (they claim) that we do measure is inequality in individual welfares.

Now, the welfarist approach continues to be associated with pro-equality policies. Why? Because if all people have the same utility function, then the optimal distribution of income is such that everybody has the same income. If from that equilibrium you take some income from A and give it to B, loss of utility of A will outweigh the utility gain of B (because marginal utility is decreasing) and thus, obviously, total utility will be less in any situation where income is not fully equally distributed.

My students then asked how I can justify concern with inequality if I reject the welfarist view that is the main ideological vehicle through which equality of outcomes is being justified. (A non-utilitarian, contractarian alternative is provided by Rawls. Yet another alternative, based on equal capabilities—a close cousin to equality of opportunity [of which more below] is provided by Amartya Sen.)

My answer was that I justify concern with income inequality on three grounds.

The first ground is instrumental: the effect on economic growth. After the period of the 1990s where, due to lack of appropriate data, the empirical work on the relationship between inequality and economic growth ended with inconclusive results, we are presently having more and more evidence that high levels of inequality slow down economic growth. We are able to show that now because we have access to micro data and a much more sophisticated view of both inequality and growth. Here, as examples, are the papers by Sarah Voitchovsky, and by Roy van der Weide and myself. But, it has to be acknowledged: if empirical literature were to come to a different conclusion, namely that inequality helps growth, we should have to drop that instrumental argument against high inequality.

The second is political effect. In societies where economic and political spheres are not separated by the Chinese wall (and all existing societies are such), inequality in economic power seeps and ultimately invades and conquers the political sphere. Instead of one-person/ one-vote democracy we get one-dollar/ one-vote plutocracy. This outcome appears inevitable, especially in modern societies, where running political campaigns is extremely expensive. But it was not very different in ancient Greece or Rome. If we hold that democracy, a more-or-less equal influence of everyone on public affairs, is a good thing, we have to be in favor of severe limits on income and wealth inequality. It seems to me that the negative impact of inequality on democracy, not only obvious in theory, is now being confirmed empirically as well (see Martin Giddens' *Affluence and Influence*).

Let me note parenthetically that even if we failed to detect such explicit influence of the rich on policy-making, the *a priori* case that it must exist (but is difficult to measure) would still be extremely strong. Because, for the opposite case to hold, i.e. rich people give money to politicians but do not get anything in return, we have to assume an entirely irrational behavior of the rich: they throw money away for no reason. That goes so much against the fundamentals of economics that if we assume it here we should also assume that when people (say) go to restaurants; they throw money randomly: "Your glass of wine costs $10. Well, I will give you $15 and you do not need to give me the wine." If that behavior seems reasonable to you, then I would agree that the rich may not influence politicians to whom they give money.

The third ground is philosophical. As Rawls has argued, every departure from unequal distribution of resources has to be defended by an appeal to a higher principle. Because we are all equal individuals (whether as declared by the Universal Charter of Human Rights or by God), we should all have an approximately equal opportunity to develop our skills and to lead a "good (and pleasant) life." Because inequality of income almost directly translates into inequality of opportunities, it also directly negates that fundamental equality of all humans. This is, I think, pretty evident on an *a priori* basis, but we have also an increasing number of papers that show the positive correlation between inequality of income and inequality of opportunity (see Gustavo Marrero and Juan-Gabriel Rodriguez; Miles Corak). Families with greater income ensure that their children have much better opportunities (which negates the fundamental equality of which we spoke) andmake sure this new inequality of opportunity is converted into yet higher income for themselves and their own children. So, a positive feedback works very strongly to maintain unequal access to opportunities.

I have to say here that, in addition, inequality of opportunity negatively affects economic growth (so we now have a negative effect going from my third ground back to the first), which makes inequality of opportunity abhorrent on two grounds: (1) it negates fundamental human equality, and (2) it lowers the pace of material improvements for society.

My argument, if I need to reiterate it, is: you can reject welfarism, hold that inter-personal comparison of utility is impossible, and still feel very strongly that economic outcomes should be made more equal—that inequality should be limited so that it does not strongly affect opportunities, so that it does not slow growth and so that it does not undermine democracy. Isn't that enough?

(Published March 25, 2023)

INEQUALITY

4.3 Why twentieth-century tools cannot be used to address twenty-first-century income inequality

The remarkable period of reduced income and wealth inequality in the rich countries, roughly from the end of the Second World War to the early 1980s, relied on four pillars: strong trade unions, mass education, high taxes, large government transfers. Since the increase of inequality twenty or more years ago, the failed attempts to stem its further rise have relied on trying, or at least advocating, the expansion of all or some of the four pillars. But neither of them will do the job in the twenty-first century.

Why? Consider trade unions first. The decline of trade union density, present in all rich countries and especially strong in the private sector, is not the product of more inimical government policies only. They might have contributed to the decline but are not the main cause of it. The underlying organization of labor changed. The shift from manufacturing to services and from enforced presence on factory floors or offices to remote work implied a multiplication of relatively small work units, often not located physically in the same place. Organizing dispersed workforce is much more difficult than organizing workers who work in a single huge plant and share a single interest. In addition, the declining role of the unions is a reflection of diminished power of labor *vis-à-vis* capital, which is due to the massive expansion of wage labor (that is, labor working under capitalist system) since the end of the Cold War and China's re-integration into the world economy. While the latter was a one-off shock, its effects will persist for at least several decades, and may be reinforced by future high population growth rates in Africa, thus keeping the relative abundance of labor undiminished.

Mass education was a tool for reduction of inequality in the West in the period when the average number of years of schooling went up from five or six in the 1950s to thirteen or more today. This led to a reduction in the skill premium, the gap between college educated and those with only high or elementary school, so much so that the famous Dutch economist Jan Tinbergen believed in the mid 1970s that by the turn of the century the skill premium will be zero. But mass expansion of education is impossible when a country has reached thirteen or fourteen years of education on average, simply because the maximum level of education is bounded from above. Thus, we cannot expect small increases in the average education

86

levels to provide the equalizing effect on wages that the mass education once did.

High taxation of current income and high social transfers were crucial to reduce income inequality. But their further increases are politically difficult. The main reason may be a much more skeptical view of the role of government and of tax-and-transfer policies that is now shared by the middle classes in many countries compared to their predecessors half a century ago. This is not saying that people just want lower taxation or are unaware that without high taxes the systems of social security, free education, modern infrastructure, etc. would collapse. But it is saying that the electorate is more skeptical about the gains to be achieved from additional increases in taxes imposed on current income and that such increases are unlikely to be voted in.

So, if the high underlying inequality is a threat to social homogeneity and democracy, what tools should be used to fight it? It is where I think we need to think not only out of the box in purely instrumental fashion, but to set ourselves a new objective: an egalitarian capitalism based on approximately equal endowments of both capital and skills across the population. Such capitalism generates egalitarian outcomes even without a large redistributionist state. To put it in simple terms: If the rich have only twice as many units of capital and twice as many units of skill than the poor, and if the returns per unit of capital and skill are approximately equal, then overall inequality cannot be more than 2 to 1.

How can endowments be equalized? As far as capital is concerned, by deconcentration of ownership of assets. As far as labor is concerned, mostly through equalization of returns to the approximately same skill levels. In one case, it passes through equalization of the stock of endowments, in the other through equalization of the returns to the stocks (of education).

Let us start with capital. It is a remarkable fact, to which little attention has been paid, that the concentration of wealth and income from property has remained at the incredibly high level of about 90 Gini points or more since the 1970s in all rich countries. This is to a large extent the key reason why the change in the relative power of capital over labor and the increase in the capital share in net output was directly translated into a higher inter-personal inequality. This obvious fact was overlooked simply because it is so ... obvious. We are used to thinking that as the capital share goes up, so must income inequality. Yes, this is true—but it is true because capital is extremely concentrated, with most of it owned by the people in the top income decile and thus an increase in a very unequal source of income must push overall inequality up.

But, if capital ownership becomes less concentrated, then an increase in the share of capital that may (let's suppose) be inevitable because of international forces, such as the Chinese move to capitalism, or artificial intelligence, does not need to lead to higher inequality within individual rich countries.

The methods of reducing capital concentration are not new or unknown. They were just never used seriously and consistently. We can divide them into three groups. First, favorable tax policies (including a guaranteed minimum rate of return) to make equity ownership more attractive to small and medium shareholders (and less attractive to big shareholders, that is, a policy exactly the opposite of that which exists today in the United States). Second, increased worker ownership through Employee Stock Ownership Plans or other company-level incentives. Third, use of inheritance or wealth tax as a means of evening out access to capital by using the tax proceeds to give every young adult a capital grant (as recently proposed by Tony Atkinson).

What to do with labor? There, in a rich and well-educated society, the issue is not just to make education more accessible to those who did not have a chance to study (although that too is obviously important) but to equalize the returns from education between equally educated people. Significant source of wage inequality is not any longer the difference in the years of schooling (as it was in the past), but the difference in wages (for the same number of years of education) based either on the perceived or actual difference in school qualities. The way to reduce this inequality is to equalize the quality of schools. This, in the US, and increasingly in the European context as well, implies improvement in the quality of public schools (a point argued by Bernie Sanders in the recent US election). This can be achieved only by large investments in improved public education and by withdrawals of numerous advantages (including the tax-free status) enjoyed by private universities that command huge financial endowments. Without the leveling of the playing field between private and public schools, a mere increase in the number of years of schooling or the ability of a rare child of lower-middle-class status to attend elite colleges (that increasingly serve only the rich), will not reduce inequality in labor incomes.

In my next post I will address the issue of the welfare state in the era of globalization and migration.

(Published March 12, 2017)

4.4 The welfare state in the age of globalization

In my previous post, which looked at policies to reduce inequality in the twenty-first century, I mentioned that I will next discuss the welfare state. Here it is.

It has become a truism to say that the welfare state is under stress from the effects of globalization and migration. It will help to understand the origin of this stress if we go back to the origins of the welfare state.

As Avner Offer has recently reminded us in his excellent book (co-authored with Daniel Söderberg) *The Nobel Factor: The Prize in Economics, Social Democracy and the Market Turn*, the origin of social democracy and the welfare state is in the realization (and financial ability to deal with it) that all people in their lives go through periods where they are not earning anything, but have to consume: this applies to the young (hence children's benefits), to the sick (health care and sick pay), to those who had the misfortune to get injured at work (worker's accident insurance), to mothers when they give birth (parental leave), to people who lose jobs (unemployment benefits), and to the elderly (pensions). The welfare state was created to provide these benefits, delivered in the form of insurance, for either unavoidable or very common conditions. It was built on the assumed commonality of behavior or, differently put, cultural and often ethnic homogeneity. It is no accident that the prototypical welfare state, born in Sweden in the 1930s, had many elements of (not used here in a pejorative sense) national socialism.

In addition to commonality of behavior and experiences, the welfare state, in order to be sustainable, required mass participation. Social insurance cannot work over small parts of the workforce because it then naturally leads to adverse selection, a point well illustrated by the endless wrangles over US health care. The rich, or those who are unlikely to be unemployed, or the healthy ones, do not want to subsidize the "others" and opt out. The system that would rely only on the "others" is unsustainable because of huge premiums it would require. Thus, the welfare state can work only when it covers all, or almost all, labor force, i.e. when it is (1) massive and (2) includes people with similar economic conditions.

Globalization erodes both requirements. Trade globalization has led to the well-documented decline in the share of the middle class in most Western countries and income polarization. With income polarization the rich realize that they are better off creating their own private systems because sharing the systems with those who are substantially poorer implies sizeable income transfers. This leads to "social separatism" of the rich, reflected in the growing importance of private health plans, private pensions, and private education. The bottom line is that a very unequal, or polarized, society cannot maintain an extensive welfare state.

Economic migration to which most of the rich societies have been newly exposed in the past fifty years (especially so in Europe) also undercuts the support for the welfare state. This happens through inclusion of people with actual or perceived differences in social norms or lifecycle experiences. It is the same phenomenon as dubbed by Peter Lindert's "lack of affinity" between the white majority and African Americans in the US, which rendered the US welfare state historically smaller than those of its European counterparts. The same process is now taking place in Europe, where large pockets of immigrants have not been assimilated and where the native population believes that the migrants are getting an unfair share of the benefits. Lack of affinity need not be construed as some sinister discrimination. Sometimes it could indeed be that but, more often, it may be grounded in correctly thinking that one is unlikely to experience the lifecycle events of the same nature or frequency as others, and is hence unwilling to contribute to such an insurance. In the US, the underlying fact that African Americans are more likely to be unemployed probably has led to less generous unemployment benefits; similarly, the underlying fact that migrants are likely to have more children than the natives might lead to the curtailment of children's benefits. In any case, the difference in expected lifetime experiences undermines the homogeneity necessary for a sustainable welfare state.

In addition, in the era of globalization more developed welfare states might experience a perverse effect of attracting less skilled or less ambitious migrants. Under "everything being the same" conditions, a decision of a migrant about where to emigrate will depend on the expected income in one country vs. another. In principle, that would favor richer countries. But, we have also to include a migrant's expectation regarding where in the income distribution of the recipient country she expects to end up. If she expects to be in the low-income deciles, then a more egalitarian country with a larger welfare state will be more attractive. An opposite calculation will be made by the migrants who expect to end up in the higher ends of recipient countries' income distributions. If the former migrants are either less skilled or less ambitious than the latter (which is reasonable

INEQUALITY WITHIN NATIONS

to assume), then the less skilled will tend to choose countries with more developed welfare states. Hence the adverse selection.

In very abstract terms, the countries that would be exposed to the sharpest adverse selection will be those with large welfare states and low income mobility. Migrants going to such countries cannot expect, even in the next generation, to have children who would climb up the income ladder. In a destructive feedback, such countries will attract the least skilled or the least ambitious migrants, and once they create an underclass, the upward mobility of their children will be limited. The system then works like a self-fulfilling prophecy: it attracts ever more unskilled migrants who fail to assimilate. The natives tend to see migrants as generally lacking in skills and ambition (which may be true because these are the kinds of people their country attracts) and hence as "different." At the same time, the failure to be accepted will be seen by the migrants as confirmation of natives' anti-migrant prejudices, or, even worse, as religious or ethnic discrimination.

There is no easy solution to the vicious circle faced by the developed welfare states in the era of globalization. This is why I argued in my previous post (Section 4.3) for (1) policies that would lead toward equalization of endowments so that eventually taxation of current income can be reduced and the size of the welfare state be brought down, and (2) that the nature of migration be changed so that it be much more akin to temporary labor without automatic access to citizenship and the entire gamut of welfare benefits. This last point in discussed in chapter 3 of my *Global Inequality* as well as in my piece in *The Financial Times* and conversation with Atossa Abrahamian.

(Published March 28, 2017)

INEQUALITY

4.5 All our needs are social

In a recent article (which is a prequel to his book), Professor Harry G. Frankfurt takes a philosophic position against our concern with inequality. According to him, our intuition does tell us that we should be worried about inequality, but that intuition is misleading for an effective moral theory where we should be only concerned about our own well-being and "good life," not in relationship to the others. He allows however that we should be concerned with incomes of those whose "resources are too little."

I have already encountered similar opinions, among economists, and written about that ("Why we all do care about inequality"), so it is with some reluctance that I have to cover the same ground again. But I must admit that this kind of argument is somewhat of a red flag to me, so here I go again. For simplicity, I divide my argument into three parts.

We are social beings. It was stated by Adam Smith very nicely that our needs vary in function of what we consider to be socially acceptable. In a much-quoted passage, Smith contrasts a man living in a relatively poor society, who is content with a roughly hewn shirt and another one, living in a richer society, who would be ashamed to be seen in public without a linen shirt. Smith was drawing on his own experience, having observed how what is socially acceptable, i.e. what are our "needs," has changed in his own lifetime as England and Scotland had become richer.

Here is the quote:

> [Under necessities] I understand not only the commodities that are indispensable for the support of life, but whatever the custom of the country renders it indecent for creditable people, even of the lowest order, to be without. (*Wealth of Nations*, bk. V, ch. 2)

Smith's observation has far-reaching consequences. If our needs depend on what is socially acceptable, then they will clearly vary as between different societies. They will depend on the wealth of such societies or the wealth of our peer groups. Consequently, our needs are (1) even in theory endless (because development has no material limit), and (2) they are thoroughly relative. We cannot distinguish between that part of the needs that is presumably due to ourselves, our "real" needs that, according to Frankfurt, determine whether "[we] have good lives, and not how [our] lives compare with the

92

lives of others" and the other part, which is presumably due to the environment.

It is futile to try to distinguish between the two. We do not know what are our needs until we live in a society and observe the needs of others. So, *pace* Professor Frankfurt, we cannot just imagine that others do not exist as he enjoins us to do. All our needs are social.

But my friend Carla Yumatle has made a point against this interpretation (I paraphrase her): yes, all our needs may be social, but it does not mean that a moral theory, whose objective is to provide us with some moral guidance, needs to take this into account. Actually, it may deplore that we have such needs. Carla draws the distinction between Rousseau's *amour propre* (which is basically vanity, or what used to be called "pride" or self-love in relationship to others) and *amour de soi* (which is concern with ourselves as such). The latter would be acceptable, according to Frankfurt, but the former (which obviously relies on our comparisons with others) would not.

Authenticity. But that too depends on a false dichotomy between *amour de soi* and *amour propre*. The two are indistinguishable. To show that they are different we have to prove somehow that only *amour de soi* is authentic, while *amour propre* is not. Or as Frankfurt claims: "It [concern with inequality] leads a person away from understanding what he himself truly [*sic!*] requires in order to pursue his own most authentic needs, interests, and ambitions."

But, similarly to the previous argument, here too we cannot tell what are authentic and unauthentic needs. I really have no idea what are my authentic needs as compared to the needs that I develop from living in New York. If I lived in Belgrade (as I did) or Chennai (as I did not), I would have had entirely different needs. Does anyone doubt that? So, what are my "authentic" needs?

Do I have an "authentic" need for an iPhone? No, I did not have an "authentic" need so long as iPhones did not exist. But now I do have an "authentic" need for iPhone. However much we might like the fact that somebody decides not to own an iPhone when everybody else has it, we cannot claim that she is more authentic or somehow unconcerned with her relative position. She might decide not to have an iPhone because she does not like to talk on the phone or because she likes to be contrarian but there is nothing more authentic in rejecting to follow the crowd than in deciding to go with it. We might like those who reject crowd-behavior or even admire them, but they are not by any means more "authentic" than the rest.

Welfare function. Finally, an economic argument against Frankfurt's position goes as follows: once we allow for our concern with the poor to enter our utility function, as Frankfurt tells us is acceptable, there is nothing to stop us from introducing in that same utility function our concern with incomes of those who are richer than ourselves.

Moreover, if Frankfurt keeps on insisting that, despite all, we should be concerned *only* with incomes of the poor, neither Frankfurt nor anybody else can tell us what is that income at which we should begin to worry about other human beings whose "resources are too little." He cannot tell us what this "too little" is. Does he want us to be concerned only with incomes of those who live below one international dollar per day, or those below $5, or those below $15? If it is only those below the absolute poverty threshold ($1 per day per capita), then we should not be concerned with poverty in the US at all because nobody lives below that level. Is this okay with Frankfurt?

But, if Frankfurt wants us to be concerned with poverty in the US, then he is introducing precisely the relative poverty measure, that is the poverty that varies with income level in a society where we live, a concept that he had banished previously, under the guise of not being "authentic." Saying resources are "too little" is to say nothing until this "too little" is defined. And, once we try to define it, it becomes immediately apparent that the concept is relative and cannot be treated in abstraction from the society where one lives. For a person living in Luxembourg, poverty is $40 per day; for a person in sub-Saharan Africa, poverty is $2 per day.

So, his reasoning brings him back to the beginning where he is unable to define needs as separate from the context where they are expressed. He is unable to do so because he is unable to distinguish between the so-called "authentic" needs and those that we develop simply by living in a society from the very moment when we are born. So, his whole edifice crumbles.

(Published August 28, 2015)

4.6 Why the focus on horizontal inequality undermines efforts to reduce overall inequality

Göran Therborn in his important new book *The Killing Fields of Inequality* lists, among the three key puzzles of the past thirty years of social and economic developments, this one: Why were rich societies much more successful in reducing "existential" inequality between various groups (blacks–whites; men–women; heterosexual–homosexual; immigrants–natives, etc.) than in reducing overall income and wealth inequality? Actually, the very opposite happened: both income and wealth inequality increased substantially.

A focus on "existential" or "categorical" inequality is what in nineteenth-century Europe used to be called a radical position, associated with the post-1789 developments. Once all formal distinctions of class between clergy, aristocracy, and people were abolished, there was, it was argued, no need to focus on the existing income differences. This view reached its peak under the French Third Republic, when inequality was increasing by leaps and bounds, while formal equality was left untouched. (The socialist position at the time was that formal equality is just the first step toward real equality, which requires also the diminution of economic inequalities.) The same radical position holds fast and true today: once you see the world as primarily composed of various groups, you quickly slip into "identity" politics, whose main objective is to equalize formal legal positions of the groups—and basically let everything else remain the same.

According to Thorborn, that's what the rich world has been remarkably successful in doing in the past thirty years. There are well-known and substantial advances in the equal treatment of different groups (listed above); there was also a strong push for "horizontal" equality, which is the term used in economics to indicate that on average there should be no wage differences between men and women, blacks and whites, etc. (that is, at least no differences that cannot be explained by better skills or experience). The progress there, although not as substantial as in legal equality, has been real too.

But the quasi single-minded focus on "existential" inequality was not always helpful and, I think in some cases, was outright harmful, to the general reduction of income and wealth inequalities. The success in the latter would—I think it could be argued—also reduce income differences due to racial or gender discrimination. In other

95

words, pushing for reduction of inequality in general would make lots of sense, even if our primary objective is to reduce specific gender or racial income inequalities. But this is not how things worked out. Rather, the focus was on "horizontal" inequalities, while the overall, general inequality was left to its own devices, namely was allowed to increase.

The focus on "existential" inequality is wrong, in my opinion, for at least three reasons.

First, the emphasis of group differences quickly spills into identity politics, splintering the groups that do have an interest in fighting for change. The joint front crumbles. The groups end up by caring just about the change in their own positions and become indifferent to the rest. I am unaware for example that gays or immigrants, once their objectives of legal equality have been achieved, have shown particular interest to fight for economic equality in general, be it in the United States or the world. Splintering has made people focus on their own complaint; once that complaint is solved, they are indifferent to the rest.

Second, the focus on "existential" inequality leaves the basic problem unsolved because the way it poses the question is wrong. I noticed this in a recent discussion regarding legalization of prostitution. For feminists, prostitution is a reprehensible activity that they would like either to ban, discourage through some ill-defined teach-ins of women, or curb its demand by punishing clients who are predominantly males. Not only do these approaches just drive the problem underground without solving it, they are futile because the root cause of prostitution is not addressed. The root cause today (and perhaps in history) is income and wealth inequality. There are many (mostly) men with huge incomes and there are many (mostly young) women with poor job prospects and no money. This drives prostitution nationally and globally (as in sex tourism). So, the point is not to address gender inequality only (men vs. women) but its economic cause. Consider what would happen even if horizontal equality between men and women were achieved, a thing which, with higher enrolment and graduation rates among women than men, and a rising number of rich women, may soon happen. The problem will simply become that instead of 90 percent of customers being men we shall have a "fair" and "gender-neutral" distribution of customers, with 50 percent men and 50 percent women. Will such gender equality solve the problem? Obviously not: prostitution, a reprehensibly activity in the eyes of the gender-focused activists, will merely become gender-balanced. Is this all they really want to achieve?

No. But, of course, it reveals that the real cause of the problem lies elsewhere, in inequality, and that their approach is misguided.

Third, the emphasis on "existential" equality is politically easy because it is not serious. It faces no real opposition from the right-wing politicians and conservatives because it does not affect the underlying structure of economic inequality and political power. Instead of fighting for meaningful general changes (e.g. increased vacation time *for all*, shorter work-week *for all*, more favorable working conditions for parents, longer maternity and paternal leave, higher minimum wage *for all*, etc.)—that is, the issues on which the success has been quasi zero, but which would cut into the profits and thus face a strong economic opposition from the businesses, proponents of the "existential" equality care only up to the point where legal equality is established. Strictly speaking, such equality is also in the well-understood interest of capitalists. We know, at least since Gary Becker, that discrimination is economically inefficient for those who practice it. But general measures that improve the position of the employees will not of course please those who have economic power. So, the proponents of "existential" equality stop midway again. Formal equality is surely a necessary condition for overall betterment, but it is not sufficient. A movement toward more generalized equalization of human condition requires not only legal equality but also substantively greater income and, especially, wealth equality.

Their approach ("formal equality and then nothing") is what Rawls calls "meritocratic equality," the lowest level of equality, where all participants are legally free to pursue whatever career they choose but where their starting positions are vastly different. All those who care exclusively about "identities" do only that: they aim to place everybody on the same starting line, but do not care if some come to the starting line with Ferraris and others with bicycles. Their job is done once everybody is on the same starting line. Case closed: just when the real issues begin.

(Published September 23, 2014)

INEQUALITY

4.7 Basic difference between wage inequality and income inequality studies

I recently wrote in anticipation of the arguments I will make in my forthcoming book (*Visions of Inequality*) that the period 1970–2000 was extraordinary barren in Western economic studies of inequality. It was similarly empty as regards inequality studies in communist economies. Only in Latin America was the situation different.

Some people objected to this by pointing to a significant number of wage inequalities papers produced in the US and elsewhere. There are indeed many them. There is also a very successful book by Claudia Goldin and Lawrence Katz *The Race between Education and Technology* that takes its cue from Tinbergen's 1970s' writing on the education premium and his expectation that the premium to college education would go down to zero, due to a high supply of university-educated people. It is not my topic here to discuss why this did not happen, or rather why the opposite, the increase in returns to education, occurred in the United States and elsewhere. What I want to show is that studies of wage inequality cannot be taken as equivalent to what we ideally expect from the work on income inequality. There are two reasons for this: technical and ideological.

Let me start with the technical. When we observe, for example, an increase in wage inequality and calculate all relevant statistics, whether it is driven by increased wage inequality among women or men, Blacks or Whites, more educated or less educated, we still know nothing about household formation. It could be that high-wage workers marry low-wage workers or the reverse. Or that they marry capital-owners or the unemployed or people outside the labor force. Or that many wage-earners do not partner at all. Each of these possibilities has significant and very different implications; yet they are, by the very nature of the topic, entirely unaddressed. The units in wage inequalities studies are different from the units in income inequality studies: individual workers vs. households (I will explain below why this is of crucial importance).

Additionally, wage studies leave out large chunks of what makes inequality: they leave out "income without work" which comes from property (dividends, interest, rents), capital gains and losses, and the entire system of redistribution through direct taxation and government cash and in-kind transfers (e.g. Social Security benefits, unemployment benefits, and SNAP, formerly known as food stamps,

98

in the United States). They also leave out self-employment income, home consumption (i.e. own produced and consumed goods and services), and imputed income from housing, all items of crucial importance in middle-income countries. Wage inequality studies are of even weaker relevance for poor countries where formal wages often represent one third or less of total income.

In other words, wage inequality studies deal with the distribution of income from one factor of production (labor) among wage-earners—which is indeed important—but ignore everything else: (1) the other factor of production, capital, which because of its concentration among the rich is often the most important determinant of inequality, (2) the entire system of government redistribution, (3) self-employment income and home consumption, and (4) family formation.

The principal problem, however, is that it misses why we care about inequality. Inequality is created and reproduced at the level of household, not at the level of individual wage-earner. It is total household income, adjusted for the number of individuals, that makes families rich, poor, or middle class and imparts to them corresponding values. The socialization is done within households, not within (whatever it may mean) individual wage-earners. It is the processes of mating, household formation, as well as contribution of other sources of income that create rich or poor households, social classes, and, most importantly, by differentiating opportunities at birth, allow for the reproduction of social inequities.

We study inequality because we care about social classes and their ability to transmit advantages across generations and create self-sustaining "aristocracies." The concern with returns to schooling is surely one of the issues, but far from the most important. People who care about inequality are concerned as much about social factors that make access to education uneven as about the fact that the returns to schooling may go up.

Wage inequality studies belong to the area of labor economics. It is an important, but subsidiary, field to inequality studies. Their position is similar to that of wage studies as affected by trade. The latter belong to trade economics, not to inequality studies.

Conflating studies of wages, whether from labor or trade economics, with studies of inequality is not only inaccurate. It displays a profound incomprehension of why we care about inequality and what is the real objective of such work: figuring out the fundamental determinants of class structure and its effects on politics, behavior, and values, and transmission of such characteristics across generations.

Tony Atkinson in his 1975 *The Economics of Inequality* did not survey wage inequality work. In his 1997 review article, he wrote: "It is indeed striking how much the recent discussion has focused exclusively on wage differentials and not asked whether such differences are associated with [income] inequality" (*Economic Journal*, 1997, p. 311). Rawls likewise thought that while inequality has to be limited both in terms of capital and labor incomes, the key concern ought to be with inequality of overall income and household-driven reproduction of such inequality.

It is important that the logic and the objectives of inequality studies be correctly understood. Such studies are at the intersection of economics, politics, and sociology, and perhaps anthropology. Not understanding it correctly is likely to lead to many mistakes.

(Published December 1, 2020)

4.8 Distinguishing incomes from capital and labor

When I recently received a copy-edited chapter from my new book *Visions of Inequality*, dealing with Adam Smith, I noticed that in several instances the editor changed my "the rate of profit on capital" to the "rate of profit on investment" or "profits on invested capital." I changed it back to the original, but I thought that the edits summarize well very different visions of capitalism. Or how capitalism, in the eyes of many, has changed from its nineteenth-century variety of industrial capitalism to the twenty-first-century version, where we often think of capitalism as financial, and of "capital" as "free" money in search of best placement. (Of course, capitalism is still industrial—somebody has to produce physical cars, smartphones, and T-shirts—but that industrial aspect is concealed under the overwhelming financialization.)

Thus to the editor, who has a background in business, a capitalist is naturally an investor; to Smith, Ricardo, and Marx, though, the capitalist was (preponderantly) somebody who used his own money to start the process of production, hire labor, advance wages, buy the machines, decide what to produce. As the business grew, the capitalist would hire others to do some of these tasks, but he would remain dedicated to, and in charge of, his business. This is still the role of capitalists/entrepreneurs in many advanced economies, and even more so in the less financialized economies, but, in common parlance a capitalist has become somebody who has enough money to "place" ('invest") it in individual stocks, government paper, mutual funds or other financial instruments.

This has led to the introduction of the misleading term "investor" that nowadays masquerades as an occupation. A number of times I have met people describing themselves as "investors" in a way that somebody would describe himself as a shoemaker, doctor, cashier, IT developer, etc. The appellation which is misleading (except in cases which I describe below) is not only the product of financial capitalism as such but of deliberate attempts to "equalize" the two factors of production, capital and labor, Thus, you may be working ten hours a day in a warehouse, and I may working ten hours looking for the best investment opportunity for my money, and we are equal: we both work ten hours per day, and I am as much of a worker as you. You are just called a warehouse worker, and I am called "investor."

Why is it misleading? Not that somebody cannot spend ten hours every day on his computer "investing," but that the real earning from his work is only the additional income that he may make on top of what he would have earned if he did nothing but simply invested that money once (and let it "work") or gave it to a mutual fund to invest. Thus, if in ten hours of work, he earns $100 from his investment, and if with zero hours of work he would earn $90 with that same money, the labor earning for ten hours of work is $10. He needs to decide whether it makes sense for him to continue spending ten hours of work for $10. But this is entirely different from a worker's situation: if our warehouse worker does not show up at the Amazon warehouse, his pay is zero. Consequently—and this is key—zero hours of work in one case give you $90 and in the other case $0. "Investor" is not just another laborer like a warehouse worker.

(When I hear somebody describe themselves as "investor" I am reminded of people who define their profession as "philanthropist," literally, a "lover of mankind"—a weird profession indeed. In both cases, they are rich people, who earn money for no work, but feel bad acknowledging it and thus, when asked "what do you do?" they do not say, "well, I do nothing, I just live on money I own/inherited," but rather "I am a lover of mankind" or "I am an investor.")

However, the term investor is not misleading in the case of individuals who are hired workers working within the investment banks and paid to find the best ways to maximize return to the rich people who entrusted them with their money. Their income is indeed a wage income—even when they are paid exorbitant bonuses. In income distribution studies, we have this problem: how do we treat a CEO of an investment company who earns a wage of $1 million, and a bonus (in the form of shares) of $2 million? The answer simply is that we treat all of that income ($3 million) as *labor* income. If the CEO decides to go off to the Bahamas, and never shows up for work, his earnings would be zero. So for him, like for the Amazon warehouse worker, presence at his job (virtual or in-person) is indispensable to earn an income. Hence that income is a wage.

Some people are confused by that classification because for them a trader for an investment company or its CEO are not workers, since their income depends on the performance of stocks and their salaries are too high. But the amount of earnings does not determine whether it is labor or capital income. Capital income can be one dollar and labor income a million, but they are still labor income, and capital income. Neither does the payment in stocks, nor whether that income is linked with the performance of the stock-market matter. Note that payment in stocks is done for ordinary workers too. When such a payment is made, it is always a wage. Only later, if the worker or the CEO decides to keep the stock, the return on that stock becomes capital income. Being paid a part of one's wage in stocks is not different from workers who are often paid in-kind, say being given free food or drinks.

Now, what is the difference, somebody may ask, between our individual "investor," whom we saw spending ten hours a day on his computer, and the trader in a wealth management company, who also spends ten hours on a computer investing? The difference is that in the first case, a person's labor earning (wage) is only the incremental amount of money made compared to what he would have earned with zero work: $10 in our example. In the second case, the trader is a hired worker and his income is entirely the result of his labor. Technically, Marx would have said that such a trader is no different from our Amazon warehouse worker. Both are working within companies they do not own, both are producing surplus value for the owners (Amazon and the wealth fund) and both are hired workers.

When, in a recent paper, Smith et al. claimed that the decrease in the US labor share was overestimated because up to a third of that decrease was due to the misclassification, that is to the failure to account for the specific labor inputs (including entrepreneurship) of individuals owning S-corporations, their point was accurate. That part that is linked to specific labor input cannot be ascribed to capital, but to labor and entrepreneurship.

(Published January 28, 2023)

INEQUALITY

4.9 Why "Make America Denmark Again" will not happen

The rise of inequality in rich countries is way over-explained. Because income inequality (evaluated at the level of households or individuals) is such a complex variable, outcome of a vast number of technological, political, demographic and behavioral factors, and its neat decomposition into these various factors is impossible, we shall always have a plethora of potential explanans. This was a point raised in a recent post by Francisco Ferreira from the World Bank. I called it TOP (technology, openness, and policy) in *Global Inequality*.

But not all explanations are equally powerful or make sense. A couple of days ago at a conference at Northwestern University, I listened to the explanation proposed by Gerald Davis from University of Michigan. Davis argued, at first very counter-intuitively (so much so that at first I thought I had misunderstood his point), that the rise of US inequality coincides with the decline of large companies, which used to employ hundreds of thousands or even millions of workers and by their substitution by much smaller companies. As shown in a graph from Davis and Cobb ("Corporations and economic inequality around the world," 2010) the share of large employers in total US employment went down simultaneously with the increase in US income inequality. (What Davis and Cobb call the "ratio of top 10 employers to labor force" is the percentage of all US workers employed by the ten largest companies.)

Why did it seem counter-intuitive? Because there is an earlier influential literature going back to Herbert Simon and Thomas Mayer that saw the behemoths of the 1960s, with their heavy hierarchical structures, as precisely driving inequality up. The more ladders you have in a hierarchical structure, the more pay grades there are, and the more likely are the top managers who lord it over thousands of employees to have high salaries. Hence greater inequality. At least that was the theory.

But Davis argues the opposite (and was helped by the data that go this way). His argument is that large hierarchical structures have to engage in some evening out of salaries (internal redistribution) in order to keep cooperation, needed for the success of the enterprise, going. On the contrary, if the big bureaucratic machines get divested, and jobs hitherto performed within company get outsourced to different contractors, there is nothing to keep the new small, lean and mean company from extracting all the surplus from each and every contractor in the way that Amazon is credited (or

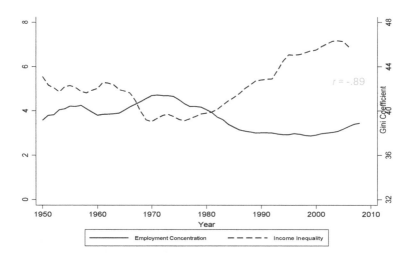

Figure 4.1 Share of labor employed by top 10 firms and income inequality in the United States

Note: The graph shows (on the left vertical axis) the share of US labor force employed by the ten largest employers (0.2 indicates 20 percent); the right vertical shows Gini coefficient (a measure of income inequality that runs from 0, theoretical equality, to 1, theoretical possibility when the entire income is received by one person).

Source: Reprinted from *Research in Organizational Behavior*, Vol. 30, No. 1, Gerald Davis and J. Adam Cobb, "Corporations and Economic Inequality Around the World: The Paradox of Hierarchy," pages 35–53, copyright 2010, with permission from Elsevier.

"credited") of doing it. So, take General Motors and break it into thousands of independent companies producing components, then outsource cleaning, marketing, food catering and legal services, offshore accounting and customer relations, and you end up with today's enterprise structure. If the accountants in Chicago feel they are paid too little, GM will gladly hire accountants in Calcutta. Those who have remained at the core can pay themselves huge salaries, since they do not depend on the goodwill and cooperation of the outsourcing companies.

This is basically, I think, Davis' idea (and I hope I presented it accurately). But my explanation for this change went, I thought, one step further. I think that the deconcentration of which Davis writes is only a proximate cause of the rise in inequality. The "deep cause" was technological change, combined in an inextricable way (as I argue in my *Global Inequality*) with globalization. What happened, I think, was that advances in technology such as stock management (just-in-time), ability of speedy "bespoke" production, and crucially advances in telecommunications made "broken up" (devolved) production more efficient. The concentration of workers in one place that, at the origin of the Industrial Revolution, was made indispensable by the importance of the energy sources available at discrete physical points, could now be reversed. We could go back to a type of production that predates the Industrial Revolution, a kind of a modernized "putting out" system.

In doing so companies were helped by globalization because the area over which the putting out system can now extend was the globe itself, not only villages 10 miles in perimeter distance from Manchester. Only then, all the elements mentioned by Davis, could follow. The companies do not need to ensure the collaboration of employees by dint of redistribution of some profits across the labor force. The broken-down units are too small to allow for any meaningful unionization, and the trade union density is less. Further, there are no labor conditions to negotiate with a company to which you sell your goods or services. At the extreme, imagine a structure where the core company divests practically all tasks to companies composed of one individual each. Inequality within each company will be zero while total inequality could be quite high.

My view is indeed one that may be called "technological determinism," but that determinism is playing itself out on an ever expanding field made possible by globalization. In other words, technological determinism is itself a function of globalization (heaving off some activities clearly could not be equally efficient in a world where you had to hire US workers only) and technological determinism in turns helps globalization. So the two go together. Moreover even things that seem to be policy-related (say, the decline of trade unions) may in many instances be driven by the combination of new technology and globalization.

It is for that reason that I am skeptical that "the happy days of the 1960s" will ever come back. This is the idea that I somewhat jokingly called "Make America Denmark Again." That world made sense with the technology and the policy as it was in the 1960s but not today. The world of large-scale manufacturing, homogenous working class, trade unions, capital controls and a quasi-closed economy (US exports and imports combined were less than 10 percent of American

INEQUALITY WITHIN NATIONS

GDP in the 1960s; they are more than 30 percent today) is over. When we think of how to address inequality today we should move from the ideas that worked half-a-century ago.

(Published May 14, 2016)

INEQUALITY

4.10 À *la recherche* of the roots of US inequality "exceptionalism"

It has been long argued that American income inequality was, in the past forty years or so, exceptionally high compared to other OECD countries. The latest (2017) results available by the Luxembourg Income Study, which harmonizes income concepts across countries, show inequality in disposable (per capita) income in the US to be 41 Gini points, that is, higher than in any other similarly rich country (Germany's Gini is 32, British 35, Italian 35, Dutch 28). So, this part is not controversial.

What is more controversial is the technical (as opposed to substantive) explanation for this "exceptionalism." Some people have argued that US market income inequality (that is, inequality *before* government redistribution through social transfers and direct taxes) is not much higher than elsewhere and that the entire explanation has to do with an insufficiently redistributive state. In simple terms, the argument is that the market generates the same inequality in the US and Sweden, but Sweden redistributes much more through pensions, unemployment benefits, social assistance, etc., and also taxes the rich more, so in the end disposable (after transfers and taxes) income inequality in Sweden is less than in the United States.

Janet Gornick, Nathaniel Johnson, and I have recently looked at this more carefully. Without going through all explanations (which can be found in the paper), we conclude that this is not entirely true: US market income inequality is generally greater than in other rich countries *and* the American government redistributes less. So, we argue, both the underlying (market) inequality is high and redistribution is relatively weak.

But, one can go further than that, and ask the following question: what part of redistribution is "weak": is it that US transfers are small and not sufficiently pro-poor, or is it that US direct taxes are not sufficiently progressive?

Now, I look at that issue in the following way. I define as "poor" the bottom 40 percent of individuals, when people are ranked by their market income inclusive of government-paid pensions (social security in the US), which can be regarded as deferred wages. I then look at how the income share of these very same people varies as we include other social transfers, and, finally, as we deduct direct taxes. (Note that this calculation can be done only if you have access to micro data because you need to "fix" these people and look at their

108

INEQUALITY WITHIN NATIONS

income share as you introduce various income concepts. The methodology is explained in my median voter paper cited below.)

Normally, we expect that the share of the "poor" increases as the state moves in to redistribute income. Indeed, in 2016 (the latest year for which we have US data), the "poor" received 11.7 percent of overall market income. Their share went up to 13.4 percent of income when we include all social transfers, and increased further to 15.8 percent when we include taxes too. (Note again that these are the same people throughout). The gain for the "poor" is thus 1.7 percentage points from social transfers (13.4–11.7) and an additional 2.4 percentage points from taxes (15.8–13.4).

We can write it out:

In the US, the "poor" gain 1.7 points thanks to social transfers and 2.4 points thanks to taxes.

So, government really "works" in the United States: it improves the position of the poorest people through government transfers and direct taxes. But the question is, does it work well enough?

One good comparator is Germany. We control for different age distributions in the two countries and the fact that people retire earlier in Germany by treating government pensions as deferred wages. But, that still leaves (as mentioned above) other social transfers like unemployment benefits, family benefits, welfare, etc. So, in Germany in 2015, the "poor" (defined in the same way as in the US) earned 15.3 percent of all market income. Their share went up to 18.3 percent when all social transfers are included, and further to 21.3 percent when we include direct taxes as well. Thus the "poor" in Germany gained 3 percentage points from social transfers (18.3–15.3) and 3 percentage points from taxes (21.3–18.3).

For Germany, we write:

The "poor" gain three points thanks to transfers and then an additional three points thanks to taxes.

Thus, not only is the starting point of the "poor" in Germany more favorable than in the United States (15.3% of market income vs. only 11.7%) but they gain more from both social transfers and direct taxes.

The results over time are shown in two graphs, 4.2 and 4.3. The "poor" always gain from redistribution but US gains are always lower than German gains. What is noticeable is that the gains from social transfers were about the same in the US and Germany until 1995, then increased in both countries (in the US they were at their peak in 2010, when unemployment benefits were extended by Obama) and afterwards, since US welfare is very modest, gains rapidly decreased.

109

INEQUALITY

Even more interesting is the evolution of the gains from direct taxes. Here we see that the American "poor" gain throughout less than the "poor" in Germany and that the level of gains does not seem to change much in the US.

Thus, when we try to find the roots of lower pro-poor redistribution in the US we can find them both in more modest social transfers and in less progressive direct taxation. Combined with our earlier finding of relatively high market income inequality in the US, this means that American income inequality is "exceptional" because (a) underlying market income inequality is high, (b) social transfers are modest, and (c) direct taxes are not sufficiently progressive.

The policy implication is that reduction in US income inequality is unlikely to be achieved through one of these three channels alone but through a combination of "improvements" in each of them. For example, through more accessible education and higher minimum wage to reduce the underlying market income inequality; through

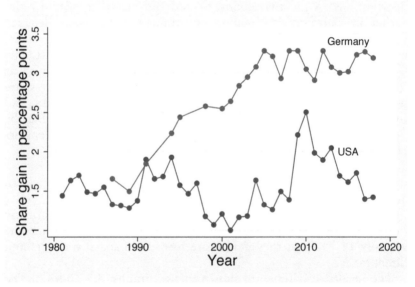

Figure 4.2 Increase in the share of the bottom 40 percent due to social transfers, 1980–2020

Note: The graph shows the increase in the income share (in percentage points) of the poorest 40% of the population (ranked by market income) thanks to social transfers. The data for Germany begin in 1985, and until 1990 refer to Western Germany only.

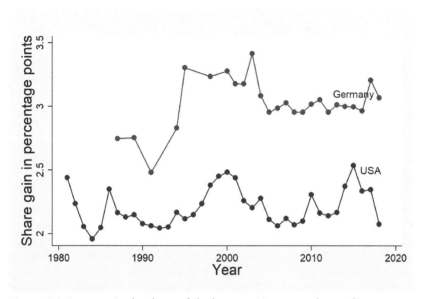

Figure 4.3 Increase in the share of the bottom 40 percent due to direct taxes, 1980–2020

Note: The graph shows the increase in the income share (in percentage points) of the poorest 40% of the population (ranked by market income) thanks to direct taxes. The data for Germany begin in 1985, and until 1990 refer to Western Germany only.

introduction of family benefits or more generous welfare; and, finally, through higher tax rates for the rich and higher taxation of capital incomes. Although this might seem like an extremely ambitious policy agenda, I think it is more reasonable to think that incremental changes in all three channels are easier to pass legislatively than a much more substantial change in any one of them alone. But it also means that if one wants to grapple seriously with high inequality in the United States, only a combination of different policies will do.

(Published July 29, 2018)

INEQUALITY

4.11 What are the limits of Europe?

We know that there is such a thing as an optimal currency area, although it is possible that the framers of the Lisbon Treaty were unaware of it. The Greek crisis has popularized the concept. As the name says, it puts limits on what should (ideally) be a single currency area.

Similarly, in the 1990s, when at one end of the European continent countries like the USSR, Czechoslovakia, and Yugoslavia dissolved into their constituent members (republics) applying to join the European Union, a similar question was asked: Why would you leave one union and join another, rather than keep your full independence? One of the answers was given in my 1996 article (see also Section 2.6 above), where I argued that there is a trade-off between independence in policy-making (say, full fiscal and monetary authority) and income growth. Countries like Estonia and Slovenia were quite willing to give up monetary and (to a large degree) fiscal independence in exchange for monetary transfers and institutional framework provided by the EU. This reasoning again posed the question: Was there a point where a country might find the cost in terms of forgone policy discretion too onerous and decide to stay out (thus placing a limit to the expansion of the union)? Perhaps Switzerland and Norway are such examples.

But, almost nobody looked at inequality as a limiting factor in the growth of a union. There at least three factors why it may be:

First, a union with members at very different income levels requires large transfers from the richer to the poor in order to function normally.

Second, a very unequal union is, by definition, composed of members whose endowments of capital and labor are very different. Hence the optimal economic policy for a poor member may not be the same as the optimal policy for a rich member. (We find here the echoes of the optimal currency area.)

Third, and presently perhaps the most important, if such a union implies freedom of movement, systematic or structural labor flows, which would then follow, with people moving from poorer to richer members, may be politically destabilizing, if richer members are unwilling to accept migrants.

The third point may be largely responsible for Brexit. It could be argued that without EU's Eastern Enlargement there would have been no Brexit. Thus the EU, implicitly, faced a trade-off of its own: it

112

could either have the UK, or Eastern Europe, but not both. Through a succession of steps, and largely unaware of this choice, the EU chose the latter.

Behind the movement of people are the underlying differences in income levels among countries. This is why Bulgaria has been estimated to have "lost" almost two million of her citizens since she joined the EU. But how large are income differences within the EU? Let us start with the most simple and most important, ignoring differences in income *within* countries and looking only at differences in income levels *between* EU countries (i.e. assuming that every French person has the mean income, i.e. GDP per capita of France, every Romanian the GDP per capita of Romania, etc.)

The results are quite striking. In 1980, when the EU was composed of only nine members, such population-weighted between-country Gini coefficient was only 3 Gini points. (Gini ranges from 0, full equality, to 100, the entire income received by one person.) It was very clear that combining the nine members into one group added to the total EU inequality (through their differences in development) an utterly negligible quantity. More than nine-tenths of EU9 inequality was due to within-country income differences (that is, to poor and rich people within France, within the Netherlands, etc.) Ten years later, in 1990, when EU12 existed, the between-country Gini had already doubled to six points. Fast forward fourteen years and, with the Eastern Enlargement, the number of members went up to 25, and Gini yet again more than doubled to thirteen points. It has increased further, but slightly (to 13.5), with the additions of Romania, Bulgaria, and Croatia. Now, the estimates of inter-personal inequality (that is, between all citizens) in the EU range between 37 and 39 Gini points. This means that one-third of overall EU (13.5 Gini points out of 37 or 39) inequality is now systemically built-in, due to the differences in underlying income levels of the members.

Compare EU28 with US50, that is the United States composed of 50 members (states). Overall US50 inequality is higher than that of EU28: Gini of the United States is in the lower 40s vs. the European Gini in the mid-to-upper 30s. But only about one-tenth of that inequality in the US is "caused" by inequality between states while, as we have seen, a third of inequality in Europe is caused by differences in income between the members.

The European inequality (which thus decomposed looks very much like Chinese inequality, which is similarly driven to a significant degree by provincial income differences) is much harder to fix. It requires strictly geographic transfers of purchasing power from rich to poor members. This translates into transfers from (say) the Dutch to the Bulgarians. But EU budget of one percent of total GDP is laughingly small for such transfers. The alternative solution is to let people migrate. This is what the EU has done, with political consequences that are obvious today,

We can then legitimately ask: are there limits to the EU enlargement, that is, limits imposed by higher inequality that would come from new and poorer members? If Turkey alone joined, the underlying between-country Gini of a new Union would become 17 points. If the Western Balkans' four candidate members joined as well, it would raise Gini further to 17.5 points. The underlying inequality, which is not subject to either domestic or EU-wide economic policies (the latter because the EU budget is so small), would then represent close to one-half of the overall inequality between 615 million citizens of the Union.

It would be an unmanageable union.

This is why the EU should not continue with its unsustainable policy, which seems to offer candidate countries potential membership at the end a very long (or rather, interminable) tunnel. That policy leads only to frustration on both sides. The EU should look at the things as they are and create a new category of countries that will not be members for any realistic period of time. Perhaps until such potential members become richer on their own, which means that EU should by all means encourage greater Chinese investment and involvement in those countries (that is, do the very opposite of what it is doing now). Or perhaps wait until the convergence of incomes within the EU members and lower all-EU inequality permits another round of enlargement—which is unlikely to happen before the second half of this century.

(Published May 14, 2019)

INEQUALITY WITHIN NATIONS

4.12 The role of economics

I wrote this in a Twitter [X] discussion about the importance of knowing and reading classical texts in economics (say, from Quesnay to Pareto, although these end-points are fairly arbitrary).

- If your definition of economics is this: "I would like to start with the one that I would have used when I was young and studied Marxist economics. Economics matters because it enables you to look at the grand political and economic changes in history and to explain them using economic factors. In other words, it is, if I can say so, a branch of historical materialism. Decisions driven by economic factors shape societies and make them change." Then you must read classics.
- If your definition is this: "A neoclassical view of economics would be more pragmatic. It would be to argue that economics matters—and to use Alfred Marshall's definition there—because it deals with our ordinary life and its objective is to improve that ordinary life, to make our incomes higher, to allow us to have more free time, and to make poverty disappear so that we can enjoy other activities that we like while having a satisfactory standard of living." Then, you should read them but perhaps not as carefully as under the first definition.
- If your definition is: "Economics is the allocation of scarce resources among the alternative ends." Then you can read only selected classic texts.
- If your definition is that economics is just what businesses and finances do now, then perhaps you should not bother with classic texts at all.

I would like to explain what I meant by these definitions. The first definition is clearly Marxist in the way it is written, but substantively it is the same definition that can be found in works as far apart historically, ideologically, and methodologically as Adam Smith and Kenneth Pomeranz. In this view of economics, its role is to illuminate economic factors that have led to systemic changes, to people moving from one way to organize production to another. It is Smith's stadial theory of economic history, from "the rude state of society" of pastoralists to the commercial society of his time. It is, of course, Marx's view too. But it is also the point of view of whoever has studied (say) Roman Empire, its economy, and the dissolution of

115

the manifold links that kept the Western Empire together: Michael Rostovtzeff or Moses Finley. It is a view of economics common to Paul Bairoch and Fernand Braudel. So, it is not a predetermined ideological position, but the methodological approach that is important here.

The second definition (due to Alfred Marshall) is, as I wrote, much more pragmatic. It looks at the ways of improving people's lives. It is related to the first definition when, under that definition, we believe that societies tend to choose more efficient ways of production over the less efficient. Through the Darwinian struggle of different modes of production, the most efficient wins, and that most efficient mode of production increases people's incomes the most. (Assuming here that we look at people's incomes broadly, and not only at the mean income, which may be misleading.) The second definition allows you not to worry about the grander historical forces but to focus, here and today, on how to make things better.

The third definition is Lionel Robbins'. That definition narrows economics very significantly. Economics becomes similar to operation research. It is not interested in the succession of different systems, not even in improvements in welfare as such, but in optimization. It could be used under any system. It is not surprising that Koopmans and Kantorovich came up with very similar findings. The "scarcity → ends" definition can be used to best allocate inputs and people in a factory, whether it is private or state-owned, to maximize work effort of inmates of a labor camp, or of the cotton-picking slaves.

The fourth definition is beyond pragmatic. It is concerned with one's own, or people one works for, immediate maximization of income; it ignores everything that is not useful for that purpose, and blurs the difference between a social science and the profit-making of a single business. It is Gordon Gekko in action.

If you think that these distinctions are too abstract, here is an example to show how they are very much concrete and are in reality applied right now. You can study China by asking the question of whether it is capitalist or not, whether its opening and marketization that began in 1978 is just one very long NEP or an irreversible change; whether Chinese economic history leads us to believe the country will evolve in one or another direction (see below Section 9.2). You are then applying Definition 1.

Or you may not bother with decisions that led China to liberalize in 1978, but focus on policies that reduced poverty, increased its income, or widened disparities between the affluent and the poor. You are applying Definition 2.

INEQUALITY WITHIN NATIONS

Or you can discuss whether the state-owned Chinese banking system is allocating the loans in the best way or not: here you are working under Definition 3.

Or you can write an article discussing if Evergrande will pay its creditors next week or not. You are in the world of Definition 4.

I was always interested in Definition 1. It gave economics its magisterial gravitas. It showed why economics matters. When I began the work on global inequality more than two decades ago, I never saw it as a mere work in empirics. Empirics is important as the first step, but one should try (if possible) not to stop there. I was not quite successful in going beyond (and I criticize myself for that in *Visions of Inequality*). Still for me global inequality was always much more about global politics, economic history, and indeed power than about numbers.

The rising global inequality in the nineteenth century was simply a reflection, in numbers, of the greatest ever divergence in power between two parts of the globe: the West and the Rest. You could not discuss these numbers without realizing that the rising between-country inequality "explained" or "reflected" (both are probably true) the 1840s Opium Wars and the Indian Rebellion of 1857. Behind increasing within-national inequalities was the class struggle: the Revolution of 1848 and the Emancipation of serfs in Russia in 1861, and the end of the slave system in the South of the United States in 1865.

Then the high plateau of global inequality in the middle of the twentieth century showed us the newly parceled three worlds: the first world of rich capitalist countries; the second world of socialism, and the third world of Asia, Africa, and Latin America. You cannot understand the work of Frantz Fanon or Samir Amin without knowing that in the background there existed three non-overlapping worlds. You cannot see where Bandung came from if you do not know these facts (or have similar knowledge anyway).

And finally, and most recently, the decrease in global inequality is simply the translation for the rise of populous Asian countries. It mirrors the Industrial Revolution: the center of economic gravity is tilting toward one region, the losing areas are deindustrializing and, as Asia catches up, global inequality is reduced. Political and economic implications of this change are obvious to all: the US vs. China conflict is written there in scarlet letters. You do not need look for its causes in politicians' speeches.

What will come in the future we do not know. Will the equalizing trend continue? Africa, with high population growth and lack

117

of income convergence, may push global inequality up again, and become additionally marginalized. Or it might replicate Asia. China may become (and is already becoming) too rich to exert a downward pressure on global inequality, and the two new hegemons (China and the US) may in two generations from now be in a group of their own.

The economic and political structure of the world today is very different from those in 1921 or 1971. All of that is not only reflected in global inequality numbers; these numbers help us better understand political and social movements. This is how I see global inequality work as proceeding according to Definition 1.

(Published October 24, 2021)

— 5 —

GLOBAL INEQUALITY

5.1 The history of global inequality studies

I recently read a very nice paper by Christian Christiansen on the origins of global inequality studies. The paper is yet to be published, so I will not quote anything from it but I would suggest to the interested readers to go to his and Steven Jensen's (editors) excellent book *Histories of Global Inequality* and especially the introductory essay that goes over the same themes.

Christiansen studies how the very idea of worldwide inequality has changed over the past seventy years. He charts the path from the post-colonialist rhetoric, where worldwide inequality was inequality between colonies and metropoles, to the Third Worldism and structuralism, to the New International Economic Order, and finally to global neoliberalism. The term "global inequality" appears for the first time in print in a 1974 article on the global food crisis by Mick McLean and Mike Hopkins ("Problems of World Food and Agriculture: Projections, Models and Possible Approaches," *Futures*). It is only in the 1990s that "global inequality" became associated with the idea of income inequality between citizens of the world.

Let me note finally that Christiansen's work may be very usefully read in conjunction with two excellent recent books that cover similar, even if wider, ideological ground: Samuel Moyn's *Not Enough* and Quinn Slobodian's *Globalists*.

Christiansen asked a question that I thought about for a while but never wrote about: how do certain ideas—in this case the idea of global inequality—arise? How do they get formulated? What explains that they become popular after not only being ignored but not even existing (as ideas) for a long time? Since I was involved in

119

this process, I thought I would try to explain how—at least to me—this seemed to have happened.

It is useful of think of the interaction between four forces: ideology, politics, data, and sociology of knowledge.

The 1980s and 1990s in the World Bank and the academia were inhospitable to the idea and study of inequality. Probably as never before. It is worth remembering for example that the World Bank was in the 1970s a pioneer in the work on inequality. I remember how excited I was (I was then working in an economics institute in Belgrade) when I first saw the 1974 compilation of income inequality statistics around the world by Shail Jain. Nothing similar existed before. Montek Alhuwalia also wrote several very important papers.

But, with the triumph of the dreary neoclassical economics, inequality was exorcised from the mainstream. It did remain in development economics though. But there too, with the neoliberalism that the World Bank espoused in the 1990s, it was soon eliminated. The toxic influence of Anne Krueger saw to it. Thus the ideology basically told you, "it is not a topic worth studying and we shall waste no resources on it."

Moreover, and somewhat ironically, the eclipse of inequality studies happened in conjunction with the increasing importance of poverty studies. The latter were, as I called them, "the moral laundering" undertaken by the rich. Those in power liked them because such studies showed them not to be oblivious or ignorant of the plight of the "less fortunate." It also buttressed their ideological hegemony. (In *The Haves and the Have-Nots* I tell the story of how the head of a prestigious Washington think tank told me to change my interest in my CV from "inequality" to "poverty"—because the rich board members were allergic to the term "inequality.")

Then there were the politics. Many World Bank member countries disliked the World Bank studying their inequality, and refused to authorize such studies, or to share the data. That applied to countries like Turkey (where for years, if not decades, the World Bank failed to do a study of inequality) and the Middle East (Algeria, Tunisia, Syria). In Eastern Europe, Romania could not stomach the idea of such a study and released no data. In Yugoslavia, too, there was strong resistance, coming from the rich republics, because a country-wide study was bound to show huge and increasing gaps between the richer and poorer parts of the country. Finally, many African countries lacked institutional capacity to mount household surveys, without which there were no data to study inequality. Thus, if there are no data (Africa), or large parts of the world do

GLOBAL INEQUALITY

not want to release the data (China should be added to my above list), or countries were not members of the World Bank (the Soviet Union and Cuba), there was hardly any sense in studying "global inequality," which would leave out one-third, or more, of the world population.

By the late 1980s, things began to change, with glasnost in the USSR and the first releases of the Soviet data, and improvements in the data-gathering capacity in Africa. China as well, from the mid 1980s, provided at least fragmentary income distribution data. All of that allowed the World Bank to move, since the 1990 *World Development Report*, into global poverty assessment and monitoring. The ideological backing for this was provided by the UN focus on global poverty alleviation. But, as all of this implies, the data were no longer the main issue: the ideology was.

The first time I had the idea of studying global inequality was around 1994, motivated (in part) by the realization that the same data that were used for the study of global poverty could be "repurposed" to study global inequality. My first paper on global inequality was published in 1999. (When prompted by Christiansen's work, I reread it yesterday. I was pleasantly surprised to see how it foreshadowed almost all the issues we still discuss today, both methodologically and substantively.)

But when ideology "militates" against studying something, very few people will bother to do it. Simply put, incentives were aligned against inequality studies. There would be no funding. Such research would be sidetracked and ignored. This is what happened within the World Bank.

On the other hand, it needs to be acknowledged that the World Bank research was never organized in the hierarchical dictatorial manner that some people imagine. You could study more-or-less any relevant topic, so long as you could show reasonable publication success. One may not receive any of the powerful World Bank financial support or media coverage (that would be reserved for politically more acceptable topics), but there was no active discouragement or prohibition; or at least I have never encountered it.

Getting involved in the work on the—not currently popular—topics is like betting on a horse that is unlikely to win a race. Most of the time, one loses and, understandably most people avoid doing it. But, at times, one may be lucky and win.

If asked what is important, a trite answer would be to say: follow one's passion or interests. But I think that, while in general this is a

121

good advice, it is of limited practical value. I would add that when choosing what to study one should keep one's expectations and ambitions for external success (within one's lifetime) low. One thus can never be disappointed.

(Published May 7, 2021)

5.2 Athenian dialogues on global income inequality

Glaucon (G). Good day, Adeimantus. I have good news for you. Perhaps you have already heard that global inequality, measured by the differences in real incomes between people, has decreased significantly during the past thirty years and this is the first such big decline since the Industrial Revolution.

Adeimantus (A). Good day to you too, Glaucon. I am extremely happy that this is happening. This simply proves that capitalism works and that the critiques of neoliberal policies were and are wrong.

G. But, you know, Adeimantus, that most of the decline in global inequality is due to China and that China did not exactly follow neoliberal policies over that period. Moreover, you have criticized China's policies of state capitalism many times.

A. Yes, I am against Chinese policies and I think they are wrong policies.

G. How can they be wrong, Adeimantus, when you just cheered the decrease in global inequality, which was achieved mostly thanks to China?

A. Difficult question, but let us go back to the discussion of global inequality.

G. Wait a minute, Adeimantus. If China's policies are so successful, should not other countries copy them?

A. No, Glaucon my friend, because I know China: China is going to exploit other countries through unfavorable loans. Borrowers would not be able to repay them and will get into the vicious circle of underdevelopment.

G. But, Adeimantus, was not the same argument made many times before by the left-wing critics of Western loans, and which you also many times, here in the markets of Athens, vehemently rejected?

A. Let me say that I think that the situation is different today. I will give you a precise answer later. But, let's go back to the convergence. I am glad that the world is converging but it seems to me that you, Glaucon, are not at all concerned that the lower parts of income distributions of the rich countries have been going down in the global rankings.

G. Sure, Adeimantus. Them going down in the global pecking order is part and parcel of convergence. If you do have convergence that means that some people who used to have income lower than yours will now have income higher than yours, and will thus get ahead of you. So, my dear Adeimantus, you cannot be in favor of global

INEQUALITY

convergence and also in favor of keeping the same people on the top. It is mathematically impossible. If convergence is good then this global reshuffling in incomes is also good.

A. But, politically, how am I going to explain that the entire distribution of my country is no longer number one, that some of my compatriots are no longer among the top decile or even top quintile of the global distribution? That creates lots of problems for us internally because the middle classes feel much poorer, relative to the rest of the world, even if their real incomes may still go up. One of the famous writers produced by the island of Britannia, Paul Collier, pines in his book *The Future of Capitalism* for the time when the British worker could stride the world, standing tall and proud because he was richer than many other people.

G. If he was richer than many other people that means that many other people were poorer than him and these people probably did not like that situation. So now they like the idea of catching up and actually perhaps even being a bit richer than Paul's Britannian worker. Moreover why should the Britannian or any other worker remain in that top position forever?

A. Because it is very difficult for us to explain it to the population.

G. I understand that, my dear Adeimantus. But this is your political problem. This is not a problem that somebody who cares about global equality and global social mobility is concerned with. From the global point of view, we must treat everybody the same. But let me ask you this: you are, I know that, in favor of social mobility in your own country. You want everybody to have the same chance to succeed. Why should there not be social mobility at the level of the world? What is different there for you to feel bad about social mobility and reshuffling of income positions in the world? If so, should you then be arguing that similar reshuffling must not take place at the national level either? Should you not argue that all people who used to be rich remain rich? If rich countries have to stay at the same positions in the world, why should not rich families stay at the same position within countries?

A. The ships are coming at noon. I have to bid you farewell now. Let's continue this discussion tomorrow.

Here comes Thrasymachus.

Thrasymachus (T). Hello, Glaucon. I am a bit upset with you. You have made a big deal of that fact that global inequality measured in relative terms (my income as a fraction of yours) has gone down. But I do not care about that. If we look at the absolute differences in income between people they have gone up.

124

G. Yes, Thrasymachus, there is no doubt that you are right but this is the case whenever overall real income and real income of individual people increase. Differences in absolute terms go up even if relative differences stay the same or go down. This is like when you take a balloon and draw by pencil different points on the balloon, and then blow the balloon up: what happens? While the relative distances remain the same (or in the case of convergence even go down) the absolute distances between the points on a bigger balloon become greater. But this is okay because the balloon (the world GDP) is greater.

T. But maybe I am a stubborn guy and I just care about the absolute distances and not about relative distances.

G. OK, Thrasymachus, but then you have to be consistent: absolute distances, for example in the US in 1860, were severalfold less than absolute distances today. The reason is simply that US GDP per capita was less than one-tenth of its level today and, when you look at the distance between any given percentile in the income distribution versus another then and compare those distances to what they are today, they were then very small. (And I am using here incomes that are all corrected for the difference in the price levels and are expressed in current dollars.) But you would not be saying, Thrasymachus, would you, that inequality in a much poorer America with 13 percent of its population in slavery was much, much lower than inequality today? Would you defend that?

T. Probably not, but let's go to the global level. Your convergence is mostly driven by China. So other countries have not really converged on Western incomes and Africa certainly did not.

G. Yes, this is a good point. China is really driving the convergence and Africa is remaining equally poor, or even the distance between Africa and the rich world is increasing.

T. So, I am right to claim that the neoliberal order has actually increased inequality between the countries and people, and you get reduced inequality only if China is included. Thus, the gap between the core and the periphery is just getting worse.

G. This is not exactly true, Thrasymachus, because even if China is excluded, the global inequality does go down although by significantly less. But then if you expel China from the "developing world" or the periphery because it has become rich, are you not permanently changing your definition of the periphery? Whoever is successful gets "expelled" from the periphery and, by that logic, there could almost never be a convergence because there would be always some poor countries that would not converge. If India converges tomorrow, you would exclude it too; if Indonesia and Vietnam, and then Bangladesh, come next you would drop them too. So, you can never have convergence by definition, since every country that converges will be kicked out of your comparison.

T. Glaucon, you make many arguments full of bad sophistry but, although I cannot rebut you now, I will think a bit and come back with a decisive proof that what you say cannot be right.

(Published June 26, 2023)

5.3 How much of your income is due to your citizenship?

It is as obvious as it is well known that the world is unequal in terms of individuals' incomes. But it is unequal in a very particular way: most of inequality, when we break it down between inequality within countries and inequality between countries, is due to the latter. Let us explain the difference between the two: the first is inequality that exists between (say) poor and rich Americans, poor and rich Chinese and so on. For simplicity, we shall call it "class" inequality. But there is also another, equally obvious, inequality: that between rich and poor nations, between the "representative" ("average") individuals in (say) Morocco and Spain, Mexico and the United States, Albania and Italy. For simplicity, we shall call it "locational" inequality.

And the world, as structured today, is such that, whatever measure of inequality we choose, the lion's share of global inequality is "explained" by the differences in mean incomes between the countries. This was not always the case. Although our data for the past are far more tentative than our data for today's global income distribution, we can still aver with little doubt that the dominant type of equality in the nineteenth century was the one within the countries. But I shall not discuss here this particular change (the reader might find more about it in my *Global Inequality* or "The three eras of global inequality, 1820–2020 with the focus on the past thirty years").

It is another implication of the fact that most of inequality is due to the differences in mean incomes that I would like to focus on. If income differences between the countries are large then one's income will significantly depend on where they live, or even where they were born, since 97 percent of the world population live in the countries where they were born. This is what I propose to call the "citizenship premium" (or "citizenship penalty"): it is a "rent" that a person receives if he or she happens to be born in a rich country, or if we use the terminology introduced by John Roemer in his "Equality of Opportunity," it is an "exogenous circumstance" which is independent from a person's individual effort and luck.

I would now like to address three questions: how big is the citizenship rent, how it varies with one's position in income distribution, and what does it imply for global inequality of opportunity and migration.

Can we estimate the citizenship rent? Yes, we can. In my "Global Inequality of Opportunity: How Much of our Income is Determined by Where we Live?" I do so by using the data from household surveys conducted in 118 countries in and around year 2008. From each country, I have micro (household level) data, which I order into 100 percentiles, with people ranked by their household per capita income. This gives 11,800 country/percentiles with "representative" per capita incomes expressed in dollars of equal purchasing parity (incomes across countries are thus made comparable). Now, I try to "explain" these incomes by only one variable: the country where people live. Obviously, people living in the United States will tend to have higher incomes, at any given percentile of the distribution, than people living in poor countries in Africa. But how will it look for the world as a whole? In a least-square dummy variable regression, I use Congo, the poorest country in the world, as the "omitted country," so that the citizenship premium is expressed in terms of the income gain compared to Congo. The premium for the US is 355 percent, for Sweden 329 percent, Brazil 164 percent, but for Yemen only 32 percent. We can "explain" (in a regression sense) more than 2/3 of the variability in incomes across country/percentiles by only one variable: a dummy variable of the country where people live. This is exactly the answer to the question we posed before: a lot of our income depends on where we live.

Does the citizenship rent vary along the distribution? But this is an average premium, country against country; does it vary along income distribution? In other words, if I were to take into consideration only people belonging to the lowest part of income distribution everywhere, would the premium be still the same? Intuition may help there. Suppose I focus only on the incomes of the lowest decile, and rich countries are more equal than poor countries. Then the gap between rich and poor countries will be greater for the very poor people than on the average. This is indeed what we find: Sweden's citizenship premium (compared to Congo) is now 367 percent (vs. 329 on the average); but very unequal, Brazil's is 133 percent (vs. 164 on the average). The situation at the top is exactly the opposite: Sweden's advantage at the 90th percentile of income distribution is "only" 286 percent, but Brazil's becomes 188 percent.

Implications for migration. The existence of the citizenship premium has obvious implications for migration: people from poor countries will have the opportunity to double or triple their real incomes by moving to a rich country. But the fact that the premium varies in function of one's position in income distribution carries additional implications. If I consider two countries with the same average income as my possible migration destination, my decision (based on economic criteria alone) about where to migrate will also be influenced by my expectation regarding where I may end up in the recipient country's income distribution and thus about how unequal the recipient country's distribution is. Suppose that the (proverbial) Sweden and the US have the same mean income. If I expect to end up in the bottom part of recipient country's distribution, then I should migrate to Sweden: the poor people there are better off compared to the mean, and the citizenship premium, evaluated at lower parts of distribution, is greater. The opposite conclusion follows if I expect to end up in the upper part of the recipient country's distribution: I should migrate to the US.

This last result has unpleasant implications for more equal among rich countries: they will tend to attract lower-skilled migrants who generally expect to be placed in the bottom part of the recipient country's distribution. So developing national welfare state would have a perverse effect of attracting migrants who can contribute less. Another element, however, has to be taken into account, even in this admittedly very rough sketch: how much of social mobility there is in the recipient country: more unequal countries with strong social mobility will, everything else being the same, tend to appeal to the more skilled migrants.

Global inequality of opportunity? The mere existence of a large citizenship premium implies that there is no such a thing as global equality of opportunity (a lot of our income depends on the accident of birth). Should we strive for it or not? It is a political philosophy question about which the philosophers have thought more than economists. Some, following John Rawls and his *The Law of Peoples*, believe that this is not an issue and that every argument for global equality of opportunity would conflict with the right of national self-determination. But other political philosophers like Thomas Pogge believe that in an interdependent world, high differences in life chances are not to be accepted lightly. I (obviously) do not propose to resolve this issue. But I believe that economists too should not shy away from addressing it. (Legal scientists like Ayalet Shachar in *The Birthright Lottery* have written about it too, proposing a much more flexible and open definition of citizenship.)

The future. As gaps between nations diminish, mostly thanks to the high growth rates of Asian countries, the citizenship rent will tend to be reduced. But it is so huge today that even a century of much higher growth of poor countries (compared to the rich) will not eradicate the citizenship rent. However, it can reduce it. As it does so, it will also

INEQUALITY

reduce the overall global inequality, and then perhaps ultimately lead us back to the world of the mid nineteenth century, where class will again become more important, for one's global income position, than the location. Do I hear "Marx"?

(Published May 6, 2015)

GLOBAL INEQUALITY

5.4 Is citizenship just a rent?

The modern idea of citizenship, after the French Revolution, is based on two pillars: one is voluntary or compulsive participation in the political life of a community, the other is the physical "grounding" in that political community. The participation means, in democratic settings, that a citizen has a voice, the right to air opinions, to vote for those who represent or lead him, and to be himself elected. In non-democratic or not fully democratic settings, political participation is often not only desirable but is required: citizens of the Soviet Union, Nazi Germany, and Francoist Spain were encouraged, or where necessary compelled, to take part in mass public celebrations of the state whose citizens they were. "Groundness" means that citizens live in their own countries (as their political participation in the affairs of the country implies), earn most of their income in own country, and spend most of it domestically.

The growth of the welfare state in the second half of the twentieth century, in the West and in the communist countries of Eastern Europe, has added another facet to citizenship: the right to a number of benefits, from child allowances to pensions and unemployment benefits that are available only to contributors (i.e. citizens who work in their countries) or to citizens as such without any contributory quid pro quo (as, for example, family allowances or social assistance). The existence of the welfare state in a world of enormous income differences between the countries has drawn a wedge between citizens of rich countries that enjoy these benefits and citizens of poor countries that do not. It has created a "citizenship rent" for those who are lucky to be citizens of the rich countries; and "citizenship penalty" for others. Two otherwise identical citizens of France and Mali will have entirely different sets of income-generating rights, which stem from their citizenships alone.

Moreover, the citizenship premium, as I show most recently in *Capitalism, Alone* carries over to other incomes: our French and Malian citizens can be equally educated, experienced, and hardworking, but their wages will differ by a factor of 5 to 1, or even more, simply because one of them works in a rich and another in a poor country. In fact, around 60 percent of our lifetime incomes is determined by country of citizenship.

In a globalized world composed of countries with vastly unequal mean incomes, citizenship has thus acquired an enormous, and well appreciated, economic value. This is evident not only from the

131

examples listed above but from the freedom to travel without visa or any other permission (luxury of the rich countries, as Zygmunt Bauman called it), support that one can expect from his country offices abroad and the like.

But, while the citizenship rent element has been reinforced in modern globalized capitalism, the other two pillars of citizenship (political participation and groundness) have been radically weakened. Citizenship has thus been effectively reduced to financial rent alone.

Groundness is still common among many citizens. But its importance fades as people move permanently, or for long periods of time, to other countries: in some cases they migrate to richer countries to make more money there (as do migrants from Africa to Europe, or from Mexico to the United States), and in other cases, migrants from rich counties move to other, also rich countries, as Americans do when they move to France (the latter category is often adorned with the title of "expatriates").

As they move to other countries, they work there, make income there, spend money there, and their financial sustenance gets "delinked" from their country of citizenship. All sources of income can become degrounded: both those of labor and capital. To see how ultimately the "degrounding" will work in a fully globalized world, assume an elderly American expatriate who lives in France. A part of his income may come from the work he does in France; another part, in the form of US social security, may come from the US. But income behind that social security check may be earned from US investments in China. Thus, both physically and in terms of the origin of his income, the American citizen will be "degrounded." Or, take a Philippine citizen who works in the US. Similarly, his income would be earned in a foreign country. If he is eligible for some citizenship-related income as a Philippine, money earned to pay such benefits may in effect be earned by other Philippine citizens working abroad, remitted back to their families in the Philippines, and then taxed by the government.

A fully globalized country may be such that its capital income comes from investments in foreign lands, its labor income from remittances sent by its workers abroad, and most of its citizens be living abroad—and yet receiving social and other benefits of citizenship.

Political participation in modern capitalism also wanes. With a much more competitive society, where one's success is measured in terms of economic power (wealth), people do not have enough free time or interest to be idealized citizens concerned with the political life of their city or nation. Hard work for money takes most of their time. The rest of the waking time is taken by social media, entertainment, family chores, or meetings with friends. Under normal circumstances, time that they can devote to political issues is minimal. Electoral turnouts in most developed democracies, by themselves a minimal requirement of participation, cheap in effort and time, confirm that. They are low, especially so among the youth. American presidential elections, where people elect a person with quasi regal powers, have only once in the past half-century brought to the polling stations more than 60 percent of the electorate (in 2020). Elections for the EU parliament manage to bestir about one-half of the eligible voters. This is not the product of apathy only, but of busyness.

The decline in political participation and increasing deground-edness imply that the two modern-era pillars of citizenship have largely been eroded. The only remaining meaning of citizenship is the stream of income and advantages that one receives if lucky to have been born or become a citizen of a rich nation. Citizenship has become an "ideal" category, a right devoid of the need to be physically present in one's own country or to be interested in it: it is physically incarnated in a passport or in an ID, a simple physical proof that one can aspire to its manifold advantages.

Countries that sell citizenship, from EU members to the small Caribbean nations, do not make a mistake. Nor do their purchasers. No one expects the new citizens either to live much of their time in their new countries (Chinese and Russians who buy Portuguese citizenship are required to spend one week there per year), nor to participate in its social life. Nor even to know the language, much less history. Countries are exchanging an ideal category (citizenship) that provides a set of rights over time against an amount of money now, equal to the net present value of the bundle of these future advantages.

The fact that citizenship has become a Polanyian "fictitious commodity" has several implications, which I discuss more fully in *Capitalism, Alone*. First, we must move from the binary version of citizen—no citizens by introducing more intermediary categories, distinguished by the amounts of rights and duties they provide (as indeed is already happening with permanent residents who are not fully fledged citizens). Second, migration can be seen as one of these intermediate positions that do not automatically lead to full citizenship. Third, we should reconsider the wisdom of giving electoral rights to people who do not live in a country for whose leaders they vote, and who hence neither benefit nor suffer from the choices they make.

(Published May 30, 2021)

INEQUALITY

5.5 Why foreign aid cannot be regressive

There are many arguments against foreign aid. Angus Deaton has forcefully argued that foreign aid, by providing resources to the governments outside normal taxation, breaks the link of reciprocity that exists between the tax payers and the state. It thus weakens national institutions, and insulates the rules from the population. Dambisa Mayo believes that aid fosters corruption. Bill Easterly has attacked aid because it goes to the governments and not to the private sector. Many of these recent critiques are reminiscent of the arguments made decades ago by Peter Bauer (*Dissent on Development*) and, even earlier, by Ludwig von Mises.

Now, when the European Union seems to be considering a significant increase in aid for Africa—led this time not by humanitarian concerns but by the well-understood self-interest, as reduction of migration is hard to imagine without a substantial convergence in incomes between Africa and Europe—it is worth pointing out that one argument against aid cannot hold. This is the argument made sometime in popular press (and at times, in academe too), that aid to the poor countries is just a transfer of resources from the poor people in rich countries to the rich people in poor countries. This is what is in economics called a "regressive transfer." ("Progressive" transfer is what we desire to achieve: tax a richer person and transfer the money to a poorer.)

The data on global income distribution clearly show that this particular argument against aid ("regressiveness") has no validity. To see this, consider as an illustrative example incomes along the entire income distributions of the Netherlands and Mali. Figure 5.1 shows annual per capita income levels (in 2011 PPP dollars) at different percentiles of Dutch and Malian income distributions. As can be readily seen, even the poorest percentiles in the Netherlands are richer than all Malian percentiles, including the top one percent. In other words, the two distributions do not overlap: the Dutch distribution starts at an income level where the distribution on Mali had already ended. (The dashed line is drawn at the income level of the poorest Dutch percentile.)

Now, this fact alone would sufficiently indicate that if one taxes a Dutch person and transfers that money to a person in Mali, it is very unlikely that he would make a regressive transfer. But the probability of a regressive transfer is even much smaller than this first impression implies. One has to ask: from whom in the Netherlands would the expected tax euro (that is used for aid) come? In other

134

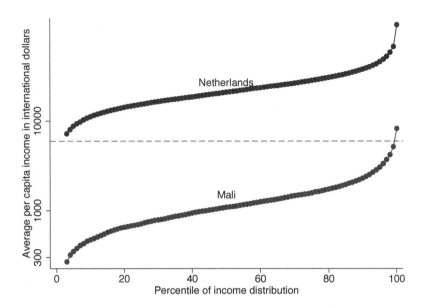

Figure 5.1 Income levels in the Netherlands and Mali

Note: The graph shows annual per capita income in international dollars In the Netherlands and Mali. It shows that even the richest income percentile in Mali (the top one percent) has an income inferior to that of the poorest income percentile in the Netherlands. The vertical axis is in logs.

words, imagine a big bowl where all Dutch income taxes are collected with, for each euro received, written the income level (or percentile position) of the person who paid it. If the Dutch system were based on a poll-tax, everybody would contribute the same amount, and the expected percentile position of the taxpayer whose euro goes to Mali would be exactly at the Dutch median income. If the Dutch system were such that the tax rate is the same regardless of income level (the so-called "flat tax" system), the expected euro would come from the person at the Dutch mean income level.

The person with the mean income in the Netherlands is located at the 63rd percentile of the Dutch income distribution.

But this is not all. The Dutch system of direct taxation is progressive, meaning that the tax rate increases with income level. Now, richer people will contribute not only more euros absolutely, but also more euros proportionally. Using LIS-provided micro income distribution data, we can calculate the average tax rate by percentile of the Dutch distribution (shown in Figure 5.2) and also calculate that a random euro that would go for aid in Africa would come from the person who is at the 77th percentile of the Dutch income distribution.

We can now go back to the first graph (Figure 5.1) and look at how likely it is that the beneficiary of the Dutch aid to Mali will be richer than the person at the 77th percentile of the Dutch income distribution. Since even the Malian top one percent has an income that is vastly inferior (it is about one-fourth) to the income at the Dutch 77th percentile, that likelihood must be quasi nil. In other words, even if we assume, rather extravagantly, that the only beneficiaries of Dutch aid to Mali are the local top one percent, the transfer would be still *progressive*. It could be of course argued that were we to slice the Malian distribution into ever smaller pieces, there may be eventually such a small slice, say the richest five or ten persons in Mali, who would be better-off than the Dutch 77th percentile. But this is simply

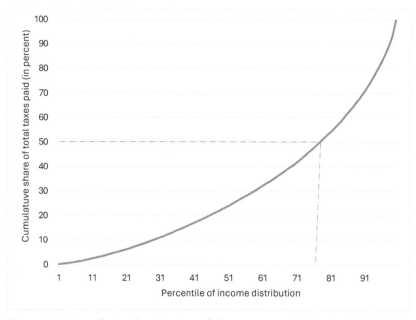

Figure 5.2 Cumulative distribution of direct taxes paid, Netherlands, 2013

Note: The figure shows the cumulative share of all taxes paid as people are ranked by their gross income, from the poorest percentile (on the left) to the richest. The bottom 77 percent of the population (horizontal axis) pays 50 percent of all taxes (line at the vertical axis); the top 23 percent pays the other half.

GLOBAL INEQUALITY

saying that—working behind the veil of ignorance of who the beneficiaries of aid are—the likelihood of a regressive transfer is somewhere
in the vicinity of one-hundredth of one percent. The onus is therefore
on those who argue that foreign aid can be regressive to show that
the beneficiaries of aid are people who are probably part of the top
Malian millesime or so. This, based on whatever we know about the
effects of aid, seems utterly unlikely.

To conclude: aid is not a panacea, it could even be detrimental to
the recipient country, but it surely does not (in most cases that we
normally have to deal with) represent a transfer of purchasing power
from a poor person in a rich country to a rich person in a poor
country. This shibboleth needs to be laid to rest.

(Published July 11, 2017)

5.6 Formal and actual similarities between climate change and global inequality, and suboptimality of the nation-state

There are obvious and (to some people) surprising similarities between global climate change and global inequality. Both are obviously global problems. Neither can be solved by a single country, group, or individual. In both cases, there are significant externalities and consequently coordination problems. Both issues are even formally linked (that is, not only conceptually): elasticity of carbon emissions with respect to real income is around one. This not only means that if a person's (or a country's) income increases by ten percent, emissions tend to increase at the same rate, but that the distribution of emitters mimics the distribution of income. Since, in the global income distribution, the top decile receives about 40 percent of global income (in PPP terms), it is also responsible for about 40 percent of all emissions.

But there are also significant differences. The effects of global income inequality are in part the product of high within-country inequalities that obviously have to be dealt with at the level of nation-states. There are only two parts of global income inequality that are truly global. The first is that high global inequality also means high global poverty; the second is that high global inequality is due to a significant extent to high inequality between countries' incomes, which in turn fuels migration.

The issue of global poverty is an ethical issue for all those who are not poor. It is not otherwise an issue that affects the non-poor in their daily lives. Moreover, since they do not share space with the global poor, they, in their daily lives, tend to ignore them.

Migration is the only concrete manifestation of global income inequality that affects people in rich countries. If some of them want to reduce migration, it is in their self-interest to help the growth of poor countries. But the benefits and costs of migration are unevenly distributed within rich countries' populations. Some groups—like employers, users of many services, and workers with complementary skills—gain from migration, while others who compete with migrants, or those who are afraid that their culture would be "diluted," lose. Thus, the overall effect of global income inequality on the lives of most people in rich countries boils down to the effect of migration.

The effect of global climate change is different in the sense that it is more remote in time and is uncertain. The winners and losers are not clear. To combat climate change requires adjustment of behavior by individuals and countries in order to forestall effects which lie in the future and whose benefits are unclear, while costs of adjustment are obvious and present. Individual adjustment, while entailing often significant monetary or convenience cost for that individual, has close to zero effect on climate change and it is therefore not rational to undertake it from a purely personal perspective. Change in behavior of larger groups, induced by taxation of especially "bad" activities, can produce effects, but the distribution of benefits from these adjustments is unknown. Even if the benefits were somehow equally distributed, a group that adjusted its behavior would receive a very small share of all benefits. It is a typical externality problem.

This implies that no group of people and no individual country has an incentive to do anything by itself: they have to be roped into an international framework, where everyone is compelled to reduce emissions and where, in the case of success, net benefits would be, most likely, unequally distributed. (Note the similarity with social insurance schemes.) This is indeed what has happened with Kyoto and Paris accords. To complicate matters further, however, nation-states are not really the best units to deal with this, although they are the only ones through which, given the current global governance structure, such policies can be agreed on and conducted. They are not the most suitable units to deal with global climate change because the main emitters who should be targeted are the rich, regardless of where they live. Thus, a much more appropriate approach would be an international (global) taxation of goods and services consumed by the rich. However, for that one would need to have an international authority that would be allowed to tax citizens of different countries and to collect revenues globally.

As I mentioned above, there is a formal equivalence between global income inequality and climate change. Migration, which is the strongest "negative" (from the point of view of some) effect of global inequality, also requires international coordination. The increased migration of Africans into Europe cannot be solved by any individual country alone. It can be "solved" or rather managed only by a joint action (distribution of quotas) involving both the emitting and receiving countries. But, unlike climate change, which is basically considered an overall "bad," migration is not an overall "bad," but rather a "good." Therefore, targeting for more action countries that are likely to be the largest emitters of migrants does not make sense.

In fact, in the case of migration, we deal with a "global good" that reduces global inequality and global poverty, even if it may in some cases produce negative effects. Because of the fears of those negative effects (economic and social) we need rules that would assuage some people, lest they wreck and stop the whole process of migration. This is where the idea of "circular migration" and differentiation between job-related rights (equal for all) and civic rights (not available to migrants) comes from (see my *Global Inequality* as well as *Capitalism, Alone*). In the case of climate change, we are dealing with something that is essentially a "bad," but we have trouble making those who are generating the bulk of this "bad" effect pay for it and forcing them to change their behavior.

Thus, in one case, we try to keep what is globally good (migration) by reducing the fears of those who may, locally, be affected negatively. In the case of climate change, we try to avoid something that is globally bad by using the only instrument that we have (nation-state), which is clearly suboptimal. We are thus in both cases trying to devise what may be called "second-best" solutions, mostly because of the political limitation called the nation-state.

(Published June 29, 2021)

— 6 —

WEALTH INEQUALITY

6.1 What is wealth?

It seems obvious. Let me start with the definitions that economists who work on inequality use. It is the sum total of all assets that you own (house, car, furniture, paintings, money in the bank, value of shares, bonds, etc.) plus what is called "the surrender value" of life insurance and similar plans, minus the amount of your debts. In other words, this is the amount of money that you would get if you had to liquidate *today* all your possessions and repay all your debts. (The amount can clearly be negative too.) The definition can get further complicated, as some economists insist that we should also add the capitalized value of future (certain?) streams of income. That leads to the problems that explained Section 6.8—but be this as it may, in this post I would like to take a more historical view of wealth.

I did that too in my *The Haves and the Have-Nots* when I discussed who might have been the richest person in history. If you want to compare people from different epochs you cannot just simply try to calculate total wealth. That of course by itself is impossible because of what is known as the "index number problem": there is no way of comparing the bundle of goods and services that are hugely dissimilar. If I can listen to a million songs and read the whole night using a very good light and, if I put a high value on that, I may be thought to be wealthier than any king who lived 1,000 years ago. Tocqueville noticed that too when he wrote that ancient kings lived lives of luxury but not comfort.

This is why we should use Adam Smith's definition of wealth: "[A person] must be rich or poor according to the quantity of labor which he can command" (*Wealth of Nations*, bk. I, ch. 5). This means that the extent of one's wealth ought to be estimated within a historical context: how many thousands of hours of labor a person could command if he were to use his entire wealth. This metric however is easier to implement in the past than now. When, say in Roman times, countries were at approximately the same level of income, taking the richest person in Roman and Chinese Empires, and comparing their wealth with the subsistence income (i.e. the usual wage at the time) made sense because that "usual wage" was the same in Rome as in China. But, if you take Jeff Bezos or Bill Gates, with whose wages should you compare their wealth? Wages of US labor or some notional global wage rate? If the former, should not then Carlos Slim's or Russian oligarchs' wealth be compared to the average wage in Mexico and Russia? This is what I did in *The Haves and the Have-Nots* and here are the results. One can see that Slim and Khodorkovsky (the Russian super-oligarch before he was jailed by Putin) were probably the richest people in history—if their wealth is measured in terms of their country's wages. And, by the same yardstick, Rockefeller in 1937 was richer than Gates in 2005.

When we do this kind of calculation, we look implicitly at billionaires' potential domestic power: their ability to move thousands of people. But, notice that here I have moved the goalposts a little. I am really measuring wealth in the space of potential *power*. Now, that power does not always require actual financial wealth. It can come from straight political power. Stalin, to take one example, could have moved much more labor by his decisions than either Khodorkovsky or Slim. The same is true for many other dictators in history.

This conflation of the amount of money as such and the power to order people around leads people to believe that absolute rules must have been extraordinarily wealthy. The view is based implicitly on the values of our own contemporary societies, which are fully commercialized, and where having wealth comes close to having power. With people like Trump, Berlusconi, Thaksin, Bloomberg, etc., it becomes even more "natural" to see wealth and power as just one and the same thing.

Wealth also, it is thought, should include the ability to leave it to your heirs. After all, many people justify their amassing extraordinary amounts by their concern for family, or maybe for some philanthropic causes. But what happens when the actual private wealth is low even if the ability to control an enormous amount of resources is huge? This was the case, in an extreme way, with Stalin, but also with most communist leaders. Whoever among them was a supreme leader within his own country had a huge power to move resources around. They

WEALTH INEQUALITY

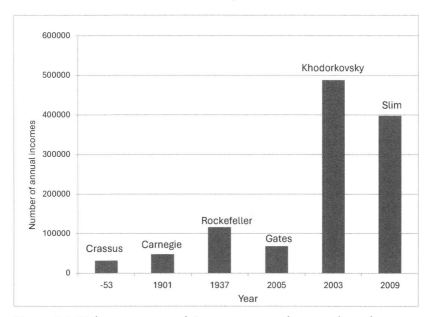

Figure 6.1 Richest man annual income expressed as number of average incomes in the year and country where he lived

Note: The graph shows estimated annual income of the richest people expressed in the number of annual incomes of the country and time where they lived. Khodorkovsky's or Slim's annual income is estimated to be equal to the 400 to 500,000 average incomes in respectively Russia 2003 and Mexico 2009.

also used for themselves many resources; not (in the case of Stalin) in an ostentatious Czarist way, but in order to showcase their own power and the power of the state (as shown very convincingly in Vladimir Nevezhin's *At Stalin's Dining Table*). Resources were also used to pay for incredibly high security demands, so that no one could track the movement of the supreme leader. (The same reason that leads American presidents always to use two or three helicopters and not one.) This resulted in Stalin having access to approximately twenty residences in different areas near Moscow and on the Black Sea coast. (Some of these residences were only for his own use, others were shared with the rest of the leadership.) Very similar was Mao's situation. Tito had at least seven residences in different parts of the country.

But, what neither of their dictators had was the ability to transfer such "wealth" to their offspring. Many of them did not much care about their nearest family—certainly in the cases of Stalin and Tito.

INEQUALITY

Table 6.1 Functions of wealth in different societies

	In despotic societies of the past	In "high" communism	In today's commercialized societies
To command people's labor	Yes	Yes	Yes
To move resources (in a macroeconomic way)	Yes	Yes	Only if you combine it with political power
To live luxuriously	Yes	Yes (but not quite)	Yes
To leave it to your heirs	Yes	No	Yes

Mao cared just a bit more, but his son inherited little; Chiang Ching (Jiang Qing), his widow, even less and died in prison. Thus, if we make a simple table (Table 6.1) of what wealth consists of, we note that in these cases it did not fulfil all the functions that we normally assign to it. The reason why it fails to do so is because we ascribe to wealth the characteristics of our own commercialized societies. In different societies, even if they are relatively close in age and technological development to ours (like Stalin's Soviet Union or Mao's China), the function of wealth was different. Power was the true wealth—not the mansions that were used ex officio and that you could not bequeath to your heirs.

We thus find that comparing wealth over different ages is not only fraught with difficulties, or rather impossible because we cannot assign values to the things that did not exist in the past and exist now, but because we have trouble comparing wealth in different societies with structurally different features. We have to realize that it is okay to compare wealth of the people on the Forbes list so long as they share similar social environments: the same ability to protect that wealth, to use it to boss people around, to bequeath it. At the moment when these underlying conditions diverge, comparison ceases to be meaningful.

(Published February 10, 2020)

6.2 Historical wealth: How to compare Croesus and Bezos

In the previous post, I wrote about wealth comparisons over time. As mentioned there, I have done such a comparison myself in *The Haves and the Have-Nots* and have used Adam Smith's argument that a person's wealth ought to be measured in the amount of labor he commands. In other words, wealth needs to be measured in its historical context. I gave two examples of misleading wealth comparisons: over time when we try to use the same bundle of commodities to compare Croesus and Bezos, and when we conflate wealth and power.

Here I would like to explain a bit more the problems with historical comparisons of wealth (or income) because they have direct bearing on our understanding of the past, and raise also some essentially philosophical points.

The difficulty of measurement of wealth between different periods derives not only because of our lack of data for most of the past but from the inability to compare wealth or consumption patterns in the past meaningfully with those of today. Some economists believe that if people in the past did not have amenities that we have today they must have been infinitely poorer. This is what one finds in Nordhaus and DeLong's view of historical progress as unfolding through reduced cost of artificial lighting, the approach that Angus Maddison (in *Contours of the World Economy: 1–2030*) termed a "hallucinogenic history."

The logic of such authors is as follows. Take the example of artificial lighting or voice recording. For Julius Caesar to read a book overnight, easily move at night around his palace, or listen to the songs he liked, would have required perhaps hundreds of workers (slaves) to hold the torches or sing his favorite arias all night. Even Caesar, if he were to do that night after night, might, after some time, have run out of resources (or might have provoked a rebellion among the singers). But for us the expense for a similar pleasure is very small, even trivial, say $2 per night. Consequently, some people come to the conclusion that Caesar must have had tiny wealth measured in today's bundle of goods since a repeated small nightly expense of $2 (in today's prices) would have eventually ruined him. Other people at Caesar's time had obviously much less: ergo, the world today is incomparably richer than before, and people then must have *felt* horribly poor and deprived of all pleasurable things. (Even if you cannot feel deprived of the things you do not know exist.)

The logic seems at first reasonable, even if somewhat extreme. But it is not reasonable. Let's extend this logic, now in a different direction, from now to the next 500 years. Suppose that in 500 years people are able to choose between Mars, Venus, or Pluto for their vacation, or perhaps even to go further than that. Suppose they can fly around our solar system, go to the bottom of the ocean, zip from one end of the Earth to another in a few minutes, or do lots of fun things that we cannot imagine today, no more than Caesar could have imagined that his singers' voices could be recorded on a tiny chip and reproduced ad infinitum at almost no cost. And when we then look at Jeff Bezos' wealth today using the consumption opportunities of the future, that wealth is likely to look to us—from the vantage point of 500 years hence—insignificant. Bezos might be rich in our own terms, but he cannot fly to Mars this weekend, no matter how much he tries.

So, should we then absurdly turn around and claim that Jeff Bezos, Bill Gates, et al. are poor? Clearly not. But thus, equally clearly, rich Romans were not poor either. In other words, we cannot compare wealth from vastly different epochs by using one yardstick, whether it be the yardstick of the past (which is on balance more reasonable) or the yardstick of the present. This is a well-known problem for empirical economic historians. If time-periods are not vastly apart or, rather, if technologies and consumption baskets are not vastly different, we can perhaps use some equal weighting of the baskets (½ of the past and ½ of the present). But that clearly will not do for the very remote periods.

This is why wealth has to be measured with a yardstick belonging to the same time at which that wealth exists. And this is why Adam Smith's approach seems the only one that makes sense. No other commodity but labor power (an hour of unskilled work) is both as unchanged over time in terms of effort exerted, and yet paid the equivalent of different amounts of real goods and services reflecting the general level of productivity of a society. It is both covariant with wealth and an unvarying numeraire.

Angus Maddison, who created the original series comparing incomes of countries over a very long-run, was perfectly aware of the problem. He directed his scorn toward those who looking at the past through today's lenses only treated everybody who lived then as "cavemen": "[Such authors as] Nordhaus and DeLong overdosing on hedonics have constructed fairytale scenarios that greatly exaggerate progress since 1800, before which they seem to believe that people lived like cavemen. These views are fundamentally wrong" (*Contours* ... p. 315).

(Published February 15, 2020)

6.3 My wealth and the lives of others

I watched tonight a BBC-sponsored discussion on inequality held at Davos meetings. It was a good discussion, and the crucial moment for me came when the moderator put down the two views of the top-one-percenters, creators or predators, and asked the audience and the discussants (who included private sector CEOs, Governor of the Bank of England, and the head of the IMF) whether one or the other category better exemplified the super-rich. The audience voted, unsurprisingly, 9 to 1, in favor of creators, but I thought that the dichotomy, while real and very important, was not sufficiently developed.

No rational person can be against people who, through their effort or brains, inventions, innovations or hard work, have become rich by also improving our lives. Without them we would be living without electricity, Internet, or washing machines. Even the person who invented pizza delivery deserves his wealth and our eternal gratitude. On a cold winter night, we would be freezing and hungry in our apartments without him.

But, I thought, there are at least six other ways that people might become billionaires without making lives of the rest of us any better. That is, their fortune could have been given to a random person and nobody (except perhaps their family) would be worse off for that. Let me list these six ways, in descending order of opprobrium.

(1) **Inheritance.** There is nothing that a person who got it did to make life better for anybody in this wide world. I think this is pretty clear.

(2) **Political position.** Presidents, kings, emirs who either got to their positions through "force and guile" or have inherited them have often (but not always) become rich without doing anything to improve other people's lives. Here, think of the Saudi rulers, presidents of the resource-rich countries (Obiang Nguema from the Equatorial Guinea), and others who simply stole billions of dollars.

(3) **Political connections.** These are people who made money by cozying up to the rulers, from billionaires in Indonesia, who were Suharto's best buddies, to Abramovich and Khodorkovsky, who were Yeltsin's. These are people who have become rich just by being close to power and being given a license to steal or to "organize" business in the best possible way for themselves.

Most of what is called Françafrique falls into this category: French businessmen cozying up to the African rulers. Many of today's Russian and Chinese billionaires belong there too. State-financed activities, from road-building to military purchases, are the ideal forms for wealth made through political connections. (Read Helen Epstein's review of several books on Zambia if in doubt about what this category exactly is.)

(4) **Political lobbying.** These are people who made money through incessant political lobbying ("having politicians in their pocket") aimed at changing the rules of the game, lowering taxation, or handicapping competitors. Here, think of pharmaceutical or insurance companies, oil and gas, and these hundreds of multi-nationals that keep offices in Washington and Brussels and make their managers and shareholders rich. Financial sector belongs here too: how else would they have gotten the legislation they needed in Washington?

(5) **Monopoly.** People who owe large shares or all of their fortunes thanks to monopolies (which are often acquired though political lobbying). Carlos Slim is often mentioning in this context; Bill Gates too. In every country where I have traveled I have heard of one, two, or three persons who have become rich by managing to obtain a monopoly or a privileged position on TV channels, mobile phones, or Internet. Berlusconi and Thaksin could be placed there before they moved to category 2.

(6) **Tax evasion.** Although it may not be strictly illegal (but then lobbying is not illegal either) it surely often implies that wealth was acquired by cleverly exploiting the rules and without making anybody else better off. Bono of the U2 fame is often cited as an exemplar of this approach and of hypocrisy of arguing for higher taxes to help the poor, while his companies are incorporated into the Caribbean islands and pay practically no taxes.

So, clearly, among the millionaires and billionaires there must be quite a few who have become rich, or who owe at least a part of their riches, to one of the six ways listed here. In other words, they have become very wealthy without any obvious contribution to anybody else's welfare.

And, thus, I thought that we are unlikely to make progress about finding out "who's who" among the top one percent (or rather 1% of 1%) until we do something that I suggested to a couple of my Oxfam friends a year ago: we have to figure out who is mostly a creator and who is mostly a predator. As in many areas, we are unlikely to make

WEALTH INEQUALITY

real progress until we quantify things. And we can quantify things by asking a simple, but powerful, question:

(1) *What percentage of your wealth was acquired through activities that benefited other people in the world?*

Obviously, we cannot get to an exact assessment, but we can try to get to an approximation. I suggested to my friends that they use the resources of Oxfam, information on the Internet, and people with specific country knowledge, to look at the way the 1,500 billionaires on the Forbes list have acquired their wealth, and then make an approximate assessment of (1). It is not an impossible, nor even a difficult, task. Most of the information is known. Very few large fortunes are made without people having an idea how somebody got rich. Not all of these ideas may be correct, but an impartial researcher can assess them, check them against the known facts, and come to a preliminary judgment. We just need to create a template where we would give negative points for acquisition of wealth under the six categories listed above (with inheritance and political position being the worse, and tax evasion being the least bad) and then make an assessment for each of the 1,500 billionaires.

To give an example. Start with the maximum of ten points (all of your wealth was acquired through activities that benefited others), and then deduct points as you find out more about how wealth was really gotten. Surely, Bill Gates might lose two or three points, but his contribution to the betterment of the world through Microsoft (I am not talking here of the philanthropic activities; see the note on the bottom of the text) is real. Then, come to the Walmart owners: they too have contributed to the world (through lower prices of the products in their stores) but have also made lives of many of their employees miserable and used political lobbying to increase their wealth. They should lose points for the latter. Then go to the Russian oligarchs: it is difficult to see how anyone could have been made worse off if the oligarch's wealth had gone into the hands of somebody else. Then, end with the heirs of large fortunes (Bettencourt in France, Forbes in the US) or Saudi princes, where it is just impossible to see what their wealth had to do with the welfare of the world.

The grades (say, from 10 to 0) would at first be rough. But they can be gradually improved. If we can grade countries' democracies, or how much governments' policies help reduce world poverty, I cannot see why we cannot make estimates about how much of the wealth of each individual billionaire was made through activities

149

INEQUALITY

that were innovative and helpful to others or not. The objective is not to shame them into being better people. Many of them do not care about that. The objective is to put some value on that unending discussion about wealth acquisition, illustrated by the question posed at Davos: was wealth deserved or not. Until we know whether we are moving toward the world where most of the wealthy have become so by doing something useful, or the opposite of it, we shall remain stuck in the sterile discussion where one opinion can be equally right or wrong as another. We shall never know if we are getting closer to the socially minded capitalism or to what Max Weber rightly called "political or exploitative" capitalism. In other words, whether we are moving forward or backward.

Note re philanthropic activities: The objective of the exercise is to assess to what extent the acquisition of wealth serves some broader purposes of general human betterment, not whether a person, after perhaps acquiring wealth fraudulently or in a violent manner, is willing to share it. The latter may be good or desirable but is a separate issue from the key one here: Is my wealth acquired through actions that have improved the lives of others?

(Published January 27, 2015)

WEALTH INEQUALITY

6.4 Dutiful dirges of Davos

You will find me eager to help you,
but slow to take any step.

Euripides, *Hecabe*

Thousands of people will gather next week in Davos. Their combined wealth will reach several hundred billion dollars, perhaps even close to a trillion. Never in the world history will be the amount of wealth per square foot so high. And this year, for the sixth or seventh consecutive time, what would be one of the principal topics addressed by these captains of industry, billionaires, employers of thousands of people across the four corners of the globe: inequality ...

Only in passing, and probably on the margins of the official program, will they get into the tremendous monopoly and monopsony power of their companies, ability to play one jurisdiction against another in order to avoid taxes, how to ban organized labor in their companies, how to use government ambulance services to carry workers who have fainted from extra heat (to save expense of air conditioning), how to make their workforce complement its wage through private charity donations, or perhaps how to pay the average tax rate between 0 and 12 percent tax (Trump to Romney). If they are from the emerging market economies, they can also exchange experiences on how to delay payments of wages for several months while investing these funds at high interest rates, how to save on labor protection standards, or how to buy privatized companies for a song and then to set up shell companies in the Caribbean or Channel Islands.

Still, poverty and inequality which are, as we know, the defining issues of our time, will be permanently on their minds.

It is just that somehow they never succeeded in finding enough money, or time, or perhaps willing lobbyists to help with the policies that they all agree, during the official sessions, should be implemented: to increase taxes on the top one percent and on large inheritances, to provide decent wages and not to impound salaries, to reduce gaps between CEO and average pay, to spend more money on public education, to make access to financial assets more attractive to the middle and working class, to equalize taxes on capital and labor, to reduce corruption in government contracts and privatizations.

Since they have been singularly unsuccessful in convincing governments to do anything about rising inequality, it is not surprising that

151

almost nothing has been done. Or rather that the very opposite policies have been conducted: Trump has, as he promised or threatened, passed a historic tax cut for the wealthy while Macron has discovered the attraction of latter-day Thatcherism. Nothing positive of note seems to have been done in the emerging market economies either (with perhaps the crackdown on corruption in China the only important exception).

This return to the industrial relations and tax policies of the early nineteenth century is bizarrely spearheaded by people who speak the language of equality, respect, participation, and transparency. None of them is in favor of the "Master and Servant Act" or forced labor. It just so happened that the language of equality has been harnessed in the pursuit of structurally most inegalitarian policies over the past fifty years, or more. And, indeed, it is much more profitable to call journalists and tell them about the nebulous schemes whereby 90 percent of one's wealth will be, over an unknown number of years and under unknowable accounting practices, given away as charity, than to pay suppliers and workers reasonable rates, or to stop selling information about the users of platforms. It is cheaper to place a sticker about the fair trade than to give up the use of zero-hour contracts.

They are loath to pay a living wage, but they will fund a philharmonic orchestra. They will ban unions, but they will organize a workshop on transparency in government.

So, in a year, they will be back in Davos and perhaps a new record in dollar wealth per square foot will be achieved; but the topics, in the conference halls and on the margins, will be again the same. And it will go on like this ... until it does not.

(Published January 19, 2018)

6.5 On luxury

Is luxury consumption bad? Should it be limited? At the time of high inequality, and especially inequality driven by the very top of income distribution (one percent and higher) these are legitimate questions. The answer however is not easy.

Keynes, in his famous opening of *The Economic Consequences of the Peace*, speaks of a social compact (although he does not use the term), which, according to him, existed between the rich and the rest before the First World War, where the rich were "allowed" to amass huge wealth but on the assumption that they would use it for investments (and thus further growth), not for ostentatious consumption.

The same idea is present in Max Weber's description of Protestantism: accumulation of wealth and austere living: "Wealth is ... bad ethically only in so far as it is a temptation to idleness and sinful enjoyment of life, and its acquisition is bad only when it is with the purpose of later living merrily and without care" (*The Protestant Ethic and the Spirit of Capitalism*, p. 163).

Recently I listened to Pierre Rosenvallon proposing the reintroduction of sumptuary laws that would not allow certain types of consumption. (This is clearly impossible to implement today, but the idea that one needs to do something with excessive wealth underlines Rosenvallon's concern.)

In last week's *Wall Street Journal*, Barton Swaim, reviewing a new book on John Adams, notes Adams' concern with American elite's accumulation of wealth and luxury consumption, which might lead to the vices of indolence and decadence.

Display of wealth is, by all these authors, and probably thousands more, criticized for two separate reasons: a social one, *viz.* that it provokes resentment and envy among those who cannot afford it, and a moral one, that it leads to personal decadence. The two critiques are different: the first is an instrumental critique: it is not a critique of the activity as such but of its social implications. It critiques a symptom of an economic system that allows for such behavior, but does not deal with the appropriateness or justice of the system itself. The second critique is concerned with the effects of wealth on people themselves who enjoy it, and perhaps secondarily on a society where the upper class becomes increasingly decadent, and separate from the rest.

Both are, in some ways, superficial critiques. They are critiques of consumption, but they do not go deeper, into the origin of wealth,

153

that is into the production process. Consider the moral effect on the wealthy individuals first. The vice that concerns John Adams is very different from the vice "diagnosed" by Mandeville. The latter is the vice of greed; it is "in-built" in the acquisition of wealth, in activities in which people engage in order to become rich. It has nothing to do with how the money is spent. Mandeville's is therefore a much more fundamental critique: the vice remains, regardless of the use to which one's wealth is put. One can live a very modest life, use all of one's money to invest or make charitable contributions, but the vice of acquisition remains.

A Marxist would also be indifferent to excessive wealth and its use by arguing that the problem does not lie with a person who has become so rich, but in the system that has allowed for such wealth through exploitation. Leszek Kolakowski in *Main Currents of Marxism* summarizes it very nicely: 'Bourgeois consumption in the face of workers' poverty is a moral issue, not an economic one; the distribution, once and for all, of rich men's wealth among the poor would not solve anything or bring about any real change." This is very different from Keynes' view, where apparent social equality is achieved through an act of concealment: becoming rich is acceptable, but not the use of riches for luxury.

For Marx (as for Mandeville—even if for different reasons), the way wealth is used is irrelevant. It might even be thought that, from the purely political point of view, extravagant ostentatious consumption is desirable because it highlights the social divide and undermines the system that creates it. Marie Antoinette by her famous (if probably apocryphal) comment on how the poor should deal with their lack of bread has probably contributed a lot to undermine the position of the monarchy. The estrangement of the elite from the majority of the people as shown in similar comments and outlandish spending may be seen as desirable by those in favor of systemic change. "Spend, spend, as much as possible and with as much visibility as possible, so that your reign can be as short as possible" may be the motto of partisans of change.

What should today's position with respect to luxury consumption be? Confiscatory taxation of excessive wealth is one possibility. Some people have argued for the wealth tax of 100 percent on all wealth above a billion US dollars. It is technically quite easy to do, but the political feasibility of such a proposal is close to zero.

Another possibility is the moral suasion, or ideological pressure that Keynes had in mind: the rich would feel uncomfortable, and would be looked at unfavorably by the other rich, if they were to spend too lavishly. That seems to be the most unlikely way to limit luxury consumption today, at the time when the media (and the public that reads such media) crave to report on extravagance. There are no moral or religious constraints that seem likely to work.

Finally, should consumption taxes on extra luxury goods be increased? That seems to me a very attractive option. The pattern of consumption of the very rich is quite well known. If private jets used by Epstein, or enormous brownstone purchased by him in New York, were taxed at exorbitant rates, even Jeffrey Epstein or similar billionaires would at some point be able to purchase fewer of them. The approach is consistent with differentiation of retail taxes (VAT tax rates) according to the type of commodity: food is often not taxed at all, hotel or restaurant consumption is taxed high. Cars, for example, at the time when they were considered much more of a luxury item than today, used to be taxed quite heavily. Exorbitant taxes on luxury items will not bring much money to the Treasury. But their objective is not that they should—their objective is either to soak as much resources from the super wealthy as possible or to make them refrain from such consumption. That, I think, they can achieve.

Unless of course your wish is for the whole system to come crashing down, in which case you should cheer up Bezos and Musk and Kardashian to spend even more extravagantly. And document it on the social media for all to see.

(Published July 9, 2021)

6.6 Absurdity of World Bank wealth accounting

For more than a decade, the World Bank has been producing global and country wealth reports. The idea is to calculate for every country its total wealth, as composed of human capital wealth, produced wealth and natural resource wealth. At first glance it seems to make sense. But, as I will argue (and indeed as when the first such report appeared I did), this is largely an exercise in tautology. Here is how national wealth is being calculated. First you take the value of assets such as machinery, equipment, physical structures, etc., or their financial equivalents, owned either by the state or by the citizens. It is estimated at world prices: if the financial wealth is one US dollar, it is counted as one US dollar regardless of country. (I am leaving aside the technical issues of this calculation as to how to avoid double-courting of real and financial wealth, and assume that everything is done perfectly.) Then you add the total value of non-renewable natural resources, estimated at world prices. Finally, you add the net present value of wages (basically current wages capitalized over time), and you thus get an estimate of total national wealth. For the rich countries, "human capital wealth" generally accounts for approximately two-thirds of total wealth, and for many poor countries, most of the wealth lies in natural resources (approximately one-half).

Now, notice the inconsistency. When you own $1 in financial wealth, or underlying that wealth, in physical equipment and machinery, in Brazil, US, or India this is counted as one dollar. When your country has one ton of oil reserves, it is counted at oil's international price, whether the oil is found in Brazil, US, or India. But when you come to "human capital wealth" it is counted at one price (domestic wage) in Brazil, another price in the US, and yet a third price in India. It is not surprising then that countries that have high wages will also have high "human capital wealth." This is because a unit of labor of the same skill is counted as being of different value, depending on the country where it is.

The inconsistency of the exercise is easily apparent from the fact that natural resources and produced capital are valued at international prices, while labor is valued at domestic. It is implicitly assumed that the movement of labor is non-existent—because this is the only way that the price for the same unit of labor can remain different from one country to another. The assumption is at odds with reality. Between-country movement of labor is becoming more important, and estimating "human capital wealth" at international prices would yield a much more accurate estimate of "human capital." Thus, with free movement of labor, the bus driver in Nairobi, whose "human capital" is estimated at much lower rate than the human capital of an identical bus driver in Hamburg, will suddenly have higher wages and the human capital wealth of Kenya will shoot up. Likewise, under full freedom of migration, human capital wealth of the United States will go down.

Real-world examples may be helpful to understand the issue. Take Japan and Germany in 1945. The countries were largely destroyed. "Human capital wealth," if it were measured by the World Bank methodology, would be minimal because wages were minimal. But both Germany and Japan had hundreds of thousands of highly qualified laborers. That labor and its skills had not suddenly disappeared when factories were burned to the ground.

The same is true in reverse, for countries that have become rich through a discovery and use of natural resources. The human capital wealth of Saudi Arabia is much less than the high wages, made possible by oil wealth, imply. If most Saudis had to move abroad or freely compete with workers from the rest of the world, they would receive a fraction of their current wages and World Bank estimated "human capital wealth" would be much reduced.

Or, consider this example, close to the experience of oil sheikdoms. Suppose that the skill level in an oil-producing country has not risen an iota since the oil, which was originally in the ground, began to be exploited and marketed. Suppose also that all labor is employed in the state sector, and that the newly acquired wealth enables the authorities to raise wages. So, when the World Bank methodologist comes to the country to calculate different components of the sheikhdom's wealth, he would conclude that the value of oil, before and after its marketization, has not changed (oil reserves are valued at international prices, whether oil is exploited or not) whereas human capital has suddenly become much more valuable. The concussion would be clearly wrong.

(Published July 13, 2019)

6.7 Repeat after me: Wealth is not income and income is not consumption

The recently published Oxfam report on the distribution of net wealth in the world, released to coincide with the Davos meeting and showing that the global top one percent own almost one-half of world's wealth, has generated lots of discussion. Some of it reflects the misunderstanding of what distribution of wealth is, and it is on that specific critique that I would like to focus.

The critique was started by Felix Salmon (and continued by the *Economist*). Salmon in his piece entitled "Oxfam's misleading wealth statistics" noticed in the Oxfam report (and in the report on which Oxfam study is based, *Credit Suisse Global Wealth Distribution for 2014*) that among the bottom decile of adults, that is, among those with zero net wealth, there are about 40 million Americans and more than 50 million Europeans. That came as a shock: how can almost 100 million people from the rich countries be among the poorest people on earth? (The other 80% of the people in the bottom decile are from Africa, India, Latin America, and Asia, as shown in Figure 6.2, the graph from Credit Suisse report.)

Salmon and others are perhaps not aware that, from the works published by Ed Wolff during the last twenty years, and based on US Survey of Consumer Finances, we have known for years (see Figure 6.3) that up to about one-fifth of American households have zero net wealth. When you exclude housing, the percentage of those with zero or negative net worth comes close to thirty. How is net wealth defined? It is the sum of housing wealth, cash, checking and savings deposits, financial assets such as stocks and bonds, and cash value of life insurance and pension plans minus all liabilities (mortgages, loans). Most of the poor and the middle class have almost no financial assets, but their main assets are the homes they "own." "Own" here comes between the quotes because a large chunk, and at times (as when housing prices go down) more than 100 percent of the value of one's home may be owned by the bank. (The outstanding portion of the housing loan may be greater than the value of the house.) A person has then a negative housing wealth. Add to mortgages, car loans, school loans, credit card loans, and you can see how a large chunk of American households may have negative or zero wealth, and how in the wake of the recent recession that percentage increased by about 3 percentage points (or about ten million individuals, as Ed Wolff shows).

WEALTH INEQUALITY

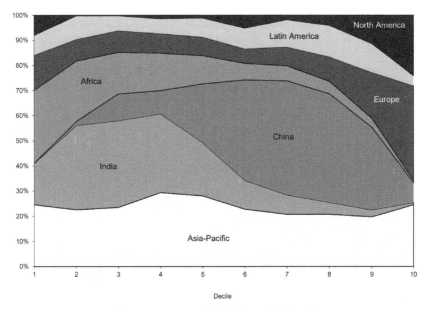

Figure 6.2 Regional composition of global wealth distribution 2014

Note: The graph shows where in the global wealth distributions are households from various regions. North American households are for most part in the top two global deciles (ninth and tenth). However, there is a non-negligable presence of North American households even in the poor (poorest) wealth decile.

Source: Credit Suisse Global Wealth Report 2014. Used with permission from UBS.

Among the advanced economies, wealth-poverty is not limited to the United States. In Germany 27 percent of households (as of 2013) have negative or zero net wealth (paper by Markus Grabka and Christian Westermeier). So, these people would also be included among the wealth-poorest people in the world, together with the poorest Indians, Africans, and Latin Americans, who have no assets at all.

Is this an anomaly? Does it make the study of wealth inequality meaningless? According to the critics of Oxfam reports it does, because the wealth-poor people from the rich countries do not necessarily lead a life of poverty. Thanks to the deep financial systems that exist in rich countries they can borrow and keep their consumption relatively high, all the while driving their net wealth down to zero. In effect, borrowing is simultaneously a way to keep consumption high (above your income) and driving your net wealth down to zero.

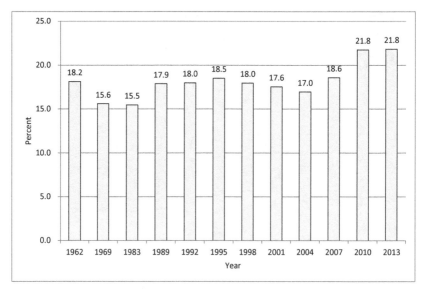

Figure 6.3 Percent of American households with zero or negative net worth, 1962–2013

Note: The graph shows that appropriately 20 percent of American households have zero or negative net worth. Negative net worth is possible when one's debts exceed one's marketable assets.

Source: From Ed Wolff's slides "Household Wealth Trends in the US, 1962–2013: What Happened over the Great Recession?" presented at CUNY Graduate Center, October 7, 2014.

Thus, we have people who are absolutely poor by wealth standards while their income or consumption levels may place them around the 60th, 70th, or even higher global percentile.

But the "anomaly" is solely in the minds of the commentators. Distribution of net wealth is not the same thing as distribution of consumption or income. Each of these aggregates has its own characteristics and uses. If one wants to look at people whose real consumption is really minimal, who live at the edge of subsistence, one should look at the global distribution of consumption, with its famous poverty line of $1 (now $1.9) dollars per capita per day. This is what the World Bank has been doing since 1990. There are no people from the rich countries among the consumption-poor. Even the poorest people from the advanced economies have a much higher level of consumption (at least around $12–$15 international dollars per day).

It is a wrong belief that there should be one and only one measure that would give us the answer to who is poor and who is rich. The three welfare aggregates (wealth, income, and consumption) are related but they are not the same. (And I leave out other "details" like the distinction between net income, that is, after-fisc income, and market income, or income before any government transfers and taxes.) There are people who are poor or middle class, according to one measure, but rich according to another, or the reverse. Wealth is not income, nor is income consumption.

Depending on what we want to study, we may focus on one or another aggregate. If standard of living is our concern, consumption is probably the best measure; it is also probably the best measure for long-term (lifetime) income. But if our interest is to look at the potential consumption that one can afford without reducing one's assets, then income is a better measure. One may consider that a decision to save out of a high income, and thus to *choose* to have a relatively low consumption, is not different from a decision to use one's income to buy restaurant meals instead of a car. It is just a decision of what to do, or not to do, with your income, which only the income-rich have the luxury to do. They can choose; others cannot.

But note also that there may be reverse cases, people with zero income whose consumption is relatively high (e.g. those who, after working for several years and saving money, might take a couple of years off to go back to school). Or, as mentioned before, there may be people with reasonably high income and consumption, and yet zero net wealth. You may even find people with very high net wealth and huge negative incomes, as happened in 2007 when the stock market crashed, and some billionaires lost millions of dollars. By income metric, they were the poorest people on the planet that year. Is it wrong? Is it silly? Does it mean that we should not study income or consumption or wealth distribution? Not at all, we need them all and we need to know what we want to find out and what the numbers mean.

There are, indeed, very good reasons to study distribution of net wealth, globally and within countries. Even for those people in the rich world who are "anomalously" placed among the wealth-poor, and who may lead nice lives despite owning nothing, a shock in the form of a medical emergency (unless there is public health care), or loss of a job, may have catastrophic consequences, since there is no wealth to fall back onto. A decline in the value of the main asset (housing) had similar consequences for many people in the US during the recent crisis. Finally, wealth, especially when we look at the rich, is the source of both economic and political power. It is not people who are running huge, and hard to repay credit card debts, who are likely to be influential players by contributing to the political campaigns, influencing policy, and setting legislative agenda. It is the global top one percent, who own half of the world wealth, or within the United States, the top one percent who own about 35 percent of net wealth, who wield political influence.

To conclude: one has to be aware of what each measures does and what your objective is, before you decide that because you think that the measure should measure something it does not, you declare it to be a "silly" or "pointless exercise."

(Published January 24, 2015)

[Note: The Oxfam report is based on the Credit Suisse 2014 report on global distribution of wealth. The Credit Suisse report in turn is based on the work done by Jim Davies, Susanna Sandström, Tony Shorrocks, and Ed Wolff on global distribution of wealth, which was published in 2011. This was a seminal piece of work. The global distribution data are pieced together from countries' household balance sheets, wealth surveys, and, finally, if data are missing, through a regression-based relationship between income and wealth inequality. Luckily, however, actual data do exist for the main countries: US, China, most of Western Europe, India, and Russia. Thus, while global wealth data are even more difficult to piece together than income or consumption data, and are subject to an even greater margin of error, their work is the best estimate of global wealth inequality that we have.]

6.8 Was everybody under socialism a millionaire?

There was, a couple of months ago, a lively discussion on the measurement of wealth. It started with two results. First, Ed Wolff's long-standing (but not widely publicized results) that the Gini for wealth inequality in the United States had reached an unprecedented high value of 87, and that some 30 percent of the population had zero net assets: second, by a comparison made by Oxfam between the wealth of the top one percent vs. the wealth of the rest. Oxfam argued, using the Credit Suisse report on global wealth, that the top one percent in the world owns almost one-half of global wealth. Some of those with zero wealth are people from rich countries who have no assets, even if their income is obviously not zero, nor can they be considered globally or otherwise poor. Actually, many of them might have relatively comfortable lives, even if they are running credit-card debts and living in homes that are almost 100 percent owned by the banks.

So, those who did not like either Ed Wolff's results nor Oxfam's comparisons went ballistic on what they termed "Oxfam misleading statistics": "Look, these guys might have zero net assets, but they are not poor." The argument was wrong, simply because there is a difference between income, consumption, and wealth. You may be wealth-poor even if you live okay; these are two different things. I wrote about that in the previous piece (Section 6.7).

But there was also another strand of attacks on these numbers, which wanted to show them to be incomplete, because the wealth definition used in standard wealth studies, like in the ones quoted here, as well as in Piketty's *Capital in the 21st Century*, is the sum total of all marketable assets; that is goods, housing, shares, bonds, patent right, etc. that you can *sell* right now. It does not include future, more-or-less secure claims on (say) social security, occupational pensions, medical benefits, and the like. (Although Ed Wolff does include the cash surrender value of pension plans if one can sell them.) Now, people who wanted these benefits to be added (in the amount of their capitalized value) did so in order to argue that the top one percent are not as rich, compared to the others, and the middle class in particular, as Oxfam and Credit Suisse claimed, and that it is not true that 30 percent of Americans have zero net assets. Indeed, if you include Medicaid, Social Security and welfare, practically nobody in the US will come out as having zero net assets. It is also true that, if you do an international comparison of the US with other wealthy countries, the inclusion of such future claims will make US wealth levels and distribution look even worse (because other rich countries generally have more developed social welfare systems), but those who argued for the change in the way wealth is defined, did not, at that point, think much about international comparisons.

However, you cannot do things in isolation, and ignore both the general rules about how wealth is defined, and how the definitions can be applied across various societies. Let me illustrate this. In a conversation over lunch, Ed Wolff and I concluded that private marketable wealth in communist countries was, for most of the population, zero. How come? First, housing was mostly state- or enterprise-owned (in urban areas), and people who lived in these apartments paid low rent, but did not own them. Second, there were no financial instruments of any kind: there was no stock market and no shares. There were, in some countries state bonds but they were less of an investment and rather a compulsory borrowing by the state. But, in any case, the state bonds were minimal. Third, the only asset that existed was savings in domestic or (even if it was illegal in many countries) foreign currencies. That was in reality the only financial asset. (And this is incidentally why people in the West did not sufficiently appreciate the pillage in which the Yeltsin's regime engaged when it destroyed overnight the years of ruble savings by millions of households.)

Most of the private marketable wealth that existed was in the countryside. In countries like Poland and Yugoslavia, land was mostly private. In addition, urban residents owned their own weekend houses (the famous Russian *dachas*) and they were indeed not only privately owned, but marketable. In addition there were owners of small-scale restaurants, bars, repair shops, etc. Thus, Ed Wolff and I agreed that if you applied the usual marketable wealth approach to communist countries you would find that perhaps 80 percent of the population had zero or wholly negligible net wealth, and 20 percent had some rather minimal wealth, and these 20 percent were not exactly the people you would associate with high incomes and certainly not with political power under socialism. Obviously, this did not mean that 80 percent of people lived on the edge of subsistence: actually most of them had "normal" middle-class urban lives. It is just that they had no private wealth.

But then I thought a bit more on this issue as I read the critics who wanted to include capitalized value of social security among private wealth. So, I said, let me see what their approach would give you for socialist countries. There first, you had guaranteed pensions for all.

164

So, let's capitalize them. Then, you had guaranteed jobs for almost all. Let's capitalize that income too. You had guaranteed other social transfers like child benefits, invalidity pensions and, of course, free medical care. And, although pensions and wages were small in dollar amounts, their capitalization produces a rather big total. Let me take the example of Yugoslavia, which I know well. In the early 1980s, the average salary was about 250 dollars per month (post-tax). The average pension was about $200 per month (also post-tax). That gives about $3,000 annually for wages and $2,400 for pensions. In today's dollars, it works out as $9,000 and $7,200 per year. Suppose then, very roughly, that wages are guaranteed for thirty years and pensions for twenty years. When you apply to the wages and pensions a low discount rate of say, two percent, you get that total wealth of almost everybody was $300,000 dollars. Throw in additional medical costs that were also borne by the state and guaranteed to more-or-less all, and you may get to $400,000 or even to half-a-million US dollars.

So, would then those who argue that US wealth data should include capitalized value of not-marketable, but almost guaranteed, future incomes streams agree also that everybody in socialism was a dollar (half-a-)millionaire and that perhaps 80 percent of the population in Yugoslavia, Hungary or Poland had greater private net assets than the corresponding 80 percent of people in the United States? Does this make sense? If it does not, then you are back to the "usual" calculations where only marketable wealth counts and where 30 percent of US population have zero wealth. So, you can choose:

(a) Either everybody in socialism was a quasi-millionaire, or
(b) 30% of Americans have zero wealth today.

Your call.

(Published May 19, 2015)

— 7 —

INEQUALITY AND LITERATURE

7.1 Literature and inequality

When I wrote *The Haves and the Have-Nots*, which is a book of inequality vignettes linked with three essays (on global inequality, inequality between countries, and inequality within countries), I stumbled upon the idea of representing inequalities in different countries and eras by using the data and stories provided by works of fiction.

The idea arose out of several dinner conversations with my wife, who is a great admirer of Jane Austen. I barely knew Jane Austen's name until twenty years ago. But, at my wife's insistence, I started reading her and was thoroughly impressed by her writing, use of irony, and sharp and critical eye for social status and conventions. I read *Pride and Prejudice* first, followed by *Emma* and then *Mansfield Park* (I have not read the others).

Then, one evening, as my wife and I were discussing Elizabeth Bennet and Mr. Darcy, I was struck when my wife reeled off the amounts in pounds that Darcy received annually, compared to Elizabeth's parents. Continuing the conversation, I hit upon the idea of including the data from *Pride and Prejudice* in a vignette. This was helped by the fact that a few years earlier I wrote, with Peter Lindert and Jeffrey Williamson, a paper that used English social tables, including Patrick Colquhoun's social table from 1801 to 1803. This coincided almost exactly with the years when the plot in *Pride and Prejudice* most likely takes place. I was thus able to locate the expected incomes of Darcy, Elizabeth (in her unmarried status) and Elizabeth if she decides not to marry Darcy but to depend on the inheritance of 50 pounds per year—a prospect menacingly dangled by the tactless Reverend Collins as he proposes to her—all three in the English income distribution at the time.

As Table 7.1 shows, the range of options for Elizabeth goes from being in the top 0.1% of England's income distribution to being at the median. The income gap between these two options is 100 to 1. As I wrote, "the incentive to fall in love with Mr. Darcy seems irresistible." The last column shows how much the gap has shrunk today compared to what it was two hundred years ago: being at the equivalent positions in the early twenty-first-century yields an advantage of seventeen to one only.

I included the story of Anna Karenina in the second vignette of *The Haves and the Have Nots*. Her social trajectory is fairly similar to Elizabeth's. We learn from just one Tolstoy's sentence that her family was around the middling income status. With her marriage to Alexei Aleksandrovich Karenin, with whom she lives in a palatial home, she moved up to the top one percent. But, with Vronsky, not unlike Elizabeth with Darcy, Anna moves to the rarefied circle of the extremely wealthy, belonging to the top 0.1% of Russia's income distribution around 1875. Her gain from switching from Mr. Karenin to Count Vronsky was 17 to 1, much more than an equivalent Anna

Table 7.1 Inequality in England in the early nineteenth and early twenty-first century (based on *Pride and Prejudice*)

	Income in 1810 (£ per annum per capita)	Approximate position in 1810 British income distribution	Income in 2004 (£ per annum per capita)
(1) Mr. Darcy	10,000/2=5,000	Top 0.1%	400,000/2=200,000
(2) Elizabeth's family	3,000/7=430	Top 1%	81,000
(3) Elizabeth alone	50	Median	11,500
Marriage gain: (1) to (3)	100 times		17 times

Note: Table shows that Elizabeth's decision to marry Mr. Darcy, compared to the alternative of remaining single, improved her income by 100 times. Nowadays, if an Elizabeth-equivalent were placed at the same income positions as was Elizabeth in 1810, the gain would be much less, 17 times. (Elizabeth's family income was estimated at £3,000 but it is shared between seven people.)

would gain from such an advantageous marriage today. (It should be noted that when income gain from both liaisons are added, Anna's lifetime gain is 250 to one; that is, even more impressive than Elizabeth's.)

I then considered adding Balzac's *Le Père Goriot*, which I liked a lot and which, as is well known, was much admired by Marx (see *Karl Marx and World Literature* by S. S, Prawer) precisely for his impitoyable depiction of financial capitalism in France. I collected lots of data, but then decided that adding a third very similar vignette may be a bit of an overkill. So, I left it out. (A few years later, Thomas Piketty employed a similar technique in his *Capital in the 21st Century* and drew heavily on Balzac.)

Now, Daniel Shaviro in his new and exciting book *Literature and Inequality: Nine Perspectives from the Napoleonic Era through the First Gilded Age* has expanded this approach to three epochs and nine books. In the first part of the book ("England and France during the Age of Revolution"), Shaviro discusses with the same

Table 7.2 Inequality in the late nineteenth and early twenty-first centuries in Russia (based on *Anna Karenina*)

	Income in 1875 (rubles per annum per capita)	Approximate position in 1875 Russian income distribution	Income around 2005 (rubles per annum per capita)
(1) Count Vronsky	100,000/2=50,000	Top 0.1%	3,000,000
(2) Karenin and Anna	9,000/3=3,000	Top 1%	340,000
(3) Anna's parents	200	Mean (around the 65th percentile)	53,000
Marriage gain: (1) to (2)	15 times		8.8 times

Note: Table shows that Anna's possible marriage to Count Vronsky (compared to while she was married to Karenin) would have improved her income by 17 times. Incidentally, the gain from marrying Karenin, compared to her income when she was single, was 15 times (3,000/200). Nowadays, if an Anna-equivalent person were placed at the same income positions as was Anna in 1875, the gain would have been 8.8 times. (Mr Karenin and Anna had a child; thus income is shared between three persons.)

objective of retrieving the facets of social and economic inequality, but in much greater detail than I, Jane Austen (*Pride and Prejudice*), Balzac (*Le Père Goriot*) and Stendhal (*Le Rouge et le noir*). In the second part (England from the 1840s to the start of the First World War) Shaviro looks at Charles Dickens, Anthony Trollope, and E. M. Forster. Finally, in the third part, he trains his gaze on the US Gilded age (Mark Twain and Charles Dudley Warner, Edith Wharton and Theodore Dreiser). I will review Shaviro's book next (see Section 7.3). I have to say that unlike the first part, I am not familiar with the authors from the second and third parts (with the exception of E. M. Forster), and I would thus have much less to say about these books. My regret is only that Shaviro did not include Francis Scott Fitzgerald in the third part. Scott Fitzgerald is, I think, a perfect writer for the Gilded Age: perhaps even better in *Tender is the Night* than in *The Great Gatsby*. But either would do.

I would like to finish this post with an observation. After publishing *The Haves and the Have-Nots* I became somewhat interested in finding similar sociologically rich but also empirically substantiated (i.e. full of details and amounts of actual incomes) books in other literatures. I looked around myself and asked several of my students from different countries for their suggestions. Interestingly, we came up with almost nothing. The books seemed to have sociological and anthropological details, but no numbers that would allow empirical economists to weave their story and place these individuals in contemporary income distributions (assuming, of course, that such distributions for the relevant countries do exist). The writers seemed much less interested in doing this than for example Balzac in his entire *La Comédie humaine*.

This is not the result of some dedicated search of various literatures and it could be that I am wrong. But it is an interesting hypothesis: was the European nineteenth-century literature exceptionally interested in social status, wealth, and income? Was it exceptionally well documented? It seemed to me that the twentieth-century literature provides many fewer empirical details. For example, Proust's *À la recherche* ... is very similar in its study of conflict and mutual accommodation between the parvenus, bourgeoisie, and the aristocratic elite, to Balzac. But, unlike Balzac, Proust gives no numbers at all. So, for an empirical economist (and for this specific purpose) Proust is not of much use. This was my impression with other writers I know, but I hope that there are out there works of fiction in many literatures that one could use as I have used *Pride and Prejudice* and Shaviro *Le Père Goriot*. One of the objectives of this post is also to

INEQUALITY

stimulate people to look around among the authors they know and to use works of fiction to tease out and trace the contours of inequality in various societies.

(Published May 7, 2020)

INEQUALITY AND LITERATURE

7.2 Was the novel born and did it die with bourgeois society?

Can we use literature to learn more about inequality? Yes, I think we can, and, as some of my readers know, I did exactly that in *The Haves and the Have-Nots*, which opens with the discussion of Jane Austen's *Pride and Prejudice* (in terms of the monetary advantage for Elizabeth to marry Mr. Darcy) and of Tolstoy's *Anna Karenina* (see the previous piece Section 7.1). Piketty has used later the same idea in his *Capital in the 21st Century*, adding Balzac—who, by the way, was cited by Marx for precisely the same reason: as an extraordinary chronicler of life in a bourgeois society.

Recently, Dan Shaviro published *Literature and Inequality*, a book in which he looked at the social structures of England and France (in the nineteenth century) and the United States (in the nineteenth and twentieth) as revealed by nine books, beginning with the unavoidable Jane Austen, going through Balzac, Stendhal, Dickens, Trollope, E. M. Forster, Mark Twain, Dudley Warner, Edith Wharton, and Theodore Dreiser.

As luck would have it, I took from my shelf a couple of days ago John Lukacs' *The Future of History*, a nice little book of essays about history written by one of foremost US historians of the Second World War. I read it when it was published, almost ten years ago, and I planned to read my book notes only. But what attracted my attention was Lukacs' discussion of the relationship between history and literature. He asks the same question as the one I asked in the beginning of this post: can we learn something about history of a given era by reading good literature?

Lukacs' answer is, "yes." Not only can we learn about how people might have felt about a historical event, whether they even knew they were participants or witnesses to such an event, but good literature, as Lukacs writes, is like good history. When you read it you are not supposed to feel that you know the outcome; it has to be open-ended, to always keep the full breadth of possibilities that exist in the present, but which we, looking at what used to be present, know did not materialize. Thus, Lukacs writes, literature and history are symbiotic. This is very much the point that I think all of us who hold that you can learn about societies and their inequality from novels would agree with.

But then Lukacs makes an additional intriguing point. Noticing that the birth of the novel was, in the mid eighteenth century,

171

contemporaneous with the Industrial Revolution, and that its peak was probably in nineteenth-century Europe, and noticing also that the type of society-revealing novel that both he and economists have in mind, has become much rarer now, Lukacs asks: Has the novel died at the same time as the bourgeois class-compartmentalized society dissolved?

He uses the fact noticed by many that, around the turn of the twentieth century, novels became much more focused on individual experiences, which did not necessarily have much to do with the surrounding society. It is not that Julien Sorel or Emma Bovary were not focused on themselves. But that self was described as it navigated and struggled in the world riven with greed, arrivisme, social mimicry, and class divisions. So, the self was seen against the background of society. At times that background moved even upfront, became the real topic of the book (which may be the case with Dickens, for example). But, in the novels of the early twentieth century and increasingly afterwards, Lukacs writes, the societal background recedes: what we see is mostly an individual with his issues, family, friends, sex, love, depression. Grand societal themes raised by the past literature are gone.

This is indeed what I noticed when, emboldened by the success of using Jane Austen and Tolstoy to throw light on the English and Russian societies of the early nineteenth century, I started looking around, and asking my friends and students to find similar novels in other settings and languages. The results were disappointing. Societies that were less developed and commercialized than the nineteenth-century Europe did not (understandably) produce such novels: if monetization is quasi non-existent, how can you quantify social positions, incomes, wealth? Novelists are not going to impute incomes the way that economists impute the value of own produced goods to farmers in household surveys. On the other hand, Western societies of the mid twentieth century and later did not seem, for the reasons Lukacs mentions, to care much for that kind of literature either.

I have not followed contemporary literature (contemporary meaning, written in the past thirty years), so I relied more on the judgment of others. But they too seemed at a loss when trying to find novels from which one could glean social inequality, or more generally social issues linked with inheritance, position in society, class distinctions, and even money. So we ended with a very meager yield.

Lukacs provides an answer to that dearth. In his view, the dissolution of classes and of typical bourgeois societies made novels of the type that I was looking for irrelevant. Society decomposed into individuals, not in classes. The subject matter of literature became individual issues, not class issues.

Now, one further element (never thought of by Lukacs, I am sure) lends credence to his explanation. Political economy stopped looking at social inequality through the lens of class, which it did: beginning from Quesnay, through Adam Smith and Ricardo, all the way to Marx. It did so precisely around the same time that the classical novel disappeared. It was Pareto at the turn of the twentieth century who introduced for the first time, studying fiscal data from a number of German and Italian cities and states, interpersonal income inequality. From Pareto onwards, we ceased to deal with capitalists, workers, and landlords; we began to deal with individuals, some rich, others poor. The class analysis was definitely pushed out, so much so that in the second half of the twentieth century, especially in the United States, even the mention of class in an economic paper would immediately classify you as an unreconstructed Marxist.

It dawned on me that this was not a coincidence: the death of the classical novel, the dissolution of the class structure of the bourgeois society, and the end of a political economy where the subjects were classes in favor of "agents" might have all been related.

But now, as the importance of capital incomes increases, and capitalist societies grow increasingly stratified, with the rich attempting to confer and transmit all the advantages to their offspring, may not both the class analysis in economics and the classical novel make a comeback?

(Published May 1, 2021)

INEQUALITY

7.3 Inheritance, marriage, and swindle: The three ways to the top

Inheritance gives a head start advantage. Marriage is the way to share in that advantage. Business swindle is a way of undermining that advantage.

The two previous posts and this one are stimulated by the just-published book by Daniel Shaviro, *Literature and Inequality*. For the sake of completeness, here is the list of nine books used by Shaviro to study what fiction tells us about inequality of status, class, and income.

The first three books are Jane Austen's* *Pride and Prejudice*, Stendhal's* *Le Rouge et le noir*, and Balzac's* *Le Père Goriot* (with *La Maison Nucingen* in continuation). They describe West European societies during the "Age of Revolutions."

The next three are Dickens' *Christmas Carol*, Trollope's *The Way We Live Now*, and E. M. Forster's* *Howard's End*. They are set in England during the Industrial Revolution, or just before the First World War.

The final three books deal with American inequality: Mark Twain's and Charles Dudley Warner's eponymous *Gilded Age*, Edith Warton's *The House of Mirth*, and Theodore Dreiser's *The Financier* (and *The Titan*).

There is obviously a lot to write about the books, their interpretation and Shaviro's very skilful analysis of societies they describe. Shaviro's book could set the tone for a new type of social study that would combine the usual empirical work with archival research and valuable fiction. Indeed, all these books of so-called fiction are grounded strongly in the "faction" of their societies and give to an economist many hints of different venues worth exploring.

I have read only four of the nine books dealt with here (indicated by the asterisks) and my discussion of others depends entirely on what I have learned from Shaviro.

I would like to focus on two themes.

The literature studied here shows us not only the common conflict between the "old wealth" (that could, in the British and French context, be aristocratic wealth, or in the US context, that of New England and Philadelphia families) and the newly acquired wealth, or between the rich and the poor. The books—all nine—show us that there are only three ways to the top of society: inheritance, marriage, and plunder.

174

Inheritance is an obvious way in which people can remain on the top. But it is tempered by marriage: if the marriage market were entirely "comonotonic" the super rich would marry only the super rich, the less rich would marry those just slightly less rich, and so forth all the way to the bottom. The ordinal rankings would not be altered, and wealth and income gaps would get ever wider. But marriages obey other laws as well: love, sexual attraction, accidents, parental influence, strategic decisions. Thus, they introduce an element of entropy into an otherwise hierarchical structure. The social order is often unsettled by marriage. This is often discussed in the case of women—most obviously among the books reviewed here by *Pride and Prejudice* and other of Jane Austen's novels that revolve around the same question: Who is going to marry whom, and how many £ of income are respective partners bringing in?

But men's marriage market is less frequently addressed. Shaviro does not discuss it as such, either; yet it pervades several of the books he reviews. Julien Sorel's career consists of amorous conquests that gradually allow him to climb to ever higher positions in society, until they also bring him crashing down onto his death. Rastignac likewise in *Le Père Goriot* and *La Maison Nucingen* plans his social ascent entirely on successful secret love relationships and marriages (often simultaneously). In both of these French novels, sexual conquest, which we typically associate with women, is used by men to move from low to high social positions. The same theme reappears in *Howard's End*, where Leonard enters into an ultimately destructive relationship with one of the much richer Schlegel sisters. Socially identical is the relationship between Lawrence Selden (aspiring youth) and Lily Bart in *The House of Mirth*. Had Shapiro decided to include Scott Fitzgerald's *Tender is the Night* in the American section, he would have had another male hero who uses marriage, consciously or not, as a climbing device.

We thus see that marriage, which some associate, and especially so in societies where the role of women was limited, to be an instrument of social promotion used by women, was in reality used by both sexes. The books reviewed here give us—interestingly—a more equal treatment of genders than we may think to have been the case.

The third tool of social advancement is to make money oneself (in this case however, it is always "himself"). Financial speculators and industrialists are the two favorite occupations: Nucingen in Balzac; Scrooge in Dickens; Melmotte in Trollope; Sterling in Twain and Dudley Warner; Percy Gryce in Edith Warren; and Frank Cowperwood in Dreiser. None of them is a sympathetic character.

It is remarkable that in all cases the self-made road to the top is described in darkest hues. It is composed of swindles, cheats, cronyism, plunder, and bribery. There is no Horatio Alger or any of Ayn Rand's heroes here. Even Dreiser's *The Financier*, discussed extensively by Shaviro, while not entirely unsympathetically depicted by Dreiser, owes his success to the readiness to use any means, however sordid, in order to prevail. It is a world similar to that we can see today in any episode of Netflix's *Succession*.

Now, whether all the climbs to economic power were possible only through bribery and swindle and plunder, I do not know. One thinks of Marx's "primitive accumulation," of Jane Austen's Henry Lascelles, whose wealth comes from slave plantations in Barbados, or of many beautiful castles and public building (Rockefeller Center in New York?) that were built on the backs (so to speak) of brutal exploitation or financial malfeasance. It could well be that huge wealth is really impossible to acquire in any other way.

But it could also be that in works of fiction we are likely to be confronted more often by such characters than in real life, simply because their lives—the contrast between enormous wealth and dearth of moral qualities—are much more compelling to both writers and readers than a more humdrum success achieved within the confines of legal and ethical rules.

Authors' uniform emphasis on unethical ways in which wealth is made should give us pause when entertaining a more benevolent view of large fortunes in capitalist societies. Perhaps the fact is that most of them were indeed made the way described in this book, and not in the way that Samuelson's *Economics* (and its various successors) would like us believe.

(Published May 15, 2020)

— PART III —

GLOBALIZATION AND MULTI-POLAR WORLD

— 8 —

GLOBALIZATION

8.1 Eleven theses on globalization

There has recently been a great deal of discussion of globalization, its effects, especially on poverty and inequality; many contradictory statements, some even absurd, were made. Here are eleven theses on globalization.

First, inequality and poverty. Globalization is a force for the global good: the globalization of economic activity has enabled production of many commodities and provision of many services in the places where it is cheapest to do so. It has released previously used resources for other activities. It has also mobilized capital and labor that was misused or unemployed. The effect was a significant acceleration in global rate of growth (when measuring global growth by using democratic and not plutocratic measures, which have also gone up) and a dramatic decrease in global income inequality and global income poverty.

Second, China. The most important positive effects, largely due to globalization and international trade, have been achieved in China. China explains most of the decrease in global inequality and poverty. But these advances have been realized by the application of non-standard or non-neoclassical policies. This has created the first dilemma for the supporters of globalization *and* neoliberalism. To defend globalization they have to praise China, but they find Chinese policies distasteful. Thus, their comments are mostly contradictory.

Third, the West. Globalization has opened a series of particularly difficult issues for the West. This was not expected when globalization was "sold" to the Western populations by Reagan/Clinton and Thatcher/Blair as a guaranteed middle-class gain. The success of

Asian countries has often been predicated on the loss of jobs, or loss of good jobs, or loss of steady wages by the Western middle classes. The feeling of insecurity and displacement has spread among those classes. Even when their real economic growth was positive, it was less that the real growth of many Asian populations, and the latter have thus often overtaken lower parts of the Western middle classes in their global income positions. When we come to the positional jostling, globalization is indeed a zero-sum game: I am either ahead of you or behind you. For many Western middle classes this is a new experience: for two centuries, most of the Western population was in the top twenty percent of the global income distribution. Some of them are no longer there and others will soon be squeezed out.

Fourth, the Great Convergence. The successes of China and India have a geopolitical aspect too. China and India cannot be pushed back to their nineteenth-century positions. They are steadily changing the balance of power, bringing the ratio between Europe/America and Asia back to the one that existed before the Great Divergence. The economic and geopolitical decline of Europe and America is not contemplated with indifference, however.

Fifth, trade blocs. One way, in some people's minds, of reversing the decline goes through a rewriting of the rules of globalization. "Globalization" would apply only to the politically friendly countries. This obviously has nothing to do with real globalization. It is the return to the world of trade blocs. It is mercantilism that does not dare say its name. Partisans of globalization will have a hard time defending it ideologically if they care for any consistency in thinking.

Sixth, wars. The geopolitical angle has sharpened global political and even military tensions. Thus, ironically, globalization, which, through the softening effect of trade (*le doux commerce*) and mutual interdependence, should have promoted a world of entente and peace has created the very reverse: conditions propitious for conflict and even war. Such a war, if led by the US, would aim to stop China from taking a preeminent position in the world and, if led by China, would be used it to propel it to that very position. If globalization preceded the First World War, can it precede the Third World War?

Seventh, disappointments and gains. What began as a globalization pregnant of advantages for many looks now very different: insecurity of jobs and relative income decline for the Western middle classes, inability ideologically to defend both globalization and neoclassical economics, abandonment of globalization by some influential circles, and even putting a stop to it by wars. But, from

180

the other point of view, globalization has created a much more equal world, both between world individuals and in terms of economic and political power between Europe/America and Asia. (Africa which has not been more successful during globalization than before is a notable absentee in terms of gains.)

Eighth, climate change. Even the positive aspects of globalization (reduced inequality and poverty) do contain some negative features. The several-fold increase in global GDP in the past thirty years, has also increased CO_2 emission by approximately the same ratio. This has made the achievement of climate change targets more difficult, and has opened up another area of contention: the targets would more readily be achieved if the West were to grow more slowly and the rich people everywhere taxed more heavily. Both are politically unacceptable propositions, so climate change problems are getting worse.

Ninth, financialization and amorality. Globalization has proceeded by the financialization of the economy, where this particular business was valued more than more solid virtues of inventiveness, steadfastness, probity, abstinence, and caution. It has favored behaviors that are short term in their vision, unconcerned with any broader good once the money can be safely withdrawn, and have propagated an overall amorality in business life. Since, concomitantly, business life has become the largest part of people's own lives, amorality has spread further into ordinary relations. When Milton Friedman stated that the role of business is to maximize profit, period, he was right in a narrow sense. But he failed to see the externalities produced by that statement. If achievement of wealth, and especially of wealth by any means whatsoever, becomes the goal of top classes, it spreads throughout the society and ultimately destroys cohesion and social bonds.

Tenth, migration. Throughout this time, globalization was incomplete. It included capital and goods first, services and ideas next, and never included the most important factor: labor. Reduction in global inequality was not achieved by moving people where they may earn the most (which would be a natural way to proceed), but by sending capital closer to wherever people are. Even the minimal migration that has taken place has produced political blowbacks.

What is to be done? We need to avoid war and trade conflicts, to accept that it is better for the world if there is an approximate equality of wealth and power between different nations and cultures, as well within individual nations, and to reduce carbon emission by a combination of high taxes on emission-intensive goods and subsidies

GLOBALIZATION AND MULTI-POLAR WORLD

to their alternatives. The nature of the current globalization makes me skeptical that we can improve steadiness and security of many jobs, accept greater migration, and make the captains of financial and IT industry behave more ethically.

(Published July 18, 2023)

GLOBALIZATION

8.2 Disarticulation goes North

In the neo-Marxist literature on under-development, one of the most important theories concerned the disarticulation of the countries in the South (the erstwhile "Third World"). What was meant by the term was that the Center, the developed North, established within a peripheral country merely enclaves of modernism, whose function was to keep the South producing for the needs of the North, without being able to create an internally connected production structure; going from raw material extraction to their processing and production of high value-added commodities. What mattered to the North was extraction of raw materials. The organization of this was entrusted to a local comprador bourgeoisie, whose economic interests coincided with those of the former colonial powers. The economy was, to use Samir Amin's terminology, "extroverted"; that is, directed only toward abroad and lacking in domestic ability to develop. The polity and the economy were disarticulated.

As a summarized history of the failed developments in the South up until approximately the 1980s, the theory did make lots of sense. No country developed without an internally integrated economy. Raw-material producers never created a successful economy. But, as a prescription to sever the links with the North and develop independently, the strategy, even when only tried half-heartedly, was a failure.

Sociologically and politically, the importance of the disarticulation story is that economic divergence of interests between the comprador bourgeoisie and the rest of society led to a class split within the countries of the South. The comprador bourgeoisie was supported by the North and was maintained in power, against the interest of the majority, by the West's constant political or, in some cases, military support.

Let us now, with this approach in mind, turn our gaze toward today's North. In a recent piece published in the *New York Times*, Paul Theroux, after traveling through the American South, was shocked by the depth of poverty there, wrought, in his opinion, by the destruction of jobs that have all gone to Asia, and the import of cheap commodities from China. He was even more distraught by the apparent lack of interest by American political and economic elites, who seemed to even fail to notice the plight of the Americans in states like Mississippi and, most ironically in Arkansas, where

183

philanthropists such as the Clinton Foundation have not been much seen, even as they proudly boast of efforts "to save the elephants in Africa."

The key issue raised by Theroux was whether trade, that is, globalization was responsible for this plight. The second issue that was raised was why there is so little empathy with the domestic poor, or interest in doing something about their destitution.

In an answer to Theroux, Annie Lowrey points out that however awful the poverty in Mississippi is, it is not as bad as poverty in parts of Africa (Zimbabwe is used as a comparator by both Theroux and Lowrey). Globalization that has lifted several hundred million Chinese out of poverty, at the cost of making ghost towns in Mississippi, is not a zero-sum game. Moreover, from a cosmopolitan point of view, the rich Americans' concern with African poverty, rather than with poverty in Mississippi or Arkansas, makes sense because people in Africa are much poorer.

Technically, Lowrey is right on all points. One can safely claim, to the extent that these things can be causally proven, that the rapid worldwide progress in poverty alleviation is due to globalization. It is also true that on any income or consumption metric, poverty in parts of Africa is much worse than in Mississippi. But, of course, none of that may be politically or socially relevant because national populations seldom care about cosmopolitan welfare functions (where happiness of every individual in the world is equally valued). They work with national welfare functions, where a given level of destitution locally is given a much greater priority weight than the same destitution abroad. There are studies (e.g. Kopczuk, Slemrod, and Yitzhaki) that show the revealed difference in implicit national vs. cosmopolitan weighting of poverty: the ratio for the US is estimated at 2,000 to 1. (In other words, when it comes to caring for non-nationals, they count as 1/2,000th of a co-citizen.) There are arguments for this, going back to Aristotle, who, in *Nicomachean Ethics* thought that our level of empathy diminishes as we move in concentric circles further from a very narrow community. And there are also political philosophy arguments (e.g. by Rawls) about why co-citizens do care more for each other than for outsiders.

But I think that it is insufficient to leave this argument at a very abstract level, where one group of Americans would have a more cosmopolitan welfare function and better perception of global benefits of trade, and another would be more nativist and ignorant of economics. I do not think that the real difference between the two groups has to do with welfare concerns and economic literacy, but rather with their interests. Many rich Americans, who like to point to the benefits of globalization worldwide, have significantly benefited and continue to benefit from the type of globalization that has been unfolding during the past three decades. The numbers, showing their real income gains, are so well known that they need no repeating. They are large beneficiaries from this type of globalization because of their ability to play off less well-paid and more docile labor from poorer countries against the often too expensive domestic labor. They also benefit through inflows of unskilled foreign labor, which keeps down the costs of the services they consume. Thus, rich Americans are made better off by the key forces of globalization: migration, outsourcing, and cheap imports; all of which have also been responsible for the major reduction of worldwide poverty. Perhaps, in a somewhat crude materialist fashion, I think that these Americans' sudden interest in reducing worldwide poverty is just an ethical sugar-coating over their economic interests, which are perfectly well served by globalization. Like every dominant class, or every beneficiary of an economic or political regime, they feel the need to situate their success within some larger whole, and to explain that it is a by-product of a much grander betterment of human condition.

A new alliance, based on the coincidence of interests, is thus formed between some of the richest people in the world and poor people of Africa, Asia, and Latin America. Those who are left out in the cold are the domestic lower-middle and middle classes, squeezed between the competition from foreign labor and the indifference of the national ruling classes. As in the neo-Marxist theories applied to the South, the divergence of economic interests within a country produces political disarticulation. The rich favor the continuation of globalization as it is, the lower middle classes are looking at the ways to change or reverse both globalization and migration that comes with it. Two political camps are thus formed, not only in the US but in practically all rich countries: the camp of the ideologically cosmopolitan rich, whose incomes keep on increasing, and the camp of the nativist lower-middle classes, who feel that nobody is defending their interests.

The disarticulation in the North produces political polarization with clear dangers of transforming democracy either into a plutocracy that would continue with current policies, or, alternatively, a populist regime that would give way to the frustration of the middle classes by reimposing tariff rates, exchange controls, and tighter migration rules.

GLOBALIZATION AND MULTI-POLAR WORLD

The idea that globalization is a force that is good and beneficial for all is an illusion. Tectonic economic changes, such as those brought by globalization, always have winners and losers. (The first sentence of my *Global Inequality* says exactly that.) Even if globalization is, as I believe, a positive phenomenon overall, both economically for the reasons Lowrey mentions and ethically because it allows for the creation of something akin to community of all humankind, it is, and will remain, a deeply contradictory and disruptive force, which would leave significant groups of people worse off. Refusing to recognize this is only possible if one is blinded by the ideology of universal harmonies or by one's own economic interests.

(Published October 16, 2015)

GLOBALIZATION

8.3 Let's go back to mercantilism and trade blocs!

I went to Rana Faroohar's book party in New York tonight. Faroohar has a new and important book, *Homecoming*, that dissects globalization as we know it and looks ahead. I have not read the book, and did not even ask Faroohar for a free copy (which were aplenty at the party tonight): the reason is that I know how authors struggle to write cute dedications in the midst of a party, and I did not feel like imposing this onto Faroohar. (In addition, I think I can afford to buy the book.) But I have read her articles in *The Financial Times*, and was told at the party tonight that she had an important— programmatic—op-ed in today's issue of *The Financial Times*. So I bought today's *FT*.

Faroohar's point is not new, but is told with unusual clarity and it comes at the right time. It is that the West should abandon globalization. Instead of it, the West should revert to trade blocs, in this case created between the nations sharing certain political values and geopolitical interests. It should use "friend-shoring," the new term invented by Chrystia Freeland, the Canadian Vice Premier, whose recent talk at the Brookings Institution in Washington is quoted with approval by Rana Faroohar.

There are two reasons why the West should abandon globalization. The first is that it was not good, economically, for its middle classes. The "elephant graph," originally produced by Christoph Lakner and myself, tells that story in a nutshell: the period of high globalization between 1988 and 2008, was good for Asian middle classes and the global top-one percent, but not for the Western middle classes. Second, geopolitically, globalization helped the rise of China, which is already now, and will even more be in the future, the main military and political competitor of the United States. China today accounts for 21 percent of the global GDP vs. America's share of 16 percent; in 1988 the percentages were respectively 3.6 percent and 20 percent.

Now, these two arguments for why globalization should be scrapped in favor of regional blocs do make perfect sense from the point of view of Western political interests. The idea was, to the great but undeclared chagrin of the American liberals, first raised by Donald Trump. Now the liberals, in this respect like in several others, are happy to follow in Trump's footsteps.

The problem is how to explain this volte-face to the rest of the world. The Western narrative has, since 1945, been built precisely

187

on the opposite view: open trade helps all the countries and it leads to peaceful coexistence. While one need not subscribe to the Montesquieu–Bloch–Angell view of trade as an engine of peace, the economic arguments in favor of open trade were always strong. The success of China, as well as India, Indonesia, Vietnam, and Bangladesh, made them even stronger.

Now, the West, which was the principal ideological champion of free trade, has soured on it because it no longer works in its favor. But, whether it does or does not, is, from a global perspective, immaterial: the idea of open trade was not based on particular benefits to one side—as mercantilism was—but to the mutual benefits for most. The gains were not, ever, thought to involve *everybody*, but the idea was that the losing parties would be compensated domestically, or at least that their particular losses would not be allowed to derail the entire process.

We are now told that we need to go back to the drawing board. But we are not allowed to call these reversals by their real names. Their real name is trade blocs. They have existed before: they were called UK imperial preferences, Japan's co-prosperity zone, Grosse Deutschland's Central European area, Soviet Council for Mutual Economic Assistance. They also responded to the geopolitical interests of the countries that introduced them. For some eighty years they were held to have been ideologically retrograde, part of "beggar-thy-neighbor" quasi autarkic policies. Now, we are to believe that "friend-shoring" is somehow different. It is not. It is just mercantilism under a new name and trade blocs in a different costume.

There is a further problem. The West was "in charge" of the dominant economic ideology. That ideology pervaded all international organizations. If the West is now going for "friend-shoring," how is the IMF to explain to Egypt, Paraguay, Mali, and Indonesia that they should continue with open trade? If globalization is (rightly) credited with raising incomes in Asia and with the greatest reduction in global poverty ever, are we now to reverse policies on global poverty and to argue that regional trade blocs should become the economic basis from which to proceed? Who is going to tell this to the IMF, the World Bank, and the WTO?

If the West abandons globalization, this is fully understandable from the mercantilist perspective of national grandeur. Colbert would approve. But, one should not delude oneself in believing that the rest of the world can just be flipped on the drop of the hat, and would not notice the enormity of the ideological change that this implies—and would not wonder about whether the initial impulse that advocated

188

economic openness might not have been based on geopolitical concerns that are now found unfulfilled.

One simply cannot maintain the universal validity of an ideology that one does not follow.

(Published October 18, 2022)

8.4 The hidden dangers of Fukuyama-like triumphalism

Tomorrow, I am attending a conference that deals with the decline of Western "liberal capitalism" and how it should be arrested. In the past year, I have been submerged by articles and books that discuss the same topic. They come from all parts of social sciences: economics, politics, sociology, anthropology, geopolitics ... It seems that you cannot write anything meaningful today unless you first address "populism" and the crisis of "liberal democracy."

Throughout all of this I have had a strong feeling of "unreality." Not only because the people who write about the crisis live the lives that are, by far, the best lives in the history of humankind, but that the talk of the crisis seems vastly exaggerated. And I was wondering about where this extravagant fear, "the end is nigh," comes from. The cause I think, is twofold: lack of knowledge of history and more importantly the Fukuyama-like narrative of post-1989 triumphalism.

The post-1989 narrative that was, often for self-serving reasons, promulgated in both the academic and popular circles in the West (and in the former Eastern bloc for obvious reasons) saw the period after the end of the Second World War as a victory of liberal capitalist democracy that was not earlier allowed to take place in some parts of the world because of the imposition of Soviet "glacis." Once the Soviet pressure relaxed, all these countries and, of course, all the others (according to the triumphalist narrative) from Iraq to China, saw, or will soon see, the advantages of liberal capitalism and will adopt the system. It was a very simple and seductive narrative. While Fukuyama's original essay was based on important, Hegelian historical and ideological precedents, it gradually got watered-down into a simplified Hollywoodesque story of a battle between good and evil—where it was even incomprehensible how the "evil" (except for its intrinsic "evilness") was able to put up such a good fight for decades.

In reality, as even amateurish students of European history know, that narrative is deeply flawed. Europe, as it emerged after the Second World War with fascism defeated in Germany and Italy, but its many tentacles present all over Europe, was deeply divided internally between the democratic and communist factions. The former eventually prevailed, but only after having to keep in check, often by very brutal and undemocratic means, one-quarter of the electorate in France and Italy and large organized trade unions linked with communist and socialist parties in most of Continental Europe. In

GLOBALIZATION

addition, it meant supporting capitalist dictatorial regimes in most of Mediterranean Europe, as well as in places as far away as Chile, Guatemala, Taiwan, and South Korea. And this is not to mention fighting innumerable colonialist and post-colonialist wars, where the "liberal democracies" invariably supported the "bad" guys: from Mobutu in Congo to Holden Roberto in Angola.

"Liberal democracy" was in a continual crisis, fighting for its mere survival, buffeted domestically by strikes, wage demands, RAF and Brigate Rose, and internationally by the challenges of the Third World emancipation and Soviet influence. It fought off all challengers and survived, not because everybody, as the triumphalist narrative would have it, saw that it was a more "natural" system but because it used power and intimidation on the one hand, and superior economic performance for the masses on the other. In 1945, the chances of democratic capitalism winning over the Soviet system were 10 percent (read Schumpeter), in 1965, they were 30 percent (read Samuelson, Galbraith, and Tinbergen), in 1975, they were 60 percent, by 1985, they were 90 percent, and, in 1989, it won. So, in the end, the system that, up to the mid 1970s, did not even dare mention its name ("capitalism"), because it was used only by the left and only as a term of opprobrium, could openly declare what it was and hyphenate it with the adjective of "liberal."

When you have in your mind this (I think) much more accurate narrative of the past half-century, the current crisis can only be seen as one of the many crises of capitalism. Like a swimmer that at times goes down under water when the winds are high and then reemerges when the winds die down, liberal capitalism is now going through one of its periodical episodes of withdrawal and weakness. There is no guarantee that it will emerge victorious from this one—it did not in 1917, nor in 1922, nor in 1933—but it allows us to think of the problem much more clearly than if we view the world through the misleading lenses of a continuous and conflictless march toward the chiliastic reign of democracy and "liberalism."

This is where, unfortunately, the vulgarizers of Fukuyama terribly misled the young Western generation. Having had no direct experience of attractiveness and importance of nationalism, fascism, populism, or communism (the Orwell of *Homage to Catalonia* is never mentioned but the Orwell of the *Animal Farm* is known by all) they imagined that no rational human being could ever entertain such views. They imagined that such beliefs had to be imposed from without—by the use of extravagant force. So, they believed (in part because it also economically suited them as many of them came of

191

GLOBALIZATION AND MULTI-POLAR WORLD

age in the last decade of the twentieth century), that the foreordained teleological march toward the system about which their parents and grandparents entertained serious doubts, could no longer be forestalled. When the march deviated from the planned course, they panicked. But they should not. They should look back at history.

(Published May 30, 2017)

GLOBALIZATION

8.5 How to dine alone ... in a hyper-competitive world

After living mostly by myself in New York for four years and having had dinner alone at least 400 times, I think I may be allowed to opine on how you should eat evening meals by yourself ... and what it tells us about the world we live in.

I have recently read that New York is the city with the highest ratio of seats that cater to solo diners compared to the total number of restaurant seats. I do not think it is an accident. The number of such seats has been, even over the last few years, in my experience, going up.

What are the advantages of solo dining? There are some obvious ones: you can decide when and where you want to eat; do not have to worry about how the bill will be split; can stay as long as you feel like. You also learn much more about the people you live with. In our ordinary lives, we are too busy to pay much attention to our surroundings: subway, work, colleagues, friends who are dissimilar in age, background, or income. When you dine alone, you have nothing else to do but to look at people around you and to listen to their conversations. You notice their body language, awkwardness or ease they have with each other, whether men talk more than women, who brags and who is silent, who pays the bill; you listen to what they say: to their job complaints, plans, political opinions, love troubles. There are some negative advantages: you do not have to put up with boring dinner companions or pretend you are interested in topics you do not care about.

What are the disadvantages? It is all vicarious. You learn some but it is a knowledge that comes not from a real exposure to things but rather from pieces of conversation, some possibly misunderstood, that you collect along the way. You never meet anybody and even those you meet (bartenders) are there, ex officio, paid to listen and entertain you.

The question you ask yourself is, what can solo dining tell us about the way of life we lead? The solo life is, I think (rather unoriginally), driven by the break-up of traditional family and communal ties. It comes with greater mobility of labor; it is enabled by higher incomes. What is not appreciated, I think, is that it is driven also by hyper-competitiveness and increasing commodification of our lives.

Hyper-competitiveness is demanding in terms of time and effort. As we compete against more people, not only does this take a toll on our time, but we become more aware that every action, every word, every comment ought to be measured and controlled, lest they come back to be used against us. Being alone provides a welcome relaxation from the pressure to perform and to project an image required by our public or business lives.

Increasing commodification means that much of our personal space and private actions have become potential money-makers. Birthday parties, reunion dinners, theaters, are occasions to meet people who may turn out to be useful and to "network." (Museums openly advertise vernissages as occasions to network.) Our "dead capitals," private time or homes, have become commercialized opportunities: we can drive own car for profit or rent own apartments for monetary gain. Being alone provides a respite from such incessant commodification. You do not network with yourself.

Is the life where we "bowl alone," dine alone, exercise alone, go to concerts alone, live alone our ultimate objective? It seems to be the case. The average size of household has been going down with higher income. Not only do richer countries have lower (or negative) population growth rates, but the richer the country the smaller the household size. The final objective will be to live in a world where each household is composed of one person. Denmark, Norway, and Germany are almost there: the average household size is 2.2 (Senegal and Mali have the average household size of 9.1 and 9.5). Japan offers a vision of a society of ultra-competitiveness combined with loneliness.

We should not be surprised by such an outcome. Being together with others always had an economic angle: expenses were less, on a per capita basis, when shared; we needed children to help us in old age and spouses to pay our bills. But, with higher incomes and higher labor participation rates, we can afford expensive utility bills, we can provide for our old age and a comfortable old-age home (so broadly advertised today). Our children (if we have any) will be too far away, swayed around by the availability of jobs and hyper-competitiveness to take care of us.

Being alone is both our preference and a response to a world of competitiveness, commodification, and higher incomes. The new world that we can glean will not be dystopian. It will be a Utopia, with a twist.

It will not be a universal concentration camp for it will be guilty of no atrocity. It will not seem insane, for everything will be ordered, and the stains of human passions will be lost amid the chromium gleam. We shall have nothing to lose and nothing to win. Our deepest

GLOBALIZATION

instincts and our most secret passions will be analyzed, published, and exploited. We shall be rewarded with everything our hearts ever desired. And the supreme luxury of the society of technical necessity will be to grant the bonus of useless revolt and an acquiescent smile. (Jacques Ellul, *The Technological Society*, 1954)

(Published November 2, 2017)

8.6 No one would be unemployed and no one would hold a job

Several days ago Steven Hill presented at the Graduate Center, CUNY, in New York his new book *Raw Deal: How the 'Uber Economy' and Runaway Capitalism Are Screwing American Workers*. It discusses the decline of trade unions, the future of jobs and robotics. It struck me that there are (in his presentation as well as in most of what we read), when it comes to the future of work, two narratives that often seem contradictory. There is a narrative of job-automatization and robotics, whereby most of our jobs end up taken by the robots. Then there is a narrative of people working more and more hours, as work intrudes into their leisure time: instead of taking it easy throughout the day as the first narrative implies, we would use our "free" time to rent apartments we own, or drive our cars as taxis. According to the first narrative, we are in danger of having too much leisure time; according to the second, of having none.

Let's consider the two scenarios in turn, and separately.

Suppose, first, that most "routine" jobs are replaced by robots. This seems quite possible (from today's perspective). If capital replaces labor easily, we shall have the elasticity of substitution exceed one (a point argued by Piketty in his *Capital in the 21st Century*), and the return to capital will not fall in proportion to the increase in the capital/labor ratio. This means that more and more of net income will belong to capitalists, and thus to the owners of the robot-producing companies. Suppose Google self-driving cars become ubiquitous, and Google drives (so to speak) out of business Mercedes, Ford, Volkswagen ... The money will be made by the owners of Google.

In that future, the distribution will move even further against labor, income inequality will increase, unemployment will be higher and there would be a generalized problem of finding a job. Since the economy will have become richer (there is just more stuff), there may be some kind of generalized income support, paid to everybody. The society would look as follows: lots of people at the minimal guaranteed income with loads of free time, the employed with incomes somewhat higher than the social minimum, working mostly in services, and relatively few fabulously rich owners of the means of productions: basically, Mark Zuckerberg, personal trainers, and the unemployed guys living in Miami.

How would the alternative scenario look? There we have robotics as well; but what robotics does is to break jobs into the tiniest

196

possible segments, parcel off each of these segments to people who are temporarily hired to work on that tiny parcel alone, and then combine hundreds of such tasks in one final product. Instead of having a worker W working for a company C full time and doing a task T, such that on the task T there is a bilateral exclusive commitment between the worker and the company, we would have task T broken into T1, T2 ... Tn, and branched off to workers W1, W2 ... Wn. Now the workers will in turn each also work on other tasks and for other employers: so the worker W1 will, on the same day, work on tasks T, Z, and Y, each for a different company. There would be multiplicity (non-exclusivity) on both sides: workers will no longer be committed to a single employer, nor will the employer depend for task T on a single worker. Since tasks are so segmented, it makes it possible to hire less professional and thus cheaper labor, often using their "free" time. This is why professional taxi drivers are now being replaced by guys who spend 1/3 of their workday as sales agents, 1/3 as bar tenders, and 1/3 driving their own cars as cabs. Or, why hotels are in competition with people who rent their own rooms. Or, why I might use every minute of my leisure time to do jobs for which I have no training, and that would replace people who have trained for them and done them for years.

Under that scenario, we should see a dramatic reduction in specialization (say, vocational education would end), blurring of the difference between leisure and work, and a pressure on the labor share. Everybody would be the jack of all trades and master of none. There would be only limited unemployment (since practically everybody could do some extremely simple tasks into which all jobs are divided).

But, perhaps it may be better to think of the two scenarios as just one scenario that would combine lots of labor substitution by capital with heavy segmentation of tasks (and much more intensive labor discipline made possible thanks to automation). In that case, jobs to which we have become accustomed would cease to exist: lots of today's functions will be automated and, for many others, "amateurs," not professionals, would do them.

And we should not be making the "lump of labor" fallacy: the amount of jobs is not limited to the jobs that we know today. There will be entirely new jobs that we cannot even imagine. Steven Hill gave one such example that exists already now: "invisible girlfriend." People pay to receive, at some intervals, text messages that are ostensibly sent by their girlfriends. In the eyes of other people their esteem goes up: many girlfriends compete for their attention. In

GLOBALIZATION AND MULTI-POLAR WORLD

reality, some moustachioed guy in short sleeves is writing these messages and getting paid for them. Or, to give another example: women whose job is to be surrogate mothers either to gay couples or to heterosexual couples who cannot have kids. Now, that job did not exist until recently, that is until (a) legal changes allowed for surrogate motherhood (and also for gay marriage) and (b) technological progress that made "artificial" insemination possible. When I give this example, people often ask me: but can male auto-workers from Detroit become surrogate mothers? No, but this is always the case in the transition period when some occupations are on their way out. But, after a while, there would be almost no more auto-workers at all and, yes, some women can become surrogate mothers and have that as their main income-earning job.

Technology will create new jobs and, if anything, I think we shall have more to worry about by not having any free time than having too much. As commercialization of our lives progresses, we shall perceive (as we already do) every hour spent, without directly or indirectly contributing to more money as wasted. Unemployment will become impossible. Being unemployed implies that you are specialized and that there is a (relative) shortage of such specific jobs. But not so in a new economy: everybody can carry Thai food from one place to another, everybody can exhibit himself or herself naked on the Internet, everybody can open doors, pack bags, or even write blogs. No one would be unemployed and no one would hold a job.

(Published October 25, 2015)

— 9 —

CHINA

9.1 Socialism with Chinese characteristics for the young person: A review of the book of Xi Jinping's sayings

Several years ago, Chinese state's People's Publishing House introduced the English translation of excerpts from Xi Jinping's speeches and, in a few cases, from his writings under the title of *Anecdotes and Sayings of Xi Jinping*. The original was published in Chinese in 2017. The link to the book is available (see below); I could not find it on Amazon though. I am unsure if it is available in the United States. I recently bought a paper copy in Belgrade and read it in Serbian translation made from the English translation. Thus, one has to take into account that the text has gone through a number of language metamorphoses.

Some may compare the book of Xi's "anecdotes and sayings" to the famous *Little Red Book*. There are similarities in the sense that both publications aim to promote the way of thinking of the leaders, and that Xi has recently begun to enjoy somewhat of a cult of personality reminiscent of the one that enveloped Mao from the Cultural Revolution to his death. There are also differences. The *Little Red Book* was a collection of relatively short excerpts from Mao's writings. The current Xi's volume is a selection of longer (on average page-long) pieces from Xi's speeches, each followed by a more detailed interpretation written by the editors of *Renmin Ribao* (*People's Daily*). Since Xi's "anecdotes" draw very heavily on Chinese history, and since the level of historical detail to which Xi refers is unlikely to be known to most non-Chinese readers (and I would guess to many Chinese too), interpretations are absolutely indispensable. I wish they were clearer and less repetitive of Xi's own sayings.

There is another important difference between Mao's and Xi's books. Mao belonged to the generation of leaders like Lenin, Stalin, and Churchill who were writing their own texts (and, in Mao's case, poems as well). So, we could be sure that whatever was published was indeed written by these old-fashioned leaders. Leaders nowadays rely on ghost-writers. This is especially the case when we deal with speeches that provide most of the text in Xi's book. We cannot be sure if this is something that Xi has really said, or that his speech-writers have written and he just approved. This is not a small issue. Why? Because the book is replete with examples from the Chinese history and literature, Marxist literature and, finally, world literature and history. Xi is, by his own admission or claim, a voracious reader, and has been so from a very young age ("What do I do with my leisure time? Of course, most of my time is spent working. The only hobby that I have retained [from my youth] is reading; it has become my way of life. It strengthens my spirits, gives me inspiration, reinforces my morality.") But did anyone who was climbing the steps of power in China (or elsewhere) really have enough time to absorb all these different schools of thought? We do not know. The reader may wonder.

The book is composed of two parts. The first, directed at the Chinese reader, discusses Chinese (but also to a certain extent global) themes, and uses mostly the examples, projected as metaphors, from the millennial Chinese history, the cases of extraordinary individuals from the Maoist times, and even some from the contemporary period of construction of "socialism with Chinese characteristics." The second (much less interesting) part is a compilation of various speeches given by Xi on the occasions of international meetings (conversations with Obama figure there twice, but there is no Putin). The second part is supposed to showcase Chinese benevolent interaction with the rest of the world, but its programmatic character makes it much less interesting. The only exception to this is where Xi discusses soccer, of which he is genuinely fond, and where his opinions are interesting.

The undisputable emphasis in the "Chinese" part of the book is on the matters of governance. By giving numerous examples from Chinese history of rulers and their aides, who cared about people's welfare, lived modestly ("One should be the first when taking care of state affairs, the last when taking care of personal affairs"), strove to improve themselves morally and educationally, Xi proposes a theory of governance that is based on virtue of rulers and results achieved, not procedure. While Western theories emphasize the procedural

CHINA

aspect (how is one selected to be the ruler—is it by a well-established democratic process or not?), Xi's concern is with the results. The tacit premise is not to discuss how one is selected to rule—and this applies not only to top positions, but to all positions from the lowest country level to the head of CPC—but how successful they are in fulfilling their functions. The success is defined in terms of improvement in the well-being and happiness of people whom they govern.

The good rule itself, as in a story from ancient China told by Xi, need not be structurally the same. Three different rulers, Xi writes, imposed the just rule by different mechanisms: one by his attention to detail and by controlling all government expenses item by item; another by his good nature; and the third by severe punishments. Corruption was eradicated under each of the three rulers but for a different reason: under the first, people could not cheat; under the second, they felt ashamed to cheat; under the third, they were punished if they cheated. Xi, who told that story in 2004, does not reveal which of the three ways he prefers.

In all cases of a good rule, there is the emphasis on individual characteristics of rulers. As editors mention, if many virtuous and conscientious rulers and government officials existed in feudal China, would not the more ideologically conscious and people-oriented communists be even more likely to care about their co-citizens? What is required, they write, is "morality inside and virtue outside"; what is sought is the rule of virtue, and by virtue.

But how to bring about such rule? Obviously, by having moral rulers. Hence—the reader begins to realize—Xi's ideological campaign: if Confucian-cum-Communist ideology is disregarded and everything is simply esteemed in terms of money and economic success, there cannot be a moral and virtuous rule. To quote Confucius, as the editors do, "if one allows oneself to follow profit in one's behavior, there will be many with cause for complaint." There could be a fair procedural selection of rulers, say, by election, but not necessarily a virtuous rule. The latter can be assured only through the education of rulers.

The key question, unanswered in the book, then becomes: is it possible to achieve an educational and moral "rejuvenation" under the current "normal" conditions of capitalism, where money-making is held by the majority of the population to be the highest objective revealing also one's individual worth? Can the examples brought up from the revolutionary era, from Yen'an forum, early Mao, etc. be relevant for a new generation raised in the world of relentless commercialization? One is allowed to doubt. This does not make

GLOBALIZATION AND MULTI-POLAR WORLD

the ideological campaign conducted by Xi (including probably through this book) less relevant—it makes it rather more so. Yet, the likelihood of success of that campaign is not very high. Xi is fighting against the spirit of the times and, while his struggle may be driven by a genuine desire to create a morally superior China, the odds of succeeding in this endeavor are, I am afraid, not particularly high.

But, perhaps, Xi could answer with the story, told by Mao in 1942, of the crazy old man who tries to move two mountains. In Mao's version the two mountains were feudalism and colonialism. They were removed. In Xi's version, they could be greed and indifference.

(Published August 11, 2022)

CHINA

9.2 The long NEP, China, and Xi

Many journalists, commentators, and political scientists see the recent policy changes in China as "the return to communism." They, in particular, point to a number of measures whose objective was to limit lending by Internet companies, to ban for-profit tutoring, and to put a squeeze on companies producing Internet games (the latter were, tellingly and ominously, likened to "the spreaders of the spiritual opium among the Chinese youth"). Western commentators are shocked by the Chinese government's apparent indifference to what such measures might do to the stock markets in Shanghai, Shenzhen, and Hong Kong. (In effect, they have all declined during the last month.) This is in signal contrast with government's concern, and even panic, when the Chinese stock market went through severe turbulence in the summer of 2015.

The commentators "transfer" or impute to China their own ideological biases. That bias consists in an excessive focus on the stock markets as almost sole indicators of an economy's health. This, of course, is not surprising in a country, like the US, where 93 percent of financial assets are held by 10 percent of the population (see Edward Wolff, *A Century of Wealth in America*). The latter are also the richest people and consequently things that affect them will be—given that they control the media either directly (as Bloomberg and Jeff Bezos do) or indirectly, because they are the main buyers of the news—reported much more extensively than things that affect the other 90 percent of the population. All of this makes the stock market acquire a hypertrophied importance compared to its real importance. It also gives us an excellent insight into who really controls the social and economic life of a country.

Donald Trump was merely an extreme example of the ruling class's singular (and fully reasonable, from the point of view of their financial interests) obsession with the stock market. Trump decided on his policy moves, not merely domestic but even foreign, in function of their effect on the stock market. One might recall that Trump's only reason for not allowing infected patients to disembark from a ship in the waters off Long Beach in March 2020 was in order not to spook the stock market. (Little did he—and all of us with him—know what would happen next.)

Let me give you a personal story that encapsulates the importance of the stock market for the rich. In August 1991, I was on vacation in Martha's Vineyard, the island rightly known as the abode of

203

very rich democrats. (The most recent house owner there is Barack Obama.) The vacation coincided with the anti-Gorbachev coup in Moscow (August 19–22). So, everybody in that small enclave where I was, rushed in the morning to watch TV news (these were the years before the Internet and smartphones). Absolutely dramatic events, with global and historical consequences, were unfolding in Moscow: the coup leaders were giving a badly organized press conference, the army had seized main buildings in Moscow, demonstrators began to descend in the streets, Yeltsin seized the Russian Parliament building, it was unclear whether Gorbachev was arrested or not ... One was watching history happening in front of us. But, after about half-an-hour of live coverage from Moscow, the liberal elite decided that it was enough, and switched the channels: they tuned in on the New York Stock Exchange and watched the developments there most attentively, probably mentally calculating how good (or bad) were the events in Moscow for their portfolios. Some of us who were more interested in the fate of the Soviet Union, communism, and the world than in stock quotations were in the minority, and we had to divine the events in Moscow from the gyrations of the stocks in the New York.

China wants to be different. In a society of political capitalism, as I argued in *Capitalism, Alone*, the state tries to maintain its autonomy. In the United States, the state generally acts as a custodian of the capitalist interest "managing the common affairs of the bourgeoisie." In political capitalism, though, the state must not allow itself to be co-opted or "contaminated" by capitalist interest. In other words, capitalist interest is one of the interests to consider—but not the only one, or even perhaps not the chief one.

This approach is consistent with the long Chinese tradition of the state keeping merchant and capitalist interests at arm's length. Ho-fung Hung, for example, nicely describes in *The China Boom: Why China Will not Rule the World*, how Qing bureaucracy sided in industrial disputes with workers, and not with "masters," as was commonly the case in the Britain in the nineteenth century. The same arguments are made by Giovanni Arrighi (*Adam Smith in Beijing*), Jacques Gernet, regarding Southern Song China (*Daily Life in China on the Eve of the Mongol Invasion*), Kenneth Pomeranz (*The Great Divergence*), and Martin Jacques (*When China Rules the World*). (All these books, except for Gernet's, are reviewed on my Global Inequality blog or Global Inequality 3.0 Substack.)

Furthermore, if one looks at the current Xi-led party from a Leninist perspective (which Xi may not be loath to do), the same conclusion is

CHINA

reinforced. The Chinese capitalism may be seen as one "long NEP"—which might last a century or even two—wherein capitalists are given a free hand in practically all areas of economics, but the commanding heights of the economy are preserved for the state (which means under the CPC control) and the political power is not shared with anyone, least of all with capitalists. Thus the state maintains freedom of action *vis-à-vis* socially the most powerful group (capitalists), and can ignore their complaints when an overarching social interest is at stake; as in the three examples of regulatory and legal crackdown was arguably the case.

Can the autonomy of the state end, and will the bourgeoisie take over the Chinese state as it did in the West? It is quite possible. The modernization theory argues that. There are, I think, three ways in which it could happen.

First, there could be a middle-class or bourgeois revolution. It should be noted, however, that no revolution against a communist regime had ever succeeded. The one that came closest was the Hungarian revolution in 1956, but it was crushed externally, by Soviet arms. So, that possibility, as long as the Party-state is united is, I think, extremely unlikely.

The second possibility is "Gorbachevization." This means that the top echelons of the Party move toward social-democracy. This makes lots of sense ideologically, given that originally communists were part of social-democracy. So the ideological gap between the two is not very wide. The end of communist regimes in Eastern Europe and the Soviet Union came when several communist parties, became, either at the top (like CPSU) or throughout its membership, social-democratic. The latter was the case, by 1988, for at least the Hungarian, Polish and Slovenian communist parties. They came close to the Italian CP, both ideologically and politically.

The third possibility is "Zhang Zeminism," whereby the Party increasingly accepts among its top members capitalists, and reflects their interests. In a recent paper in the *British Journal of Sociology*, Yang, Novokmet, and Milanovic find indeed that while CPC membership (by the end of Zhang Zemin's rule) was more similar to the overall composition of China's urban population than before, the top (richest) CPC members were increasingly diverging from the rest of the membership and the population. Here is our conclusion: "While the structure of CPC membership in the recent period approximates better the population structure than in 1988, the CPC top is moving further away from both CPC overall membership structure and that of the urban population as a whole."

205

The "insinuation" of the rich into the top Party ranks was rationalized by Zhang Zemin under the ideology of "the three represents." One does not hear much about "the three represents" nowadays (it seems to have been replaced by Xi Jinping Thought) so that path to change is currently being blocked.

The future will tell us if in one of these three ways the Chinese state gets taken over by the rich, or not—that is, whether it remains autonomous in its decision-making.

(Published August 3, 2021)

9.3 Hayekian communism

You think it is a contradiction in terms, a paradox. But you are wrong: we are used to thinking in pure categories, while life is much more complex; and seeming paradoxes do exist in real life. China is indeed a country of Hayekian communism.

Nowhere, I think, is wealth and material success more openly celebrated than in China. Perhaps it was stimulated by the 40th anniversary of the opening up, which is this year [2018], but more fundamentally, I think, it is stimulated by the most successful economic development in history. Rich entrepreneurs are celebrated in newspapers, television, conferences. Their wealth and rags-to-riches stories are held as examples for all. Ayn Rand would feel at home in this environment. So would Hayek: an incredible amount of energy and discovery was unleashed by the changes that transformed the lives of 1.3 billion people, twice as many as the combined populations of the "old" EU-15 and the United States. People discovered economic information that was inaccessible or unknown before, organized new combinations of capital and labor in a Schumpeterian fashion, and created wealth on an almost unimaginable scale (certainly, unimaginable for anyone who had looked at China in 1978).

At a large banquet in Beijing, we were presented with first-hand stories of five Chinese capitalists, who started from zero in the 1980s, and became dollar billionaires today. One spent years in the countryside during the Cultural Revolution, another was put in prison for seven years for "speculation," the third made his "apprentissage" of capitalism, as he candidly said, by cheating people in East Asia ("afterwards I learned that if I really wanted to become rich, I should not cheat; cheating is for losers"). Hayek would have listened to these stories, probably transfixed. And what news would he have loved better than to read in today's [September 23, 2018] *Financial Times* that the Marxist society at the Peking University was disbanded because of its support of the striking workers in the Special Economic Zone of Shenzhen.

But, there is one way in which Hayek went wrong. These incredible personal (and societal) successes were achieved under the rule of a single party, the Communist Party of China. Celebration of wealth comes naturally to Marxists. Development, widespread education, gender equality, urbanization, and, indeed, faster growth than under capitalism, were the rationale, and sources of legitimacy, of communist revolutions, as they took place in the less developed world. Lenin said so; Trotsky confirmed it when he canvassed for large-scale industrialization; Stalin implemented it: "We are fifty or a hundred years behind the advanced countries. We must make good this difference in ten years. Either we do it, or we shall be crushed."

I remember, as a precocious high-school student in Yugoslavia, how I scanned the newspapers for the indicators of industrial growth. Since Yugoslavia was then among the fastest growing economies in the world, I was deeply disappointed when the monthly growth rate (annualized) would fall below ten percent. I thought ten percent was the normal growth rate of communist economies: why would you care to become communist if you would not grow faster than under capitalism?

So, the celebration of growth—new roads, new super-fast trains, new housing complexes, new well-lit avenues and orderly schools—comes naturally to communists. Not any less than to Hayekian entrepreneurs. (As an exercise in this, read Neruda's beautiful memoirs, where he exudes enormous pleasure at seeing Soviet-built dams.) The difference, though, is that the Hayekians celebrate private success, which also helps society move forward; in communism, success too was supposed to be socialized.

But this did not happen. Collectivist efforts worked for a decade or two but eventually growth fizzled out and the efforts flagged. Cynicism reigned supreme. It was left to China and to Deng Xiaoping to stumble (in the immortal phrase of Adam Ferguson) on a combination where the rule of the Communist Party would be maintained but full freedom of action, and social encomium, would be given to individual capitalists. They would work, become rich, enrich many others in the process, but the reins of political power would remain firmly in the hands of the Communist Party. Capitalists will provide the engine and the fuel, but the Party will hold the steering wheel.

Would things be ever better if the political power too was in the hands of capitalists? This is doubtful. They might have used it to recreate the Nanjing government of the 1930s, venal, weak, and incompetent. They would not work hard but would use political power to maintain their economic privileges. It is one of the key problems of US capitalism today that the rich increasingly control the political process, and thus skew economic incentives away from production and competition into creation and preservation of monopolies. Much worse would likely have happened in China. It is precisely because the political sphere was largely insulated from the economic sphere that capitalists could be safely kept busy with production, and at arm's length (as far as possible because the Party is exposed to growing corruption) from the politics.

How did China stumble on this combination? There may be many reasons, including the millennial tradition of being run by imperial bureaucracies, the historical alliance—even if it became unraveled—between the Communist Party and Sun Yat-sen's KMT (an alliance the like of which never existed elsewhere in the communist world)—but one cannot but ask oneself, could it have happened elsewhere too? Perhaps. Lenin's New Economic Policy was not much different from Chinese policies of the 1980s. But Lenin saw NEP as a temporary concession to capitalists—because he believed that socialism was more progressive and thus "scientifically" generated higher growth. Perhaps it is only the failures of the Great Leap Forward and the chaos of the Cultural Revolution that chastened Chinese leadership and convinced Deng and others that private initiative was more "progressive" than social planning and state-owned enterprises. Lenin could not have seen that. It was too early.

I also wondered what Stalin would have made of China. He probably would have been glad that his name is still enshrined in the official pantheon. (In a large bookstore in downtown Beijing, the first row of books are translations of Marxist classics: Marx himself, Engels, Lenin, and Stalin. Very few people look at them. The next rows that display books on wealth management, finance economics, stock market investments, etc. are much more popular.) Stalin would have been impressed by Chinese growth; by the extensive power of the state and the country (for sure, no longer a country to which he could send his advisors to help it technologically), by the Party's ability to control the population in a very sophisticated and unobtrusive manner.

Stalin would have loved economic success and the military power that comes with it, but would probably have been shocked by private wealth. It is hard seeing him coexist with Jack Ma. Hayek's reaction would have been the opposite: he would have been delighted that his claims about the spontaneous market order have been vindicated in a most emphatic fashion, but would have failed to understand that this was possible only under the rule of a communist party.

No one would have been left indifferent by the most successful economic story ever. And no one would have fully understood it.

(Published September 24, 2018)

9.4 *The World Turned Upside Down*: A critical review

This may be the most difficult book review to write. I have decided to break it into two parts. Writing it is difficult because one has to have huge admiration for Yang Jisheng, a former journalist, now a historian, who has amassed an incredible amount of information about the political maneuvering, personal relations, events and, most importantly, victims of the Cultural Revolution, and presented all of this in his new book *The World Turned Upside Down* (published in English only two months ago). Yang reminds me of those few courageous authors, indignant by the inequities of communism, who, beginning with Djilas, then the Medvedev brothers, and even Solzhenitsyn himself, or Dmitri Volkogonov in his biographies of Lenin and Stalin, have written valuable testimonials about the system.

But, alas, most of them were almost fully ignorant of political science, economics, and historiography. Yang is perhaps an extreme example: on the one hand, extraordinary evidence that he has collected (I think that the book must contain several thousand names of people involved) and, on the other hand, equally extraordinary absence of any reflections about that evidence. The book is thus a succession of events, many of them tragic, conferences and rallies, gossip and innuendoes, intrigues and betrayals. Yang is the type of writer whom Cicero two thousand years ago dismissively called "narratores rerum."

So, in my first review I will focus on these defects and problems.

Yang's explanation for many events during the Cultural Revolution, including ritualistic vows of fealty to Mao, is "totalitarianism." It is repeated a number of times. It is a cool word to say, but the Cultural Revolution was anything but totalitarianism. It might have been started by Mao (although I will explain later that Yang never tells us why) but, while totalitarianism is absence of agency by individuals, the Cultural Revolution was the opposite: hundreds of millions of individuals had agency. They had too much of it. The Cultural Revolution was not totalitarianism, but its very reverse: a Hobbesian world where everyone fought everyone else. The most tragic revelation about the Cultural Revolution (an observation that Yang does not make) is that it shows us what the withdrawal of the state and government does: it reveals human nature at its worst. Without state's monopoly on violence, we would simply go out fighting each other. Forever. Imagine the United States, when suddenly the President, Congress, all politicians, judges, and

CHINA

police simply decide to go home and never return to their jobs. Within a week, the country would be in a "Cultural Revolution." (Actually, with Katrina, it took less than a week for New Orleans to descend into the "Cultural Revolution.") China during the Cultural Revolution was not Stalinism redux, but Libya today.

Under totalitarian regimes, every individual, spontaneous action is proscribed. Writing on your own a letter of support to Stalin was as likely to land you in jail as writing a letter criticizing Stalin. Not so under the chaos of the Cultural Revolutions: everyone wrote big-letter posters, organized rallies, attacked "traitors," called themselves followers of "Mao Zedong's line." It is just that nobody knew what that line was today, or what it might become tomorrow. Neither did Mao.

But if not totalitarianism, was it autocracy? That too is difficult to justify in standard terms. Mao did not rule like an autocrat; he ruled like a God; which meant that he appeared just from to time, when needed. Yang shows that Mao, uninterested in management of the country and the economy, and even in foreign affairs, simply delegated all of the day-to-day running of the affairs to various people, mostly to Zhou Enlai. But, even saying "delegated" is an exaggeration. Mao just ignored the running of the country, and whoever managed to get to it, did. If, in this management, "the delegate" did something that eventually displeased Mao, he could end up dismissed, expelled from the Party, wearing a dunce hat, being driven to suicide or pushed by a mob from a tall building. But Mao's ruling style was not the style of a usual autocrat. Mao was neither a Stalin who worked twelve hours per day and personally authorized (or ordered) executions during the Great Terror, nor a Hitler with his obsessive control of every detail. People were persecuted or killed without Mao having had the slightest idea what was happening to them. In daily affairs of government, Mao's involvement was significantly less than, for example, the involvement of Joe Biden or Angela Merkel, let alone that of an autocrat like Vladimir Putin. He would disappear for weeks, sometimes for months; would come to Beijing without his "closest collaborators" being aware of it. We do not even seem to know how Mao was spending his days: was he writing poetry, editing Central Committee's communiques, sleeping, having long meals, sharing beds with mistresses—but, whatever he was doing, he was not running the government in the way governments are commonly run by autocrats.

Perhaps the closest parallel that we have is the power of a prophet (Weber's charismatic power?) The prophet does not need to show up

211

GLOBALIZATION AND MULTI-POLAR WORLD

daily—perhaps it is even better for him that he does not. But prophets are not normally prototypes of autocratic leaders.

Then, why did Mao start the Cultural Revolution? Yang does not tell us. There are some very vague hints that it was a revenge for Mao's relative loss of power after the failed Great Leap Forward. Was it a pay-back time for Peng Zhen and Liu Shaoqi? But to get rid of the two, Mao did not need to turn 800 million people upside down, nor to have Collective No. 6 fight Collective No. 5 with sticks and stones (and at times firearms) in X'ian or Shanghai. Another possibility is his fear of being replaced by a within-Party coup as happened to Khrushchev in 1964. It is possible, but we are never provided with any evidence nor a narrative about why the Cultural Revolution might have been a solution to that fear. It is also possible, Yang mentions in passing, that it was sheer idealism: "permanent revolution" and the desire to recreate the Paris Commune. But many lovers of the Paris Commune (Lenin was buried wrapped up in its flag) did not see the need to start the war of all against all in order to replay it.

Since this is a critical review, let me just end in the same spirit. The book suffers from many editing problems. There is, for example, a direct quote from Mao that is, midway, suddenly interrupted by the introduction of the third person, "Mao observed." There are typos. There are statements in the introduction that are plainly contradicted by the text. The quality of American publishing has steadily deteriorated—probably under the pressure of time and money-making. This was a super difficult book to translate and edit (the translators had to convince the author to drop four chapters from an already very lengthy book). I can only hope that the translation was better than the editing.

(Published April 26, 2021)

CHINA

9.5 License to kill: *The World Turned Upside Down*: A laudatory review

Yang Jisheng's *The World Turned Upside Down* (whose methodological approach I reviewed just above, Section 9.4) is an extraordinarily rich book. The ten-year period that it covers, from 1966 to 1976, was an amazingly turbulent period in Chinese history, with implications that do not carry over only for today's China, but that have response (and precedents) in the rest of the world.

When it comes to the narrative alone, Yang's book is fascinating. It is impossible to describe in a short review the chaos wrought by the Cultural Revolution that Yang studies, not only chronologically, but in various parts of China. A part of the challenge of describing what was happening lies with the decentralized nature of anarchy and violence that engulfed the whole country. The reader often thinks of analogies with Stalin's Great Terror, but the differences are perhaps even more telling. While the Great Terror was a centralized terrorization of certain groups and individuals, often specifically selected by Stalin, the Cultural Revolution was a decentralized permission to settle accounts given to everybody. Thus, the nature of conflict varied from one locality to another, from one town to another.

The beginnings in the summer of 1966 were limited to high school and university students and were almost entirely Beijing-based. It was a permission, even encouragement, given to high-school kids to take over schools and universities, berate and humiliate teachers, and do as they please. If one were to do the same thing anywhere in the world, the results would be the same: the kids would enjoy "turning the world upside down," as the young Nero and Caracalla did. At that early stage, the attacks were mostly directed against "the five black classes" (landlords, rich farmers, counter-revolutionaries, bad influencers, right-wingers). Offspring of high government and Party officials (all studying at various Beijing universities) were often in the lead, using a bizarre "blood lineage" theory that, they argued, gave them the right to rule by virtue of being of the right class (and genetic) background.

The escalation was not only geographical, as the student movement widened to cover all of China, but "sectoral" as well. Mao first authorized the movement to spread among workers, and encouraged the alliance of revolutionary students and workers (a thing which, by the way, eluded the "revolution" in France only a year later), and finally—despite the strong opposition from the military—allowed the

213

"support-the-left" movement to sow havoc in the Army as well. The military was asked to supply weapons to the left factions, or to ignore such factions' stealing or simply taking the weapons themselves.

Within some twelve months, the country descended into full chaos, led by a bewildering number of factions with quasi-identical names (e.g. "The Red Alliance" against "The Revolutionary Alliance," in Daoxian, p. 351), which all fought in order to further Mao Zedong thought. "Thousands of large-scale armed conflicts throughout the country resulted in deaths of more than a hundred thousand people" (p. 228). At the risk of simplification, it could be said that the factions can be divided into two groups, and Yang uses the two groupings consistently through the book: rebels and conservatives.

The rebel faction was originally started by the children of the nomenklatura but then gradually was taken over by malcontents, low-paid workers, and those with grievances, or just a taste for violence; that is, those who had most to gain from anarchy, as well as by those who ideologically believed in "the permanent revolution." As Yang explains:

A genuine rebellion requires taking political risk, but the old Red Guards [the original rebel faction] with their privileged backing, had little to fear from attacking teachers ... When the situation of the Cultural Revolution changed and the parents of the Red Guards were attacked as capitalist roaders, the old Red Guards openly protected the cadres and attacked the rebel factions, and in that way became a conservative faction in name as well as practice, however they might disavow the label. (p. 151)

Was the rebel faction the people's faction? The negotiations in Shanghai between the rebel faction of the workers and the city government eerily resemble those between Solidarity and Polish government, some fourteen years later. So, workers in Shanghai and workers in Gdansk united? The difference was that in Shanghai workers had the support from the top, namely from Mao, who in 1967 "allowed China's people to enjoy the freedom of association enshrined in the constitution, [and] mass organizations proliferated" (p. 149). So, is it a revolution of freedom, or "revolution because of lack of freedom"? Moreover "The Sixteen Articles [the CPC rules on handling the Cultural Revolution] prevented party committees from attacking the rebel masses, while giving the masses the freedom and confidence to rebel, and the higher the rank of the leader denounced, the more revolutionary the critic was considered to be" (p. 154).

CHINA

Against the rebel factions were arrayed the conservative factions, supported by most of the top military (old marshals whom Mao alternatively cajoled and berated), the government apparatus, health and education workers, factory managers, and all those who wanted to impose some kind of order over a society that was looking more Hobbesian by the day.

Yang's unstated, but clear, objective in the book is to overturn the current official narrative. The officially sanctioned view of the Cultural Revolution is that most of the crimes were committed by the "rebel faction" and that eventually the country was saved, thanks to those who managed to ensure the return to normal life. But, Yang writes, "mainstream public opinion has blamed all the evils of the Cultural Revolution on the rebel faction, but the vast majority of victims died while the rebel faction was suppressed under the new order of military and administrative bureaucratic control" (p. 230). In that revision of official history, neither Liu Shaoqi, who initially, whether for opportunistic or genuine reasons, supported the Cultural Revolution, nor (especially) Zhou Enlai are spared at times scathing comments. (Deng Xiaoping hardly appears in the story.)

The "new order"—which basically means a major turning point in the Cultural Revolution—occurred when Mao himself personally witnessed the chaos of pitched armed battles in Wuhan in August 1967, and had to flee the city. It was followed by investigations and suppression of the rebel faction, linked to the May 16 [1967] incident, when the rebel faction directly accused Zhou Enlai.

The three central chapters of the book (chs. 16–18) describe in gory detail the enormity of the massacres. "The cleansing of party ranks" gives a review of local campaigns against various class enemies (who in many cases were the same people who themselves previously conducted campaigns of cleansing of the enemies); the next chapter describes the cases of famous victims, mostly scientists and old Party members (in a way strongly reminiscent of Roy Medvedev's *Let History Judge*) and the most gut-wrenching chapter describes the appalling massacres conducted at the local level by whatever faction managed to do it against neighbors. The randomness and brutality of killings (including ritualistic murders and cannibalism) is both shocking, and not entirely unexpected for those who know, from history, that humans freed from any constraint and given a license to kill, will often do so. We are not there in the presence of a systematic targeted killing, as performed by the Nazis and Stalin's Great Terror, but of decentralized massacres common to civil wars.

215

GLOBALIZATION AND MULTI-POLAR WORLD

It is a book that anyone interested in Chinese or communist history should read. But it is a book whose main messages are about the role of government, freedom from constraint, and human nature.

(Published April 26, 2021)

9.6 Interpreting or misinterpreting China's success

I recently read a review of China's long-term economic progress by two well-known scholars of Chinese economy: Loren Brandt and Thomas Rawski. I have read and cited both. Just to give some examples: I liked very much a paper on inequality in the Chinese countryside in the 1930s co-authored by Brandt; or Rawski's work on growth (and, also on inequality) in pre-war China. As these examples show, my interest in both authors was, not surprisingly, more on what they wrote on inequality in China, not on the issues of growth and long-term development. The latter however is the topic they address in their new paper "China's Great Boom as a Historic Process" (which is also a chapter in the recently published *Cambridge Economic History of China*, vol. 2).

I thus read their new piece with great interest. Alas, I was disappointed. I will criticize the paper in two respects: first, the implicit, or at times quite explicit, narrative regarding China's development from the end of the nineteenth century to today, and second, internal contradictions among the arguments made in the paper.

Brandt and Rawski's (B–R) narrative can be summarized as follows. Late Qing and early Republican China, while backward in many respects, has shown the signs of remarkable ability to quickly adopt Western production and financial techniques. Coercive and discriminatory rules imposed by Western powers, Russia, and Japan were, in reality, helpful for the Chinese development. (It is unlikely that China could have experienced this early development burst without Western semi-colonialism.) The Nanjing KMT government adopted many more pro-state policies (compared to the late Qing), although this was short-lived because of the war and internal conflict. The Maoist government, when it came to power in 1949, continued KMT's line of state-led development and made it more planified (even if it never approached the Soviet extent of planning). Because such policies blunted the incentives, they created a huge gap between the potential and actual output. The gap was "mopped up" during Deng's pro-market episode. The recent approach by Xi Jinping is a reversal aiming to give a greater role to the state ("an inward-looking Soviet-style plan"), accompanied by a "retreat from ... global cooperation." It is very unlikely that China will be able to make the technological leaps that the Party and the government promise and have made the cornerstone of their policies.

GLOBALIZATION AND MULTI-POLAR WORLD

I believe that this, hopefully fair, review of the B–R argument highlights several important points on which the authors insist. First, the quasi-colonial relations were good for China's development ("privileges won through foreign military pressure encouraged domestic economic growth," p. 787). Second, there was a continuum between KMT's and Maoist policies. Third, China's spectacular post-1978 growth is to be explained simply as a "rebound," the clever use of the already existing capacities and capabilities.

Let me focus on these points. The principal argument for the first is the existence of economically dynamic parts, or rather cities, in the coastal region of China. B–R mention for example that Shanghai was a sleepy country seat but that its growth rate in the Republican period was comparable to the growth rates of Japan, India, and the USSR. Such examples of individual successes in a country as enormous as China (500 million inhabitants in the 1930s) are a form of cherry-picking, if they are used to claim something more than that there were a few poles of growth. One could almost at will find cities or areas that have prospered in any country in the world, while that country as a whole had stagnated, or had even gone backward. Maddison's data on China show its GDP per capita to have increased from $985 in 1913 to $1,003 in 1938 (all in international dollars), which gives an average annual growth rate of hardly above zero. Thus, Chinese growth in the pre-war period merely kept up with the increase of population (which was about 0.6 percent per year). This is hardly extraordinary.

As the quote below from a survey of villages undertaken by the China Cotton Mill Owners' Association for the purpose of estimating the demand for textiles in the 1930s shows:

[we] found disastrous conditions: women in Szechuan were not wearing skirts because the rural devastation had left farmers without the means to purchase cloth, and in many households family members shared one item of clothing. (Shiroyama 2008, p. 127; quoted in Milanovic, *Capitalism, Alone*, p. 80)

China, for most of its inhabitants, was a land of almost unimaginable poverty and backwardness. A few entrepots' bright lights here and there made little difference to the country as a whole. This holds even more if we believe that the lack of domestic agency (that is, the quasi-colonial relationship) is a negative thing per se.

The continuation of policies between KMT and Mao's government has been noted by many authors. It is not a new point. But in B–R it

218

plays a paradoxical role. They aim to situate the post-1978 Chinese advances not on the basis created by Mao's policies but very implausibly, given the short duration of the KMT government, on pre-revolutionary developments. The authors' narrative becomes inconsistent: on the one hand, a number of glaring inefficiencies of socialist planning are rightly cited, but then the Dengist success is explained by the claim that it simply exploited the existing gap between the potential and realized output created during the Mao era. But, if Mao's era created the possibility of having a much higher output, it must have done something right. Since the authors cannot bring themselves to mention anything positive to have happened during Mao's period, we are left in a quandary as to how a thoroughly inefficient system such as Mao's could have created the basis for Dengist revival.

B–R come to this impossible position because they tend to see the Dengist revival not so much on its own terms, to have been the greatest long-term expansion in economic history, but they treat it as filling up the gap, almost mechanically, between the possible and the actual. Thus, the narrative undervalues the importance of Dengist reforms (which are not discussed in any detail), explicitly dismisses the Maoist period (while indirectly acknowledging its importance), and all but explains China's 1980–2008 successes by the Nanjing government policies.

The authors here face a real problem: in order to dismiss Deng, they need to claim that the potential for growth already existed under Mao; but they cannot credit Mao for that potential because they criticize all of his policies. Thus, somehow, that potential has to be shown to have originated in a government that lasted less than ten years, never controlled the entire territory of China, and operated in an entirely different intellectual and global environment more than half-a-century before Deng.

My last point already hints at one—of many—internal contradictions in the paper. The authors document low productivity growth of state-owned enterprises (SOEs) by, among other things, pointing to their low profitability. But they do not seem to notice that SOEs low profitability may be due to extra-economic tasks that these enterprises are supposed to fulfill, as well as to higher effective taxation. Moreover, in order to explain the Belt and Road initiative, they have to acknowledge large profits of SOEs; so, suddenly, we read that the share of SOE profits in GDP has risen. But, if SOEs profits are increasing faster than the total value added, this is hard to reconcile with the earlier statement that low profitability of SOEs is due to their inefficiency.

B–R write with a Thatcherite glee about the industrial restructuring that took place in the 1990s (urban reforms). The employees of SOEs are "culled" (p. 809), the reforms "decanted" tens of millions of workers "into the grip of market discipline" (p. 825) at the time when companies were "bulging with surplus employees" (p 827). The dogma of efficiency, which comes on the heels of privatization, is so extravagant that, reading this in 2022, when in many countries the gains from privatization of the *existing* companies have been found to be minimal (if any), the text seems slightly embarrassing and anachronistic. The authors would probably not imagine using this cheerleading language if they were to describe Thatcher's or Reagan's policies. But, this kind of language and, more importantly, the cheerful interpretation of driving thousands of middle-aged workers out into the street, seems to be de rigueur when writing of former socialist economies and China. Its costs are never mentioned.

After celebrating the unemployment and "sharpness of incentives" that it brings, the authors strangely blame CPC for high inequality that "resembles" the late Qing era (p. 824). Leaving aside that their quote of 15 percent of total income received by the top one percent is highly contested (because it is based on imputing SOE profits to individuals with the highest private capital incomes—a most dubious assumption), a 15 percent share is still much lower than the 24 percent share of the top one percent in the 1880s obtained from a study of the incomes of Chinese gentry.

But, even if (1) the 15 percent share were somehow correct (the just released 2018 nation-wide household income survey gives the share of the top one percent to be 7 percent), and (2) even if the 15 percent share "resembled" the 24 percent share, the entire tenor of the article celebrates inequality as a force that, when unleashed, explains Chinese growth—so what is then suddenly wrong with inequality? There again, we encounter an internal contradiction: the current CPC is criticized for not being more market- and incentive-friendly (in contrast to Jiang Zemin's policy of "three represents"), and is then, in a strange reversal, also criticized for allowing inequality to be too high. So, is Xi Jinping in favor of too little or too much inequality?

Now, one can reconcile the two (which B–R never attempt). Perhaps the fact is that the government hogged all income, and everybody on the top is corrupt. But this line of argument has to be defended. As Yang, Novokmet, and I show (reference below), the elite at the top of China's income pyramid has markedly shifted toward private sector entrepreneurs and large capitalists. While people linked with the private sector accounted for one quarter of those in the top five

CHINA

percent in 1988, their share exceeded one-half in 2013 (see figure 3 in our article and the discussion around it). This is in contradiction with the possible claim that inequality is due to the state and Party functionaries *alone* being inordinately rich. On the contrary, it is the private sector that is the richissime. Moreover, that line of argument cannot explain at all the anti-corruption campaign that was directed against people whose state and Party connection enabled them to amass money. So, if B–R celebrate greater market incentives and inequality throughout their article, and people at the top in China are rich private-sector entrepreneurs, why is CPC's insufficient market-orientation taken to task for allowing high inequality?

In conclusion, it is deeply dispiriting that such a unidimensional view of Chinese long-run growth, which fails to deal with very important questions of (just to name a few) the emergence of TVEs, *de facto* privatization of land, its later commercialization, the dilemmas of the Big Bang vs. gradual reform (on which scores of papers and books have been written; see, e.g. books by Isabella Weber, Julian Gewirtz, Yuen Yuen Ang—all of them reviewed on my Substack), and adopts a simplistic, and at times even dogmatic, narrative, may be read as a valid summary of one hundred years of China's development. This is especially important because China's experience is influencing other countries and a unidimensional Washington-consensus interpretation favored here is likely, if accepted, to have harmful consequences for global development.

Note 1. Even the choice of some references by Brandt and Rawski is rather unusual. For the share of the state sector in value added, B–R cite the journalistic article "The State Never Retreats," published in *Gavekal Dragonomics*, rather than the most detailed study of the state sector importance done by the World Bank's Shunlin Zhang in 2019 (and which, on the contrary, shows a steady decline in the state-sector share in value added and employment). The finding of lower growth of total factor productivity among state firms is seriously challenged (see Hsieh and Song, "Grasp the Large, Let Go of the Small," *Brookings Papers on Economic Activity*, 2019), but this is never mentioned.

Note 2. Lin Chen's *Revolution and Counterrevolution in China* represents a perfect antidote to the interpretation presented by Brandt and Rawski. I would suggest reading the two texts one after another.

(Published August 6, 2022)

— 10 —

RUSSIA

10.1 Russia's circular economic history

Today I participated in a nice web-based program started by the Central Bank of Russia. An economist is being interviewed by another, and then the one who has been interviewed becomes in his/her turn the interviewer of yet a third one. My friend Shlomo Weber, the head of the New School of Economics, interviewed me, and then I interviewed Professor Natalya Zubarevich, from the Lomonosov Moscow State University and a noted scholar of Russian regional economics.

Just a couple of days ago Natalia gave a very well-received talk at the Gaidar Forum in Moscow on (what one might call) "unhealthy convergence" of Russian regions. In fact, Natalia shows that most recently Russia's regional per capita GDPs have started a mild convergence, but that this is due first to low growth rate of most of them and the economy as a whole, and to the redistribution mechanism (mostly of the oil rent) between the regions. A healthy convergence, Natalia says, would be the one where economic activity, and especially small and medium-size private businesses, were much more equally distributed across some ninety subjects of the Russian Federation. She also had very interesting insights into the excessive "verticalization" of economic power and decision-making in Russia, and the economic growth of Moscow (much faster than of any other part of Russia) driven by centralization of that power, and concentration of large state-owned or state-influenced enterprises, as well as bureaucracy in Moscow.

But what most attracted my attention during Natalia's presentation at the Gaidar Forum was her description of the current period of low growth rates in Russia as *zastoi*, or stagnation. Now, *zastoi* has a very special political meaning in the Russian language because it was a disparaging term used in the Gorbachev era, and by Gorbachev himself, to define the Brezhnevite period of declining growth rates, lack of development perspectives, unchanging bureaucracy, and general demoralization and malaise.

But I asked Natalia the following question. Looking over the past 150 years of Russian history (and I think it is hard to go further back), were not really the best periods for ordinary people exactly the periods of *zastoi*: incomes rose by little for sure, but the state repression was weak, there were no wars, and if you look at violent deaths per capita per year, probably the lowest number of people died precisely during the periods of *zastoi*. So, perhaps *zastoi* was not so bad.

Natalia said, "I know I lived through the Brezhnevite period. Many people were demoralized; but I used it to study. I never read so many books and learned so much as then—you could do whatever you wanted because your actual job really did not matter much." (Even art, as I saw in the Tretyakovska Gallery, even if some of these paintings were never exhibited in the official museums, seems to have done well during the Brezhnevite *zastoi*. The recent film *Leto* appears to argue this indirectly as well.)

The best growth periods, as Natalia said, and as is generally accepted by economic historians, were the 1950s up to about 1963–1965, and then the period of the two first Putin's terms. In both cases, the growth spurs came as a ratchet effect to the previous set of disasters: in the Khrushchev period, to the apocalypse of the Second World War; in the Putin period, as a reaction to the Great Depression under Yeltsin during the early transition.

So, this then made us think a bit back into the past (say, going back to 1905) and put forward the following hypothesis: that Russian longer-term economic growth is cyclical. The cycle has three components. First a period of utter turbulence, disorder, war, and huge loss of income (and, in many cases, loss of lives as well), followed by a decade or so of efflorescence, recovery, and growth and, finally, by the period of "calcification" of whatever (or whoever) worked in that second period—thus producing the *zastoi* or stagnation.

I do not know if this is something specific to the Russian economic history. It made me think of Naipaul's observation on successful and unsuccessful countries. The history of the former consists of a number of challenges and setbacks indeed, but certain things are solved forever, and then new challenges appear. Take the United

GLOBALIZATION AND MULTI-POLAR WORLD

States: the Indian challenge and then the independence from Britain were not easy to overcome/acquire but, eventually, they were and they never came back; then the Civil War and the Emancipation; then the Great Society, etc. But unsuccessful countries, according to Naipaul (and he had, I think, Argentina in mind), always stay within the circular history. The same or similar events keep on repeating themselves forever, without any upward trend—and no single challenge is forever overcome. In each following cycle everything simply repeats itself.

(Published January 17, 2019)

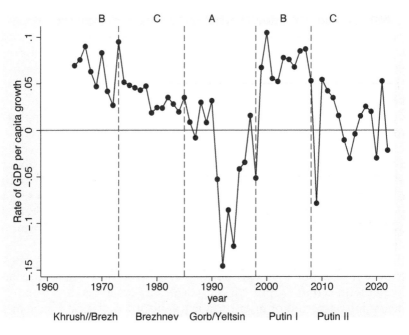

Figure 10.1 Growth rate of real GDP per capita, Russian Federation, 1962–2019

Note: The graph shows how real (inflation-adjusted) growth rate of per capita GDP has evolved in Russia under different leaders. The vertical axis displays the growth rate (0.1 means growth rate of 10% per capita per year; minus 0.1, growth rate of minus 10%) The figure illustrates the period of very strong income contraction (negative growth rates in the 1990s). A stands for depression and decline, B for recovery, C for *zastoi*.

RUSSIA

10.2 The lessons and implications of seizing Russian oligarchs' assets

The first and the most obvious lesson that we can draw from the confiscation of Russian oligarchs' assets is that the pre-February 24 Russia was not an oligarchy, as many believed, but an authoritarian autocracy. Instead of being ruled by a few rich people, it was ruled by one person. To draw this (rather obvious) conclusion, we need to go back to the initial rationale given for the threat of asset seizure. When the US government spoke of the seizure of oligarchs' assets, it was *before* the war and with the expectations that the oligarchs, faced with the prospect of losing most of their money, will exert pressure on Putin not to invade Ukraine. We can assume that 99 percent, or perhaps all, targeted oligarchs (and even those who feared possibly being targeted) realized the stakes and must have been against the war. But their influence was, as we know now, nil. So, ironically and perhaps paradoxically, they were punished not because they were powerful, but because they were *not*.

If their influence on such an important matter, on which their entire assets and lifestyle depended, was nil, then the system was clearly not a plutocracy, but a dictatorship. There is a distinction to be made between the early Russian billionaires who controlled the political system (one should not forget that it was Berezovsky who brought Putin to Yeltsin's attention because he thought that Putin could be easily manipulated), and the more recent billionaires who were treated as custodians of assets that the state may, by political decision, take from them at any point in time. It happened – unexpectedly—that it was not the Russian state that took their assets, but the American state. But it did so precisely because it thought that billionaires were "state oligarchs."

This is the lesson about the nature of the Russian political system. But what are the implications of the seizure of assets? There are, I believe, two kinds of implications: global and Russia-specific.

The global implication is that foreign plutocrats, who often moved their money from their own countries to the "safe havens" of the US, UK, and Europe will be much less sure that such decisions make sense. This applies in the most obvious way to the Chinese billionaires, who might experience the same fate as the Russian. But this may also apply to many others. The frequent use of economic and financial coercion means that if there are political issues between the West and (say) Nigeria or South Africa or Venezuela, the same

225

recipe will be applied to the billionaires from these countries, whether simply as a punishment or because of the expectation that they should influence the policy of their governments. Under such conditions, they would be very unwise to keep their money in places where it may be as insecure as in their own countries. We can thus expect the growth of other financial centers, perhaps in Gulf countries and India. Financial fragmentation would not be driven only by the fears of billionaires but by obvious fears of potential US adversaries like China that their governments' and central banks' assets may also prove to be just pieces of paper.

What are the likely implications for Russia? Here we have to take a longer-term view, and to look past the Putin regime. The conclusion that billionaires and people close to power will draw is the one that was drawn a few times in Russian/Soviet history only to be forgotten. Leaving aside the conflicts between boyars and the czar, consider similarities with what is happening presently with Stalin's regime. Stalin, too, was able, through skillful maneuvering, to move from being a "grey blur" (as characterized by Trotsky) to the position of complete power, including, in the last years of his rule, over the entire Politburo. Putin has not yet started executing people around him, but he has shown that politically they do not matter at all. The conclusion that the future Russian oligarchs (including the top figures in state-owned companies, those that used to be called "the red directors") will draw is the same that the Politburo members did: it is better to have a collective leadership where individual ambitions will be checked, rather than to let one person take the full power.

I think that the future oligarchs will realize that they can either stick together or hang together. Under Yeltsin, when they did dictate government policy, they preferred to fight each other, brought the country close to anarchy and even civil war, and, by doing so, facilitated the rise of Putin, who introduced some order.

Another implication is very similar to what I called the global implication. Again, it is useful to go back in time. When the original privatizations happened in Russia, the commonly used economic logic was: first, that it does not matter (for efficiency) who gets the assets because they would be outbid by better entrepreneurs; and second, everybody will have an incentive to fight for the rule of law simply to protect their gains. Communists will not be able to come back. The comparison was made with American "robber barons," who often became rich by dubious means, but had the interest to fight for the safety of property once they became rich. The expectation was that the Russian billionaires would do the same.

RUSSIA

These expectations were upended by billionaires' finding a (seemingly) much better way of making their money safe: move it to the West. Most of them did so and it seemed an excellent decision—all the way to February 24, 2022. The new post-Putin billionaires will probably not forget that lesson: so we may expect them to favor the creation of a true oligarchy, and to insist on the domestic rule of law—just because they will no longer have any place where to move their wealth.

(Published April 17, 2022)

10.3 The novelty of technologically regressive import substitution

In the next decade or so, the history of economic policy will be enriched by a new, never imagined, experiment: how to accomplish technologically regressive import substitution? This is the problem that Russia will have to face, and that is entirely new. To explain why it is new, consider first what is import substitution. It was originally, at the time of Alexander Hamilton and Friedrich List, a policy whose objective was the technological catch-up of less developed countries through the use of high-tariff barriers to enable local production of things that were previously imported. The policy was imitated by many other countries, including the Imperial Japan after the Meiji Restoration, and Czarist Russia under the Prime Minister Sergei Witte. Soviet industrial policies in the 1930s, and even after the Second World War, were also in the same mold. And, finally, domestic policies in Brazil and Turkey in the 1960s–1980s (among other countries) defined the meaning of import substitution for several generations of economists.

In all these cases, not surprisingly, the aim of policies was technological modernization. No one has ever tried to implement import-substitution policies with the objective of going backwards in the development chain. Neither would Russia, were she not under the pressure of Western economic sanctions. Why does it have to go backwards? The reason is that Russian "inclusion" in the world economy over the past thirty years has left the country fully dependent on foreign technologies, as Russia has specialized in the production of raw materials, food, and relatively unprocessed products. The industrial areas that are normally the backbone of traditional (predigital) development were well developed in the Soviet Union, but have been abandoned, left to deteriorate and, even if barely existing, are today technologically obsolete. Almost all of what is technologically advanced was produced, or was dependent in part, on Western-made technologies.

In the next decade Russia will try to revive these industries (e.g. machine building for petroleum and gas exploration, avionics, car production) on the basis of technologies that have been left rusting for thirty years. For sure, Russia would prefer to catch up with Boeing and Airbus, but an endeavor of that kind requires years and years of development, and tens of thousands of specialists. Instead, as the Russian Ministry of Transport's just published plan for the period up to 2030 envisages, in order to (re)create domestic aviation industry, Russia will have to go back to the Tupolev-like technologies and that of the rather unsuccessful Sukhoi Super Jet. Even if Russian regressive import substitution is successful in terms of output, which is very doubtful, as it projects the increase of production from eighteen domestic aircrafts in 2022 to almost 200 in 2030 (the rate of growth of 35% annually!), once the Russian market gets reopened and sanctions lifted, all that effort will be shown to have been in vain because the new and created-from-scratch Russian models would be less efficient than Western. Thus, in the year X when sanctions are removed, Russia will be, under the most optimistic scenario, in the same position that the USSR was in the 1980s: it will have an industrial base but that base will not be internationally competitive.

To further complicate matters of technologically regressive import substitution, we need to take into account the labor force. In past import substitution episodes, workers were relatively low-skilled and import substitution policies were supported by policies of improved education, in order to have workers able to "man" the new and more sophisticated machinery. In the Russian case now, the problem is exactly the reverse. Russia has a labor force that is highly educated and tends to move toward post-industrial areas, like that of other advanced economies. But here it would have to go down in its skills levels to be adequate for the operation or (re)creation of the technologically regressive import substitution. To put it in graphical terms: while the original import substitution required that semi-literate peasants learn a bit of arithmetic in order to "service" the machines, here we would expect software engineers to become metal-bashing workers, or foremen in large factories. This is because the demand for their (advanced) kind of skills will be reduced, as Russian economy is cut off from the global market, and domestically there will be few similarly advanced sectors that would employ them.

There will thus be a mismatch between the skill level of the labor force and the skill level technologically needed. Suppose that workers of high skill level (HW) are needed to work with highly sophisticated machines, say robots (HM). But if HM are unavailable, because previously they were all imported and they cannot be produced at home, the technological level of home-produced machines will be medium; call it MM. For MM however, one does not need HW workers but medium skilled workers MW. Thus, one needs to proceed to the de-skilling of highly skilled workers, or just simply to ignore their level of education and "allocate" them to the jobs for which they are over-qualified. It is hard to believe that workers would find such repositioning attractive, whether in terms of income, or challenge of, or interest in, the work they do.

From the economic point of view this forced experiment will be interesting to observe, since nothing similar in modern history has ever happened, but I do not think that it will very much fun for the participants.

(Published April 30, 2022)

10.4 Russia's economic prospects: The short-run

I will consider in two parts what seem to me to be the short-term and long-term prospects for the Russian economy (see Section 10.5 below).

I begin with the short term. It is based on the assumption that the shooting war in Ukraine ends within months (that is, that it does not continue at its current intensity for years) and that there are no drastic internal changes in Russia, in the form of a coup, revolution, etc.

To answer the question of the short-term effects, it is useful to go through some history, for which, unfortunately, Russia, thanks to its circular economic history (see above Section 10.1), provides several examples. The most calamitous declines in income in the past 100 years occurred during the later stages of the First World War and the ensuing Civil War, as well as during the transition to capitalism in the 1990s. (Enormous declines in GDP, and especially consumption, also happened during the Second World War but they are more difficult to interpret.)

Between 1917 and 1922, Russian GDP was halved (all numbers given here are in real terms, i.e. adjusted for inflation); the industrial output in 1921 was 18 percent of the pre-War level; the agricultural production was 62 percent of the pre-War level. (The data are from Kritsman, 1926, quoted in Pipes, 1990; and from Block 1976; see also chapter 1 of my *Income, Inequality and Poverty During the Transition from Planned Economy.*)

During the transition episode, Russian GDP per capita decreased between 1987 and 1995 by almost 40 percent. This was a much greater decline than that which the United States experienced during the Great Depression. The greatest one-year decline was in 1992 (16 percent), followed by the next two years of respectively 8 and 13 percent. (The data are from the World Bank.)

We can also take the third example of the 1998–1999 financial crisis and Russia's default on government debt. In 1998, Russian GDP went down by 5 percent. The financial crisis and the general disorder of 1998–1999 probably led Yeltsin to the realization that he could no longer control the Russian society and the economy: in a quick succession he appointed several prime ministers (all of them in one way or another linked to KGB—seemingly realizing that no one else could salvage the situation), and the rigmarole ended with Putin's appointment on December 31, 1999. This opened to Putin the venues of being elected president after Yeltsin's early resignation (Yeltsin's term would have normally ended in June 2001).

The 1920s civil war (obviously) and the transition were both greater economic shocks than the current one. The period of the early 1990s involved a wholesale change in the way enterprises functioned, the break-up of almost all economic ties with other Soviet republics, privatization, government's inability to implement policies, and corruption on an epic scale. Today's sanctions, however onerous for the economic activity, are unlikely to have the same impact in the short run. But they would certainly have much more of an impact than the 1998–1999 financial crisis. One can thus, very roughly, put the expected decline in 2022–2023 at high single digits, or low double digits: it is not going to be as sharp as in 1992, nor as (relatively) mild as in 1998.

It is of course unclear how the costs of the decline will be distributed. The Russian government has recently introduced a new, more favorable, indexation of pensions (30% of Russia's population are pensioners) but it is doubtful that, under the new conditions, it would be able to deliver that policy. The same is true for greater income-tested child benefits, voted in by the Duma. The withdrawal of many foreign firms, *de facto* embargo on a number of imports, and surely a decline in foreign and domestic investments, will increase unemployment. Currently, Russian unemployment is low, but it could go back to 7–8 percent or more, as it was in the 1990s. The Russian safety net is simply not institutionally nor financially strong enough to maintain these people's incomes at a reasonable level. The institutional weaknesses were revealed by the effects of covid: the total number of registered covid deaths was 360,000 and Russian excess deaths are, according to some estimates, among the highest in the world. One can compare these results with those of China, which had 4,600 registered covid-related deaths, i.e. about one percent of Russia's, with a population almost ten times as big as Russia's.

Inflation that will accompany the fall in the ruble will also affect the poorest the most. Although Russia's food prices may not increase as much as in food-importing countries, they will go up (domestic production in some areas not being able to compensate for lower imports, and foreign input costs increasing, due to the depreciation of the ruble). Sporadic shortages might develop, The news already report the run on a number of essential items, including the shortage of sugar. Faced with such unstable and volatile relative prices, under the condition of return of high inflation, the prudent policy would be to impose rationing for all essential items. In the Soviet Union, rationing was eliminated in 1952, and then briefly reintroduced for some goods in Russia during the early 1990s. It may have to be reintroduced, probably more broadly. The rationale of rationing is, of course, to protect the welfare (and even the survival) of the poorest classes, but it obviously blunts the incentives for producers. In the Soviet Union, this did not matter much, since production was based on planning, but in the Russia of today, incentives do matter.

Government policies, unveiled so far, whose objective is reduce the impact of sanctions, are very weak. To declare a temporary tax holiday for small and medium-sized enterprises makes sense in order to avoid massive layoffs, but it cannot be a medium-term policy. It obviously affects the budget, and also opens the way to what seems inevitable, namely a monetary expansion followed by inflation. As already mentioned, inflation was extraordinarily high in the early 1990s (the annual level was at three figures between 1992 and 1995) and also in 1999, when it reached 90 percent. It is hard to see how it may not return: already by February, the inflation was 10 percent on an annual basis. The March numbers will certainly be higher.

Another government measure aims to encourage repatriation of Russia's foreign investments. But why would people bring back to Russia money that, under the regime of capital controls that are already in place and will become stricter, will be impossible to move back abroad, if needed?

The problem is not that the government is making wrong policy choices; the problem is that, in the current situation, there are almost no good policy choices to make. The range of what the government can do is extremely limited, and is determined by foreign-policy decisions made by Putin (probably without any consultation of the economic ministries) and by foreign sanctions. Between the two, there is very little that any economic policy can do, other than be led by the events in becoming more and more restrictive, i.e. dirigiste. It is important to point out that the restrictiveness will be mostly forced by the events. Ideologically, the Russian government is technocratic and neoliberal. Putin himself had always had a neoliberal approach to the economy. The first day after the invasion of Ukraine, he called a meeting with the big business and promised them a "fully liberalized economy" (in actuality, practically asking them to do whatever they want). He, and probably they, might not have been at the time fully aware of the deleterious effects of sanctions. As that becomes increasingly clear, the field of decision-making for economic policy will be drastically reduced. It will no longer be the question whether one likes price controls or not: it will be a question of having massive

GLOBALIZATION AND MULTI-POLAR WORLD

riots without them. Thus restrictive policies will be dictated by the events. But, once adopted, they will be difficult to alter.

Another aspect should be also mentioned. Sanctions and any kinds of limitations always call for work-arounds. They are indeed possible: imports may be made from (say) Armenia and then resold in Russia; Russians abroad might share their credit cards with cousins at home, etc. But such "creative solutions" are expensive. People who engage in them take risks for which they have to be compensated. The Russian papers have already reported the emergence of "specu-lators," a term which hails back to a revolved era. The increase in prices due to clever work-arounds is not the only effect. A more socially pernicious one is the emergence of smuggling and crime networks that will control such schemes. This is the same as with drugs. Once a good is illegal, underpriced or difficult to obtain, it will be brought to the market, but at a high price, and by people who are willing to defy the law. The criminalization of the Russian society, which has gone on since the 1990s and that exploded under Yeltsin, will come back in force.

The coming years of Putin's rule will thus look very much like the worst years of Yeltsin's rule. Putin was brought out of the deep shadows with the idea that he would protect the gains of Yeltsin's family and the oligarchs, while reimposing some degree of internal stability. In his first two terms, he was successful in doing that. But at the end (or whatever the current point it is) of his reign, he brought all the original diseases back and made them in some sense worse because his foreign policies stuck the country in an impasse and closed off all the venues of escape.

In the next post I discuss the longer-term prospects.

(Published March 12, 2022)

10.5 Long term: Difficulties of import substitution and delocalization

When we look at Russia's long-term economic prospects, it is also useful to begin with some assumptions and to look at historical examples. We can make two assumptions.

First, that the current Russian regime, in one form or another, might continue for some ten to twenty years.

Second, we can assume that American and Western sanctions will continue throughout the entire period of say, fifty years that we consider here. The arguments for this are as follows. US sanctions once imposed are extraordinarily difficult to lift. As of today, there are already 6,000 various Western sanctions imposed against Russia (see *Novaya Gazeta* article referenced below), which is more than the sum of sanctions in existence against Iran, Syria, and North Korea put together. History shows that US sanctions can last almost without any time limit: sanctions on Cuba are more than sixty years old, on Iran, more than forty years old, and even the sanctions on the USSR (e.g. the Jackson–Vanik amendment) that were imposed for one reason, continued on the books during twenty years after the end of the USSR, even after the original reason that led to sanctions (Jewish migration) had entirely disappeared.

When the post-Putin government tries to have sanctions lifted, it will be faced by such a list of concessions that it would be politically impossible to satisfy. Thus, sanctions, perhaps not in exactly the same form, may be expected to last for the entire duration of what we call the long term here (fifty years).

It seems obvious, then, that Russian long-term economic policy will have to follow two objectives: import substitution, and the shift of the economic activity away from Europe toward Asia. While these objectives are, I think, clear, the realization will be extremely difficult.

As before, consider the historical precedents. Soviet industrialization can be seen as an attempt to substitute imports by creating a strong domestic industrial base. That process, however, was based on two elements that would be missing in Russia's future.

First, Soviet access to Western technology, which was at the origin of most large Soviet complexes like the Krivoy Rog in the Donbas, and the largest factory of tractors in the world in Tsaritsyn (later Stalingrad). The surplus, extracted through collectivization, and hunger and the death of millions, and even the gold taken from the Orthodox churches, was used to purchase Western technology. There

GLOBALIZATION AND MULTI-POLAR WORLD

was never any doubt among the Bolsheviks, from Lenin to Trotsky to Stalin to Bukharin, that for the USSR to develop it had to industrialize, and to do so it needs to import technology from the more developed countries. (That consciousness of relative underdevelopment of Russia was extremely strong among all Russian Marxists, who were all also modernizers.) The ability to import similarly advanced Western technology, which could provide the basis for downstream import substitution, will not exist under the regime of sanctions. Therefore, such technology would have to be invented locally.

There, however, there is a huge temporal break. Had anyone proposed that import substitution approach in 1990, it would have been difficult to implement but not impossible: the USSR (and Russia) had at that time a broad industrial base (production of airplanes, cars, white goods; largest world producer of steel, etc.). The sector was not internationally competitive but it could have been improved, and with right investments made competitive. But most of these industrial complexes have in the meantime been privatized and liquidated, and whatever was not is technologically obsolete. In the thirty years after the beginning of the "transition," Russia has not been able to develop any technologically advanced industry, except in the military area.

Take the example of passenger airplanes. In the 1970s, USSR was certainly ahead of Brazil, and even ahead of Europe, which only began developing Airbus in 1972. But that industry was destroyed during the transition, and the only remnant of it is Sukhoi Superjet, which is currently used by several Russian airline companies but has not been sold (almost) anywhere else in the world. In contrast, Brazilian Embraer operates in sixty countries.

Doing import substitutions in conditions where both the base of such substitution will have to be recreated and then new industries created without much (or any) input through investments from the more advanced parts of the world is almost impossible. This is the problem that China was able to solve only after a dramatic foreign-policy shift in the mid 1970s. But that option, by definition, will be unavailable to Russia.

The second factor underpinning Soviet industrialization was the increase in the labor force. It came from the supply of surplus agricultural labor, increased overall population and, very importantly, from the improving level of education. The USSR in the 1930s used to produce annually hundreds of thousands of various types of engineers, scientists, doctors, etc. None of these elements will hold in the next half-century. The Russian population is urbanized, shrinking

236

in size, and well-educated. Hence, gains cannot come from any of the three sources that were used in the 1930s.

Of course, a highly educated labor force is a plus. But that labor, in order to produce its maximum, needs also to work with top technology. If top technology is unavailable (for the reasons explained above), highly educated labor will be wasted. Due to the shrinking population, even the overall pool of such labor will be smaller every year. Since it will not find adequate use and adequate pay in Russia, it will tend to emigrate, thus further shrinking the available number of highly skilled workers. It is not impossible that Russia might return to the Soviet policy of not allowing free migration—now under the pressure of economic factors. It was precisely the outflow of highly qualified workers that led East Germany to erect the Berlin Wall.

We can thus conclude that all factors that made import substitution feasible in the 1930s and 1950s in the Soviet Union will not work in tomorrow's Russia.

What are the prospects of shifting the gravity of the economic life from West to East? Technically, one can imagine a new type of "Peter the Great" move, where Russia does not open a window on Europe (what St. Petersburg was supposed to be) but a window on East Asia, by, for example, moving its capital to Vladivostok and trying to shift as much as possible of economic and bureaucratic life, together with the population, to the East. If things could be moved by a decree, such a shift could even arguably be seen as quite reasonable. East Asia is, and will remain, the fastest growing part of the world. Leaving Europe, which in many ways is also a declining continent, could be seen as a right move. Russia is, with the United States, the only country in the world that can make such a radical move; for others, geography is much more of a destiny. Politically too, Russia is unlikely to be exposed to sanctions and political pressures by China, India, Vietnam, or Indonesia in the same way as it is by the UK, France, and Germany. Finally, a Pacific vocation could be seen as a replay of the American thrust to open the new frontier a century and half ago. Climate change might also help by making the Northern Russian territories more habitable.

How feasible is such a change? It would require massive investments in infrastructure, including much better communication between the two far-flung parts of Russia: the flight from Moscow to Vladivostok takes almost ten hours and the train ride more than a week. Developing new cities along the way, expanding the existing ones, etc. does not only require investments that a shrinking Russian economy cannot provide; it would also require the creation of new jobs in such cities, which would be the only thing that could attract the population to move from European to Asian Russia. The Soviet Union tried to do so by opening many Northern outposts in Siberia and paying workers higher salaries to move there. It did have some limited success. However, these towns and settlements have almost all died in the past thirty years. It is difficult to see how such a massive shift of activity can be accomplished without huge investments and, indeed, some comprehensive urban and production planning.

Both policies, namely import substitution and shift toward the East, will therefore meet with almost insuperable obstacles. It does not mean that they cannot be undertaken; some of them will be done, by necessity: Russian softwares will have to be produced to replace the 95 percent of Western-origin software that is currently used in automated Russian plants (Russian newspaper sources). Closer economic ties with China would also imply some movement East of companies and people. A Siberian or a Pacific city can become the second capital (as Ankara did in Turkey). But a significant success in either of these two domains seems—the best that can be seen from today's perspective—simply unreachable.

So, what happens next? As I mentioned several years ago in the introduction to the translation of my *Global Inequality* in Russian, the future of the Eurasian continent looks very much like its past: the maritime areas along the Atlantic and the Pacific coasts will be fairly rich, much better-off than the significant large continental areas in the middle. This opens up the question of how politically viable such an uneven distribution of economic activity would be: will migrations, or political reconfigurations, "solve" such disequilibria?

(Published March 12, 2022)

RUSSIA

10.6 What if Putin's true goals are different?

By any standard indicator that measures achievements by the extent to which the stated objectives have been realized, Russia's war against Ukraine has been a failure. Ukraine is much more militarized than ever; it is probably one of the most militarized countries in the world right now; Russia's security has markedly deteriorated; NATO has not returned to its 1997 positions, but has further advanced and become much more consolidated. The West is stronger than before. So, is Putin failing?

Perhaps. Or perhaps not. For suppose that the real objectives of the "special military operation" were not the announced ones, but very different.

Sovereignty vs. income. To see what they might be, I have to go back to my October 1996 paper, published as a World Bank Working Paper, and later in an edited volume, which I also discussed here (see Section 2.6). The paper is pretty complex because it deals with economic and political forces that lead countries to create unions and conglomerates, or to prefer secession, but its core model is simple. It is as follows. Countries (and their leaders) aspire to two goods: sovereignty and wealth. Sovereignty means freedom to make political and economic decisions as little constrained by other countries as possible; wealth means having high income level (high GDP per capita). Now, the problem is that there is a trade-off between these two objectives. Countries can become rich only if they become less sovereign, that is, more globally integrated. To be rich requires trading, developing technology jointly with others, sending people abroad to learn new skills, consulting with, and even hiring foreigners. All of this implies much greater interdependence between the economies and observance of international norms and rules regarding trade, intellectual property rights, domestic economic policies, convertibility of currencies, and the like.

To fix the ideas take the two extreme examples of North Korea and Belgium. North Korea is practically unconstrained in its economic and political decision-making: it can make nukes because it is not a signatory to the non-proliferation treaty; it can impose tariffs or ban imports of goods as it likes; it can print as much or as little money as it wants because its currency is not exchangeable for any other, etc. But, for all these reasons, it is also very poor. On the other end of the spectrum is Belgium, which does not have its own currency, whose fiscal policy is hemmed in by the EU rules (the Maastricht

239

treaty), trade determined by the EU and WTO (Krugman: "Europe's 1992 is not so much a trade agreement as an agreement to coordinate policies that have historically been regarded as domestic"; cited in my 1996 working paper, see below), foreign policy decided by the EU, and military engagement by NATO. In terms of domestic policy, autonomy, or sovereignty, it practically has none. But it is rich.

Other countries are aligned along the different points of the sovereignty–income trade-off. The size of the country will also matter: the US enjoys more sovereignty for a given level of income because it is a big country: it issues a reserve currency, it is the main actor in a number of trade negotiations, it leads NATO, etc. But it will not be immune to the trade-off. Consider Trump's decision to start the trade war with China. It gave greater political space to the US (including the very ability to impose new tariffs), but it probably reduced its income.

Russian isolationism. Now, with this idea of a trade-off between these two desirable things, let's go back to Putin and his group of advisers from the power ministries. Suppose that they came to the following conclusion: Russia's attempts to Westernize since Peter the Great have been a failure. Russia failed to catch up with the West prior to 1917, it then it adopted an extreme Westernizing doctrine that diminished Russia by giving independence outright to Finland, Poland, etc., and then proclaimed equality of nations and self-determination, all of which ultimately led to the break up of the country in 1992. Afterwards, it adopted liberalism, also imported from the West, whose results were the dramatic impoverishment of the population, increased mortality and suicides, and the astounding stealing of assets created by the millions of Russian citizens. During that period, Russia lost its ability to decide alone on its policies: it blindly followed the West. It offered its military bases in Kyrgyzstan to the US; it got nothing in return; it acquiesced to limited expansion of NATO, but was treated to an expansion up to its borders; it joined various European bodies, only to be criticized by them; it privatized its economy, as Western experts suggested, but all the money went abroad. Thus, in order to regain its economic and political autonomy, it needs to break decisively with the West. It needs to become an independent Eurasian power, whose interaction with Europe will be limited to the necessary minimum. Eventually, Russia has to move in the direction opposite from the one charted by Peter the Great in the early eighteenth century.

West builds the Iron Curtain. Such increase in sovereignty would lead to lower income. But the problem is: neither the break with

Europe, if announced by the leaders, nor lower income, would be welcomed by the population. Russian government cannot thus, on its own, begin to create a new Iron Curtain. But, what if the Iron Curtain were built by the West against Russia, as a punishment for something that, from the Russian point of view, could be considered an entirely justified policy? Enter Ukraine. Reconquista, in some ways, was always popular among the Russian public. But the West will not see it as such but will impose sanctions and pile up costs on Russia. The West would, by its own will, cut Russia off from Europe. It would build a new, impenetrable Iron Curtain. The objective of detaching Russia from the West—desired under this scenario by the Russian leadership—will be achieved not by the Russian leadership, but by the West. The Russian leaders will not be seen by its population (or at least not by the majority of the population) as being responsible for undoing Peter the Great's dream. On the contrary, the West will be seen as unwilling to accept Russia as an equal partner, and Russia hence will have no option but to become a Eurasian power, fully sovereign, untrammelled by treaties and rules, and free of the Western ideologies of Marxism and liberalism.

The new Brest–Litovsk. But, in the longer-run—the leaders might fear—would not people, having realized that the greater sovereignty comes with lower income, try to find some accommodation with the West? How to avoid this? How to make the rupture permanent? The only way to do so is to make the costs of returning to the West extraordinarily high. That is, to make sure that, when the first feelers of reconciliations are sent by the post-Putin governments, the bill submitted by the West will be so high that most of the Russian policy-making elite and the public opinion will reject it out of hand. Think of another Brest–Litovsk, but this time without Lenin, who put all his power and authority on balance to have it accepted. The new Brest–Litovsk may include not only the withdrawal of all Russian forces from the Ukraine, and the return of Crimea to Ukraine; it might include reparations, extradition of officers responsible for war crimes, reduction in the size of the army, limits to military exercises, even possibly control of Russia's nuclear program. Thus, the Putin government has an incentive to make the West pile up demand upon demand from which it will have a hard time climbing down. For only such extensive and even unreasonable demands will ensure that they are rejected by the successor Russian governments, and that the anti-Petrine policy favored by Putin and his entourage will remain in force for a very long time.

GLOBALIZATION AND MULTI-POLAR WORLD

This does not mean that the current government is totally indifferent to the cost of sanctions. But it will accept increased sanctions so long as the income cost of new sanctions is less than the gain in sovereignty. At some point, it will decide that the trade-off had gone far enough, and at that point it will negotiate. But before it does so it will make sure that it has gained sufficiently, and for a long time, in the ability to decide on its policies independently.

The implication of this way of seeing the Russian objectives is that sanctions and decoupling between the West and Russia are no longer seen only as costs that Russia is paying but, rather, as the West doing what the current leadership believes is in the fundamental long-term interest of Russia: breaking off all links between Russia and the West, and thus freeing Russia to follow its own course.

(Published June 2, 2022)

— PART IV —

HISTORY

— 11 —

ECONOMIC HISTORY

11.1 Byzantium: Economic reflections on the Fall of Constantinople

This Sunday, May 29, marks the anniversary of the Fall of Constantinople in 1453. I have recently been reading (and in some cases, rereading) books on the last period of Constantinople, after the reprieve of 1402, brought about by the Ottoman defeat by Tamerlane, and how and why this period was not better used. But, thinking of Roman Empire and of what is called (somewhat inaccurately) Eastern Roman Empire, led me to two, I hope interesting, observations.

First, why did the Industrial Revolution not happen in the Eastern Roman Empire? Asking this question is going back to the famous query posed by Michael Rostovtzeff in the 1920s: "Why was there a detour of some ten centuries; why did not seemingly modern-looking market institutions of Rome produce at least a Lombardy-like economic development, not in the fourteenth but in the fourth century?" There are many answers to that question. From those who emphasize external factors like the "barbarians at the gate" to those who, like Rostovtzeff himself, believe that the weakening and the break-down of the Empire came because of its inability to incorporate lower classes and because of the "dead hand" of a rising military bureaucracy; to those like Marx and Aldo Schiavone and Bob Allen who believe that the culprit was slavery: cheap labor that provided no incentive for the use of labor-saving machines that technically could have been developed. Finally, there are those who in the debate between "modernists" and "primitivisms" thought, like Moses Finlay and Karl Polanyi, that Roman

245

HISTORY

institutions did not contain at all the seeds that could have led to capitalist development.

Where does Eastern Empire come into that discussion? It seems to me that the most appropriate answer to Rostovtzeff's question would be to look to the "country" about which he posed the question: the country that was the continuation of the Roman Empire, nay that *was* the Roman Empire itself (Constantinople had become the capital in 330 AD, some eighty years before the first sack of Rome) and that lasted for another 800 to 900 years with no interruption. (That is, if we want to date the end of the Roman Empire to 1204 when Byzantium was conquered by the Crusaders.)

Wasn't there enough time to find out if ancient institutions could become capitalistic? Eight or nine centuries seems plenty. Moreover, what culturally and institutionally better place to develop than the Eastern Empire: direct continuator of the larger Roman whole, with an educated elite, same institutions, stable currency (solidus, "the dollar of the Middle Ages"), reasonable protection of property rights, people knowledgeable in Greek and Latin, and thus able to read everything from Herodotus to Columella's agricultural treatises without the intermediation of translation, with Roman laws codified and simplified by Justinian. Why did not there develop "bourgeois virtues," "inclusive institutions," Landes' "culture"? Or does it all have to do with "serendipity," of having coal and expensive labor (Pomeranz)? Yet, despite all of these advantages, no one reading the history of the Eastern Roman Empire would come thinking that there was almost any chance of it developing in the capitalistic direction. It was as feudalistic as they come.

I do not know why a market economy with wage labor failed to developed there and can only speculate that it might have been because of a militarized bureaucracy, land magnates (and thus high inequality), obsession with Christian theology, which sucked the best minds into sterile disputes (it would be nice to have an anti-Christian like Gibbon tell us why the Eastern Empire could not become a capitalistic power!), its frequent wars with Arabs, Persians, Russians, Normans, Bulgars, Pechinegs, Avars, Ottomans ... Any other candidate explanations?

There is plenty of recent scholarly work on why China failed to become capitalist and start the Industrial Revolution (for an excellent discussion see Peer Vries' *Escaping Poverty*, and especially the chapter entitled "Why it does not make sense to call Qing China capitalist ..."), but it seems to me that equally revealing and rewarding would be to study why the Eastern Roman Empire, seemingly full of all the

246

ECONOMIC HISTORY

necessary prerequisites, failed to do so. The ingredients were present in both China and Eastern Rome, but in neither case did development occur: why?

The second observation has to do with trade and war. The reading of Eastern Mediterranean history is extremely instructive for a way in which we should think of trade. A benevolent approach, starting with Ricardo, always regarded trade as an activity freely undertaken by two parties with no extra-economic compulsion. No reader of history of the Eastern Roman Empire can share that view. Trade and military underpinning of it went hand-in-hand. This is at its most obvious not in large empires, which anyway had to have armies, but in trading city-states like Venice and Genoa. If you believe that trade is all about peace, there would be no reason why these city-states had to maintain large naval fleets, fight battles, conquer islands, negotiate, under military threat, special rights to tariff-free imports and exports. Trade, debt, and the army always moved together. No tourist to any Greek island today will fail to observe large Venetian and Genoan fortresses, which could not have been built without money and labor, but also without a naval presence that allowed the control or conquest of the islands in the first place.

When the Fourth crusade started, the first city to have been sacked by the Crusaders was the Christian port-city of Zara (today's Zadar in Croatia), a rival to Venice. The doge paid the Crusaders to start their path of destruction with a city populated by their co-religionaries. The association between trade and war, which continued throughout the rest of history, and certainly throughout the nineteenth century, helps us have a much more clear-eyed view about colonialism too. As said by a Dutch Proconsul in Batavia in a letter written to the directors of the Dutch East India Company:

> Your Honors should know by experience that trade in Asia must be driven and maintained under the protection of Your Honors' own weapons, and that the weapons must be paid for by the profits from the trade, so that we cannot carry on trade without war nor war without trade. (Jan Pieterszoon Coen, Dutch East India Company Proconsul in Batavia, to the board of directors of the company, December 27, 1614; quoted in Landes' *Wealth and Poverty of Nations*)

Trade followed the flag in Africa and Asia (Leif Wenar and I wrote an article on that, criticizing Rawls' rather quick acceptance of the "doux commerce" view of trade). "The unequal treaties" with China would be unimaginable without European military superiority and

247

the threat it implied; the Opium War—another example of the close association between the two—was won by arms. The road to free trade, that time in narcotics, was cleared by gunboats and rifles. "Free trade" came to India and Africa "out of the barrel of a gun."

Trade, helped by arms, was often at the origin of the fortunes, which grew further by monopolistic or monopsonistic practices, lending, or usury, or, in some cases, through entrepreneurship. The origin of fortunes was thus often extra-economic. But, that need for military power, if one wishes to trade and be rich, is best seen in the example of trading city-states that, in a world without coercion and ruled by benevolent comparative advantage, would not require fleets, cannons, and mercenaries.

(Published May 26, 2016)

ECONOMIC HISTORY

11.2 Global poverty over the long term: Legitimate issues

I became somewhat peripherally involved in the debate on long-term trends in global poverty that is raging these days in the WebSphere, prompted first by some very strong claims by Steven Pinker and Bill Gates, summarized by Jerry Coyne, followed by an equally strong rebuttal by Jason Hickel.

Max Roser, whose work is to be strongly commended became somewhat of a lateral casualty in this debate; it was his graph (based essentially on the work of Martin Ravallion and the World Bank) that Pinker and Gates quoted, and with which Hickel disagreed. Joe Hassel and Max Roser have now written a detailed explanation of the data they used to create the graph and how others (and themselves) have calculated global poverty over the long term. So, to be clear, I find Martin's and Max's work absolutely crucial and indispensable for the understanding of long-term trends in this and a number of other dimensions. But I disagree with the excessively political and strident tone in which this work has been promoted by Steven Pinker (and more recently by Bill Gates) and their disregard of many caveats, which come with some of these numbers.

There are (in my opinion) at least four such caveats that Hickel rightly brings out explicitly. (He uses other arguments too, but I do not comment on them.)

First, Angus Maddison's and Maddison-project data, which are the only game in town for both global poverty and global inequality and which I also use in my work, do tend, like all GDP calculations, to overestimate the increase in real income, where there is a transition from activities that are not commodified to the same activities becoming commodified. GDP, as is well known, is geared to measure mostly monetized activity. At the time of industrialization, as well as today during the ICT revolution, such underestimation is likely to be significant. It is odd that people today would question this—while we are going through a similar period of increased commodification and a rising share of activities, which are now marketable but hitherto were not. Until Airbnb and Uber came along, your hosting friends of friends or driving them to the airport was not part of GDP. Nowadays, it is because you will be paid for such services. (The same is true for home activities that used to be performed without monetary compensation mostly by women—and which, at some point, become commercialized.)

Even more dramatic were, as Hickel points out, the changes that occurred during the Industrial Revolution. Many activities performed

249

HISTORY

within households became monetized, while people were often physically chased away from, or disposed of, land, water, and other rights that they enjoyed for free. I do not need to go into too many examples here—just take the enclosures, or the land dispossession of Africans. This was not solely a transfer of wealth, but seriously reduced income of those who had the right to the *usus fructus* of land, water, or other resources. Their reduced access to the actual goods and services was not recorded in any income statistics, meaning that the previous income from such activities was ignored. It is thus reasonable to think that both GDP growth rates and the decline in poverty were overestimated.

Second, income distribution data for the nineteenth century, which we all use, come almost entirely from the 2002 seminal paper by François Bourguignon and Christian Morrisson (B–M). There are two more recent papers, one by van Zanden, Baten, Foldvari and van Leeuwen and one by myself that used a somewhat different methodology (that is, more diversified sources) in order to check the robustness of B–M findings. Both conclude that B–M results stand, but in both papers (van Zanden et al., and Milanovic) the number and/or reliability of these new sources are extremely limited. (I use social tables to estimate countries' distributions in the nineteenth century. But the number of social tables that we have is very limited; both in terms of country and temporal coverage.)

Furthermore, Morrisson's original distributions, while made available by the author, are unsourced. So, one cannot tell if they are right or wrong. In addition, even if individual country distributions were right, many of them are made to represent a vast variety of other countries' distributions too (say, Colombia, Peru, and Venezuela; or Côte d'Ivoire, Ghana, and Kenya; or "45 Asian countries"; or "37 African countries"). B–M divide the world into 33 "regions" or "blocs," with identical distribution for all countries within the bloc simply because information from most of countries is lacking. Note that it also means that the evolution in time of each country's distribution is the same as the rest of the bloc.

Fragility of such distributions has a particularly strong effect on poverty numbers. It affects inequality somewhat less because, from other (fragmentary) sources we know what are the ranges within which inequality moves. But we know that less for poverty. The bottom line is that income distributions for the nineteenth century are, to put it mildly, fragile.

Third, Hickel questions the use of $PPP1.90 absolute poverty line. There is a huge debate on this, and I will not enter it—but it suffices

250

to look at the critiques made by Thomas Pogge and Sanjay Reddy (regarding the underestimation of the price level faced by the poor), a large degree of arbitrariness with which the poverty line of, at first $PPP1, and now $PPP1.90, was drawn (see e.g. Angus Deaton), or, more recently, the methodological questioning of the World Bank approach by Bob Allen. Hickel simply mentions these issues. They are real and they should not be ignored.

Fourth, Hickel makes a more philosophical point that economists (unlike, say, anthropologists or historians) are less well-equipped to deal with: human costs of the Industrial Revolution, from England to the forced labor (and probably ten million dead) in the Congo and Java, to Bengal famine (more than ten million dead) to the Soviet collectivization (more than five million dead) and China's Great Leap Forward (about twenty million dead). The dead enter our calculations only to the extent that their deaths affect the estimated life expectancy. (And in the B–M paper there is an attempt to calculate global inequality over the past two centuries, taking into account also changes in life expectancy.) But, otherwise, so far as poverty calculations are concerned, the deaths have the perverse effect of reducing the population and increasing per capita output (since the marginal output of those who die as forced laborers or from famine is zero or close to zero). Jason is right to bring up this point.

The effect of this last point is ambiguous though. While it would— were we somehow able to account for it—increase the costs of industrialization and make the gains, compared to the pre-industrialization era, less, it would on the other hand improve the relative position of the present with respect to the era of industrialization— simply because such massive famines do not occur today, or occur less frequently (e.g. North Korea, and before that in Ethiopia).

To conclude. In my opinion, Jason Hickel had brought up several valid issues that most economists acknowledge as well (and have actually frequently written about). However, others, once a graph is created, tend to use the results less scrupulously or carefully in order to make political points. This is why bringing these issues to the fore is valuable and should be encouraged—and not shot down.

(Published February 6, 2019)

HISTORY

11.3 On Eurocentrism in economics

Sebastian Conrad's book *What is Global History?* is in many ways important for economists and economic historians. This is not only because Conrad illustrates the way in which global studies differ from other ways of looking at the world (modernization theory, world-systems theory, post-colonial studies), but also because he takes many examples from economics.

The problem of Eurocentrism, defined by Conrad as "Europe/ the West ... seen as the locus of innovation, and world history ... understood as a history of diffusion of European progress" (p. 74), is especially acute in economics because the very notions of "modernity," "economic growth," "welfare," emerged in Europe, were propagated by European thinkers, and were later adopted by thinkers from other regions of the world. What passes for global economic history is thus often a teleology that sees the non-European "peripheral" regions as retracing the steps through which the "core," i.e. Western countries, have already passed. This is, rather obviously, true of the main variant of Marxism and of modernization theory, and perhaps even of the world-systems theory (projection of the economic dominance of Europe and the US in the twentieth century back to the sixteenth, according to Conrad).

This is also true of economic histories that, in their standard format, begin either with colonization and "the discovery" of the Americas, or with the Industrial Revolution. "Interaction" or "connectivity" in these histories means simply, as Conrad writes, interaction with the West, almost never interaction between non-Western parts of the world (e.g. India with Malaya and East Africa, China with South Asia). Some are almost caricaturally Western-centric: David Landes' (*The Wealth and Poverty of Nations*), or Daron Acemoglu's and James Robinson's (*Why Nations Fail*) who, as Peer Vries writes in *Escaping Poverty*, present "a stylized generalization of a very specific, positive interpretation of the modern history of Great Britain and the USA" and simply reproduce "all the clichés when it comes to Asian institutions."

But it is also true of books like *Global Economic History: A Very Short Introduction* by Robert Allen. This is an excellent book, but its approach is very standard: it begins with the Industrial Revolution, England, and Western Europe, moves to the Americas only as the United States becomes an economic powerhouse, then introduces Meiji Japan, Czarist and Soviet Russia, and finally China. Now, Allen

252

ECONOMIC HISTORY

can sensibly defend his approach by arguing that it does not privilege Europe (or the West) as such but that it simply retraces economic development measured by an objective criterion: how much above the subsistence is the average income of a society? This is a general standard, and we go following that standard wherever it takes us. This is a good defense that can be made also with regard to such classics as Colin Clark's *The Conditions of Economic Progress*, Angus Madison's *Contours* ... or Paul Bairoch's *Victoires and déboires*—all of them, in my opinion, brilliant works of *global* economic history.

However, one could also argue that the seemingly objective criterion that is being used (had the society overcome the level of physiological subsistence for its members) is itself Eurocentric, insofar as the objective of economic growth was born with economic growth itself. The yardstick that we claim to be universal is, on the contrary, a product of a specific era—the Age of Enlightenment and the European Industrial Revolution. Both of them are local or, at best, regional events. There is no reason why we should take economic growth as the organizing principle to study economic history. We could, it may be argued, equally validly take social stability, or the caste-like inheritance of division of labor, or sedentary-nomadic division as key economic principles, and write a book on global economic history from one of these perspectives.

It does seem to me that the latter perspectives are deficient compared to the "desirable" objective of overcoming the niggardliness of nature and generating greater wealth. But, I cannot reject the notion that I hold that the organizing principle of a good book on global economic history should be a study of economic growth because I have learned that by privileging one way of looking at economics. We are back to the beginning, where the "I" is simply the reflection of the dominant narrative. There is nothing independent there: if the narrative were different, the "I" would have been different.

How should we then write economic history or history of economic thought? For economics, which is so intimately connected with Eurocentrism, the question is exceedingly difficult to answer. One way would be, as Conrad mentions, to do comparative history (à la Pomeranz), another would be to take more seriously postcolonial studies—even if they, as Conrad I think rightly argues, tend to degenerate into cultural essentialism. Integration of studies of slavery and serfdom is perhaps a good way for economic history to move toward becoming "global." This is because slavery and serfdom are global phenomena that long predate capitalism and Western exceptionalism. In fact, when I think of all the global economic history works mentioned in this post, I cannot see any of them integrating or paying sufficient attention to the unfree labor.

The approach we should avoid is to pay lip-service to non-Western thinkers by including one or two sentences from their work without any analysis or contextualization. I have seen this done in recent histories of economic phenomena: it is now *de rigueur* to quote a couple of non-Western authors, mostly (I would guess) by grabbing a few sentences from a Wikipedia entry. It makes a mockery of the entire idea, but it does (formally) satisfy the thought police who look at the "diversity" requirement as a purely quantitative target: are there quotes from a sufficiently diverse crowd of authors? (On the other hand, a good example of real substantive engagement with non-Western thinkers is Pankaj Mishra's *From the Ruins of Empire*.)

Perhaps it is the case that global economic histories will remain difficult to write unless they are organized around a single overarching *topic*; for example, global economic history of gender inequality (as Alice Evans is writing now), or global history of capitalism or socialism. Writing global economic history could thus be organized around the non-spatial and long-term (perhaps beyond Braudel's long durée) ideological constructs. It would fragment global economic history, but the alternatives would be either to continue with the standard Western-centric narratives, or be reduced to thoughtless listing of economic facts around the globe and over time. Still, even so, we would have difficulty including, without doing violence to the approach, the recent emergence of China as a global economic power. It is hard to place under any of these headings.

(Published July 27, 2021)

ECONOMIC HISTORY

11.4 Net economic output in history: Why we work

Physiocrats. It is well known in the history of economic thought that the founders of political economy, the Physiocrats, and Quesnay in particular, thought that only agriculture is productive and manufacturing is "sterile." Their use of the word "sterile," and insistence on it, is unfortunate because the reality of what they argued is more sensible and sophisticated.

What they meant by "sterility" of manufacturing is that the price of manufactured goods decomposes into depreciation of capital, subsistence wage, "normal" return to the capitalist (which they, rather generously, assumed to be 10% per year), and even "recompense" for entrepreneurship. So, why is it different from what economists believe today? In effect we use exactly the same components. But for the Physiocrats there was no surplus (on top of these four components, which they saw as simple inputs) that could be taxed to provide income for the elite: the people who do not directly participate in the process of production, namely landlords, clergy, and government officials.

In a certain way, it was quite sensible: one cannot tax subsistence wages, nor can one tax profit that is at a "normal" rate, if he believes that driving it below that rate will result in no production being undertaken at all. However, absence of surplus in manufacturing was at odds with what was observed in France at the time. As Georges Weulersse, the author of the most detailed analysis of physiocracy, explains, large fortunes—by definition made of accumulated surpluses—existed in manufacturing. Yet, Physiocrats stubbornly refused to admit that, and argued that these fortunes existed only because of special protection given to individual industrialists. Manufacturing, they held, could not produce surplus on its own without state protection.

It was only in agriculture that there existed a surplus that could be taxed: ground rent. For, in agriculture, price decomposes into depreciation, return to capital advanced by the tenant-farmer, entrepreneurial profit, subsistence wages paid to the hired labor and ... the rent. Rent is not an income necessary to bring forth output. It is (as the nice formula has it) price-determined, not price-determining. It is the only net income that can be taxed and used to maintain a civilized society, which needs government for the protection of property and administration of justice, and clergy for the provision of spiritual sustenance.

255

HISTORY

Physiocrats, quite consistently with this view, argued in favor of policies that would raise agricultural production through longer land-leases (so that tenant farmers have incentive to invest in land improvement), freedom of movement of grain (laissez-passer) and freedom of exports. Such measures would increase both the quantity of agricultural output and the relative price of food, and therefore doubly yield a greater net product, the goal of economic activity as defined by them.

This is, in essence, the logic behind the view that only agriculture is productive, which, without looking at it more closely, seems strange to the modern ear. But thinking of it, poses the all-important question: what is net income? There is no general answer to that question. It depends on what the social structure is, and what is the goal of economic activity. Incomes that Physiocrats disregarded, i.e. wages, depreciation, interest, and entrepreneurial profit, are all parts of the gross value added as presently defined. Their and our components were not different. It is just that they were not interested in the components, like wages, that appear to us to be a valuable goal of economic activity.

SNA and online work. And, indeed, the same questions regarding the definition of gross value added are discussed today: how should GDP account for the use of exhaustible resources, or should it include net income from financial services and insurance? (For a nice book on GDP measurement, see Diane Coyle's *GDP: A Brief, but Affectionate History*; for a critical review of the book see Moshe Syrquin's long essay in the *Journal of Economic Literature*.) When the System of National accounts (SNA) and GDP in its more-or-less current version were defined, Simon Kuznets thought that transportation services should be considered an intermediate good and not included in value added. This was not accepted even if Kuznets' logic was impeccable: if you use bus, metro, or your own car, to go to work, depreciation of the car and the expense of gas, etc. have to be deducted from your wage. Travelling to work is a means, not a goal. Kuznets' argument reappears rather unexpectedly today with the "explosion" of online work during and after the pandemic. Online work reduces the travel cost but, since we have decided that transportation to and from workplace should be counted as value added, less of commuting traffic lowers GDP. We thus have a paradoxical situation that what is clearly an improvement in the welfare of workers is counted as a reduction of GDP.

Output of goods only. There was a very important difference between the System of National Accounts and the System of Material

Balances (SMB) used in centrally planned economies. The difference was due to what was considered to be the goal of economic activity. SMB excludes all activities that result in non-material output: government administration, education, and health services. Gross output in centrally planned economies was thus systematically lower than when expressed in the SNA. The difference was estimated at between 10 and 15 percent, and in some cases even 20 percent.

On the other hand, given that productivity growth is slower in education and health than in the production of material goods, underestimation of gross output in socialist countries was combined with an overestimation of the rate of growth. We thus had, judged from the standpoint of SNA, two opposite biases in centrally planned economies: lower level of output, but its higher rate of growth.

Surplus value. The SMB claimed to have been based on Marx's view of productive labor, but this is not obvious because we do not know what exactly was seen by Marx to be the goal of economic activity in socialism. Marx believed that "productivity" (and thus the goal) is a historic concept, defined from a systemic point of view. In a capitalist system, productive is the worker who produces surplus value for the capitalist. This is the origin of Marx's famous example of an opera singer, who is a productive worker if he is hired by a capitalist, but not when he works for himself. Productivity of labor is not, according to Marx, deduced from labor being embodied in goods as opposed to services but from labor's contribution to what is the goal of economic activity in a given system. Under capitalism, it is profit. So, if the opera singer generates profit for the impresario who employed him, he is a productive worker. Similarly, if the goal was to provide net income for the elite, as Physiocrats thought, and if the only source from which this can be extracted is agriculture, the correctly defined net product is indeed as they defined it.

What we call value added or useful output in one system is not necessarily the same as what we call useful output in the other. It depends on what the ruling ideology tells us is the reason why we engage in economic activity at all.

(Published March 12, 2023)

HISTORY

11.5 Capital as a historical concept

In a recent thesis written by Mauricio de Rosa, the last chapter is dedicated to the discussion of what is capital in Marxist and neoclassical worlds. Mauricio very carefully translates Marx's concepts of constant and variable capital into national accounts that we use now, and distinguishes Marx's rate of profit from the neoclassical rate of return. (I am sitting on his dissertation committee and cannot say anything more.)

That chapter made me think (again) of the definition of capital. In the neoclassical world, capital is the sum of values of productive and financial assets. Because capital is extremely heterogeneous, we cannot express it in physical, but only in value terms. This has led to the Cambridge Controversy, which petered out but was never resolved. In our usual work on wealth inequality, we also add the value of non-productive assets like jewelry, paintings, etc. And, for some assets that do not yield cash return but are used by their owners (like housing), we add them too at their estimated value.

Marx's concept of capital is very different. Consider for example a shoe-maker who works in his own shop. In our usual work as neoclassical economists, we would estimate the value (price) of all the tools that he owns and include this in our national capital. For Marx though this is not capital. Capital is "the characteristic the means of production acquire when they are used to hire labor and generate surplus value." Our shoe-maker does not hire anyone. His machines are simply the means of production, the physical tools. They are not capital until he expands his store, takes over its management, and hires workers to work with the tools he owns. At that point, the tools become capital. For the national accounting, Marx's concept of capital will therefore exclude the value of all machines and tools owned by either worker-owners (like our shoemaker) or cooperative firms and most of non-incorporated businesses. In countries where owner–worker (self-employed) sector is relatively large as, for example, in Latin America, lots of what is today considered "capital" would cease to be so. From household surveys we know that about one-third of total income in Latin American countries comes from the owner–worker sector. We can then venture a guess that perhaps (a bit less than) one-third of what is today considered capital will be "lost." Since that part of capital is less unequally distributed than the "capitalistic" capital, it is very likely that we would empirically find that the concentration of capital à la Marx is significantly greater than currently estimated.

258

ECONOMIC HISTORY

There is yet another, more difficult, issue. Marx, like all classical authors (Quesnay, Smith, Ricardo), takes wages to be advanced before the process of production begins. It means that if our shoemaker decides to become a capitalist, he not only would have to own the tools (which we already assumed he does), but enough cash on hand to hire workers. This assumption seems much more reasonable than the neoclassical (tacit) assumption that wages are paid at the end of the process of production. Why? Because if wages are paid at the end, then workers are co-entrepreneurs, since their (promised) wage depends on whether our shoemaker-capitalist is able to sell his shoes at the expected price or not. This is clearly unrealistic, or even absurd. Workers do not bear the risk of the enterprise; in fact, the crucial difference between labor and capital owners is that the risk is entirely borne by the latter. If workers' wages have to be paid before the process of product begins, somebody has to have the wherewithal to do so. That somebody is a capitalist. This is his "variable capital" in Marx's terminology. Thus, in terms of national accounts and calculations of wealth inequality, we would have to allocate all wage income accrued in capitalist enterprises to their owners. This means that the wages fund of, say Tesla or Google has to be imputed as capital, in its aliquot proportions, to all owners of shares in Tesla or Google. Marx's concept of capital would therefore include a significant chunk of what goes under the name of labor income today. If I am the owner of one percent of Google shares, my capital will not be only the current value of these shares (equal, in principle, to the expected discounted amount of profit), but also one percent of the wage-bill paid by Google.

Thus, while we "lost" one part of capital before because we did not include the value of worker-owned tools and machines, we expand the concept of capital now by including all the wages paid by the capitalist sector. These wages are imputed to the owners who have in principle advanced them. Whether this would increase or not the calculated inequality in distribution of capital is not clear. Owners of shares in heavily capital-intensive sectors, where the wage-bill (the variable capital) is relatively small, will not register a large increase in their capital. The outcome in terms of inequality will depend on whether more capital- or less capital-intensive sectors have more concentrated ownership. This is, by the way, a topic which, regardless of whether you subscribe to Marx's definition of capital or not, is worth exploring. It does not seem to have been studied.

If we use the following notation, A = value of productive and financial assets used in the capitalist sector, B = value of productive and

259

HISTORY

financial assets used in the owner–workers sector, C = non-productive wealth, D = wages paid in the capitalist sector, the current concept of capital is equal to A + B, the current concept of wealth adds to that C, while Marx's concept of capital would be equal to A + D. It then becomes clear that whether neoclassical or Marxist concept of capital will be larger depends on the relationship between B and D. In less-developed (capitalist) economies, the size of the self-employed sector may be large, B would consequently be high and D small. But in a hyper-capitalized economy, B might tend toward zero and D would be high.

In other words, as capitalism becomes more "capitalistic" the very size of what is deemed to be capital expands. This seems to make sense. In an economy composed of small producers, say thousands of small land-holders, the overall capital will be small. There will be very few capitalist enterprises (hence A is small) and wages paid by them will be a small share of the overall labor income. Thus, we come to the conclusion that what is capital is historically determined. When we compare capital in France and Cameroon, we are not just comparing how many tools exist in France and in Cameroon: we are really comparing how many tools are put to work to generate profit for their owners. There is, in conclusion, no capital as such, outside of the concrete reality and existing relations of production.

It will be interesting to have empirical estimations of Marx's concept of capital and find how the capital/income ratios and inequality in the distribution of capital change with the definition of capital.

(Published December 4, 2022)

ECONOMIC HISTORY

11.6 The plight of late industrializers: What if peasants do not want to move to cities?

In a paper that I wrote with Boško Mijatović on the real wage in nineteenth- century Serbia, we deal with an interesting and not novel problem. In a society where 90 percent of the population lives in the countryside and all farmers cultivate their own (small) landholding, and there is no landlessness, how do you industrialize?

All the contemporary evidence points to the fact that peasants were not at all keen to move to cities and work for a wage. Since there was no landlessness very few people were pushed by poverty to look for city jobs. Political parties that strongly (and understandably) represented peasantry further limited mobility of labor by guaranteeing homestead (3.5 ha of land, house, cattle, and the implements) which could not be alienated, neither in the case of default on the loan, nor in the case of overdue taxes.

This situation was very typical for the late industrializers in South-East Europe. Greece, Bulgaria, and Serbia were all overwhelmingly agricultural, with small peasant landholdings and little landlessness. All displayed slow or arrested capitalist development and half-hearted urbanization. The reason was simple: farmers had no incentive to move from being self-employed to being hired labor. And who would prefer to switch from being one's own boss, and dependent perhaps only on the elements, to become a hired hand, working six days a week all year round, in "satanic mills"?

The issue is noted by Fukuyama (among others) in *Political Order and Political Decay*. He explains slow industrial development in Greece (and he could readily have added Serbia and Bulgaria) by political clientelism, which in his view stemmed from premature democratization; that is, before programmatic and not clientelistic political parties could be formed. But he fails to see the economic origin of the problem: lack of incentive to move to cities.

The question is, how do you industrialize under such conditions? Reluctance of peasants, whenever they had their own land, to become industrial workers has been discussed (Gerschenkron, Polanyi). In England they had literally to be chased from land through enclosures; in France, the process was much more overdrawn and took a century; in Germany, Poland, and Hungary, large estates owned by nobility and consequent landlessness did the job. In Russia, it was bloody and occurred through forced collectivization.

261

HISTORY

Which introduces the following interesting topic. Suppose, as a counterfactual, that the October Revolution never took place, as it seemed most likely until the very day when it occurred, and that Russia, after the March revolution, became a democracy. Tsarism was overthrown, the elections of the Constituent Assembly were held in December 1917, and the largest party in the new Duma (later disbanded by the Bolsheviks) were Social-Revolutionaries (SR), who, combining their Russian and Ukrainian branches, held about 50 percent of the seats. (Bolsheviks got 24% of the vote.)

SRs were the party of the peasantry. By 1918, after the forced seizures of large estates, the land reverted to peasants, and the bulk of them acquired their own plots. Landlessness was relatively small.

Then, how do you industrialize? Peasants are quite happy to stay on land; SRs, who depend for their parliamentary majority on peasantry, might have passed laws similar to the ones passed in late-nineteenth-century Serbia, guaranteeing peasant property from creditors and the state. Why, under these conditions, would peasants move to Moscow or St. Petersburg to become wage workers, unless they got a much higher wage—most unlikely—than was their net marginal return from farming? So, unlike in the Lewis model of development, with an infinite supply of labor, here we deal with development, or rather attempted development, with close to zero new supply of labor.

Could high export taxes be imposed on Russian/Ukrainian grain to provide savings that would be invested in industrial development (a policy followed by Peronists in Argentina)? It is hard to imagine that a party (SRs) that did not depend on industrial proletariat but on peasantry would have done that. Thus, we quickly reach an impasse. To develop industrially, you need landless peasants looking for city jobs. But, in a society where peasants own farms and their parties control government, there is neither incentive nor desire to move to cities. Stasis, or equilibrium of sorts, ensues.

Now, going back to what really happened in Russia, we see better what was the problem faced by Bolsheviks. The war that Stalin launched on peasantry in 1928, and which resulted in at least an estimated six million deaths from famine and destroyed the Soviet agriculture for the entire period of the existence of the USSR, was to some extent on the cards from the very moment that the March revolution happened. Russia could have more easily become capitalist with the pre-1917 large landed estates and the attendant landless peasantry that gravitated toward cities for jobs. But, once small landowners became dominant, the (non-violent) road to indus-trialization was either blocked or had to be very long.

262

ECONOMIC HISTORY

The process whereby agricultural economies industrialized was wrenching. The displacement and unhappiness of the population dragged into industrial centers either through empty stomachs or outright terror, was incomparable in its human costs to today's similar transfer of labor from manufacturing to services (or to unemployment). The transformation in the underlying economic structure is never easy but it seems to me that the one from the fresh air and freedom of one's own farm to being a cog in a huge soiled machine of industrialization was the most painful.

(Published January 16, 2023)

HISTORY

11.7 Can Black Death explain the Industrial Revolution?

Every schoolchild knows that the Industrial Revolution started in England. But the question no schoolchild knows the answer to is why did it start in England? One theory (from Kenneth Pomeranz) sees it as a combination of serendipitous developments (invention of steam engine and presence of coal deposits), another (from Daron Acemoglu and James Robinson) as the result of long-term institutional developments: limited franchise and protection of private property. David Landes thinks it was English culture. But, for me, the most persuasive explanation was offered in 2003 by Bob Allen's "Progress and Poverty in Early Modern Europe": the Industrial Revolution happened because capitalists had an incentive to substitute capital for labor, since English labor was expensive. This led to the invention of labor-saving technology and technological revolution.

The argument is relevant for the students of ancient economies too: to the famous question posed by Michael Rostovtzeff in 1926, why did not Roman economy directly transit to the commercial capitalism of the Renaissance, if all the prerequisites were there? Why a ten-century detour? The answer, made already by Marx, is: because of the prevalence of cheap slave labor.

(Allen's 2003 paper also rejects two favorite shibboleths: that property was more secure in England than in pre-revolutionary France and that taxes were higher in France. Actually, the reverse is true for both.)

But Allen's solution still needs to deal with an additional issue: why is it that labor in England was more expensive than elsewhere in Europe? In his 2001 and 2005 papers, Allen has documented wage divergence between Northern and Southern European cities: while in the fourteenth century real wages were about the same in the North as in the South, by the 1800s, real wage in London and Amsterdam was thrice as high as in Vienna and Valencia. What led to this?

At a recent conference organized by the Santa Fe Institute and Sam Bowles, a young Italian researcher, Mattia Fochesato proposed an intriguing answer to that problem. The reason why European wages diverged between the North and the South was the difference in the response to the Black Death-driven increase in real wages (Orhan Pamuk was, I think, the first to argue that the North–South wage divergence started with the Black Death). In the South, where feudal institutions were stronger, land-owners responded to the increase in wages caused by the decline in population by renegotiating

264

share-cropping contracts, restraining movement of labor, and doing everything they could to reduce wages through extra-market mechanisms. In the North where feudal institutions were weaker, the ability to check wage increase was less. The feudal laws that limited the movement of labor were not always implemented. Fochesato constructs more-or-less annual series of population and real wages for Northern and Southern countries (England and Netherlands are the "North"; France, Italy, and Spain are the "South") and shows that the response of real wages to a given increase in population, that is, population recovery after the decimation due to the plague, was very different. In the North, population increase had negligible influence on wages; in the South, population increase reduced wages, eventually back to their pre-1350 levels.

There are, of course, still the questions that the paper in its present version does not answer satisfactorily: what exactly were the feudal institutions responsible for the "wage squeeze"?, how did they function?, was feudalism in the North *really* that much weaker? Also, there must have been some underlying economic reason (like increase in productivity) that allowed population to increase in the North without producing negative effects on wages. Obviously, these are the questions that Fochesato's paper (or perhaps another paper) might try to address. But, for now, we have here a set of very interesting hypotheses that link the events of 1350s with those some four centuries later, and that were crucial for worldwide economic development.

Combining this hypothesis with Allen's nicely eschews the mono-causal explanations that are all too current. It is both institutions (as reflected in the response to the population decrease) and capitalist incentives (as reflected in the substitution of labor by machines) that led to economic development. Any single story is bound to provide only a partial explanation.

(Published January 11, 2015)

HISTORY

11.8 Why were the Balkans underdeveloped?
A geographical hypothesis

The Balkans is an odd man in Europe. Its income level is much lower than the average income level of Western and Central Europe. This is a well-known fact but is worth another look. The median GDP per capita in Western Europe is around $40,000 (expressed in constant 2005 international dollars used by the World Bank). Balkan countries' incomes range from a little over $10,000 to just over $20,000 (excluding Greece). In other words, the gap between Western Europe and the Balkans is at least 2 to 1, and on average about 3 to 1. (Obviously, by taking the richest to the poorest country, the gap would be much higher.) If you look at the map of Europe without knowing much history, you should be surprised by such gaps: the distances are small; the flight time between Vienna and Belgrade is about an hour, but the income gap between the two cities (after adjusting for the lower price level in Belgrade) is probably around 4 to 1. Why is that the case?

I would agree with the standard explanation that sees the type of colonial power as the main "culprit." The areas controlled by the Ottomans for between three and four centuries do have lower incomes, lower educational attainments, lower levels of trust in institutions, etc. than the areas that were part of the Habsburg Empire (see Woessmann and Becker). Moreover, this is not a new phenomenon: the gaps, in non-income variables (like literacy or numeracy rates) were even wider in the past, and especially so in the early nineteenth century, when most of Balkan countries (as well as the dissatisfied nations under the Habsburgs) began their movements toward independence. This is the first part of the standard explanation.

The second part of the standard explanation is slower growth due to communism. This may perhaps best be seen in the income gap between Greece and other Balkan countries, a gap that was smaller in the 1930s than in 1989. For example, according to the 2017 Maddison Project data, the Greece–Romania GDP per capita ratio was 1.4 just before the Second World War but increased to 1.9 by 1989.

This is, I think, so far a standard explanation with one detail that I find rather puzzling. In the multitude of papers and books that deal with the colonial origins of today's institutions and thus income levels, there is—rather inexplicably—hardly any mention of the Ottoman colonial influence, which of course does not apply solely to

ECONOMIC HISTORY

the Balkans but to the Middle East and North Africa as well. I hope it is one of the lacunae that future work will fill.

But, my interest here is to speculate as to why the Balkans were not more developed, even at the time of the Roman Empire. Looking at the map again, this presents an even greater puzzle. Balkans (which at the time did not have a single name since the appellation of the Balkans comes from the Ottomans) were "squeezed" between two most advanced and developed parts of the then known world: Greece/Asia Minor and Italy (Rome). Why were then developments in the Balkans so slow?

If one looks at the data on urbanization, the Balkans (excluding Greece) were not much urbanized. The distribution of the largest ten cities around 150 was as follows: three in North Africa (Carthage, Lepcis Magna and Ptolemais), two in Egypt (Alexandria, Memphis), two in Greece (Athens and Corinth), two in Italy (Rome and Syracuse), one in the Levant (Antioch). The smallest of them was estimated to have had 80,000 inhabitants. The biggest Balkan city was Iader (today's Zadar in Croatia) with 30,000 inhabitants (data from Andrew Wilson, "City Sizes and Urbanization in the Roman Empire").

In terms of income, around the same time, the differences were also large. Maddison's data show the Balkans (again without Greece) to have had per capita income of a little over $400, approximately the same level as Gaul. But this is a surprise, since the Balkans are wedged between the two wealthiest parts of the Euro-Mediterranean world: Greece and Asia Minor with more than $500 per capita and Italy with almost $700 per capita. Normal expectation would be that the area's income should be some weighted average of Italian and Greek incomes and thus perhaps 50 percent higher than it was (and certainly higher than the faraway, in civilizational terms, Gaul, not to speak of the end of the world: the British Isles). (The data and the graph are from Maddison; also discussed, with some extensions, in my 2019 paper.)

Gibbon wonders about that too and mentions what is an interesting hypothesis, and perhaps the answer to our query: geography. The geography of Dalmatia and Moesia (to take the provinces as they were in Trajan's time) is such that there is only a narrow strip of the Mediterranean coast along the Adriatic, followed almost instantly, as one moves toward the hinterland, by high and impassable mountains. They make for spectacular contrast, as anyone who has travelled to the Bay of Kotor in Montenegro can vouch, but they also make communication with the hinterland difficult.

HISTORY

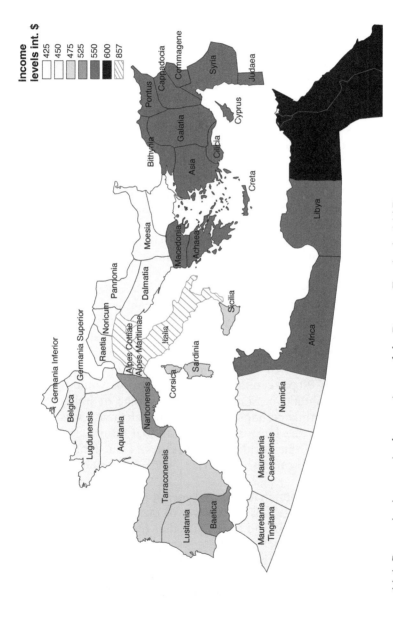

Figure 11.1 Per capita income in the provinces of the Roman Empire in 14AD
Source: Reproduced from Angus Maddison, *Contours of the World Economy, 1–2030 AD: Essays in Macro-Economic History*, copyright 2007. Reproduced with permission of Oxford Publishing Limited through PLSclear.

It is then not surprising, when one reads about the multiple travels of poets, writers, soldiers, and emperors between Italy and Attica and the Aegean, that the travel was always done by naval route crossing the Adriatic, preferably at its narrowest point, Otranto, between today's Puglia and Albania. It would have been much more perilous and longer to take the land route. So, two things happened: the part that communicated directly with the most advanced world was limited to the coastal areas of the Adriatic and never expanded into the hinterland; and the inconvenience of the land route between Italy and Greece made hinterlands additionally underdeveloped and less urbanized than we would expect.

The "worst" part, however, is that after several mountain ranges end, the terrain, as one moves further East and gets closer to the Danube, becomes flat and thus is ideal for all kinds of invasions from the steppes. This is, indeed, what happened, and the number of peoples who took that route, attacked and pillaged the area, is innumerable. Rome as it expanded eastward had to build its famous limes along the Danube (and later to expand it by annexing Dacia) and while the region became more important in the second, third, and fourth centuries its importance was translated mostly in military and strategic terms. Not only did many emperors hail from the Balkans (which is not surprising, since in the later Empire only generals could realistically aspire to become emperors) but the cities that grew in the "frontier" area were basically military garrison towns. They had some luxurious buildings, where top officers and emperors resided, but little signs of a lively middle class that one finds in the cities that dot the coastal areas of Asia Minor or the Levant. Balkan cities, if I can venture this generalization, were military encampments. Marcus Aurelius who spent most of his late years on the "frontier" fighting there did not seem to have left any trace. Had Constantine chosen Serdica (today's Sofia) instead of Byzantium, as he seemed to have thought at one point, the situation might have become different: a true city life could have been born. But this did not happen.

So, if the mountains were some 400 km to the East would the entire history of this part of Europe, and quite possibly Europe too, be different?

(Published May 11, 2018)

— 12 —

ADAM SMITH

12.1 Through the glass, darkly: Trying to figure out Adam Smith, the person

Dennis Rasmussen's book *The Infidel and the Professor* is a pleasure to read. It is an excellent introduction to the thinking and the friendship of David Hume (*le bon David*, as he was dubbed by the *philosophes* during his wildly successful sojourn in France) and Adam Smith. I had a book recommended to me by a friend, and I read it with two objectives in mind: first, to get a bit more of a feeling for Adam Smith as a person, and second, to learn more about his relations with the physiocrats while he lived in France, On both accounts, I learned nothing. Still, the book was a pleasure to read: it is well structured, not overly technical, and very well written.

Of the six economists I discuss in *Visions of Inequality* (Quesnay, Smith, Ricardo, Marx, Pareto, and Kuznets) I find Smith the most enigmatic. This book confirms him as being reserved, a somewhat distant and lonesome character despite dinners and company that he seemed to have, *intermittently*, enjoyed. Rasmussen's thesis about the very close friendship between Hume and Smith is somewhat dubious, or is at least exaggerated. Rasmussen, for example, claims that it was the closest and/or the most important intellectual friendship in history. But, just going over the authors I mentioned, there are intellectual friendships that seem stronger: Quesnay and Mirabeau, as well as Marx and Engels, coauthored articles and books; Ricardo and Malthus, and Pareto and Pantaleoni, corresponded much more frequently than Hume and Smith.

So, how close was the Hume–Smith friendship? They did not spend almost any time living in the same place: when Smith was in

ADAM SMITH

Glasgow, Hume was in Edinburgh; when Smith finally moved to Edinburgh, Hume was dead for a year. According to Rasmussen, they exchanged 170 letters, of which only 56 are still extant (15 from Smith to Hume and 41 from Hume to Smith). Hume and Smith met in 1749 and Hume died in 1776. That means, on average, 6.3 letters per year—not an extravagant number for a seemingly very close friendship. In this relationship, Hume is the insistent partner, often beseeching Adam Smith to visit him, reinviting him over again, finding schemes that might please him and induce him to come. Smith's letters are mostly technical in nature: they ask for Hume's recommendations (especially during Smith's stay in France) and bring to Hume's attention this or that of Smith's students or friends. Lack of Smith's engagement with Hume's incessant invitations can also be read—a hypothesis Rasmussen does not mention—as being a slight annoyance with an obstreperous friend: rather than having to find endless excuses, Smith just prefers to keep quiet.

Hume's open, vivacious, and friendly temperament, attested by all, was very different from Smith's. In this partnership the usual roles between a younger and older partner were reversed: while usually a younger partner tends to seek out the older and better-established partner's friendship and to ask for his advice, here we have a twelve-years-older, and more famous, Hume asking for Smith's company, and Smith often proffering advice to Hume. In fact, Smith's advice is always on point: good, rational, cautious, and mindful of the intellectual and political climate. The role reversal was due to the temperamental difference between the two men: the less guarded and much more lively older man, and the very deliberate and thoughtful younger one.

Other than confirming Smith's reserved and prudent nature, as well as his wisdom, both in dealing with people and in his writings, the book does not throw new light on Smith's life: his relations with his mother and the family, his amorous life (apparently non-existent), or his wealth. This is not the primary objective of the book, since it tries to document Hume's and Smith's intellectual mutual influence (Smith seems to have in many instances benefited from Hume's—the reverse is practically non-existent), not their lives. However, Rasmussen's early emphasis on their friendship inevitably drives the book toward the personal side of both thinkers. The book thus falls somewhere between intellectual history and a biography *à deux*.

On my second topic of interest, the influence of physiocrats on Smith, there is nothing in the book. Smith's stay in France (from January 1764 to the Fall of 1766) is given in chronological order but with very few details. I do not think that this is due to Rasmussen's choice: other books on Smith's travel in France are equally vague. There is simply not enough information on what Smith did in France, and by whom he might have been influenced.

Rasmussen makes the usual nod to Smith having met with d'Alambert, Voltaire, Quesnay, etc. in Toulouse and Paris, but this is all that we know. Even the word "met" is, I think, hardly appropriate in this case. Smith's spoken (unlike reading) French was not very good; his understanding was probably not much better, especially not in a salon where several people would speak at the same time, and where topics would easily mix personal intrigue and gossip with philosophy. So, it may seem more appropriate to say that Smith was a few times (we do not know how many: three, five, ten, twenty?) in the presence of the French luminaries. No document referring to their discussions or conversations exists.

One wonders how Smith was spending his days in Toulouse with his young charge, the Duke of Buccleuch. Were they made of the same solitary routine as his ten years in Kirkcaldy, during which he wrote most of *The Wealth of Nations*? What did Adam Smith do evening after evening in Toulouse? Surely, he was not conversing with the eight-year old Duke, nor did he have any French acquaintance to visit or entertain (as he himself complains in his letter to Hume— asking, as usual, for Hume's intercession on his behalf). Spending eighteen months like that, at the age of forty-one, must not have been especially pleasant.

The combination of intellectual and personal history is at its best in the chapters that describe the nasty *querelle* between Rousseau and Hume (actually, the querelle was almost entirely in Rousseau's mind and was of his creation); Smith's refusal, in the last months of Hume's life, to publish his strongly anti-religious *Dialogues*, and, finally, the Socrates-like Hume's final days when "everyone" was curious to see whether the impious philosopher would succumb to the dread of annihilation and, as many have done, espouse religion in the last hours of his life. As is well known, Hume did not do so.

But, in the end, it is worth mentioning Smith's reaction to Hume's request to publish his *Dialogues* posthumously. Rasmussen provides several hypotheses for Smith's decision, and I think that the most sensible one has to do with Smith's self-interest. Given Hume's terminally declining health, the posthumous publication of the *Dialogues* would have come just months after the publication of *The Wealth of Nations*. At that point—especially at that point!—Smith was not keen on getting embroiled in a row over religion, which could not only taint him with the epithet of atheist but would eclipse his just-released book, in whose writing he had spent, on and off, two decades of his life.

Smith's decision was fully comprehensible and in keeping with his personal interest. By unfortunate coincidence, it happened to mean the rejection of a favor being asked by a dying man who was his friend, and from whom he has learned a lot. Smith had to choose between the philosophy *of The Theory of Moral Sentiments* that applies to our relations with family, friends, and others close to us, and the philosophy *of The Wealth of Nations*, that applies to our relations with the rest of the world. He chose the second even if, by his own criteria, he should have chosen the first.

(Published November 25, 2021)

HISTORY

12.2 America's Adam Smith: A review of Glory M. Liu's *Adam Smith's America*

This is an excellent book. The objective of Glory Liu is to describe how the reception of Adam Smith in America has changed over the past two hundred years, and, using Adam Smith to some extent as a foil, to describe the changes in the intellectual climate and even in political economy over that period. That Adam Smith is an ideal person, in whose "reception" and in whose discussion will be reflected broader intellectual trends, is obvious. Smith's work is well known, respected by his admirers and detractors, and covers vast areas, going from moral philosophy and jurisprudence to political economy, and even astronomy. It is thus an ideal object to refract political and ideological trends.

One could divide the reception of Smith in America into three eras. The first, which lasted from Independence until the early twentieth century, was dominated by the discussion of free trade vs. protectionism in *The Wealth of Nations*. The second, from the early to the mid twentieth century, by the debate on the roles played in Smith's overall work by sympathy vs. self-interest. The third, which continues, was dominated by the disagreement over the roles of the price system (free market) and government. As these antinomies illustrate, the broadness of Smith's oeuvre allowed a sensible discussion of all three themes, and made each of the six positions defensible.

In fact, it could be said that whenever there was an important economic issue in America on which two sides were formed, Smith always played an important part in the debate because each side could, with some justification, bring Smith's views to their support. This may be due to some internal inconsistencies in Smith (especially if one includes *The Theory of Moral Sentiments* and *Lectures on Jurisprudence*, and not only *The Wealth of Nations*), but the more important reason is that Smith's work always had a pragmatic and eclectic character. Absence of dogmatism allowed him to take nuanced positions, and then these different nuances provided the *matériel* with which the two sides attacked one another. For example, even in the case of free trade that Smith, according to all readings, strongly championed, he nevertheless extolled the Act of Navigation. Why? "As defence, however, is of much more importance than opulence, the act of navigation is, perhaps, the wisest of all the commercial regulations of England" (*WoN*, bk.1, ch. 2).

274

ADAM SMITH

Liu fails, in my opinion, to acknowledge sufficiently that there never was nor will there be a "real" or "true" Smith: our readings of Smith will always be colored by what is the issue at hand, by our interests, location, and time (as the book indeed shows). Moreover, the ways that people come to Smith, precisely because his work is so vast and he influenced many, are diverse. I came to Smith through Marx. That particular channel played no role in the American intellectual discourse but illustrates the spread of Smith's influence. My original Smith was the one of the stadial theory of development, labor theory of value, definition of the three key classes in capitalism, their conflict over the distribution of the net product, and the dumbing effect of the division of labor. Do these themes remind you of somebody else? They do. Is this the entire Smith? No. But this is nevertheless the Smith that was, at one point of time and location, of interest.

Similarly, the subject that Smith argued about in the early decades of the US Republic was the one of free trade. Although there was a ritualistic invocation of Smith's name by many Founding Fathers (there are in the book quotes from Jefferson, Hamilton, Adams, etc.), his policy prescriptions were ignored. The young Republic, under Hamilton's impulse, went for protectionism. As Liu shows, it was Friedrich List, whose ideas developed while he lived in the United States, who was much more influential. Even in terms of textbooks, Smith's *Wealth of Nations* was eclipsed by the translation of Jean Baptiste Say's *Treatise* (first published in French in 1803; American translation in 1821).

There are ironies aplenty in the use of Smith during that period. The strongest supporters of free trade were, as is well known, the Southerners. They liked Smith's stance on free trade, but disliked his condemnation of slavery. The very opposite was true for Northern intellectuals and industrialists. Moreover, once we take free trade/protections, and slavery/abolitionism as political positions, we have four quadrants that will be filled by various people. Some, in the North, might agree on abolitionism, but disagree on trade. As we see here clearly, every side took from Smith what it found convenient, and questioned, or even simply ignored what it did not like.

This becomes very clear in chapters 5 and 6, which are in my opinion the best, and that deal with the first and second Chicago school. The Chicago school disregarded entirely Smith's political philosophy, considered the *TMS* an inferior work and decided to ignore the whole second era of the discussion of Smith in America, which revolved around the contrast between the advocacy of sympathy in the *TMS*

275

HISTORY

and an equally strong advocacy of self-interest in the *WoN*. The Chicago school took only the economic part. The older Chicago school (Frank Knight and Jacob Viner), more sensibly saw Smith not only as a partisan of laissez-faire but also ready to accept a limited role for government: "economics must be political economy," as the chapter title says, quoting Frank Knight.

The second, and to us better known and influential, Chicago school (George Stigler and Milton Friedman) continued with the reductionism of Smith. Not only was he shorn of moral philosophy, his work was now shorn of political economy as well. It became price theory. The emphasis turned entirely to the informational role of prices, the invisible hand, and (the "granite" of) self-interest. Liu rightly emphasizes the very narrow and reductionist view of Smith taken by the Chicago school. But, going back to my previous question: was this wrong? The answer is "No." Was this the entire Smith? The answer again is "No." Chicago's "filleting" of Smith may be disagreed with, but Chicago did not invent a new Smith. It took key elements that were there, jettisoned the rest, and created a Smith that it needed for its purposes. I do not think that it is an illegitimate approach—simply because every ideological movement, when it needs to "clothe" itself in earlier writers and to appropriate some of their aura, must do it.

All three elements of the Chicago school that I mentioned here are extremely important, and are present in Smith. But many others, perhaps equally important, are present too, and they can be, no less legitimately, taken and defended. The (slight) weakness of Liu's book is, as I mentioned, that it does not fully accept this point of view, and does not realize that every description of reception of an influential author will always be a story of intellectual development in *that* location and place. The mirage of "recapturing" the real Adam Smith does float in the book, especially in the beginning and the end.

The most recent (post-Chicago) period is dominated by Irving Kristol and Gertrude Himmelfarb's "reintegration" of Smith, where *TMS* (that was earlier supposed to support a more benign, even socialistic, interpretation of Smith) has now been repurposed for "bourgeois" virtues. The conservative reinterpretation reunified the "two Smiths" but, again, at a cost of significant simplification, and possibly misinterpretation. The discussion in the last chapter of *Adam Smith's America* ("Turning Smith Back on the Present") also includes discussion of some, in my opinion, silly issues (namely whether Smith really thought that the metaphor of the invisible hand was important or not), and, strangely, does not mention Amartya

276

Sen's important contribution to a different reading of the *TMS* (and even its superiority to the contractarian theories like Rawls').

Regarding the style, I would have one minor complaint. Liu does not always wear her formidable scholarship lightly: there is, at times, a surfeit of quotations that are only tenuously related to the subject matter. Finally, the reader, or at least this reader, may get annoyed by the excessive use of "[sic]." There is no need to "sic" differences in spelling between the English of Smith's time and ours. The use of "sic" often tends to convey the feeling of the writer's superiority both with respect to the author he or she is citing, and with respect to the readers (who may not be, in the author's view, sufficiently aware of the problem). It must be used sparingly.

(Published June 6, 2023)

HISTORY

12.3 People, associations, and government policy in Adam Smith

Sameness of people and accidents of birth. I would like to begin by highlighting three features of individuals and society that I think are assumed or believed by Adam Smith. The first is that all people are fundamentally the same, which implies that we can understand motivations behind people's behavior and accept a form of "egalitarianism." The second point is that accidents play a large role in life and, here, by accidents I mean the accidents of birth, location, and parental wealth. The third point is that no organized groups of individuals are to be fully trusted. We have to maintain healthy skepticism toward any organized group, whether it is the businessmen's association, trade unions, government, or even organized religion. This skepticism combined with Smith's view about the evolution of factoral income shares explains, I will argue, his negative attitude toward the influence of capitalists on government policy.

Regarding the first point, I would like to begin with a personal reflection. I asked myself the following question: when Adam Smith published *The Wealth of Nations*, what were my ancestors doing then? And, although I don't know the details because my knowledge of my background does not extend that far into the past, I do know that they lived in the then Ottoman Empire, in what is today Serbia, Macedonia, and Greece and I think that all of them, with the possible exception of one or two persons were fully illiterate or functionally illiterate. The situation in Scotland at that time was better. The question I then asked myself is whether Smith would have been surprised to have somebody like me deliver a talk on his work in his house. And the answer that I thought I would get from him was that he would not be surprised. The reason why I think he would not be surprised is because of his belief in the fundamental sameness of people, and in economic growth. Economic progress not only makes people materially richer but is associated with better education. better health, and, very importantly, greater self-awareness. Self-awareness is needed for self-expression. There would be no books like *The Wealth of Nations* were it not for the ability of individuals to reflect on society and on their own place in it. Without economic growth, there would be no "commercial society," and nothing like that to observe; and, most likely, without economic growth there would be no Adam Smith.

There were millions of people who have lived prior to us and of whom very little is known. Practically nothing remains of their

278

thinking. It is not that they were unable to think as clearly as we. But, in the less developed or more primitive societies, the thinking about social matters was the prerogative of a few select groups. For others, it was difficult or impossible to transmit whatever they thought and felt without sufficient education and, obviously, without being literate. Economic growth changed all of that.

I would now continue with the discussion of what I defined as the three important ideas that feature in Adam Smith's view of individuals and society.

The fundamental *sameness* of people is critical: it means that we are able to understand other people's behavior and to have empathy for them. This is the bedrock principle *of The Theory of Moral Sentiments*. But we are also able to understand that self-interest influences what people do, the principle that is the bedrock of *The Wealth of Nations*. Thus, the sameness of people, in terms of their motivations and behavior, is treated in *TMS* and *WoN* as the basis for the main principles that activate the two books: empathy and self-interest. Without people's being the same, we could not feel empathy with the other, simply because we could never mentally place ourselves in their position. And, without people being the same, we could never understand self-interest as the engine of economic activity, nor figure out that other people's interests and ours may be complementary, as in the famous lines from *The Wealth of Nations* about the butcher, the brewer, and the baker ... and ourselves. Nor would we understand that the desire for material improvement is common to most people. As Smith writes: "An augmentation of fortune is the means by which the greater part of men propose and wish to better their condition" (*WoN*, bk. II, ch. 3, p. 436).

The sameness of individuals also rules out, by definition, as good societies those based on claiming that there are intrinsic differences between people. These could be differences between free people and slaves, men and women, legally defined social estates, or any other ascriptive differences like the caste. The sameness of people represents the basis for treating everybody equally, both in a legal and an economic sense. And, if I am allowed to jump to the twentieth century, it allows us to require that any departure from economic equality be justified by the appeal to some higher good, such as, for example, that greater inequality would improve the absolute position of the worst-off.

The second principle is the importance that Adam Smith places on social conditions under which we are born, and under which we live, for our "observable" success. If accidents of birth, and what

HISTORY

John Roemer calls "the episodic luck," explain most of the differences in wealth and status, then these differences cannot be due to intrinsic differences in intelligence or capabilities. In the *Lectures on Jurisprudence*, Smith writes (or more exactly teaches): "The difference between a porter and a philosopher in the first four or five years of their life is, properly speaking, none at all" (p. 113). The fundamental variance between people is small or hardly existent; it is much smaller than the observable variance. This is expressed frequently *in The Theory of Moral Sentiments*, where even the happiness of the poor is contrasted with the insecurity of the rich: "In ease of body and peace of mind, all the different ranks of life are nearly upon the same level, and the beggar who suns himself by the highway, possesses that security which kings are fighting for" (*TMS*, pt. IV, i, 10). While that particular statement can be interpreted as a justification of economic inequality, it can also be interpreted as a statement that the differences that we observe are much less "real" than they seem to us. The same principle is illustrated by Smith's idea of what may be called "the hiding hand," which prompts us to seek income and power in the hope that they would make us much happier, only to discover, to our disappointment, that this is seldom the case.[1]

Skepticism toward all associations, including government

The third fundamental proposition is that associations of people that are formed to pursue a particular interest are always to be looked upon with a very skeptical eye. Every such association tends to promote a special interest, often to the detriment of the interest of others or of social interest. That, of course, opens up the question what is the social interest, but one might sidestep that question by arguing that social interest, according to Smith, is the improvement in the material conditions for the majority of people. It was a novel statement at the time (mercantilism holding a very different view) and one that Adam Smith frequently invokes:

> Servants, laborers and workmen of different kinds make up the far greater part of every great political society, But what improves the circumstances of the greater part can never be regarded as an inconvenience to the whole. No society can surely be flourishing and happy

---

[1] See *The Theory of Moral Sentiments*, pt. IV, i, 10, p. 158.

ADAM SMITH

of which the far greater part of the members are poor and miserable. (*WoN*, bk. I, ch. 8, pp. 110–111).

Government. The skeptical approach toward organized individuals, i.e. associations, carries over to all such organizations. Indeed, the most frequently quoted parts of *The Wealth of Nations* are those where Smith speaks with a very heavy dose of skepticism about the role of government. He sees the people in the government (and it is important to underline that he looks at the *people* in the government, not the government as some transcendental or separate entity) as pursuing their own interests. He sees them as unfit to tell other people what to do because they themselves are often transgressing the norms that they try to impose upon others. As Smith writes in a famous paragraph:

> It is the highest impertinence and presumption, therefore, in kings and ministers, to pretend to watch over the economy of private people, and to restrain their expense, either by sumptuary laws, or by prohibiting the importation of foreign luxuries. They are themselves always, and without any exception, the greatest spendthrifts in the society. Let them look well after their own expense, and they may safely trust private people with theirs. If their own extravagance does not ruin the state, that of their subjects never will. (*WoN*, bk. II, ch. 3, p. 442)

Indeed, civil servants never forget to overpay themselves:

> The emoluments of offices are not ... regulated by the free competition of the market, and do not, therefore always bear a just proportion to what the nature of the employment requires. They are, perhaps in most countries, higher than it requires; the persons who have the administration of government being generally disposed to reward both themselves and their immediate dependents rather more than enough. (*WoN*, bk. V, ch. 2)

Capitalists. Less frequently cited are similar statements that express negative or skeptical attitudes toward the organized groups of employers or, as Adam Smith called them, before the term "capitalist" was invented, "masters."

> People of the same trade seldom meet together, even for merriment and diversion, but the conversation ends in a conspiracy against the public, or in some contrivance to raise prices. It is impossible indeed

HISTORY

to prevent such meetings, by any law which either could be executed, or would be consistent with liberty and justice. But though the law cannot hinder people of the same trade from sometimes assembling together it ought to do nothing to facilitate such assemblies; much less to render them necessary. (*WoN*, bk. I, ch. 10, p. 177)

Moreover, "[t]he masters, being fewer in number, can combine much more easily and the law besides authorizes or at least does not prohibit their combinations (*WoN*, bk. I, ch. 8, p. 94).

Thus masters, as opposed to workers, enjoy the coordination advantage since it is easier to bring together and find common interest among very few than among the dispersed many. One must be suspicious of masters not only because of their tendency to collude but also because of the way they have acquired their wealth. Smith is not more gentle toward them than Marx: "the primitive accumulation" is done through the exercise of monopoly power (*WoN*, bk. IV, ch. 8, p. 807), collusion to raise prices (*WoN*, bk. I, ch. 10), Ponzi-like schemes (*WoN*, bk. II, ch. 2), sheer plunder (*WoN*, bk. IV, ch. 7, p. 722), crusades (*WoN*, bk. III, ch. 3, p. 513), and enslavement (*TMS*, pt. V, i, 19, p. 178),[2] among other fine means. This negative view regarding the original acquisition of "masters'" wealth and the role of their associations, will, joined with Smith's view that the road to "natural opulence" of societies implies a decrease in the rate of profit, lead him to take a strong stance against the political role of capitalists. But he will also acknowledge that thanks to their cleverness and ability to handle sophistry, capitalists are most likely to influence government's policy. This should make us twice wary when we listen to them.

Churches. Smith's unwillingness to take at face value what organizations claim for themselves extends to organized religion. It is shown, for example, in Smith's ironic statement about the Quakers' release of their slaves: "The late resolution of the Quakers in Pennsylvania to set at liberty all their negro slaves, may satisfy us that their number cannot be very great" (*WoN*, bk. III, ch. 2, p. 496).

Organized religion plays on people's prejudices, and even good government must yield to such prejudices in order to preserve "public tranquillity."

---

[2] "Fortune never exerted more cruelly her empire over mankind, than when she subjected these nations of heroes to the refuse of the jails of Europe, to wretches who possess the virtues neither of the countries which they come from, nor of those where they go to, and whose levity, brutality, and baseness so justly exposed them to the contempt of the vanquished." (*The Theory of Moral Sentiments*, pt. V, i, p. 19B).

ADAM SMITH

The laws concerning corn may every-where be compared to the laws concerning religion. The people feel themselves so much interested in what relates either of their subsistence in this life, or to their happiness in a life to come, that government must yield to their prejudices, and, in order to preserve the public tranquillity, establish that system which they approve of. It is upon this account, perhaps, that we so seldom find a reasonable system established with regard to either of those two capital objects. (*WoN*, bk. IV, ch. 5; pp. 682–683)

Workers. Smith is also skeptical of workers' associations but they come in for less criticism. There are several reasons for this: (a) the already mentioned difficulty of organizing many people hampers the efficiency of workers' organization and thus requires from the philosopher and the economist a less probing or suspicious eye; (b) the lack of influence of workers on government's decisions because they are not close to the centers of power, and (c) lack of education, which prevents workers from effectively presenting their case.[3] The last reason has, interestingly, in its origin a phenomenon that is at the heart of economic progress and, indeed, one of the key ideas that rendered Smith famous: the division of labor. The division of labor, the author of the first chapter of *The Wealth of Nations* holds, leads to the dulling of thinking or to the lack of interest in social matters among people who are subjected to it. Smith, followed in that by Marx and Tocqueville, tends to see the division of labor as being destructive of intellectual interests because a working day of ten or twelve hours spent in accomplishing a single task does not leave any time for mental activities. He contrasts the much broader knowledge and interests of farmers or countryfolk compared to workers: "How much lower ranks of people in the country are really superior to those of the town is well known to every man whom either business or curiosity has led to converse much with both" (*WoN*, bk. I, ch. 10, p 175).

Perhaps the most important reason why workers' associations are less to be worried about is that they represent the largest class in society. Their combinations are therefore less likely to be deleterious to the public interest. As Smith writes: "When the regulation ... is in favor of the workmen, it is always just and equitable; but it is

---

[3] "But though the interest of the laborer is strictly connected with that of the society, he is incapable either of comprehending that interest, or of understanding its connection with his own" (*Wealth of Nations*, bk. I, ch. 11, p. 337).

283

HISTORY

sometimes otherwise when in favor of the Masters" (*WoN*, bk. I, ch. 10, p. 195).

The conclusion is that Smith is the least critical of workers' associations because he believes that they are simply less powerful, they are unlikely to influence government policy, and, even if they do, they stand for the interest of the majority of the population. As we have seen, it is the improvement in the position of the largest classes that is by definition the attribute of a progressive society.[4]

But the situation is exactly the opposite with employers' associations, to which I turn next.

Evolution of income distribution and capitalists' influence on government policies.

Here we have to take into account Smith's views regarding the evolution of incomes of the three major classes. It will be from that distributional angle that Smith will look at the undesirability of capitalists' advice on economic policy.

As already mentioned, Smith sees capitalists as the most influential group, so far as economic policy-making is concerned. It is interesting to note here that Smith did not change this opinion, or that at least it was not contradicted, by his own experience as the Commissioner of Customs in Scotland. Revisions of *The Wealth of Nations* were done while Smith was the Commissioner: the third edition of *The Wealth of Nations* was published in 1784, in the seventh year of his job as a Commissioner. A new text of some 24,000 words (about 6% of the total length) was added. *The Theory of Moral Sentiments* was revised, significantly in parts, and was republished in 1790, shortly before Smith's death, in the twelfth year of his job as Commissioner of Customs.[5] Had he changed his mind or had he began to doubt that the influence of capitalists on government policy is less than he originally thought, there was ample time and opportunity for this to

---

[4] The term "progressive," as opposed to "stationary" and "declining," is a technical term used by Smith for a society that has a positive rate of economic growth. It exhibits different states of mind among its population. "The progressive state [of society, in economic terms] is in reality the cheerful and the hearty state to all the different orders of the society. The stationary is dull, the declining melancholy" (*WoN*, bk. I, ch. 8, p. 114).

[5] Based on Gary M. Anderson, William F. Shughart II, and Robert D. Tollison, "Smith in the Customhouse," *Journal of Political Economy*, 93 (4) August 1985: 740–759.

ADAM SMITH

be reflected in the revisions *of The Wealth of Nations*. But this never happened.

What is the problem with such influence? It is less welcome compared to that of other classes because the natural course of opulence implies, according to Smith, a decrease in the rate of profit, and that means that the interests of capitalists are, whether they are aware of that or not, opposed to the interests of society on the whole and to the interests of the other two classes, whose incomes tend to increase with the advancement of society. Real wages go up, Smith holds, because an improved society pays more to those who "feed and clothe it." And the land rent goes up because of the increased demand for food and for products of the earth, including mining. We thus have only the rate of return to capital, which, because of competition among the owners of the ever-increasing amounts of "stock" (i.e. capital intensity of production increases with per capita income), tends to go down.[6] Contemporary Holland is often adduced by Smith as a perfect example. As he writes:

> The rate of profit does not, like rent and wage, rise with the prosperity and fall with the declension of the society. On the contrary, it is naturally low in rich, and high in poor countries, and it is always highest in the countries that are going fastest to ruin. The interest of this third order [capitalists], therefore, has not the same connection with the general interest of the society as that of the other two. (*WoN*, bk. I, ch. 11, p. 338)

This is why—and let me give here three strong quotes from *The Wealth of Nations*—one should not trust the advice coming from this class:

> The proposal of any new law or regulation of commerce which comes from this order, ought always to be listened to with great precaution, and ought never to be adopted till after having been long and carefully examined, not only with the most scrupulous, but with the most suspicious attention. (*WoN*, bk. I, ch. 11, p. 339)

> [The capitalists] are an order of men, whose interest is never exactly the same with that of the public, who have generally an interest to deceive and even to oppress the public, and who accordingly have,

---

[6] The evolution of factoral income shares is discussed in an important section concluding Book I *of The Wealth of Nations*.

285

HISTORY

upon many occasions, both deceived and oppressed it. (*WoN*, bk. I, ch. 11, p. 339)

But the mean rapacity, the monopolizing spirit of merchants and manufacturers, who neither are, nor ought to be, the rulers of mankind, though it cannot perhaps be corrected may very easily be prevented from disturbing the tranquility of anybody but themselves. (*WoN*, bk. IV, ch. 3, p. 621)

We thus come to the conclusion that the mistrust expressed by Smith toward the self-proclaimed objectives of all organizations is particularly strong when that organization's interests run contrary to the "natural progress of opulence." It is these interests in particular that should be the subject of scrutiny.

Two distinct parts of Adam Smith's economic and political thinking—his skepticism toward associations and his theory of evolution of income shares in progressive societies—come together to fashion his views on economic policy. This is not sufficiently appreciated. On the contrary, his critiques of government and of organized labor are more frequently cited than his critique of organized capital, or what we would today call business lobbyists. Yet, for the reasons explained, it is really the latter whose advice is, according to Smith, most likely to hold sway and to be pernicious.

Implications for today

Smith's views in these areas have clear implications for today, some two and a half centuries after they were put on paper. Smith would, I think, regard with profound suspicion the idea of a deserving or meritocratic elite that is today often touted. He would know that "meritocracy" is often the product of happen-stance, of more favorable conditions enjoyed at the outset, and even of the use of disgraceful means to get ahead. It may be speculated that one of his disagreements with the physiocrats, who saw themselves in a position of such a meritocratic elite, was that Smith simply did not believe in meritocracy as a reflection of individuals' superior ability.

Today's Smith would be an anti-elite Smith, sympathetic to the workers' cause but without supporting them in all instances, skeptical of all capitalists' associations, Davoses, Renaissance Weekends, and similar gatherings organized in order to "deceive the public." He would be an adversary of crony capitalism, yet on guard against the

286

ADAM SMITH

political capitalism, where many economic decisions are taken by the state, or rather by the people who pretend to act on behalf of the state. His legacy is thus, I think, one of abiding commitment to equality of people, suspicion toward the do-gooders and special interests who do not dare show their true colors; and belief that if public opinion is sufficiently strong to prevent the most egregious misdeeds by different organized groups, including the government and organized religion, the road to prosperity will nevertheless remain open. His common sense made him believe in things being sufficiently good, not ideal.

(The Adam Smith Lecture, delivered in Edinburgh, February 29, 2024)

HISTORY

12.4 Is democracy always better for the poor?

Who has read Adam Smith's chapter 7, book IV in *The Wealth of Nations*? It is an unusual chapter, located toward the end of the book that deals with the systems of political economy, more exactly with mercantilism (and physiocracy briefly at the end), and discusses at great length mercantilist trade policies of European empires, from Portugal to England. It is no surprise that Adam Smith has very few nice words for imperial policies, including a ban on production of goods that may compete with metropoles' production (like the famous case of steel in North America), prohibition of direct exports to other markets than metropole's, and obligation to carry trade using metropole's ships (the Navigation Act). Smith is even more scathing about merchant companies, the two famous East India Companies, the Dutch and the English ("The government of an exclusive company of merchants is, perhaps, the worst of all governments for any country whatever").

The chapter "On Colonies" is the second longest chapter in *The Wealth of Nations*. In the edition I was using, it has more than 100 pages, which is about eight percent of the entire book (the whole book is about 1,200 pages long in the same edition). Having been written in 1774, it spends considerable time on North America and the "disturbances" that were brewing up there. As is well known, Smith was right both in seeing the inevitability of American secession and in forecasting the great future for the continent.

But he also presented a ledger where the British expenses on behalf of American colonists were much greater than what Britain received in return ("under the present system of management, therefore, Great Britain derives nothing but loss from the dominion, which she assumes over her colonies")—and this despite discriminatory trade policies mentioned in the previous paragraph. He explained British stubbornness in not granting independence by pride ("No nation ever voluntarily gave up the dominion of any province, how troublesome soever it might be to govern it, and how small soever the revenue which it afforded might be in proportion to the expense which it occasioned") but also, and importantly, by the economic interests of the English elite that, unlike ordinary people, did benefit from colonies: "[granting of independence] is always contrary to the private interest of the governing part of [a nation], who would thereby be deprived of the disposal of many places of trust and profit, of many opportunities of acquiring wealth and distinction, which

288

ADAM SMITH

the possession of the most turbulent, and, to the great body of the people, the most unprofitable province seldom fails to afford" (*WoN*, bk. IV, ch. 7, p. 783).

This Smithian sharp distinction, within the metropole, between the interests of the elite and those of the rest of the population is something that Thomas Hauner, Suresh Naidu and I use in our paper on the world prior to 1914 to argue that the imperialist expansion in the nineteenth century was driven by the narrow interests of the metropoles' rich, that is, by the people who disproportionally owned colonial assets, which provided them with returns superior to those they could have obtained at home. Now, we can "rope in" Adam Smith to our case, in a foundational book on political economy written more than a century before the period we discuss. (We do not quote Smith in the current version of the paper but might decide to do so in the next.)

Overall, Smith comes to the conclusion that British colonies are treated better than any others, but, in one very important respect, he qualifies this statement: it is in relation to the treatment of slaves. There he makes an interesting, and I think not sufficiently appreciated (at least I have not seen it mentioned), observation. More democratically governed colonies (like the British) treat slaves worse because the elite which, in a system of oligarchic republicanism, controls the levels of power is reluctant to punish its own members, who are particularly brutal toward slaves. An authoritarian or autocratic state however has less compunction about punishing members of the elite whose behavior is especially outrageous (even if the state does not care much for the welfare of slaves as such). Here is the full quote from Smith:

> In every country where the unfortunate law of slavery is established, the magistrate, when he protects the slave, intermeddles in some measure in the management of the private property of the master; and, in a free country, where the master is perhaps either a member of the colony assembly, or an elector of such a member, he dare not do this but with the greatest caution and circumspection. The respect which he is obliged to pay to the master renders it more difficult for him to protect the slave. But in a country where the government is in a great measure arbitrary, where it is usual for the magistrate to intermeddle even in the management of the private property of individuals, and to send them, perhaps, a lettre de cachet if they do not manage it according to his liking, it is much easier for him to give some protection to the slave; and common humanity naturally disposes him to do so. The protection of the magistrate renders

the slave less contemptible in the eyes of his master, who is thereby induced to consider him with more regard, and to treat him with more gentleness … That the condition of a slave is better under an arbitrary than under a free government is, I believe, supported by the history of all ages and nations. (*WoN*, bk. IV, ch. 7, pp. 744–745)

Smith's lesson here has broader applicability. An oligarchic democracy may be worse for the poor than an arbitrary government. A state, relatively autonomous from the elite, may care more about the "general interest" than an ostensibly democratic government that is in reality the government of the rich. Smith highlights, I think, both in his discussion of social cleavage in interests when it comes to colonies, and in his discussion of slavery, the ambivalence of the connection between the state and class. In more democratic (but exclusivist) settings the state may be less autonomous and more directly "hitched" to the interests of the ruling class. In an autocracy, the state may be less subject to the power of moneyed interests, and more concerned with the position of the poor. Our facile and somewhat lazy approach—that more democracy implies a greater concern or improvement for the poor—is shown here, by the founder of political economy, to be possibly—at times—wrong.

(Published August 30, 2021)

12.5 Why slave-owners never willingly emancipated their slaves

When I wrote my chapter on Adam Smith in the *Visions of Inequality* I considered including a section discussing Smith's views on slavery. I eventually decided against it because slavery plays only an incidental role in Smith; most of his analysis in *The Wealth of Nations* assumes the three standard social classes that are all formally free, and the interplay between them generates their incomes and social positions. In that context, slaves who no longer existed in countries with which Smith was mostly concerned, namely England, Scotland, France, Netherlands, and the rest of Western Europe, were somewhat outside the main scope of his interest.

However, Smith's views on slavery are, as is well known, fairly complex. I wrote about his argument that the position of slaves was better in autocratic than in oligarchic democratic governments (see above, Section 12.4). The reason is that in an oligarchic and representative government the power is held by the people who themselves are the largest slave-holders (US comes to mind) and they are very unlikely to emancipate slaves because they would thus deprive themselves and their friends of a large amount of capital. They are wary of treating them well because they are permanently afraid of slaves' insurrection. In richer societies (Smith explains this at some length), the income and social gap between the master and the slave is much greater. The slave has also much more to covet. Hence, in more democratic and richer societies the treatment of slaves, in order to forestall their insurrection, must be particularly harsh. In one of perhaps the most striking passages in the *Lectures on Jurisprudence* Smith says:

> Opulence and freedom, the two greatest blessings the men can possess, tend greatly to the misery of this body of men, which in most countries where slavery is allowed makes by far the greatest part. A humane man would wish therefore, if slavery has to be generally established, that these greatest blessings, being incompatible with the happiness of the greatest part of mankind, were never to take place. (*LoJ* (A), February 16, 1763)

The passage is, I think, so seldom cited because it questions the two most cherished beliefs: popular government and opulence. If both can exist only if slaves are terrorized, what good are they? It is a striking statement.

HISTORY

In more autocratic forms of government, the kings are not necessarily dependent on slave owners for their power and, as Adam Smith explains regarding the abolition of serfdom in Western Europe, they might even like to get rid of forced labor if it reduces the power of local lords that could use slave armies to challenge the king.

But the most important part which attracted attention of the economists, and I want to single out a recent paper by Barry Weingast, is the following. Smith very clearly in his *Lectures on Jurisprudence* states that slavery, as an economic institution is, inefficient. That means that a slave-toiled land would yield to the owner much less than if the same land were leased for a reasonable rent to the tenant. The reason is obvious: the tenant farmer has an incentive to increase production even if he has to give one-third (Smith's estimate, but we can substitute any number) of the crop to the owner. The owner can easily calculate that over a period of x years, the Net Present Value (NPV) of the rent he gets would exceed the amount of the surplus product that he receives from slaves, to whom he pays only the subsistence wage. We are not talking here about high mathematics. Things are pretty simple. We can introduce different discount rates, and different amounts for rent, different productivity differentials for the land worked by free vs. slave labor, etc., as Weingast does, but whatever set of (reasonable) assumptions we choose the final result is the same. The landlord should just dismiss his slaves, offer to some of them to continue working as free tenant-farmers, find new tenant famers if needed, and spend the rest of his time at leisure enjoying the rent.

So why did not slave owners do precisely that? Why do we never observe in history *endogenous* scrapping of slave-holding when it is such an inefficient system and when the owners could actually make more money by hiring free labor than by using slaves?

It is a fair question and Weingast solves it by using a game theoretic framework showing that neither side can credibly commit to their part of the bargain. (He does this because he introduces, in my opinion, totally unnecessarily, the further assumption of slaves, buying over time their freedom. Yes, slave owners can try to extract that too, but in a simple model, it is superfluous. For slave owners are better off, even if they emancipate slaves for free.)

The reason why this spontaneous emancipation has never happened in the real world is the following. What would be the reaction that our emancipatory landlord would meet from his peers at the news that he has just released all his slaves? How would such an act be viewed by them? Certainly not with pleasure and warmth. As Smith

292

ADAM SMITH

writes, slave-owners, like all property owners, the richer they are the more they live in a perpetual fear of expropriation by the poor. Every slave-owner forms part of that implicit compact. Everyone who, as a slave-owner, does not observe the compact is as much of a threat, if not more, to other slave-owners as the slaves themselves.

Smith holds that in richer countries, where the slave-owners are much richer than slaves, they are especially fearful of rebellions. The only way to hold slaves down is to apply brutal control that Smith details, with gory detail: from whipping them on a daily basis, keeping people in chains during most of the day, or even in the most gruesome example crucifying them for trivial offenses, hacking their bodies into pieces and then feeding them to the fish. In such an atmosphere of fear of constant rebellion a landlord who would follow the economic logic described above would find no sympathy from other landlords. Moreover, other landlords would do everything to stop the manumission: they might claim that our economist-landlord has lost his mind, has been bewitched by slave wizards, is mad, a traitor, foreign agent, anything. They would do everything to make his life impossible, to make him change his decision and short of it, to punish him by seizing the land, which in their view he is mismanaging. So, in calculating gains and losses from slavery on a piece of paper is a very different proposition from acting on what the calculation reveals.

But, let us go further and assume that for some reason the rationality prevails and that his decision to emancipate the slaves gets imitated by many, and enjoys a sufficient momentum so that at a certain time a large number of slaves become free, as it were, spontaneously. Make even further a very unrealistic assumption that the powers-that-be that Smith very clearly associates with people who own slaves and who, as he says, "hate them," overcome the hatred because of material interest and agree to the emancipation.

We have to ask the new question then: what will happen next? If the land was originally toiled by five slaves and can now be worked equally productively (yielding the same output) by one tenant, this means that all the released slaves will not be able to find a job on the land on which they worked before. Perhaps only a fraction would. Others would congregate in the urban areas looking for jobs there.

And, that's where the problems begin. There will be a massive surge of brutalized, poor, and unskilled people, who would get into a cut-throat competition with the urban proletariat, driving the wages

HISTORY

down and getting into conflicts, perhaps riots and fights, with the working class. Moreover, in the urban areas there would now be two large classes of malcontents with unstable jobs, subsistence wages, deep hatred of each other, and even deeper hatred for the rich. This is something the top politicians among slave-owning elite are unlikely to overlook.

This is not a very different situation, just more dramatic, than what many contemporary developing countries have faced: immense inflow of labor from the countryside into the urban areas, which has created political instability, violence, crime, and conflict between different parts of the lower classes, and then, ultimately, the conflict between the lower classes and the upper classes.

Only a little dose of reality shows that the Panglossian idea, shared by some economists (but not by Adam Smith), that proving that slave holding was not profitable for the individual landlord should have led to the spontaneous emancipation of slaves. Such economists make several logical mistakes: they make a composition error by assuming that what is true for one might also be true when it is extended to everybody, and they ignore political externality by assuming that other slave-owners are not affected by the decision of some of them.

Most importantly they make a mistake that Smith did not make: they disregard the political forces and political implications of such a big move. After all, by now we have sufficient historical evidence that no society has ceased being slave-holding spontaneously through the working of economic factors alone: not the slave-holders of Egypt, nor Persians, nor the Arabic slave-holders, nor the slaveholders of Justinian's Eastern Roman Empire, nor the slave-holders of the Western Roman Empire, nor the slaveholders among the Visigoths and Ostrogoths, nor was forced labor abolished spontaneously in France, nor in the Habsburg Empire, nor in Russia, and obviously not in the West Indies and the American South. And it is not because slave-owners were not numerate enough to calculate Net Present Value that economists have discovered.

The way slavery was crushed and abolished was almost always through the use of violence: riots, revolution, threats to government, and civil wars. Adam Smith, who believed that anti-slavery forces will never be strong enough to abolish slavery: "Notwithstanding those superior [economic] advantages it is not likely that slavery should be ever abolished, and it was owing to some peculiar circumstances that has been abolished in the small corner of the world in which it now is"—was wrong on that score, but he offers us a

294

cautionary tale, showing that looking only at economic advantages, without considering them in their political context, is insufficient. We can draw game theoretic boxes but they are a paltry substitute for what we observe in reality. They may be a starting, but never an ending, point.

(Published August 15, 2023)

HISTORY

12.6 How Adam Smith proposed to have his cake and eat it too

It is this deception which rouses and keeps in continual motion the industry of mankind. It is this which first prompted them to cultivate the ground, to build houses, to found cities and commonwealths, and to invent and improve all the sciences and arts, which ennoble and embellish human life; which have entirely changed the whole face of the globe, have turned the rude forests of nature into agreeable and fertile plains, and made the trackless and barren ocean a new fund of subsistence, and the great high road of communication to the different nations of the earth ... It is to no purpose, that the proud and unfeeling landlord views his extensive fields, and without a thought for the wants of his brethren, in imagination consumes himself the whole harvest that grows upon them. The homely and vulgar proverb, that the eye is larger than the belly, never was more fully verified than with regard to him. The capacity of his stomach bears no proportion to the immensity of his desires, and will receive no more than that of the meanest peasant. The rest he is obliged to distribute among those, who prepare, in the nicest manner, that little which he himself makes use of, among those who fit up the palace in which this little is to be consumed, among those who provide and keep in order all the different baubles and trinkets, which are employed in the oeconomy of greatness; all of whom thus derive from his luxury and caprice, that share of the necessaries of life, which they would in vain have expected from his humanity or his justice. The produce of the soil maintains at all times nearly that number of inhabitants which it is capable of maintaining. *The rich only select from the heap what is most precious and agreeable.* They consume little more than the poor, and in spite of their natural selfishness and rapacity, though they mean only their own conveniency, though the sole end which they propose from the labours of all the thousands whom they employ, be the gratification of their own vain and insatiable desires, they divide with the poor the produce of all their improvements. They are led by an invisible hand to make nearly the same distribution of the necessaries of life, which would have been made, had the earth been divided into equal portions among all its inhabitants, and thus without intending it, without knowing it, advance the interest of the society, and afford means to the multiplication of the species. When Providence divided the earth among a few lordly masters, it neither forgot nor abandoned those who seemed to have been left out in the partition. These last too enjoy their share of all that it produces. In what constitutes the real

296

ADAM SMITH

happiness of human life, they are in no respect inferior to those who would seem so much above them. In ease of body and peace of mind, all the different ranks of life are nearly upon a level, and the beggar, who suns himself by the side of the highway, possesses that security which kings are fighting for. (*The Theory of Moral Sentiments*, pt. IV.I.10; my emphasis)

Who has not read this long, and famous, paragraph in Smith's *Theory of Moral Sentiments*, and been left absolutely speechless? Not only because it is the first (of only three) mentions of the invisible hand, but because after the most eloquent critique and even ridicule piled upon the rich landlords, it ends with a Panglossian conclusion that everything, in this world of inequity, is actually done in the best possible manner. Who, but the most stone-hearted writer, would *seriously* aspire to defend a distribution of whose injustice he is so critical, and to do this by using the threadbare excuse that the rich really overestimate the worth of their wealth and comforts, and that the poor, "sun[ing] ... by the side of the highway" may be as happy as the rich. It seems so presumptuous a statement that our facilities of reacting to it appear, for a moment, to have been stunted.

David Wootton in a new book *Power, Pleasure and Profit: Insatiable Appetites from Machiavelli to Madison* opens his chapter dedicated to Smith with this long quote. He relates it to the discussion about the two Adam Smiths, the one of the *TMS* (a moralist) and another of the *WoN* (a realist). Wootton argues that Smith's introduction of self-delusion among the rich is crucial to downgrade the moral significance of acquisition of wealth. Smith needs people to believe that wealth will provide them with happiness in order to make them work hard, take risks, and invest, and thus make us all benefit as the society gets wealthier—but he also needs self-delusion to make sure that there is equality in the space of happiness.

The self-delusion is thus the key link that ensures that there is no trade-off between growth and equity. Self-delusion acts as a deflator of all actual wealth: yes, I have a big house, but if I use a delusion deflator of 100, the happiness that it gives me makes it feel like a hut. The social order which produces such inequitable outcomes in the space of actual incomes and wealth, is not impugned: actually existing inequality is immaterial.

But did not Smith really delude himself about that delusion? Wootton writes: "Thus Smith failed to acknowledge the amorality of market forces ... He failed to recognize that speculators and gamblers, thieves and fraudsters often flourished, while people

297

of industry, prudence, and circumspection were broken by forces outside their control" (p. 279).

Had Smith accepted that amoral and often immoral ways in which wealth is acquired (mentioned in innumerable examples in his two books) can still lead to greater happiness of those who engage in such acts, this would have validated the rationality of such behavior. A commercial society could be seen not only as having produced a visible hierarchy in which fraudsters were on the top but allowed them to live happier lives than the rest. How could then such a society be morally justified? Religion came with the answer that such riches are ephemeral: the real riches lie beyond. For Smith, the delusion does the job: it comes in to erase the importance of undeserved gains. Adam Smith can have his cake and eat it.

I do not think that anyone would have defended this point of view today because it relies on something that is manifestly false: that higher income or wealth do not (at a given point in time and given society) lead to greater happiness. This is true empirically (as the studies on happiness show), and it is revealed in our daily behavior through permanent striving for more. Thus, the argument which denies the relevance of massive inequality in the distribution of "earthy" goods by minimizing their importance—or by claiming that in the end, we would all be dead—is indeed one of the most brazenly dishonest arguments. For, if the authors of these kinds of arguments seriously believed them, they should have nothing against the poor and the rich changing their places. But they have seldom proposed to proceed to such a swap.

(Published November 16, 2018)

— 13 —

RICARDO AND MARX

13.1 Ricardo, Marx, and interpersonal inequality

It is a question often asked: what do Ricardo and Marx have to say about interpersonal inequality of income? The answer is, strictly speaking, very little. In writings of neither Ricardo nor Marx does inequality in personal incomes feature at all, and I even think that the concept of what we call "interpersonal inequality" or "size distribution of incomes" does not appear.

The reason why this is the case is both simple and revealing. Ricardo and Marx were concerned with functional (between factors of production) distribution of income, that is with the distribution of net product between workers, capitalists, and landlords (the three big classes introduced by Adam Smith). In Ricardo, this concern was such that he wrote on page 1 of *The Principles*, the famous sentence that the principal problem of political economy is to study the distribution between "proprietors of land, the owners ... of capital and the labourers." Actually, the entire book is organized around that idea. Marx likewise (with a few exceptions) dealt with functional distribution only.

The omission of interpersonal distribution is revealing of the type of society that Ricardo and Marx had in mind. To see this, consider the decomposition of a standard inequality measure like Gini coefficient. It is decomposed into three components: the gap between mean incomes of different groups into which we break a society, inequality within each of these groups, and the "overlap" term, which is non-zero when some members of a mean-poorer group have higher incomes than some members of a mean-richer group.

HISTORY

Now, consider a society that is strictly segregated into classes such that (say) capitalists are rich and workers are poor. Interpersonal inequality looked at through the lenses of a Gini coefficient will not include the overlap term because of a tacit assumption shared by both Ricardo and Marx that all capitalists are richer than all workers (and, if landlords are included, that they are all richer than the other two groups). If, in addition, all workers are paid subsistence or close to subsistence, the within-group inequality for them will be very small. Capitalists and landlords may be differentiated depending on how much capital or land each possesses but, because of their small population size, they will not add much to inequality (Gini within each group is weighed by the group income and population shares).

The bottom line is that most of interpersonal inequality will boil down to the gaps in mean incomes between the two (or if landlords are included, three) classes. Studying only that is not different from being concerned with income shares of the three groups, that is, with functional income distribution. Thus, the question of income inequality between individuals dissolves into the question of income shares of landlords, capitalists and workers. In such a society, it is indeed of little practical import to go beyond functional distribution.

This picture which is, I think, basically accurate, is still a bit simplified, especially as far as Marx is concerned. In Ricardo workers are seen as a homogenous mass facing capitalists such that every increase in the wage rate implies a direct reduction in profit: "a rise of wages, from the circumstance of laborer being more liberally rewarded, or from the difficulty of procuring necessities on which wages are expended, does not ... produce a rise in prices but has a great effect in lowering profits" (*Principles*, ch. I, section 7, p. 31). Or even more clearly: "There is no adequate reason for a fall in profit but a rise in wages, and ... it may be added the only adequate and permanent cause for the rise of wages is the increasing difficulty of providing food and necessities" (*Principles*, ch. XXI, p. 197).

Note that the increase in the wage comes either from an improvement in (what we now call) real wage or from the greater cost of providing subsistence, which, while keeping real wage unchanged, raises the share that belongs to labor, and reduces that of capital. Throughout, not only are the interests of workers and capitalists directly opposed but workers are supposed to be paid subsistence, and when, in very unusual circumstances, they are not, the Malthusian checks kick in to drive them back to subsistence (*Principles*, ch. V).

300

In Marx, the opposition between workers and capitalists is similar but the labourer distinction between simple and complex labor introduces some variability among workers' wages, even if Marx seldom speaks of it. In fact, workers with greater skills will earn more. The rationale is very similar to "human capital" approach. In principle, workers are paid the amount necessary for the reproduction of their class. That could be subsistence only for unskilled workers, who are plentiful, while for skilled workers the costs of reproduction may be above subsistence because it costs more to produce a skilled than an unskilled worker: "[the difference in wages] can be reduced to the different values of labour-power itself, that is, its varying production costs" (*Theories of Surplus Value*; see also Rosdolsky, pp. 515ff.); or "all labor of a higher or more complicated character than average labor is ... labor power whose production has cost more labor and time and which therefore has a higher value than unskilled or simple labor" (*Capital*, vol. I, ch. III, section 7). In contemporary terms we could say that the skilled wage must compensate for the forgone earnings during the period of training and for the cost of additional education.

Income inequality among workers thus moves us a bit further from a narrow functional distribution of income. If, in addition, we allow for the differentiation of capital stock among capitalists, which is implicitly present in both Ricardo and Marx, within-capitalist income Gini will be positive too.

The situation present in today's capitalism but uncommon in classical capitalism, namely that either (i) a worker may be richer than a capitalist, or (ii) that people could have both labor and property incomes, is not envisaged by either Ricardo or Marx. They must have thought both of these possibilities remote and thus not worth complicating the analysis. Possibility (i) existed as some (few?) members of liberal or scientific professions, say doctors or engineers, probably commanded higher incomes than petty capitalists. Possibility (ii) existed only among the self-employed but they could rightly be considered remnants of a past social order and not representative of capitalism. The British social tables, whether in their original form, or as they had been reworked by Lindert and Williamson, or more recently by Bob Allen, can be read as the ranking of different non-overlapping classes where the lion's share of inequality is explained by income gaps between these classes. In other words, we do not lose much in our estimate of total inequality if we ignore both the overlap component, and assume all members of a given class to have the same incomes.

HISTORY

It was thus left to people like Pareto, who were, at the end of the nineteenth century, witnessing less segregated and less hierarchical societies and were lucky to have access to tax data, to move the study of inequality from functional to interpersonal.

(Published April 24, 2020)

13.2 Reading David Ricardo's letters

While redrafting the chapter on Ricardo in my *Visions of Inequality*, I reread, his letters published in the excellently edited (by Piero Sraffa and Maurice Dobb) and handsomely printed volumes of Ricardo's collected writings. Ricardo's letters take four volumes and run from 1810 to 1823, the year of his death. The Sraffa and Dobb edition includes letters written by Ricardo, as well as those sent to him, with very useful notation as to which letter replies to which, so that the correspondence can be easily followed. The letters are not corrected for orthographic or spelling errors.

The letters exchanged between Ricardo and Malthus have been often cited, but less so those between him and James Mill, John Ramsey McCulloch, and Hutches Trower. The latter are perhaps the most interesting, and they were published in a separate volume that contains only Ricardo's letters. Trower was Ricardo's friend from business, from the stock market, where Ricardo made his enormous fortune, before deciding to dedicate more time to other activities, including political economy and politics (he became a member of parliament, by buying the seat in 1818 and remained in the parliament until his death).

The letters deal only sporadically with mundane personal matters; practically all are discussions of economic and political issues. A lot of space is taken by the discussion of the theory of value or by the search for a commodity unchangeable in value, such that all other prices could be reflected in it. Ricardo correctly criticizes Malthus, who decided that such a standard of value should be the average of wage level and price of corn. We know that this search for an unchangeable standard of value ultimately led to Sraffa's "standard commodity." Some of Ricardo's letters that deal with it are very hard to read, and make *Principles*, which too is in parts excessively abstract and dry, seem easy by comparison.

But there are also some lighter parts: "our Princes have certainly not refrained from marriage from the consideration of Malthus' prudential check, and from a fear of producing redundant royal population. If they had they would be now actuated by different motives and we might expect that the great demand for royal infants be followed by so ample supply as to occasion a glut" (Letter to Trower, December 10, 1817).

I find very interesting Ricardo's discussion of the Poor Laws. As is well known, Ricardo was in favor of abolishing Poor Laws on the

HISTORY

grounds that, by entitling poor people to an open-ended assistance, they promoted idleness and, here partly agreeing with Malthus, improvident behavior by the lower classes who might marry earlier and have more children than otherwise. There is still a perceptible difference in tone between Malthus and Ricardo, even if both were against the Poor Laws. While Ricardo expresses sympathy for the poor and, to some extent, believes that they may be, in the longer-term, better off without the Poor Laws, Malthus shows an almost undisguised disdain, and perhaps even hatred, for the lower classes.

I think that one could make a case that Ricardo's rejection of the Poor Laws and his championing of capitalists (as against the landlords) have the same origin: Ricardo's view of political economy as preeminently concerned with economic growth. It is, at first, strange to think that the person who famously wrote on the first page of the *Principles* that the most important problem in political economy is one of distribution should be a champion of economic growth above all. But, as I write in my chapter, this is not surprising if one realizes that for Ricardo change in distribution, that is lower income for landowners and higher income for capitalists, was precisely the indispensable condition for economic growth. It is only capitalists who are regarded as active agents of change and economic growth—since all investments come from profits.

Similarly, I think, one could argue that high spending on the poor (what we would call today high expenditures on social programs) would ultimately detract from profits and hamper economic growth. One can easily recognize in these views today's standard right-wing policy position, but I think that in Ricardo, who obviously had many left-wing continuators, from Marx to Ricardian socialists, to Sraffa's neo-Ricardians, the pro-capitalist position was not motivated by class interest, but by the single-minded focus on economic growth.

In fact, when in a letter to Trower, Ricardo describes his 1822 European continental tour and his dinner with Sismondi, the famous underconsumptionist, this pro-growth concern readily comes through. Ricardo writes:

M. Sismondi who has published a work on political economy, and whose views are quite opposed to mine, was on a visit at the Duke's [de Broglie] house ... Notwithstanding my differences with M. Sismondi on the doctrines of political economy, I'm a great admirer of his talents, and I was very favorably impressed by his manners. I did not expect from what I've seen of his controversial writings to find himself so candid and agreeable. M. Sismondi takes enlarged

RICARDO AND MARX

views, and is sincerely desirous of establishing principles which he conceives to be most conducive to the happiness of mankind. He holds that the great cause of the misery of the bulk of the people in all countries is the unequal distribution of property, which tends to brutalize and degrade the lower classes. The way to elevate men, to prevent him from making inconsiderate marriages, is to give him property and an interest in the general welfare—thus far we should pretty well agree, but when he contends that abundance of production caused by machinery, and by other means, is the cause of the unequal distribution of property, and that the end he has in view cannot be accomplished while this abundant production continues, he, I think, entirely misconceives the subject, and does not succeed in showing the connection of his premises with his conclusions. (Letter to Trower, December 14, 1822, pp. 195–196)

I would like to finish with two remarks made in passing by Ricardo, which, when "unpacked," are pregnant of deep meaning and have a thoroughly contemporary ring to them. The first is made in connection to James Mill's *History of India*, which Mill was in the process of writing during the period of correspondence. (By the way, James Mill who was of the same age as Ricardo appears in the letters as a benevolent elder on whose unerring advice Ricardo much depends.) There, Ricardo reflects on our inability to ever fully comprehend other cultures, not because they are irrational and not because we are not smart enough, but because our worldview is fashioned by our experience, which may be entirely different from that of people from other cultures.

However well we may have examined the end to which all our laws should tend, yet when they are to influence the actions of a different people we have to acquire a thorough knowledge of the peculiar habits, prejudices and objects of desire of such people, which is itself an almost unattainable knowledge, for I am persuaded that from our own peculiar habits and prejudices we should frequently see these things through a false medium, and our judgment would err accordingly. (Ricardo to James Mill, November 9, 1817, p. 204)

This penetrating observation should give us pause, I think, when we too readily pronounce on matters we do not know sufficiently or on cultures with which we are only superficially acquainted. (One can, of course, imagine that the observation was influenced also by Ricardo's own past, rejection of Judaism, and conflict with his parents.)

HISTORY

The second note is on the role of political economy. Ricardo writes:

Political economy would teach us to guard ourselves from every other revulsion, but that which arises from the rise and fall of states—from the progress of improvement in other countries than our own, and from the caprices of fashion—against these we cannot guard. (Letter to Trower, October 3, 1820)

There are, he says, three exogenous changes that even the best economics cannot deal with. The first are exogenous political changes that affect economic matters. What better example than today's war in Ukraine—from the point of view of domestic economics, whether in the US, Russia, Ukraine, or the European Union—an entirely exogenous shock with, nevertheless, huge economic repercussions.

The second exogenous shock is the arrival of new technologies. Here, interestingly, Ricardo seems to say that the exogeneity occurs only if the shock is externally generated, that is, comes from abroad. That could be, for example, the development of synthetic rubber in Germany in the 1910s, or the agricultural revolution in Asia in the 1960s, or the invention of the "just-in-time" system in Japan in the 1980s: all were exogenous technological shocks for the American producers. But, by circumscribing exogeneity of technology only to abroad, Ricardo seems to be saying that domestic technological development is endogenous; that is, is determined by domestic policy instruments (say, interest rate, exchange rate, subsidies, and taxes) and that technology is not a manna from heaven but the outgrowth of economic management. However, since we do not have control over foreign countries' economic management, technological developments there (which are from their point of view endogenous) appear to us as exogenous, and hence as something that we cannot control.

The third exogenous element is "the caprice of fashion" or what in today's eco-lingo would be called "change in preferences." This, of course, is a very wide field. It could include many things, from ordinary fashions to a change in taste for working long hours and making money. Today's still marginal but growing "culture of withdrawal," which we observe in Japan and China can be one such change in fashion. There too, Ricardo is right, economics cannot do much. If you want to stimulate growth but people are content with their incomes and just wish to work less, economic policy will, in the end, be powerless to change it.

306

It is often in these dispersed observations, made in his letters, that we can better appreciate Ricardo the man, and the fundamental decency and gentleness of his character, and Ricardo, not only as one of the founders of political economy, but a deep thinker about the limits of power of economics and our own knowledge.

(Published October 2, 2022)

HISTORY

13.3 The Ricardian windfall: David Ricardo and the absence of the equity-efficiency trade-off

David Ricardo is rightly famous (among other things) for being the father of functional income distribution (distribution between the three factors of production: land, labor, and capital). For it is in *The Principles* that the definition of each factor of production, with its distinct source of income, is most sharply made: to the landlords, the rent; to the capitalist, the profit; to the workers, the wage. But, Ricardo, like other classical writers and later marginalists too, never cared to develop, or even look at, personal income distribution. To Ricardo, like to Marx, what happens to personal income distribution was self-evident, even redundant to explain because individuals were basically defined by their class incomes. Workers' income was always at subsistence and landlords' income was determined by the cost of production of corn at the worst parcel of land such that it allowed "reasonable" profit of (say) 5 percent to the capitalist tenant.

As is well known, the entire Ricardian apparatus was created to show the irrationality of the Corn Laws. With the Corn Laws and an increase in population, less and less fertile land will have to be cultivated to provide food for workers. The price of food will increase and, since the real wage (in our usual terminology) is fixed, it would imply that capitalists will have to pay more of their net income to workers (so that the capital-to-labor income will move against capital; which in Ricardo's terminology is called the increase in the real wage). Thus, capitalists' profits will go down (say to 3%), workers' wage will remain fixed, and landlords' income will go up.

As Ricardo quite emphatically writes (*Principles*, ch. XXI): "however abundant capital may become, there is no other adequate reason for a fall in profits but a rise of wages, and further ... the only adequate and permanent cause for a rise of wages [compared to profit] is the increasing difficulty of providing food and necessities for the increasing number of workers." (Note that Ricardo does not believe in diminishing returns to capital with capital deepening.)

If we now translate this "class-based" outcome in terms of personal income distribution, where all workers are at the bottom of the pyramid, capitalists in the middle, and landlords at the top, we can derive a growth incidence curve (which charts the increase of real income against one's initial position in income distribution). To make the figure more realistic we can use the approximate incomes and population shares of the three groups. From Colquhoun, social

308

tables for England and Wales (drawn up for the period between 1798 and 1801) and recently systematized by Bob Allen in his *The Industrial Revolution: A Very Short Introduction*, we know that the average income of the landlords was about 54 times greater than subsistence, bourgeoisie (which we assimilate to capitalists) had an income 37 times greater than subsistence, and workers four times (that is, they were not at the physiological subsistence minimum as Ricardo tended, without data of course, to assume). Their respective population shares were 1.3%, 3.2%, and 61% (I omit the other intermediary classes).

Take now that over the medium to long term landlords move to have an income 64 times subsistence, capitalists 27 times, and workers stay where they are. The growth incidence curve will look approximately as in Figure 13.1, and the share of the top one percent (that is, of the landlords) will increase from 16% to 20%, while the mean income declines.

Thus, with the continuation of the Corn Laws, not only will functional income distribution move in favor of the rich landlords, but the personal income distribution would get worse too.

What was, as is also well known, Ricardo's counter-proposal? Eliminate the Corn Law and let the foreign corn (from Russia, US) flow freely into England. Now, the reverse happens: landlords lose (as the production on their land becomes too expensive to compete with foreign corn), workers' real wage stays the same but, to capitalists, workers become "cheaper," since for the same quantity of food they have to pay them less out of their net income. The growth incidence curve now changes: the top loses, the middle gains, the bottom is unchanged. Income concentration becomes less. (I do not draw it here; it can be easily done.)

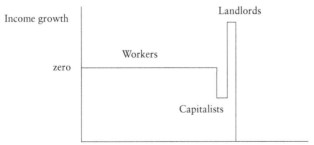

Figure 13.1

Moreover, as Ricardo argued, if you do not follow his advice, the food produced in England will ultimately become so expensive that the entire capitalists' income will be swallowed by wages, the net (after-wage) rate of profit will tend toward zero, capitalists will invest less and less, and the economy will go back to its historical stationarity. Thus, higher inequality will be associated with slower growth, and ultimately with zero growth.

If the Corn Laws are repealed, however, capitalists' profit will increase, they will save and invest more and the economy will grow. Therefore, lower interpersonal inequality will be associated with faster growth.

Pace Okun, there is no trade-off between equity and efficiency for David Ricardo. In effect, just the very opposite: lower inter-personal inequality leads to faster economic growth. It took thirty years after *The Principles* ... for the Corn Laws in England to be rescinded, but one can easily see how attractive was the sketch of development that Ricardo presented to his readers: he promised to deliver both faster growth and to reduce inequality. Shall we term it the "Ricardian windfall"?

(Published March 11, 2016)

RICARDO AND MARX

13.4 The influence of Karl Marx—a counterfactual

The two-hundredth anniversary of Karl Marx's birth is giving rise to many conferences dedicated to numerous (and God knows there were many) aspects of Marx's work and life. (I am going to one such conference in Haifa.) Add to it an even greater number of reviews of his work and influence (Peter Singer just published one a couple of days ago), new books on his life, a movie on Young Marx—and the list goes on.

I will also look here at Marx's intellectual influence—but from a very different angle. I will use the counterfactual approach. I would ask what would have been his influence had not three remarkable events happened. Clearly, like all counterfactuals, it is based on personal reading of history and guesswork. It cannot be proven right. I am sure that others could come with different counterfactuals—perhaps better than mine.

The first event: had there been no Engels. This counterfactual had been discussed but it is worth reviewing. When Karl Marx died in 1883, he was the coauthor of *The Communist Manifesto*, a number of political and social short studies, newspaper articles (in the *New York Daily Tribune*) and a thick but not well-known or much translated book called *Das Kapital* (volume 1). It was published sixteen years before his death and, during the intervening years, he wrote a lot but published little. Toward the end of his life, he even wrote little. Similarly unpublished and in a mess were hundreds of pages of his manuscripts from the late 1840s, and the 1850s and 1860s. Marx was known among the rather small circle of worker activists, and German, French, Austrian, and increasingly Russian social-democrats. Had it remained so, that is, had not Engels spent more than ten years putting Marx's papers in order and producing two additional volumes of *Das Kapital*, Marx's fame would have ended at the point where it was in 1883. It would have been rather minimal. I doubt that anyone would have remembered his birthday today.

But, thanks to Engels' selfless work and dedication (and Engels' own importance in German social-democracy), Marx's importance grew. Social-democrats became the largest party in Germany and this further carried Marx's influence forward. Under Kautsky, the *Theories of Surplus Value* was published. The only other countries where, within a very narrow circle, he was influential, were Russia and Austria-Hungary.

311

HISTORY

The first decade of the twentieth century saw the increasing influence of Marxist thought, so much so that Leszek Kolakowski in his monumental *Main Currents of Marxism* rightly calls it "the golden age." It was indeed the golden age of Marxist thought in terms of the caliber of people who wrote in the Marxist vein, but not in terms of global influence. For Marx's thought made no inroads into the Anglo-Saxon world (the first English translation of *Das Kapital*—which is still, strangely, referred to by its German title— was in 1887, that is twenty years after its original publication). And, in Southern Europe, including France, he was eclipsed by anarchists and by "petty bourgeois socialists."

This is where the things would have ended had there not been the Great War. I think that Marx's influence would have steadily gone down as the social-democrats in Germany moved toward reformism and "revisionism." His picture would have probably been displayed among the historical *maîtres à penser* of the German social-democracy but not much of his influence would have remained, neither in policy nor (probably) in social sciences.

But, then, the October Revolution came (the second event). This totally transformed the scene. Not only because he was "allotted" the glory, unique among social scientists, to be single-handedly ideologically responsible for a momentous change in one big country and in world history, but because socialism, due to its worldwide reach, "catapulted" Marx's thought and fame. His thinking, whether for good or ill, became unavoidable in most of Europe, whether among intellectuals, political activists, labor leaders, or ordinary workers. Evening schools were organized by trade unionists to study his writings; political leaders, due to the particularly dogmatic turn taken by the communist parties, planned their moves and explained them by the references to the hitherto little-known Marx's historical writings.

Then, as the Comintern began to abandon its Eurocentrism and to get engaged in anti-imperialist struggle in the Third World, Marx's influence expanded to the areas no one could have predicted it would (the third event). He became the ideologue of the new movements for social revolution and national liberation in Asia, Afric,a and Latin America. Whether political leaders stuck to his precepts or abandoned them (as Mao did by putting peasantry rather than workers in the role of the revolutionary class), Marx influenced them—and it is in the reference to him that they explained their policies. Thanks to Trotsky and Stalin in Russia, to the left-wing republicans in Spain, popular front in France, Mao in China, Ho

312

Shi Minh in Vietnam, Tito in Yugoslavia, Castro in Cuba, Agostino Neto in Angola, Nkrumah in Ghana, Mandela in South Africa, Marx became a global "influencer." Never had a social scientist had such a global reach. Who would have thought that two bearded nineteenth-century Germans would adorn on special occasions the Gate of Heavenly Peace in Beijing?

And, not only did he have global influence, but his influence cut across class and professional lines. I have already mentioned revolutionary leaders, politicians, and trade unionists. But the influence spread to the academe, to high schools. It influenced both those who opposed him and those who extolled him. That influence went from elementary Marxism, which was taught to high-school students to sophisticated philosophical treatises or "analytical Marxism" in economics. The publication of Marx's manuscripts from 1848–1850, brought us the unknown young Marx and that moved the discussion to an even higher plane: there was now a philosophical battle between the Young and classical Marx.

None of that would have happened without the October revolution and a decisive turn away from Eurocentrism and toward the Third World. It is the latter that transformed Marx from a German and European thinker into a global figure.

As communism's crimes became better known, and gradually increasingly laid on Marx's door, and as communist regimes sputtered and their mournful and poorly educated ideologues regurgitated predictable phrases, Marx's thought suffered an eclipse. The fall of communist regimes brought it to its low point.

But then—the third event—globalized capitalism that exhibits all the features that Marx so eloquently described in *Das Kapital*, and the Global Financial Crisis, made his thought relevant again. By now he was safely ensconced into the Pantheon of global philosophers, his every extant word published, his books available in all the languages of the world, and his status, while still subject to vagaries of time, safe—at least in the sense that it could never fall into obscurity and oblivion.

In fact, his influence is inextricably linked with capitalism. So long as capitalism exists, Marx will be read as its most astute analyst. If capitalism ceases to exist, he will be read as its best critic. So, whether or not we believe that in another 200 years, capitalism will be with us, we can be sure that Marx will.

His place is now there with those of Plato and Aristotle but, were it not for the three favorable and unlikely turns of events, we might

HISTORY

have hardly heard of an obscure German émigré who died long time ago in London, accompanied to his grave by eight people (as reported by *Der Sozialdemokrat* on March 22, 1883; that is, a week after his death).

(Published May 2, 2018)

RICARDO AND MARX

13.5 Marx for me (and hopefully for others too)

Yesterday I had a conversation about my work, about how and why I started studying inequality more than thirty years ago, what was my motivation, how it was to work on income inequality in an officially classless (and non-democratic) society, did the World Bank care about inequality, etc. The interviewer and I thus came to some methodological issues and to the inescapable influence of Marx on my work. I want to present it more systematically in this post.

The most important of Marx's influences on people working in social sciences is, I think, his economic interpretation of history. This has become so much part of the mainstream that we no longer associate it with Marx very much. And surely, he was not the only one, or even the first, to have defined it. But he applied it most consistently and most creatively.

Even when we believe that such an interpretation of history is common-place today, this still is not entirely so. Take the current dispute about the reasons that brought Trump to power. Some (mostly those who believe that everything that went on previously was fine) blame a sudden outburst of xenophobia, hatred, and misogyny. Others (like myself) see that outburst as having been caused by long economic stagnation of middle-class incomes, and rising insecurity (of jobs, health care expenses, ability to pay for children's education). So, the latter group tends to place economic factors first and to explain how they lead to racism, etc. There is a big difference between the two approaches—not only in their diagnosis of the causes but, more importantly, in their view of what needs to be done.

The second Marx's insight, which I think is absolutely indispensable in the work on income and wealth inequality, is to see that economic forces that influence historical developments do that through "large groups of people who differ in their position in the process of production," namely through social classes. The classes can be defined by the difference in the access to the means of production, as Marx insisted, but not only by that. Going back to my work on socialist economies, there was a very influential left-wing critique of socialist systems, which held that social classes in that system were formed on the basis of differential access to state power. Bureaucracy can indeed be seen as a social class. And not only under socialism, but also in pre-capitalist formations, where the role of the state as an "extractor of the surplus value" was important, from ancient Egypt

HISTORY

to medieval Russia. Many African countries today can be usefully analyzed using that particular lens. In my *Capitalism, Alone* I use the same approach with respect to the countries of political capitalism, notably China.

But, to underline: class analysis is absolutely crucial for all students of inequality, precisely because inequality before it becomes an individual phenomenon ("my income is low") is a social phenomenon that affects large swathes of people ("my income is low because women are discriminated," or because African Americans are discriminated, or poor people cannot access good education, etc.). To give a couple of examples of what I have in mind here: Piketty's work, especially in *Top Incomes in France*, and Rodriguez Weber's book on Chilean income distribution over the long term (*Desarrollo y desigualdad en Chile (1850–2009): Historia de su economía política*). On the other hand, I think that Tony Atkinson's work on British and various other income and wealth distributions failed to sufficiently integrate political and class analysis.

This is also where the work on inequality parts ways with one of the scourges of modern micro- and macro-economics, the representative agent. The role of the representative agent was to obliterate all meaningful distinctions between large groups of people, whose social positions differ, by focusing on the observation that everybody is an "agent," who tries to maximize income under a set of constraints. This is indeed trivially true. And, by being trivially true, it disregards the multitude of features that make these "agents" truly different: their wealth, background, power, ability to save, gender, race, ownership of capital, or the need to sell labor, access to the state, etc. I would thus say that any serious work on inequality must reject the use of representative agents as a way to approach reality. I am very optimistic that this will happen because the representative agent itself was the product of two developments, both currently on the wane: an ideological desire, especially strong in the United States because of the McCarthy-like pressures to deny the existence of social classes, and the lack of heterogeneous data. For example, median income or income by decile was hard to calculate, but GDP per capita was easy to get hold of.

The third extremely important Marx's methodological contribution is the realization that economic categories are dependent on social formations. What are mere means of production (tools) in an economy composed of small-commodity producers becomes capital in a capitalist economy. But it goes further. The equilibrium (normal) price in a feudal economy, or in a guild system, where capital is not

316

allowed to move between the branches, will be different from the equilibrium prices in a capitalist economy with the free movement of capital. To many economists this is still not obvious. They use today's capitalist categories for the Roman Empire, where wage labor was, in the words of Moses Finley, "spasmodic, casual and marginal" (*Ancient Slavery and Modern Ideology*, p. 68).

But, even if they do not realize it fully, they *de facto* acknowledge the importance of the institutional set up of a society in determining prices, not only of goods, but also of the factors of production. Again, we see it daily. Suppose that the world produces exactly the same set of commodities and the demand for them is exactly the same, but it does so within national economies that do not permit movement of capital and labor, and then does it in an entirely globalized economy, where borders do not exist. Clearly, the prices of capital and labor (profit and wage) will be different in the latter, the distribution of income between capital owners and workers will be different, prices will change as profits and wages change, incomes will change too, and so will consumption patterns, and, ultimately, even the structure of production will be altered. Indeed, this is what today's globalization is doing.

The fact that property relations determine prices and the structure of production and consumption is an extremely important insight. The historical character of any institutional arrangement is thereby highlighted.

The last among Marx's contribution that I would like to single out—perhaps the most important and grandiose—is that the succession of socio-economic formations (or more restrictively, of the modes of production) is itself "regulated" by economic forces, including the struggle for the distribution of the economic surplus. The task of economics is nothing less than global historical: to explain the rise and fall not solely of countries but of different forms of organizing production: Why were nomads superseded by the sedentary popula-tions? Why did the Western Roman Empire break into a few large feudal-like demesnes and serfs, while the Eastern Roman Empire remained populated by small landholders? Whoever studies Marx can never forget the grandiosity of the questions that are being asked. For such a student, then, using supply and demand curves to determine the cost of pizza in his city will indeed be acceptable, but surely will never be seen as the prime or the most important role of economics as a social science.

(Published December 28, 2018)

HISTORY

13.6 Marx on income inequality under capitalism

Among those who have read Marx, it is well known that Marx was rather indifferent to the issue of inequality under capitalism. Among those who have not read him, but know the left-wing views from social-democracy and assume that Marx's view must have been similar (but just more radical) this is not well known, nor are the grounds for such an attitude well understood.

(Marx's views on the topic are dispersed: they are in *Grundrisse*, *The 18th Brumaire* ... *Capital*, *Critique of the Gotha Program*. A very nice and succinct recent discussion can be found in Allen W. Wood's piece "Marx on equality.")

There are several grounds on which Marx treats inequality as we currently understand it—that is, inequality of income or wealth between individuals—as relatively inconsequential.

The first ground has to do what is the main, as opposed to derivative, contradiction in capitalism: that between owners of capital and those who have nothing else but their labor-power. As in Ricardo, for Marx, class determines one's position in income distribution. Class is therefore prior to income distribution. It is the abolition of classes that matters. Engels (who certainly on this had the same opinion as Marx) wrote: "'The elimination of all social and political inequality' [as stated in the social-democratic program that he is criticizing] rather than 'the abolition of class distinctions', is ... a most dubious expression, as between one country, one province and even place and another, living conditions will always evince a certain inequality which may be reduced to a minimum but never wholly eliminated" (Letter to August Bebel).

Once classes are abolished, the "background institutions" are just and this is the moment to begin any real discussion about what is a fair distribution. This is the topic about which Marx wrote (more) relatively late in his life, in *Critique of the Gotha Program* in 1875. He introduced there the famous distinction between the distribution of income under socialism ("to everybody according to their work") and under communism ("to everybody according to their needs").

Under socialism, as Marx writes, equality in treatment presupposes an original inequality because people of unequal physical or mental abilities will be rewarded unequally: "This equal right is an unequal right for unequal labor" (*Critique*).

Under communism, however, in a Utopia of abundance, the real equality may imply an observed *inequality* in consumption, as some

318

people whose "needs" are greater decide to consume more than other people whose "needs" are less. If, in a hypothetical communist society, we observe a Gini coefficient of 0.4 like in today's United States, it tells us nothing about inequalities in the two societies—and certainly not that the two societies display the same level of inequality. In one (communism), it is a voluntary inequality, in the other involuntary.

One is, of course, reminded here of Amartya Sen's "capabilities approach": achievement of equality might require unequal treatment of unequal individuals.

The second ground of relative unconcern comes from Marx's insistence that production and distribution are "unified": capitalist mode of production, with private ownership of the means of production and hired labor, results in a given distribution of income. It does not make sense to focus on a change in distribution so long as the endowments are distributed unequally, and some people, thanks to such unequal distribution of endowments, are allowed to collect income, while hiring others to work. Marx here disagrees explicitly with J. S. Mill, who thought that the laws of production are "physical" or "mechanical," while the laws of distribution are historical. For Marx both are historical.

> Any distribution whatever of the means of consumption is only a consequence of the distribution of the conditions of production themselves. The latter distribution, however, is a feature of the mode of production itself. The capitalist mode of production, for example, rests on the fact that the material conditions of production are in the hands of non-workers in the form of property in capital and land, while the masses are only owners of the personal conditions of production, of labor power. If the means of production are so distributed, then the modern-day distribution of the means of consumption results automatically. (*Critique of the Gotha Program*)

And, quite importantly:

> Vulgar socialism has taken over from the bourgeois economists the consideration and treatment of distribution as independent of the mode of production and hence the presentation of socialism as turning principally on distribution. (*Critique …*)

This point of view can be criticized by pointing to the redistributive role of the state. In Marx's time that role was minimal and, hence, distribution of income perfectly mirrored the distribution of endowments.

HISTORY

But, if the link between the two is broken or modified through the intermediation of the state, the mode of production no longer uniquely determines the distribution of "the means of consumption."

The third ground for unconcern is more philosophical. Hired labor implies alienation of the worker from the meaning and product of his work. If the fundamental issue is alienation, it cannot be overcome by mere improvements in the distribution of income. As a hired worker in Amazon, I am as alienated from my work at Amazon, whether my wage is $10 per hour or $50 per hour. To transcend alienation, both private property and the division of labor have to be abolished.

All of these grounds lead to the rejection of the salience of inequality *as such* under capitalism. How is it then that trade union activity, or social activism in general, is justified if the improvements in the material conditions of workers cannot be the ultimate objective of a Marxist-inspired movement operating under capitalist conditions? Here, Marx takes a very different stance from the usual social-democratic. The struggle for the increase in wages, the shortening of the working week, lower intensity of work, etc., are all valuable because they highlight the antagonistic nature of capitalist relations and, more importantly, because the joint work and unity of purpose implicit in social activism create bonds that presage the future society of collaboration and even of altruism. As Shlomo Avineri writes: "[Workers' association] does not have a narrowly political, nor a trade union significance: it is the real constructive effort to create the social texture of future human relations" (*The Social and Political Thought of Karl Marx*, p. 142).

The primary objective of such social activism is ... pedagogical: the learning of social cooperation and, only secondarily, the improvement in the economic conditions of the working class—or any other group whose interests are thus promoted: gender, race, or ethnicity. (One can even go further and say that such social activism is the essence of praxis: "man's conscious shaping of the changing historical conditions" [Kolakowski, *Main Currents* ... vol. 1, p. 138]).

For all these reasons, a student of income distribution, in the current sense of the term, or the social activist who proposes one or another meliorative measure, is involved in something that, from Marx's perspective, while not useless, as it makes the underlying contradictory class interests more apparent, fundamentally does little to move the reality of life under capitalism toward the creation of just "background institutions."

(Published February 13, 2022)

13.7 Transcending capitalism: Three different ways?

After the crisis of 2007–2008, capitalism has entered among some parts of the public opinion into an ideological crisis. (I have written elsewhere why I think that this is not a general crisis of capitalism but a limited response to the decline of Western economic and political power; see the *Guardian* article cited below.) However, the question of durability or of non-permanency of capitalism has, unlike in the years after the fall of communism, re-entered the public discourse. In many ways, in the West, the situation is returning to the 1970s or earlier, when the ideas of alternative socio-economic systems were hotly debated. This is something that had disappeared in the next several decades, driven away by neoliberalism in economics, the collapse of Soviet socialism, and the imposition of the pensée unique.

Now, things are changing, and, understandably, many people bring their own ideas about how capitalism can be "transcended," that is replaced by a different socio-economic system. I want here to highlight three different ways in which this subject has recently been addressed.

In a new paper "What is Socialism Today?: Conceptions of a Cooperative Economy," John Roemer starts with three essential pillars of all economic systems: an ethos of economic behavior, an ethic of distributive justice, and a set of property relations. In capitalism the three pillars are: (1) individualistic ethos, (2) laissez-faire (no redistribution), and (3) privately owned means of production with profit accruing to capitalists. Until now, Roemer argues, all attempts to transcend capitalism focused on element No. 3, replacing privately owned capital with state or socially (collectively) owned capital. They have all failed.

Instead of that, our emphasis should be, according to Roemer, on developing a solidaristic ethos. Using the terminology from the game theory, Roemer contrasts the Nashian ethos, where each individual behaves to maximize his or her gain (and which, in some cases, like the prisoner dilemma, may lead to the paradoxical outcomes) and the Kantian ethos, where we behave in the way in which we wish that everybody else would behave. This is a form of a golden rule (behave toward others the way you wish that they behaved toward you), or, in more narrowly economic language, we try to internalize (account for) the behavior of everybody else.

In a presentation given recently at the Graduate Center, CUNY, Roemer gave the example of the "tragedy of the commons," where

HISTORY

Nashian (narrowly profit-motivated individuals) maximize their own fishing with the result that eventually no fish remain vs. a Kantian type of solidaristic behavior, where one would think that if he increases his fishing everybody else would do the same. The person would thus "internalize" the behavior of others and presumably avoid the tragedy of the commons.

Roemer argues that, as societies get richer and as a conscious effort is made, the percentage of "Kantians" would increase compared to the "Nashians," and we would gradually move toward more solidaristic and cooperative societies. A nice example that Roemer used to buttress his case is the increasing attention given to environment, where many people make an extra effort to adjust their own consumption or sort different types of trash, even if neither is monitorable and defections are costless. Still, many do it the way they wished everybody else did.

A different way of "transcending capitalism" was recently proposed in Piketty's new book *Capital and Ideology*. In the last part of the book, Piketty, after reviewing on some 800 pages the ways in which various hierarchical and property relations that seem abhorrent to us today (slavery, patriarchy, racism, serfdom, etc.) have been ideologically justified, argues in favor of ending the fetishism of private property. In terms of Roemer's taxonomy, Piketty is clearly back to the pillar No. 3 but, unlike Marxists and the Soviets, Piketty does not require a dogmatic thoroughgoing elimination of all private property but looks at the ways in which the economic power held by property holders could be limited. To that objective, he deploys a radical yet realistic proposal, whereby all enterprises after a certain size would have obligatory workers' shareholding, with workers holding 50 percent of the shares, and no single capitalist (regardless of the amount of capital he has invested in the company) could hold more than one-tenth of the capitalist half of shares. (Thus, even the largest owner would be limited to five percent of total voting power). The system, however, would allow small enterprises to be managed as they are now, with capitalists holding the full power, and workers being a hired labor, but, as soon as such enterprises would go over the threshold, obligatory workers' shareholding would kick in.

This two-tier system at the production level would be combined with the system of the so-called "temporary ownership," consisting of severe annual taxation of private wealth and progressive taxation of inheritance.

The aim of the two systems (production-stage and fiscal) is to fundamentally alter the relations of production in favor of labor and to limit the accumulation of private wealth. The latter will not only change levels of inequality that currently exist but would structurally constrain the ability of the rich to control the political process and to transmit their wealth across generations. It would thus significantly change inter-generational mobility. But, more importantly, perhaps, it would change the intra-enterprise hierarchical relations between owners and workers.

(Piketty's ideas have been criticized, including in a debate with Frédéric Lordon, for being un-Marxist, in the sense that they do not go beyond the logic of capital or social-democracy, do not dispense with all power relations derived from ownership, and that his concept of social change is idealistic, as opposed to materialistic.)

A third way to envisage the change in modern capitalism is somewhat different, and I briefly mention it at the end of *Capitalism, Alone*. It is materialistic and grounded in the "objective" relationship between the two factors of production (labor and capital), or, more exactly, in their relative scarcities. It is based on a standard Marx-Weber tripartite definition of capitalism (used in the book): (a) production is carried using privately owned means of production, (b) labor is legally free but hired (that is, the entrepreneurial function is exercised by owners), and (c) coordination of economic decision-making is decentralized. Now, as I argue in *Capitalism, Alone*, the current apotheosis of capitalism is largely due to the weakening power of labor, brought about by the doubling of the global labor force that works under capitalist conditions, following the transition to capitalism of the Soviet-bloc countries, China, Vietnam, and India. Furthermore, the digital capitalism of today has enabled commer-cialization ("commodification") of many activities that have never been commercialized before and has thus made further inroads into our private life. The dominion of capitalism has become extended, both geographically (to encompass the entire globe), and "internally" to move to our individual private sphere.

But, if the underlying relations of relative scarcities between labor and capital change in this century or the next, if the world population reaches its peak and remains there (as all projections indicate), and if the capital stock keeps on increasing, we might face an entirely different situation between capital and labor—very much the reverse of the one the world is facing after 1990. The relative abundance of capital may allow individuals to become entrepre-neurs by simply borrowing capital and not letting the suppliers of funds have a decisive role in management. This is what we currently observe in the start-up world. It might seem not important, but it is: the agency which is now almost exclusively vested in capitalists would be transferred to "workers." The component (b) of the standard Marx-Weber definition of capitalism—the existence of wage labor—would disappear. The system would still maintain the private ownership of the means of production and decentralized coordination: it would be a market economy, but it would not be a capitalist market economy.

This "transcending" would be different from the other two. Unlike Roemer, it would not rely on the change in our ethos and, unlike Piketty, it would not depend on constructivist change in the rules but would arise "organically" from the changed relationship between the two factors of production. Being "organic" would also make it stronger and more durable.

(Published February 7, 2020)

13.8 On unproductive labor

Today I read an article on shortages and economic collapse in Venezuela. The reason why there are huge lines in front of the stores was the same known to any student of socialist economies: state stores sell heavily subsidized goods and the demand for such goods exceeds their supply. Then, many people buy much more than they need and engage in selling the goods at higher prices to those who are either sufficiently rich to pay higher prices or who have been unlucky that the supply ended before their turn came.

The buyers and resellers of such goods in Venezuela are called, according to the *New York Times*, *bachaqueros*. Ricardo Hausmann, from the Kennedy School at Harvard, who was Venezuela's planning minister in the 1990s, was then quoted by the *New York Times* as saying: "This is the crazy thing about the system. A lot of people are putting in effort [to buy the goods and resell them], and none of that increases the supply of anything. This is perfectly unproductive labor."

That statement made me stop. "Perfectly unproductive labor"? But that "unproductive labor," as every economist knows, improves the allocation of goods. The goods flow toward those who have greater ability to pay and, since we tend to associate greater ability to pay with greater utility, the goods, thanks to bachaqueros' activities, are better allocated. If one argues that bachaqueros activity is unproductive because it "does not increase the supply of anything," then one should argue that the activity of any trade or intermediation is unproductive because it does not produce new goods, but simply reallocates. The same argument could be used for the entire financial sector, starting with Wall Street. The entire activity of Wall Street has not produced a single pound of flour, a single loaf of bread or a single sofa. But, why we believe that financial intermediation is productive is that it allows money to flow from the places where it would be less efficiently used to the places where it would be used more efficiently. Or, for that matter, from the consumers who cannot pay much to the consumers who can. Exactly the activity done by bachaqueros.

Haussmann's view is identical to the (falsely) Marxist view of productive and unproductive activities reflected in socialist countries' national accounts, called Material Net Product. Socialist countries' approach was that all services (including health, education, and government administration) were unproductive because they did not produce new physical goods. Obviously, speculators like bachaqueros were the very epitome of unproductive, and, even (it was held) "socially noxious" or "abhorrent" labor. This view had practical consequences for the calculation of national income because the level of national income in socialist countries was underestimated, compared to what it would be according to the UN's System of National Accounts, but the rate of growth was overestimated because productivity increases were generally greater in production of goods than of services.

Marx had a distinction between productive and unproductive labor which was more sophisticated. Productive was all labor that resulted in the production of the surplus value. Thus, Marx, in a well-known example, shows that a singer (a prototype of activity that does not produce anything tangible) is engaged in productive labor so long as he is hired by a company or an individual and creates profit for his employer. In Marx's view productive-unproductive dichotomy was not given forever but changed depending on the socio-economic formation. The problem with socialist governments in Eastern Europe was that they had trouble deciding what should be productive and unproductive according to Marx in a socialist society, and took the easy road to declare unproductive whatever activity did not produce tangible physical goods.

There was also a categorization introduced by Ann Krueger in the 1970s, who defined the so-called "directly unproductive activities" or "rent-seeking activities." The idea was to classify under such headings all activities whose objective is to extract some government concession that would result in higher incomes for those successful in lobbying. Pharmaceutical and IT companies that pay hundreds of K Street lobbyists in Washington today would fall under that category—even if Krueger's classification was originally intended mostly to push developing countries' governments to be less interventionist (it was directed especially against "India's Licence Raj"; see, e.g., Bhagwati's *Why Growth Matters*). Lobbying was, it was argued, unproductive, because it led to the creation of rents. And rent is, of course, an income that can be taken away, without affecting the supply and allocation of goods.

Finally, it leads us to the topic of theft. It is not easy to put theft in its right place in economics. Theft for private use can be justified by arguing that the bread stolen by a poor person from a rich one is almost certain to increase the amount of "social happiness." (I have often thought of that in New York, where that old-fashioned idea that one should keep $20 in his/her wallet to give it to a mugger certainly made sense in raising the happiness for the greatest number.)

The issue is more complicated when we come to the theft for resale: burglary of a jewelry store and resale of the jewels might increase overall welfare, if burglars are very poor and the jewelry owner very rich, but it cannot be defended on better allocation grounds because the jewels could have been equally accessible to those who wanted to buy them, whether they are sold by the owner or by thieves.

The issue of preventing theft leads us to yet another category of labor that can also be considered unproductive: security personnel, or what is called the "guard labor." Their salaries are paid in order to prevent theft. They clearly do not increase the supply of goods, nor do they improve goods' allocation. The only defense that their labor does produce something is in the argument that prevention of theft improves protection of property, which makes for more investments and increases long-term growth. But this is, as can be seen, a rather convoluted justification, which, by the way, can also be used to argue why theft, even if it might improve short-term welfare, is likely to be pernicious in the longer-term, a point of view that goes back to Adam Smith.

Deciding for a capitalist economy what is productive and what is unproductive labor is not always easy. How much more difficult if we study economic history: how to classify monks and priests when they are paid by legally compulsory tithes; Robin Hood could be defended on the maximization of utility principle, but criticized as inimical to long-term growth; Francis Drake stole goods owned by the Spaniards, who extracted them by using forced labor ...

(Published May 30, 2016)

HISTORY

13.9 When Tocqueville and Marx agreed

While writing the chapter on Marx and on how he thought about inequality for *Visions of Inequality*, I reread most of his writings (and read some that I have not read before). Because Marx's discussion of class structure—crucial also for his understanding of inequality—is most clearly exposed in the discussion of the 1848 revolution in France contained in *The Class Struggles ...* and *The 18th Brumaire ...* I reread them. *The Class Struggles* is a compendium of articles, written during the Revolution, for a German newspaper. *The 18th Brumaire* is Marx's analysis of the rise and fall of the proletarian power between February 1848 and the assumption of dictatorial powers by Louis Napoleon at the end of 1851. On my new reading, *The 18th Brumaire* seemed much better than I remembered it, perhaps because reading one after another *The Class Struggles* and *The 18th Brumaire* allows one to follow the events described by Marx much better, and thus to understand his analysis and conclusions.

It is, however, unfortunate that the English edition that can be found on Amazon is old, with the translation dating from 1897, and with a number of typos and odd turns of phrases. The book absolutely cries out for a new translation and a good editor, because many events mentioned there are not well known, and Marx's numerous allusions to historical or mythical parallels are difficult to follow unless one knows very well both the French history and Greek myths.

Reading Marx on 1848 reminded me that I read many years ago Tocqueville's *Souvenirs*, which cover the same period. Moreover, both Marx and Tocqueville write "à chaud" as the events proceeded. Tocqueville's *Souvenirs* were written in 1850 and 1851 and published only in 1893; Marx's *The 18th Brumaire* was written and published in 1852.

In an excellent introduction to the French edition of *Souvenirs* and an equally remarkable postface, written respectively by Fernand Braudel and J. P. Mayer (the editor of Tocqueville's collected works), they both make direct comparisons between Tocqueville and Marx. J. P. Mayer finds *Souvenirs* "infinitely superior," although he admits that Tocqueville was never as close in his social analysis to Marx as he was here. Tocqueville (unlike Marx) "does not judge his time using the norms that were not those of the time itself"; moreover, "Tocqueville was a realistic sociologist, Marx was a utopist," writes

328

RICARDO AND MARX

Mayer. Braudel is not so sure in the comparison, avoids a direct judgment, and seems to put the two works *ex aequo*.

Our two authors (Marx and Tocqueville) start from almost opposite personal and ideological positions. Tocqueville was a member of parliament until the 1848 Revolution, and remained in parliament after the Revolution, having won in his ancestral region (by garnering 110,000 votes out of 120,000) in the first election with a full adult male franchise in history. In 1849, after the second wave of the revolution was crushed, he became briefly the Minister of Foreign Affairs. Marx, thirteen years younger, was a revolutionary exile in France, soon to be expelled to England. Tocqueville directly participated in the events; Marx was an observer and during much of the period in Germany. Tocqueville's *Souvenirs* are obviously a personal and insider's view of the revolution; Marx's are a study done by a revolutionary outsider. Tocqueville was against the revolution, Marx in favor.

There are three elements, however, where their views fully converge. They are the nature of the 1830 Louis-Philippe regime, the politics of Parisian proletariat, and the role of the peasantry.

The 1830–1848 regime was, for Marx, the rule of "high finance, large industry, large commerce, i.e. [of] Capital with its retinue of lawyers, professors, and orators ... [It] was but the political expression for the usurped rule of the bourgeois upstarts" (p. 26). The power was held by an "aristocracy of finance" legitimized by a monarchy.

Tocqueville, while being an MP for almost ten years during Louis-Philippe's reign, and bitterly opposed to the 1848 Revolution, has only damning things to say about the rule of the bourgeoisie between 1830 and 1848:

> The particular spirit of the middle class became the general spirit of government; it dominated foreign policy as well as internal affairs: an active spirit, industrious, often dishonest, generally orderly, bold out of vanity and egoism, timid by temperament, moderate in all things except in its taste for comfort, and mediocre; a spirit which, mingled with that of the people or of the aristocracy, can do wonders, but which alone, will never produce but a government without virtue and without grandeur. (*Souvenirs*, p. 40; my translation)

Because it is a very personal book (after all, it is *Souvenirs*) and because it deals with contemporary France, Tocqueville expresses more candidly than elsewhere his anti-bourgeois aristocratic prejudices. It is notable that the only unambiguously positive portraits in

329

HISTORY

the book are of those socially inferior to Tocqueville (peasants in his ancestral village who are shepherded by Tocqueville to vote *en masse* for him, and his own man-servant), while the short sketches of the ruling bourgeoisie, other MPs, Tocqueville's friends, and even of his sister-in-law (as well as of Louis-Philippe and Louis Napoleon), are often "deadly" in their detail, where every personal virtue mentioned is followed by a much more serious vice.

The second thing on which Marx and Tocqueville agree is the egalitarianism of the Parisian proletariat. In *The 18th Brumaire*, which presents a uniformly negative description of all social groups except for the Parisian proletariat, its egalitarian spirit is exalted; in Tocqueville, it is considered unrealistic and dangerous, born of "cupidity and envy": "I saw in Paris, a society split into two: those who had nothing united in a common envy [convoitise]; those who possessed something, in a common worry [angoisse]" (p. 162). Yet, Tocqueville makes two extremely important points.

First, he argues that after all other social privileges, from class-based legal inequality to differential taxation, had been abolished by successive revolutions, inequality in property has remained in many people's minds the only visible obstacle to full equality:

... and [unequal property] remaining the only obstacle to equality among men, and seemingly its only obvious sign, wasn't it necessary ... that it should be abolished in its turn, or at least that the idea of abolishing it came to the mind of those who did not enjoy it [property]? (*Souvenirs*, p. 130; my translation)

The elimination of inequality in property, and perhaps the elimination of private property, remained, for some, the last and necessary step toward full equality. Tocqueville, of course, does not approve of it, but notes the logic of political developments leading in that direction.

Then, in just two paragraphs below he makes an even stronger statement:

I am tempted to say that what we believe are necessary institutions are just institutions to which we are accustomed, and that in matters of social organization, the field of the possible is much vaster than men living in any given society can imagine. (*Souvenirs*, p. 131; my translation)

One could just copy that sentence and put it into *The 18th Brumaire* and nobody would notice anything strange.

330

RICARDO AND MARX

The third topic of agreement is the role of peasantry. Marx does not have nice thigs to say about French small landholders who tasted the pleasures of private property after the land was distributed widely after the 1789 Revolution.

The allotment farmers are an immense mass, whose individual members live in identical conditions without however entering into manifold relations with one another. Their method of production isolates them from one another, instead of drawing them into mutual intercourse. This isolation is promoted by the poor means of communication in France, together with the poverty of the farmers themselves. Their field of operation, the small allotment of land that each cultivates, allows no room for a division of Labor, and no opportunity for the application of science; in other words it shuts out manifoldness of development, diversity of talent, and the luxury of social relations. (*The 18th Brumaire*, p. 78)

He argues, moreover, that they were the main supporters of Louis Napoleon when he decided to take power. Tocqueville does not cover this last issue because it falls outside the chronological limits of his book, but he agrees that the opinions in the countryside were very different from those in Paris.

A certain demagogic agitation reigned among the city workers, it is true, but in the countryside, the property-owners, whatever was their origin, their antecedents, their education, their very property [biens], became closer to each other ... Property, among all those who enjoyed it, became a kind of fraternity. The richest were like older cousins, the less rich like younger cousins; but they all considered each other like brothers, having all the same interest in defending their inheritance. Because the French Revolution [of 1789] has extended the possession of land to infinity, the entire [rural] population seemed to be included in that huge family. (*Souvenirs*, p. 146; my translation)

Thus despite markedly different preferences and points of views, the convergence between Tocqueville and Marx on these three important points in the study of the same historical event is remarkable, and worth noting.

(Published on May 8, 2021)

HISTORY

13.10 A short essay on the differences between Marx and Keynes

This short piece is stimulated by my recent reading of the French translation of Joan Robinson's 1942 *Essay on Marxian Economics*, published together with several additional texts on Marx, Marshall, and Keynes written by Robinson over the years. (The translation and preface by Ulysse Lojkine.) It was also stimulated by a very nice review of Joan Robinson's life and *The Essay* just published by Carolina Alves in the *Journal of Economic Perspectives*.

Before I begin, let me set the knowledge limits right. My knowledge of Marx had always been good and, since only a couple of months ago I finished writing a long chapter on Marx's views on income distribution (for *Visions of Inequality*) that deals with the usual topics of the real wage, rising organic composition of capital, tendency of the profit rate to fall, etc., all of that is fresh in my mind.

Keynes is much less so—although I have to say that I had, many years ago, an extraordinary person as my tutor in Keynes' *General Theory*. I had a year of tutoring (one-on-one) from Abba Lerner, who, of course, was one of the earliest disciples of Keynes. Lerner's approach was to make me read a chapter from the *GT*, then to summarize it and discuss it and send it to Abba, who next week would bring my text all corrected in red. I admired Keynes for his brilliance. I still remember vividly (and I am writing this very far from any book by Keynes) his chapter on the "own rates of interest" and the "carriage cost of money" that Lerner made me read and reread. But, I have not at all followed Keynesian macroeconomic developments, and I am generally quite uninterested in macroeconomics. So, here I will speak of what I think of Keynes, not of Keynesians.

The objective of Joan Robinson's *Essay* was to enact a "rapprochement" between Marx's and Keynes' economics, by showing similarities between Marx's view of capitalist relations of production resulting in a lack of effective demand and the themes from *The General Theory*. Here is one of the supporting quotes from Marx: "The ultimate reason for all real crises always remains the poverty and restricted consumption of the masses, in the face of the drive of capitalist production to develop the productive forces as if only the absolute consumption capacity of society set a limit to them" (*Capital*, vol. III). One can produce more, and Joan Robinson does. Or, as Marx writes—I paraphrase—for every individual capitalist, his own workers are his antagonists: he wants to pay them less; but

332

workers of other capitalists are his "friends," they are his customers. When all capitalists try to squeeze workers, and when they all succeed, the outcome is the economic crisis.

The other explanation of economic crises in Marx is the unbalanced growth of departments that produce consumption goods and those that produce investment goods, but this explanation holds less interest for the Keynesians. Robinson also provides a very nice summary of other ideas of Marx, including the labor theory of value, the transformation problem, the tendency of the profit rate to fall, etc., but the emphasis is, as I mentioned, on the origin of crises and the effective demand.

When she contrasts Marx, Marshall, and Keynes, Robinson argues that we should try to separate, in the study of each, the "scientific" prepositions about the functioning of the economy from the "ideological" drivers present in all three authors: in Marx, the conviction that capitalism is a historical (and thus transitory) mode of production, in Marshall, the assumption of capitalism as the "natural" way to organize production, and, in Keynes, a desire to improve capitalism or to save it from self-destruction.

To me, it seems that the difference, at least between Marx and Keynes, is not so much ideological (although I would not deny that it is real) but in the time-horizon they use in their analyses.

For Marx, the time horizon is always long term, even when he discusses crises. Crises are temporary manifestations of the long-term (inherent) issues faced by capitalist production, and it is thus not surprising that Marxist authors like Grossman, Bukharin, and Mandel would—I think closely following Marx—see the overlap between the long-run declining rate of profit and the short-term instability of crises as bringing capitalism to an end. (It is also not surprising that Robinson rejects the tendency of the rate of profit to fall, but supports the explanation of the crises.) Everything in Marx, as Joan Robinson rightly says, is historical. The reader is always directed to look forward, to think about the fundamental forces that drive capitalism.

In Keynes, the situation is different, almost the reverse. The entire Keynes' edifice (not necessarily Keynesian) is short term: the objective is to stabilize the economy and to return it to the condition of full or near-full employment. Keynes is not particularly concerned with capitalism's long term. Implicitly, I think, he believed that capitalism can go on forever, so long as it is "fixed" in such a way as to produce full employment of resources. "Fixing" it might involve government-directed investment, or the euthanasia of the rentier, but Keynes is not a purist: he would take any, including seemingly socialist, tool to mend things.

Let me illustrate the difference between Marx's long-run and Keynes' short-run on two concepts where our authors seem to speak of the same thing: "the animal spirits" and "the reserve army of labor." "The animal spirits" was, as is well known, the idea that Keynes introduced to explain capitalists' investment decisions; capitalists are most of the time not led by the exact calculation of expected gain and loss but act on their gut feeling ("animal spirit"), and if, for whatever reason, that gut feeling changes, the economy can experience sudden expansions or contractions of demand. Joan Robinson mentions how this largely irrational (in the strict sense) incentive to invest is similar to Marx's point of view, where capitalists *qua* capitalists always strive not only to achieve maximum profit *but also* to reinvest it. For Marx, they become capitalists only when they do not consume profit but reinvest it. Accumulation is (to use another famous quote) "Moses and all the prophets." In both cases we see that the incentive to invest is given from outside the economics proper: through sudden bursts of optimism or pessimism, or by the definition of what we may call "the capitalist spirit." But, in Keynes' case, the concept is used to explain short-term fluctuations; in Marx, it is the definitional feature of the whole class, and thus obviously long term.

Or take the "reserve army of labor," which shrinks and expands as the economic activity waxes and wanes. It is very similar to the cyclical unemployment that plays such a big role in Keynes (actually, one could say, motivates the entire book). But Marx's "reserve army" is an ever-present, hence long-term, feature of capitalism. Capitalists need it in order to discipline labor, and if, in some periods, the reserve army shrinks, thus reducing the relative power of the capitalist class, it immediately sets in motion forces that will bring it back to life: labor-saving investments. The reserve army can never disappear in Marx. In Keynes, however, cyclical unemployment is ideally to be reduced to zero. It is something that capitalism, being judiciously managed, can eliminate. Again, the horizons are different: for Marx, it is the long-term structural feature, for Keynes, it is the short-term interplay between key economic variables.

Marx was the first student of fundamental historical features of capitalism, Keynes, the last cameralist. Marx was a philosopher who believed that economics shapes history, Keynes, the smartest adviser to power. In *Capital*, we have a *Bible* of capitalism, in *General Theory*, we have *The Prince* for economic management of capitalism.

(Published June 29, 2022)

13.11 Marx in Amerika

Karl Marx is back in the West. After having done a *tour du monde* that took him from a German émigré philosopher to a *maître à penser* of German social-democracy to global revolutionary thinker, his influence is back in the parts of the world that he studied and where he lived. The current crisis of capitalism, provoked at first by the financial sectors' swindles (something which would not have surprised Marx), and then exacerbated by rising inequality, pandemic, and seemingly unsolvable climate issues, is making Marx's readings more relevant than they were to several past generations, and his ideas more attractive to the young.

But, is Marx's capitalism at all similar to the capitalism of today? Can his ideas be relevant now, more than a century since they were formulated, and during which time the world's per capita income was multiplied by seven, and US per capita income by more than eight times?

The main differences between the classical capitalist world of the nineteenth century and today is not, however, that wages are higher (Marx would not have been much surprised since he held that wages reflect "moral-historical" conditions of each country) or that the welfare state is much broader. The main differences are in the nature of the ruling class, and the effects on the middle classes in the globally dominant countries.

Today's top of income distribution in advanced economies consists of people who have high incomes both from labor and capital. This was not the case in the past. Landlords and capitalists were the top class under classical capitalism, and they hardly had any incomes other than what they derived from their property. Many of them would have probably found it unthinkable or even insulting to complement their incomes by wages.

This has changed. Currently, among the richest ten percent of Americans, one-third also belong to the richest capital owners *and* richest workers. Less than fifty years ago, that share was less than one in five; previously, probably even lower (Berman and Milanovic). This makes the class conflict very different from what it was. There are no longer two groups, markedly different by their income levels and the origin of that income, whether it was obtained through work or property; only inequality remains, and in an attenuated state. Moreover, instead of the books dealing with the leisure class (Thorstein Veblen, Nikolai Bukharin), the coupon-clipping elite

HISTORY

("to grow richer was nothing more than a passive activity for the wealthy," wrote Stefan Zweig about the pre-First World War European rich), the top class today is more likely to be chided for working too much: "[t]oday's Stakhanovites are the one-percenters" in the words of Daniel Markovits in *The Meritocracy Trap*.

The hard-working rich, who either inherit their original capital or build it up through savings over their working lives, marry each other, and play an increasing political role through political donations, are in many ways a new elite. They wish to transmit their advantages to offspring by paying expensively for the best education. That they have succeeded is seen in numerous studies that find decreasing inter-generational income mobility (see, e.g., Mazumdar). Thus, both the origin of the elite's income and their behavior are different from the capitalist class with which Marx was familiar.

The second major difference is international and has to do with globalization. In the latter part of the nineteenth century, British real wages were increasing. Marx's explanation for the increase was largely based on hegemon-led globalization, the Pax Britannica. The British elite was willing to share some "crumbs from the table" from its imperialist plunder with lower classes, and to use workers' rising standard of living as a tool to exact quiescence or sullen acceptance of the existing order.

Would not then Marx think that the US elite, exercising today a similar role to that of the British, would pursue similar policies? He would have been surprised that it did not. The American elite was largely indifferent, as its own country's middle class was hollowed out by globalization, and middle-class incomes remained stagnant. Unlike the British elite, the American elite probably did not think that its political power could be challenged from below. Whether it thought so because it believed that it would be able to manipulate the political process, or because it thought that the losers of globalization would never be able to organize themselves, or perhaps because it was blinded by its ideology, is impossible to tell. All elements, and probably many more, played a role.

But the awakening came in the form of the so-called populist protests in France, Spain, UK, Germany, and in the United States, too, where Donald Trump mounted, perhaps largely by accident, a coalition of "malcontents." It took a special effort by the elite and a worldwide pandemic to take the control back.

These two developments show how much today's capitalism in leading capitalist countries has evolved. The developments are ambiguous, from the political or philosophical perspective. Breaking

336

the explicit class distancing and having an upper class that does not privilege its own nationals, could be considered an advance. But, having an upper class whose position is invulnerable to the movements in the labor market (because it can fall upon its capital assets) and in the stock market (because it has high level of skills and high labor earnings), and is keen to transmit these advantages across generations, may show the same developments in a much less positive light.

(Published May 6, 2021)

— 14 —

COMMUNISM

14.1 A secular religion that lasted one century

The death of Fidel Castro made me think again of the idea that I had for a while about our lack of understanding of what is the place of communism in the global history of mankind. We have thousands of historical volumes on communism, and similarly thousands of volumes of apologia and critiques of communism, but we have no conception of what its position in global history was—e.g. whether colonialism would have ended without communism, whether communism kept capitalism less unequal (see Section 14.12 below), whether it promoted social mobility, or made transition from agrarian to industrial societies in Asia much faster, etc. As Diego Castañeda mentioned in today's tweet, we probably will not be able to assess communism for a while, probably until the passions that it aroused have died down.

The death of Fidel Castro is a useful marker because he was the last canonic communist revolutionary: the leader of a revolution that overthrew the previous order of things, nationalized property, and ruled through a single-party state. We can pretty confidently state that no communist revolutionary in that canonic mold that was so common in the twentieth century, from Lenin, Trotsky, Stalin, Mao, Liu Shaoqi, Tito, and Fidel, will arise in this century. The ideas of nationalized property and central planning are dead. In a very symmetrical way, the arrival of Utopia to power that began in glacial Petrograd in November 1917 ended with the death of its last actual, physical, proponent, in a far-away Caribbean nation, in November 2016.

Let me go over some grossly simplified ideas that, perhaps one day, I will expound more fully in a book format.

COMMUNISM

What was communism? It was the first global secular religion. Its appeal was truly global, both geographically and class-wise: it drew to itself sons and daughters of the rich as well as of the poor, it appealed to the Chinese and Indians no less than to the French or Russians. Like Christianity and Islam, it asked from its followers self-sacrifice and self-abnegation. Like Christianity (as was of course noticed) it had its prophet, dead in semi-obscurity, whose subversive works were propagated by foreigners using the communication means provided by the hegemon, whom they tried to undermine and destroy. Unlike capitalism, it was heavily ideological. While the ideology of capitalism is pretty light (and often malleable and pragmatic), the ideology of communism was inflexible. The system took its ideology seriously, no less seriously than (again) Christianity and Islam. But, taking it so seriously led to the many splinter movements, doctrinal disputes, conflicts and killings—again similarly to the transcendental religions.

Although communism was ideologically an economics-based movement whose objective was the creation of a classless society of abundance, its features are particularly difficult to understand within the narrow economistic confines. For it combined extreme concentration of political power with large economic equality: modern economists like Acemoglu and Robinson can neither understand that nor fit it into their scheme. Most people today cannot either, since they believe that the objective of all political power must be economic (that is, wealth acquisition).

Communism promoted and achieved social mobility but that mobility often came with a cost: workers escaped from low-paying and hard-working occupations in order to become much better-paid bureaucrats, bossing around those workers who failed to "escape." It thus created something akin to a class society, although it promised to abolish classes. In its most degenerate form, it created monarchies, like in North Korea and to some extent in China (with princelings).

Why did it fail? In the most general terms, it failed because it opposed two strong human impulses: to be free (in expressing opinions and doing what one likes) and to own property. Both were the desires created or ratified by the Enlightenment. In the pre-modern past, a majority of people took political oppression and absence of own property as given. However, communism was not a movement arising in the Middle Ages, but in the modern era, a true inheritor of the Enlightenment.

Because it was a secular religion, it promised to deliver the goods on this Earth, which is a fact susceptible to empirical observation.

339

HISTORY

The goods were freedom of labor from the oppression by those who possess property (which it delivered only in part) and economic abundance (which it did not deliver). It increasingly failed to provide economic advancement, largely because the nature of technological progress changed: from large centralized network industries to much more decentralized innovations. Communism could not innovate in practically anything that required for success acquiescence of consumers. It thus provided tanks but no ball-point pens, spacecraft but no toilet paper.

Will it come back? We cannot tell for sure, but today the chances of a comeback of non-private property and centralized coordination of economic activity seem nil. Capitalism, defined as private property of capital, wage labor and decentralized coordination, is for the first time in human history the only economic system that exists across the globe. It could be monopoly capitalism, state capitalism, or competitive capitalism, but the principles of private ownerships are as accepted in China as in the United States.

However, some ideas of communism will always appeal to groups of people: its egalitarian ethos, internationalism, and expectation of self-sacrifice are as intrinsically human as are the impulses it tried to suppress (quest for freedom and property). It will thus permanently find partisans among those who find the greed and acquisitive spirit that inevitably undergird capitalism too distasteful. But, seen from today's perspective, such groups appear condemned forever to remain on the margins of societies, creating their own communities or penning little-read treatises: exactly where they seemed to be doing in the latter part of the nineteenth century.

(Published November 27, 2016)

COMMUNISM

14.2 State capitalism one hundred years ago and today

A few days ago I re-read the book of Lenin's final years' speeches and letters. The book covers the years 1922 and 1923 (Lenin died in January 1924). I grabbed the book simply because I saw it on my shelf and, having read it probably twenty years ago, I could not remember exactly what was there, and thought, as I was proof-reading the section on inequality in socialism in my forthcoming *Visions of Inequality*, that there could be something in the Lenin book that might be relevant for my chapter. In reality, there was nothing.

But there were several topics that have not lost their relevance even 100 years later. There are at least two that are very relevant today: Lenin's views on the New Economic Policy (NEP) and state capitalism, and his views on the nationality problem during the process of the creation of the Union of Soviet Socialist Republics. (Even the name was still debated: Lenin writes of the Union of Soviet Republics of Europe and Asia.) I will discuss the first topic only.

In a very long speech (which takes fifty closely printed pages) to the 11th Congress of Russian Communist Party in 1922 Lenin summa-rizes the results of the first eighteen months of the New Economic Policy. (I also use his speeches to the Comintern Congress in 1922 and to the Moscow Soviet the same year.) He presents NEP as a necessary retreat from the construction of socialism. Why was the retreat needed? First, in order to restore the links with the small-holding peasantry who during the War Communism reduced their production of agricultural goods, as there was nothing to exchange them for (since the industrial production plummeted), and second, to learn how to manage the economy. "Learn from capitalists" could have been the key slogan of the NEP.

Lenin argues that communists, having studied ideology and the technique of political struggle, simply do not know how to manage the economy: "Communists do not know how to run the economy ... they are inferior to the ordinary capitalist salesmen who have received their training in ... big firms" (*Lenin's Final Fight*, p. 35); "we must organize things in such a way as to make possible the customary operation of capitalist economy ... because this is essential for the people" (p. 41). It was not part of communists' tool-kit. They have gained political power but they do not know how to use it to make the economy work. They are utterly bureaucratic and thus they mismanage the economy. (Lenin has a ten-page "excursus" on

341

HISTORY

how complicated it was to buy canned food when hunger reigned in Moscow because different Soviet bureaucratic bodies could not agree among themselves. Finally, the issue came to the Politburo and it was decided there. Lenin exclaims: "But Kamenev [the Politburo member] cannot be dragged into every transaction, dragged into the business of buying canned food from a French citizen," p. 57).

But he fails to recognize, and perhaps it was difficult to recognize at that time, that the problem was not just learning how to manage large enterprises but that there was a problem of incentives. It was not that the communists were necessarily worse in management skills than capitalists. The problem was that the incentive structure is very different for a bureaucrat or a manager who runs a large state-owned company from the incentive structure faced by an individual capitalist.

For Lenin, however, the problem lay in lack of knowledge of management: he would have loved MBAs and mentions as a very positive development, the creation of a similar institute in Moscow and the role of the journal *Ekonomicheskaya Zhizh* as somewhat of a Soviet *Forbes* (in today's terms, obviously). The problem, Lenin believed, could be remedied by working alongside capitalists in the so-called mixed enterprises created by the state, and Russian and foreign capitalists (fourteen of them existed at the time of Lenin's 1922 speech) and by imitating capitalists' skills.

NEP is a learning experience; once communist cadres have learned how to do business, and run the economy, NEP can be shut down ("state capitalism is capitalism that we shall be able to restrain, and the limits of which we shall be able to fix," p. 40). The justification of the NEP is thus that while it is a retreat from the ideals of socialism, it is a temporary retreat, and after its objectives have been achieved, future advances will be much more powerful because better organized and sustainable. And the country would be richer.

In that context, Lenin discusses state capitalism. He makes a distinction between (a) state capitalism under capitalist conditions, and (b) state capitalism under socialist conditions. He rejects the view that the two of them are the same, and he criticizes Bukharin, who wrote that the term "state capitalism" under socialism is a logical absurdity. In Lenin's view (a) is when the state, ruled by the capitalist class, takes over some of the private-sector functions, while the substantial part of the economy remains capitalist. And there is (b), state capitalism, where the state is controlled by the Party and the proletariat, and allows capitalists to function in order to boost productivity and to learn management skills from them. So, state capitalism under socialism, according to Lenin, is entirely different,

342

in the political sense, from state capitalism under capitalism. The political power is not vested in the hands of the capitalist elite and this enables communist rulers, whenever they decide to do so, to curtail capitalists' involvement in the economy. The power remains solidly with the Party.

This last point is very relevant for the understanding of the Chinese approach to state capitalism today. As argued in Section 9.2 above, we can see the current Chinese state capitalism as a protracted NEP that began in 1978 and continues until today. But Lenin seems to overlook the possibility that with a very long NEP the economic and political power will gradually seep from under the Party and the very nature of the state would change. Those who have money will dictate things as in capitalist countries. The state may not be able to control them and the commanding heights of the economy may change ownership. This happened under Jiang Zemin and Hu Jintao: the development of state capitalism under socialist conditions led to the increasing influence of rich people and capitalists, including their inclusion in most of the Party organs, and through the idea of "the three represents," it gave a pretense of ideological acceptability to such evolution. The change in the elite composition, evident in a study done by Li Yang, Filip Novokmet, and myself, is another product of such policies. The social structure of the Chinese elite had evolved enormously between the late 1980s and 2013 (when our study ends). While the private sector was marginal among the elite (the top 5 percent) in 1988, twenty-five years later almost one-third of the people in the elite were private businessmen (owners of small enterprises and large-scale capitalists). If one includes professionals who are employed in the private sector, a bit over one-half of the elite is private-sector dependent.

It is in this context that one can look at Xi Jinping's policies: as an attempt at the reassertion of the power of the state vs. the capitalist sector and the rich. Or, to use Lenin's distinction between the two, as an attempt to move from state *capitalism* to *state* capitalism. It is an adjustment in the political power between the two sectors: the state, ruled by a bureaucratic stratum, and the rich. It represents the analog of the populist reaction in the Western democracies: the feeling that the business elite has become too powerful, has no discernible interest in the problems of ordinary people, and has to be reined in. We can thus see Xi Jinping as both an heir to Lenin's New Economic Policy and, in much more contemporary terms, as a populist response to the excesses of the new rich.

(Published June 26, 2023)

HISTORY

14.3 Milton Friedman and labor-managed enterprises

In the spring of 1973 Milton Friedman visited Yugoslavia. A few weeks after his trip, he recorded a very interesting conversation (the link was unearthed by my friend Miloš Vojinović). Friedman's impressions and conclusions are remarkably clear and spot-on. They were not something new: the problems that he mentions regarding Yugoslav cooperatives (or more exactly, self-managed enterprises, SMEs) were quite well known by 1973. Nevertheless, Friedman summarized them very accurately. He also must have had a very well-organized visit and good interlocutors. I vaguely remember reading that his main host was an excellent journalist from Belgrade's outstanding economics weekly *Ekonomska Politika* (some of my first ever writings were published by them, so I am always a bit biased in their favor).

I would suggest to everyone to listen to Friedman, but let me say a bit more regarding three major flaws of SMEs identified by Friedman too (and of course others). This is of special importance now because the ideas of workers' management and ownership are becoming popular again.

The first flaw has to do with the maximand of SME. Like US cooperatives, they maximize average output per worker because at that point the wage is the highest. This means that SMEs will not go all the way to marginal product of labor=wage and would thus employ fewer workers than an entrepreneur-run company. This is indeed something that was confirmed in practice. Yugoslav SMEs were loath to expand employment. Unemployment in Yugoslavia, despite massive workers' emigration mostly to Germany, always stayed around 10 percent through the 1970s and 1980s. Some writers, like Susan Woodward, see high youth unemployment combined with IMF policies of austerity imposed after the debt crisis of 1980s as being responsible for the break-up of the country. (I will leave this aspect aside.) However, the reluctance of SMEs to hire more workers led the government in the 1980s to enact the law on "obligatory employment of new workers," whereby each SME had to increase its employment by two percent per annum: not the most market-friendly and reasonable policy.

The second problem mentioned by Friedman was that all SMEs can be in equilibrium, while having vastly different average products per worker and wages. Since wage depends also on capital-intensity of the enterprise or even of the branch of production, workers in highly

344

COMMUNISM

capital-intensive areas (like electricity generation) will have much higher wages than those in textile production. And, for the reasons explained in the previous paragraph, there would be no tendency to move from one enterprise to another. (The high-wage enterprise will have reached its maximum and would not hire more workers.) This was, like the previous problem, noted already in the seminal paper by Benjamin Ward published in 1958. It was expanded in Jaroslav Vanek's monumental *The General Theory of Labor-Managed Market Economies*, and, of course, numerous articles on that problem (and the previous) were published in the *Journal of Comparative Economics* and *Economic Analysis and Workers' Management*, the two prime journals that dealt with market socialism. (I would also like to recommend an excellent paper by Dinko Dubravčić, published in 1970, as well as James Meade's 1972 article.)

The third problem had to do with the fact that capital was "socially" owned. It could not be alienated by workers, i.e. sold to somebody else. Workers enjoyed only *usus fructus* rights. That led to the following problem (which, by the way, was also obvious in the Basque Mondragon cooperatives). When workers had to decide how much of net income to use for wages as opposed to plowing back into investment, they tended to go for higher wages. It was not simply because of pure time preference but because wages were fully privately owned (obviously), and could be used to open a savings account in which the worker both owned the principal, and received interest. But if that same amount were reinvested in his company, he will get only the return on investment; the principal will be merged in the rest of "social" capital and will never revert back to the worker. Now, imagine that you are a year before retirement, and you have the option of increasing your wage by $100 or reinvesting that amount in your company. What will you choose?

As Friedman rightly says in the interview, Yugoslav policy-makers constantly complained that companies were distributing too much in wages, and tried to set, through heavy wage taxation, incentives to move more money into investment. But the results were nugatory.

These are some intrinsic drawbacks of labor- or self-managed firms. Most of them stem from non-privately owned capital. This is why this model of cooperatives should not be confused with privately owned cooperatives, where workers are also shareholders. In that case, the last problem, for example, disappears entirely. The first two do not however, but they are "solved" by the introduction of two types of workers: those who are workers–shareholders and others who are hired workers. Mondragon did precisely that.

345

The advantage of SME was workplace democracy. Workers indeed had much more extensive rights and power than in similar capitalist firms that are, by definition, hierarchical and are actually run as mini-dictatorships. Whether the democratic nature of SME had positive effects on productivity (adjusted for all the mentioned deficiencies) I do not know, although I think that there were such studies.

Finally, when assessing intrinsic advantages and disadvantages of such a system one should leave aside other characteristics, which had nothing to do with the system as such but with specific Yugoslav conditions. They are at least two.

First, for large and important enterprises, some workers' rights were curtailed because Republican governments, and through them the Republican Communist Parties, appointed their nomenclatura members to top positions. It was thus a "controlled" workplace democracy. Very often these appointees were not well qualified to run companies. They were basically Party hacks, who tried to pretend to be businessmen. Slobodan Milošević is the most famous example. He became the head of one of the largest Yugoslav banks and, although he always bragged of dealing skillfully with Rockefeller and Chase Manhattan, he probably knew very little about banking (having graduated in law).

Second, Yugoslavia, after the Constitution of 1974 (that was just being discussed as Friedman was visiting the country, as he briefly alludes), functioned as a confederation ruled by Republican Communist Party oligarchies. Each of the republics not only tried to control better its SMEs and especially the banking system but to undermine the unitary market by imposing restrictions on free movement of capital, or even in some cases of goods. Thus, SMEs worked in an ever-more restrictive market, and under a greater control by political oligarchies.

These two last features (one-party system and extreme decentralization leading toward autarky) need not be present in other countries.

(Published May 3, 2021)

COMMUNISM

14.4 Socialist enterprise power structure and the soft-budget constraint

Yesterday's bizarre and rather ignorant discussion of the Komsomol in the US Congress, and the recent passing of Janos Kornai, the famous "inventor" of the soft-budget constraint, reminded me that I planned for several years to describe in very simple terms how the socialist companies of labor-managed kind, as in Yugoslavia, really functioned. Having worked in one, and having read a fair amount on it, I know the topic, I think, quite well. Especially so when I think that most people in capitalist countries never had a clear idea of how labor-managed (LM) enterprises differed in their internal structure from capitalist firms, and nobody younger than fifty-five or even sixty in the former communist countries has any direct experience of how such companies worked. The structure described here is fully relevant for Yugoslavia in the period 1965–1990, and probably for Hungary and Poland after 1968–1970, and even for the Soviet Union and China in the part dealing with the role of Communist Party (CP) in management.

Shareholders and workers. Take the standard capitalist firm. It is run by shareholders, whose individual power is equal to the amount of shares they own. Shareholders elect a board that does closer oversight of management, and the board elects chief executives who do the daily work. Now, just replace shareholders with workers employed in the enterprises, each with equal voting power, who elect the workers' council, which, in turn elects the enterprise director, and you have the management structure of an LM enterprise.

This is not at all very difficult to understand. Some features are obvious, even from such a simple sketch. First, workers will have the power to decide about how the company will be managed (in Yugoslavia, since it was a market economy, they were involved even in decisions about what to produce, how to make profit and the like). Second, ability to enjoy only the *usus fructus* rights from capital (a worker could not sell his share in the enterprise; it simply did not exist) led workers to focus on short-term gains; and third, workers' power to decide on hirings led to their tendency to restrain enterprise membership. These problems were amply discussed in the economic literature at the time (I explain them also in Sections 14.3 and 14.5). But my objective now is not to discuss them but to explain the internal structure of the enterprise.

347

HISTORY

So far, that structure seems relatively simple. But now the complicated part kicks in. We have to explain the role of trade unions and enterprise-level Communist Party organization (ELCP).

Trade unions. Their role was basically nil. The reason is obvious. If the company is run by workers' assembly and the workers' council, the very same people being members of the trade unions (trade union membership was compulsory and thus 100%), have already made their decisions. There is nothing for them to do through trade unions. Trade unions were thus a redundant organ and very little attention was paid to them.

Communist Party organization. ELCP was important. Its members were employees who were CP members. This could, I guess, range from 10–20 percent of the labor force to 80 percent. They too met in assemblies (strictly speaking, after the work hours while the organs of workers' management, including the assembly and the workers' councils, met during the work hours), and elected either a small committee and/or the head of enterprise-level Party organization. We shall still have to talk more of him/her.

Election of the director. Now, let's go back to the management structure. The company has a director. The director is elected by the workers' council. However, the Party organization within the enterprise has also an informal veto power. So, the director, in order to be elected, has also to have support of the ELCP, which essentially means of the head of the enterprise Party organization.

Here, the *duality of power* immediately becomes apparent. It is reinforced by the fact that the director is almost always a Party member himself and, within the Party organization, he is below the enterprise Party leader. But, as director he is his boss within the company. Not an easy situation.

But it gets more complicated. The enterprise director in any medium- or larger-scale company would also need, in order to be elected, to have tacit support or even explicit clearance of the territorial Party organization, where the enterprise is located. Decisions on management promotions of very large enterprises were not left to the total discretion of the workers' council. Its sovereignty was limited. Thus, our director needs to court three constituencies: workers in his company, CP organization and its enterprise leader, and the territorial-level Party organization. Moreover, the ELPC leader is structurally linked with the Party decision-makers at the territorial level. Consequently, he can exercise pressure on the director through two channels: internally, by being the leader of a large part of workers (who are members of the CP), and externally,

348

COMMUNISM

by having close links with the territorial Party organization that needs to vet the election of the director.

The director is thus hemmed in from all directions. Unless he himself has powerful allies at the territorial level and a compliant enterprise Party boss, his power of decision-making is quite restrained but responsibility, if enterprise does badly, is all his. The enterprise-level Party boss bears no responsibility for profit or loss of the enterprise.

This duality of power within the enterprise, and the divorce between power of decision-making and responsibility, is responsible for the emergence of the soft-budget constraint and for the constant friction between the more technocratically minded managers (directors) and the more bureaucratically minded people who made their careers within the Party. (The latter topic was much studied in the sociological literature of the 1960s and 1970s dealing with socialist economies.)

Soft budget constraint. Mixed hierarchical lines between the managers and CP enterprise leaders not only give large indirect power to the latter, but might stimulate in them desire to become managers themselves (and be paid more: enterprise-level Party boss was a non-remunerated position). Now, people who would make their careers through the Party were generally less knowledgeable and interested in economic matters and would often have close to zero knowledge of how to manage companies. This was different for "normal" directors, who would rise by gradually going from managing a section within a company, to a larger branch, and eventually the whole company. But, if the enterprise-level CP leader succeeded in being elected (garnering the support of the workers' council and the territorial CP organization), he would not necessarily pay much attention to the functioning of the company, relying rather on his political connections. With good political connections (at the territorial level) he could be sure that almost any amount of enterprise losses would be covered by the banking system (which was government-controlled). He may even be very popular among workers. He can relax labor discipline, workers can work much less, and then cover all the losses through credits that would never be repaid, or through outright subsidies. Thus, for workers it was often preferable to have an incompetent, but well-connected, Party hack as a director than a more technocratically minded person: workers' salaries might be higher, while they would work less.

Inefficiency. As this makes clear, the soft-budget constraint was an endogenous part of the system. Its origin is, I think, in the unwillingness of the CP to relinquish the power of enterprise

HISTORY

decision-making (which in theory it conferred on workers' councils). It thus created a dual power structure that had many inefficiencies of its own (long discussions, permanent canvassing of support, creation of factions, etc.) and, on top of that, it created the soft-budget constraint. The softness was the greater the more powerful the enterprise director, and the most powerful would be those managing large companies ("too big to fail") and who had good connection with the territorial Party organizations. Thus, the center of power decisively shifted toward the Party and bureaucracy, and away from managers or technocrats. And this in turn reduced the enterprise efficiency.

Nota bene. Some of these undesirable features might appear in Chinese enterprises (private and public), where enterprise-level CP organizations are re-introduced. In my opinion, for an efficient management, political organizations, like CP, must not be made part of power structure within the enterprise. They can remain on the territorial level. But then, of course, their real economic power would be much diminished. This is the conundrum.

(Published November 19, 2021)

COMMUNISM

14.5 Disciplining workers in a workers' state

When, yesterday, I reviewed Fritz Bartel's excellent new book *The Triumph of Breaking Promises*, where he describes how governments in both the West and East in the late 1970s and early 1980s had to break tacit promises (of economic growth and welfare state) with their citizens, he speaks of "disciplining labor." In a capitalist context, it is clear what it means: reduce the power of trade unions, make the labor market more flexible (i.e. firing easier), reduce the duration and amount of unemployment benefits, etc. Almost everyone understands it.

But some people wrote to me: they did not understand what "disciplining labor" meant in the East European (and probably Soviet) context in those years. To understand what it meant one has to start with the position of labor in socialist societies. In those societies, and in those years (because it was different under high Stalinism), workers were seen as the "privileged" class in theory. While they were not high in income distribution, they benefited from many egalitarian policies, and it is they, and their position, that provided the legitimacy to the Communist Party rule. Since that rule could not be legitimated through elections, it had to be legitimated through the claim that it ensured the "dictatorship of the proletariat," i.e. made workers, rather than capitalists, the ruling class. Obviously, they were not the ruling class in truth: Party and government bureaucracy was, but the ideological claim of "the dictatorship of the proletariat" could not be openly ignored and it meant that a special social contract did exist between the powers-that-be and the working class.

The contract included the following items: (1) low intensity of work effort, (2) guaranteed employment, (3) low wage differences between skilled and unskilled workers, (4) less hierarchical plant-level relations than under capitalism, (5) social benefits linked to jobs.

The most important thing to realize is that work effort was much less, and the number of hours of effective work probably even less than in an equivalent capitalist-run firm. There were several reasons for it. Socialist enterprises were organized much less efficiently. There were no real owners who cared about profitability and, in consequence, they did not care whether labor was employed for eight hours per day or four. On top of that, the overall system was less efficient: so often raw materials would not show on time and there would be no work to do. Then, there was surplus labor within companies hired, just in case they needed it, to fulfill the plan quota

351

HISTORY

(or, as in Yugoslavia, which was not a planned economy, just in order to hire family and friends). Companies were encouraged to increase hirings because local politicians were afraid of unemployment in their area and under their watch. They wanted companies to hire as many people as possible, regardless of whether it made economic sense or not (the soft budget constraint will somehow mop all of this up: somebody else will pay). Finally, hours and hours were lost in political meetings, or, as in Yugoslavia, in interminable discussions of workers' assemblies or workers' councils.

All of these things combined meant that for an individual worker, he or she effectively worked much less than in a corresponding capitalist firm: the intensity of work was less, the duration of work was less, the idling was much greater. Workers' shop-floor positions were stronger than in an equivalent capitalist firm because it was almost impossible to fire them. So they were both more powerful, and worked less.

Comes the need for reform. "Breaking promises" under socialism meant principally disciplining labor along the three dimensions: make them work harder, reduce their shop-floor powers, and allow (timidly) for possibility of firing. As a careful reader might have noticed, disciplining labor had mostly to do with "internal" elements of the shop-floor organization, and establishment of stricter rules and hierarchy, not with the usual "external" elements, as in capitalism (amount of unemployment benefit, etc.).

I remember observing clearly these differences during the years when, to complement my student income, I worked with Yugoslav trade unions. They had very close relations with French trade unions (CFDT in particular), and I knew them well. When the French trade unions would visit Yugoslavia, they would be taken to the management of the company and to the plant-floor to chat with workers. When Yugoslav trade unions went to France, they would meet in trade union offices (very nice, by the way), but they would never meet the management (obviously the management would ignore us), nor would they ever be allowed onto the shop-floor. The internal organization of work was entirely the "province" of capitalists and managers. Of course, unions may be consulted, or could strike, but the rules of work organization, the pace of work, the hierarchy within the company, were not the object (or were seldom the object) of negotiations.

It is that very hierarchical work organization that technocrats, or reformers, in socialism wanted to establish, so that the system would be more efficient. Consequently, they had to fight the acquired rights

352

of workers. This was ideologically difficult because workers were the "ruling class." If they are the ruling class, how—and for what purpose—can you force them to work harder, be less consulted, and even face unemployment?

This was the perennial battle between technocrats, often company directors, and the working class. Whenever crisis would hit, technocrats would gain the upper hand. They would make temporary inroads, but would be thwarted and pushed back by a coalition of bureaucrats in the Party and workers. It was a battle that was, for ideological reasons, impossible to win by technocrats. "Disciplining labor" was thus much more difficult in Eastern Europe in the 1970s than in the West and, especially so, in the United States, where the power of labor (and the ideology legitimating that power) was always weak.

(Published November 11, 2022)

HISTORY

14.6 How I lost my past

In almost all recent literature that analyzes Br-exit and Trump-entry, there is an almost constant theme of a fall from the heady days at the end of the Cold War, of pining for a time when unstoppable victory of democracy and neoliberal economics was a certainty, and liberal capitalism stood at the pinnacle of human achievement.

Such narratives always filled me with discomfort. It is in part because I never believed in them and because my personal experience was quite different. Rather than believing in the end of history, I saw the end of the Cold War as an ambivalent event: good for many people because it brought them national liberation and the promise of better living standards, but traumatic for others because it brought them the rise of vicious nationalism, wars, unemployment and disastrous declines in income.

I know that I was influenced in that by a very clear realization that, once the Berlin Wall fell, the civil war in Yugoslavia was inevitable (I still remember a rather somber dinner that I shared with my mother on that day in November) and by the first-hand experience of sudden misery that befell Russia in the early 1990s, when I travelled there working for the World Bank. So, I was aware that my discomfort with triumphalism could be explained by these two, rarely found together, circumstances. It was perhaps an idiosyncratic discomfort.

But, reading other books, and especially the highly acclaimed Tony Judt, I realized that the discomfort went further. In a deluge of literature that was written or published after the end of the Cold War, I just could not find almost anything that mirrored my own experiences from the Yugoslavia of the 1960s and 1970s. However hard I tried, I just could not see anything in my memories that had to deal with collectivization, killings, political trials, endless bread lines, imprisoned free thinkers, and other stories that are currently published in literary magazines. It is even stranger because I was very politically precocious; without exaggeration, I think I was more politically minded than 99 percent of my peers in the then Yugoslavia.

But my memories of the 1960s and the 1970s are different. I remember interminable dinners discussing politics, women and nations, long summer vacations, foreign travel, languid sunsets, whole-night concerts, girls in mini-skirts, the smell of the new apartment in which my family moved, excitement of new books and of buying my favorite weekly on the evening before the day when it would hit the stands ... I cannot find any of that in Judd, Svetlana

354

Alexievich, or any other writer. I know that some of the memories may be influenced by nostalgia but, as hard as I try, I still find them as my dominant memories. I remember too many details of each of them to believe that my nostalgia somehow "fabricated" them. I just cannot say they did not happen.

Thus, I came to realize that all these other memories from Eastern Europe and communism that pop up on today's screens and "populate" the literature, have almost nothing in common with me. And yet, I lived under such a regime for thirty years! I know that my story may not be representative, not the least because the 1970s were the years of prosperity in Yugoslavia and because that peripheral part of Europe then played, thanks to Tito's non-alignment, a world political role that it never had in 2,000 years—but still, after I adjust for all of that, I believe that some other, non-preordained, stories of "underdevelopment" and communism have the right to be told too. Or should we willfully destroy our memories?

Yet it is very difficult to tell these other stories. History is written, we are told, by the victors, and stories that do not fit the pattern narrative are rejected. This is especially the case, I have come to believe, in the United States, which has created during the Cold War a formidable machinery of open and concealed propaganda. That machinery cannot be easily turned off. It cannot produce narratives that do not agree with the dominant one because no one would believe them, or buy such books. There is an almost daily and active rewriting of history, in which many people from Eastern Europe participate: some because they do have such memories, others because they force themselves (often successfully) to believe that they have such memories. Others can remain with their individual memories, which, at their passing, will be lost. The victory shall be complete.

When I was in 2008 in Leipzig to watch a World Cup game, I was struck to see, displayed in a modest store window, a picture of the East German soccer team, which, in 1974 in the World Cup played in West Germany, unexpectedly beat the West German team by 1–0. None of the players in that East German squad went on to become rich and famous. They were just home boys. It was, I thought, a small, even in some ways pathetic, attempt to save the memories and say: "We also did something in these forty years; we existed; it was not all meaningless, "nasty and brutish."

Thinking of those years in political terms, one moment now, perhaps strangely, stands out for me. It was the summer of 1975. The Helsinki conference on peace and stability in Europe was just taking

HISTORY

place. It was closing a chapter on the Second World War. It came just months after the liberation of Saigon. And I recall being on a beach, reading about the Helsinki conference and thinking, linking the two events: there will be no wars in Europe in my lifetime, and imperialism has been defeated. How wrong was I on both counts.

(Published September 16, 2017)

COMMUNISM

14.7 The red bourgeoisie

June 3, 1968 was a beautiful late spring day in Belgrade. The school year was just about to end and, for me, the best days were about to begin: until mid July, when many of my friends who had either relatives in the village or second homes on the seaside would go on vacation and I would not see them for two months. But now, during the beautiful, clear June days with long sweet evenings, we could stay out in the streets seemingly forever, play soccer, tell tall stories and talk about the girls.

During that day, June 3rd, just for a few moments, probably to pick another soccer ball, we went to the apartment of one my friends. Only his grandmother was there. The phone rang. His mother called. She worked for the federal government whose HQs were across the river. In deep panic she called to tell her son, my friend, not to go out in the streets, but to stay at home because (and I do remember her words well) "the students are out trying to overthrow the government."

For sure, as soon as we were told by the grandmother that we should stay indoors, we promptly went outside. My friend's apartment, like mine, was close to one of the main university buildings in Belgrade. When we, kids, got there, it was already occupied by students, surrounded by the police, who did not let anyone get into the university perimeter (in those days, the old-fashioned rules of the "university autonomy" were still observed, even under communism), and we could just look at the seemingly feverish activity inside and listen to the incendiary speeches carried on loudspeakers.

We were attracted to the "forbidden" things happening there. So, I remember when several days later, as the insurrectionist students communicated with the city only through large banners, I first saw the words "Down with the Red Bourgeoisie." It was a new term. The students were protesting against corruption, income inequality, lack of employment opportunities. They renamed the university of Belgrade, "The Red University Karl Marx." It was very difficult for an officially Marxist-inspired government to deal with them. The days of uncertainty ensued: the newspapers attacked them for destroying public property and "disorderly conduct," but rebellious students continued skirmishes with the police, and proudly displayed the name of their new university. I remember a bearded student with a big badge "The Red University Karl Marx" standing in the bus,

HISTORY

and everyone around him feeling slightly uncomfortable, not sure whether to congratulate him or curse him.

But the slogan was true. It was a protest against the red bourgeoisie, the new ruling class in Eastern Europe. It was a heterogeneous class: some came, especially so in the underdeveloped countries like Serbia, from very rich families; others from the educated middle class, many from workers' families. Their background was similar to the background of students who were protesting against them now. Had the students won in 1968, they would have become the new red bourgeoisie.

The red bourgeoisie itself was the product of huge inequities of underdeveloped capitalist societies. From my mother, who got the story from my father (who came from an impoverished merchant family) I learned that on the last day of his high school, when he managed to save enough money by giving private math classes to the rich parents' kids and proudly came to school in his new coat, one of the rich kids took the inkpot and poured it on my father's jacket: "you will never wear what we wear." Many years later when I told the story to my North European friend, he said you me: "this is the European class system in a nutshell."

It is against such a system that the students in the 1930s, who would later become the red bourgeoisie, stood up. But, by 1968 they were the new ruling class and the new students stood up against them.

This ruling class is insufficiently studied and known. It varied between the countries. I liked a lot a book by Tereza Torańska about the new bourgeoisie in Poland, entitled *Them*; a young Serbian journalist Milomir Marić wrote in the 1980s a popular book called *Deca komunizma* (*The Children of Communism*). The story of the red bourgeoisie's very top is narrated in the Russian novel *The House of Government* by Yuri Slezkine. One can find it in Solzhenitsyn's "First Circle" too. Emma Goldman noticed it very early on, just a few years after the October Revolution. I was pleased to re-discover that I had discussed some of its empirics (income level, housing ownership) in my 1987 dissertation. But this is all very little. The class is unexplored, both in literary terms or in its economics.

Like all ruling classes, its members did not think they were a ruling class. I asked many years later one of my close friends, who, thanks to her belonging to the upper echelons of the red bourgeoisie, spent several summer holidays on the three small islands off the Dalmatian coast that Tito took for his exclusive resort. I asked her how were social relations among the people there: powerful indeed, but each with their own different agendas, wives, children, preferences, drinking habits, and the like. (Very similar to the US Martha's Vineyard in the summer: people who may not suffer each other politically, but are "condemned" to be there together, sharing the same beaches, restaurants, tennis courts, with children fighting each other or falling in love.) She told me nothing: she saw none of the political infighting or personal feuds reflected on the beaches, or in the altercations over the umbrellas. She did not think people there were special in any way. It was just another workers' rest home, with better food and more comfortable rooms.

The Yugoslav red bourgeoisie was perhaps specific because it was self-created (i.e. came to power by itself), and developed among its members a feeling of pride connected with non-alignment policies and the huge role that Yugoslavia, compared to its objective importance, played in the world. Eventually, that bourgeoisie splintered along the republican lines, everyone deciding that it would be more powerful if it could break the country in smaller pieces and rule their own small piece unmolested by others. That's how democracy was born.

I thought of that recently—as indeed I had for many years—as I read about the background of many among the capitalist rulers of Yeltsin's Russia and today's Putinism. Their origins are typically in the affluent upper middle class of the red bourgeoise. That ensured for them all the privileges of the Soviet system, including (in the Soviet case) the ability to travel to the West, to trade in foreign currencies, to listen to the latest rock albums from England. They were the ones who, when Gorbachev came to power, most eagerly embraced democracy, adulation of the United States, and gaily participated in the plunder of the country. They bought villas in the Riviera, and then, either disappointed at the treatment they received in their summer resorts by their new Western neighbors, or having outgrown their infatuation with the things Western and the United States in particular, moved to the other side, championing nationalism not only as a way of staying in power, but of creating an ersatz ideology that would justify their continued rule.

(Published September 25, 2023)

HISTORY

14. 8 On charisma and greyness under communism

Several years ago, in a conversation about politics and history, a friend asked me something about the durability of Tito's regime in Yugoslavia (35 years). I cannot remember what my answer was, but I remember that he explained it by saying how Tito must have been a charismatic leader. That statement struck me then and I still remember it today. My friend lived in Latin America for a decade or more, and I thought that perhaps it came naturally to him to ascribe the long rule of leaders to their "charisma." Yet, as far as Tito was concerned, I do not think that anyone could think that he was a charismatic leader. Toward the end of his life, he was quite popular, liked by most, even adored by many—but "charismatic": no.

That led me to think about the absence of charismatic leaders among the communist leaders. For sure, communists had some charismatic leaders: Trotsky and Fidel Castro (but not Raul) come to mind. Even Mao—although I will treat him below separately. But nobody else. Stalin was certainly not a charismatic leader. Nor were the leaders whom I remember well from my youth. Todor Zhivkov, János Kádár, Gustav Husak, and Władysław Gomułka, were the greyest shade of grey. In no crowd, would they stand out. Rather, they seem to have cultivated the desire for greyness and "averageness." Others were not much better. Khrushchev was mercurial and often unpredictable, but not charismatic. And Brezhnev, Kosygin, Andropov, Chernenko, were of the same grey greyness variety. Jaruzelski stood out a bit, but this was because he was an unusual communist leader: a military man with dark glasses. He looked more like an East European Pinochet than a communist leader. Ceauşescu was better known because of his independent foreign policies and crazy domestic policies, but he too was far from charismatic—as we can easily ascertain from his much-replayed last speech at the Victoria Square in Bucharest.

An easy answer to this absence of charisma or individuality is to point out that all post-revolutionary communist leaders were men of the "apparat": skilful in bureaucratic machinations and back-room manoeuvring: they did not need to appeal to the population, run for elections, or gather votes. And bureaucratic organizations prefer greyish technocrats (like Kosygin and Kádár) or just grey people with zero individuality (like the rest of the characters I mentioned above). Reading recently Halberstam's *The Best and the Brightest*, I thought: was not McNamara, the man of the system, the same: grey, even if he was in certain intellectual ways surely more impressive than this list

360

COMMUNISM

of communist "apparatchiks" (a term I dislike but, *faute de mieux*, have to use).

Nonetheless, I think that this bureaucratic explanation is not fully convincing. I think that there was another ideological explanation. When my friend mentioned as an explanation for Tito's longevity of rule his presumed charisma, I felt like correcting him, by saying that for communists charisma was never an ideologically desired property. No true communist leader would explain his popularity or longevity by charisma. They were tools of history; individuals who just embodied the historical Geist. Thus, ideally, and I think that this is a correct context within which to place their "greyness," they as persons would not natter. What mattered was history, was what the Party decided. Every individualism and every flamboyant individual was suspicious. (My cousin, who was a perfect Party man: scrupulously honest and dedicated, would never answer any personal questions directly: asked what are his plans re. work and life he would invariably—and honestly—reply: "I have none. It will be as the comrades decide." End of story.)

The submission of individuality meant of course no place for charisma. This seems strange because some of these rulers, Stalin in particular, but also Tito, Enver Hoxha, and Mao, enjoyed and even encouraged a cult of personality without claiming charisma. The other leaders (the Husaks and Kadars) neither had a cult of personality, nor encouraged any individual adulation.

Communist ideology was, fundamentally, an ideology of ordinary, working-class men and women. It was an ideology of masses. It thus frowned on all displays of individualism and, I think, even favoured an aesthetic of orderliness, of utilitarianism, of non-standing out in the crowd. Greyness of the leaders was exactly how ideologically the leaders should be: not any different from you and me, dressed boringly, speaking softly, monotonously, and for a long time in a mixture of Marxist and economistic jargon that would put most listeners to sleep.

The point was to be "the average man."

I think that there was a distinct communist aesthetic of greyness, derived from the ideology, where what might be judged as colourless and dull was precisely what was sought. Every aesthetic is deeply subjective. There is no reason to believe that an aesthetic of grey, dusty colours is inferior to the aesthetic of a rainbow. I have thus come to the conclusion that what is often ridiculed or criticized as a lack of aesthetics in leaders, apartment buildings, and art in general, is the application of foreign (to communist ideology) aesthetic

361

HISTORY

criteria. The conventional ugliness of communist constructions was not a defect. It was something that was sought after. It was an alternative aesthetic where nothing would stand out. The grey leaders were beautiful—on their own terms.

(Published March 5, 2023)

COMMUNISM

14.9 Trotsky after Kolakowski

As people who follow my blogs know, I have recently reread all three volumes of Leszek Kolakowski's magisterial *Main Currents of Marxism*. I read them first in the mid 1980s (the date when I bought them, inscribed on my copy, is June 1982), and am rereading them almost forty years later. They are even more impressive now—because I know more and because the world has changed.

Kolakowski discusses many writers, from the Greek founders of dialectics, and Hegel, to Mao Zedong. His knowledge is simply astounding. With many of them he disagrees strongly, and yet Kolakowski is—discussing them on their own terms, not his—at times admiring. This is the case of Lukács (especially) and Lenin. Lukács indeed is, after Marx, the most impressive thinker, among more than a hundred discussed in the three volumes. Young Kolakowski was, it seems evident, very influenced by Lukács.

But, a person of whom Kolakowski is probably the most contemptuous (leaving aside Marcuse—who is not worth discussing) is ... Trotsky. If I were to summarize it in one sentence, I would say that it is because Trotsky was a Stalin without Stalin's convictions, or rather without Stalin's ruthlessness and readiness to make difficult decisions when left alone (i.e. without having Lenin to back him up).

How do we reconcile this with (I think) the undeniable fact of Trotsky's brilliance in many spheres, from writing to war-making, and his particular attraction for intellectuals? Indeed, when intellectuals who dream of changing the world think of an exemplary life, it is hard not to see that Trotsky's probably fits the bill as one of the most brilliant such lives in history. How many intellectuals are there sipping coffee in the Central Café in Vienna on a Friday, and leading to victory the largest army of workers and peasants in the world next Monday? How many are there writing book reviews on a Saturday, and taking hostages on the next Tuesday? Is it common to go to an art exhibition in Paris on Sunday, and to negotiate a peace treaty that gives away a third of a country's industry on Wednesday?

The extraordinary combination of a brilliant intellectual life (for Trotsky was indeed an excellent writer) with the life of a man of action, not being afraid or deterred by obstacles, is straight out of a Greek playbook of heroic lives.

What went wrong? Why is it that the architect of Bolshevik victory already by 1924 received the second lowest number of votes in the

363

HISTORY

elections for the Central Committee? A person who was clearly number 2 to Lenin was already, in May 1924, the No. 2 from the bottom, in terms of Bolshevik's top echelon's preferences (see J. Takiguchi).

The reason is that Trotsky's manifold abilities could only be fully displayed and used so long as he was put in a position of command, but was ultimately controlled by a person whom he saw as his intellectual and political equal or superior. That was Lenin. As soon as Lenin was gone from the scene, all the negative features of Trotsky came to the fore: his haughtiness, conceit, arrogance. His ideologically extreme positions (collectivization, willing contempt for the trade unions and workers) were later applied by Stalin, and Trotskyists—many of them in labor camps across the Soviet Union— briefly rejoiced in their ideological victory over the "grey blur" of bureaucracy, Stalin.

It was never clear if that extremism in the 1920s was true or fake. And this is where we come to Kolakowski's contemptuous judgment: Trotsky was a poseur. After the anchor of Lenin was gone, he did not want to take any responsibilities: he was the head of the Red Army, technically commanding millions of people, yet he refused to attend meetings; he would decline positions he was offered, including the one of Prime Minister; he would treat his comrades with contempt, so much so that they would stop talking to each other as soon as they saw him walking the corridors of the Kremlin, afraid of his biting remarks. (All of these examples are from other writings, not Kolakowski's book.)

His unwillingness to take charge when it was manifestly his duty to do so sowed the seeds of later defeatist outlook, and not only of the Trotskyist movement, which broke up into ever smaller groupuscules. It affected many left-wing movements that preferred to claim grandiose ideas, but were unwilling to even try to take power. Examples include the French and Italian Communist Parties in the 1960s–1970s, who totally gave up the idea of winning elections, or gaining power.

Trotsky personally did not want this to happen: he continued fighting to the end, including against his own assassin, a strong man thirty years his junior, whom Trotsky, with his bleeding head, was able to wrest to the ground. Yet, by avoiding the responsibility when it was his for the taking, he charted the future path of many left-wing parties. It was reinforced by Gramsci's oft-repeated defeatist "pessimism of the intellect, optimism of the will." All of that meant that many left-wing politicians lost any desire to win.

364

"Trotskyism" eventually became a "movement" (if this term can at all be applied) of Western intelligentsia that wanted to pretend they were doing something—while in reality doing nothing. It made no inroads anywhere in the world, with the possible exception of the Spanish Workers' Party of Marxist Unification (POUM) in the 1930s. It became, after the Second World War, a useful "movement" to have nice dinner conversations and to meet clever girlfriends and boyfriends—it might have served as an *eHarmony* of post-war Western Europe—but it was little else. Even worse, in its US form, it converted itself from the left to the extreme right as many formerly young Trotskyists ended up, not only supporting, but defining, the neocons' imperialist project.

Trotsky still haunts the left: if you really do not want to win, you never will. If it is more fun to drink cappuccinos on a square at noon, then to get up at 6 am to canvass support, you will end up drinking cappuccinos.

(Published August 6, 2021)

HISTORY

14.10 Notes on Fanon

As I was writing the third chapter of my book (*Global Inequality*), which deals with the change in the factors underlying global inequality (from being driven by within-national inequalities to becoming driven by between-national inequalities and, perhaps in the future, going back to within-national inequalities), entitled "From Karl Marx to Frantz Fanon and then back to Marx?," I decided that I should also reread some of Fanon.

A couple of days ago, in Washington, I found my 1973 copy of the Croatian–Serbian translation (with a very nice introduction) of *Les damnés de la terre*, which I read probably in 1974 or 1975. Now, I reread basically only my notes and, as in 1975, I skipped the last chapter on the psychological effects of violence (Fanon was a psychiatrist.)

What are my impressions, reading now a book published at the height of decolonization and when the income gap between the First and Third World was at its peak, in 1961? First, I noticed how much the world has changed. Fanon was one of the "prophets" of the Third World. Well, neither the Third, nor the Second, world exists anymore. He spoke of colonies in Africa. None exists today. He spoke of Western left-wing Marxist intelligentsia. It is all gone. Even the copy of the book I held in my hands added to this eerie feeling. It was published in Yugoslavia, which no longer exists. It was published in Croato-Serbian, the language which (at least under that name) no longer exists. Did everything he wrote about disappear?

What can we say about Fanon today? I divide my impression under three headings: violence, new man, and economics.

Violence. Fanon is perhaps best known for his support of violence, used by movements for national liberation. He never glorified violence like Sorel and many European writers, who glorified the First World War. But he thought that violence was necessary to fight the colonizers: "eye for an eye, tooth for a tooth," knife for a knife, gun for a gun. Was he right? In some sense yes. There is no doubt, I think, that in Vietnam, Algeria, Angola, Zimbabwe, Burma, Kenya, the colonizers never wanted to give up power. They were the first to use violence and national liberation movements had to do the same. Moreover, the violence used by the weaker side is not the same as the violence used by the stronger side.

But Fanon's language is not guarded. Although I think that his chapter 1, "On violence," is the most interesting part of the book

366

(perhaps the only one that he really finished; the book was published posthumously), he seems at times to view violence as a "cleansing tool," to believe that there is something valuable in it as such, and not to realize that once it ceases to be used carefully and in very controlled and instrumental doses, it turns against the one who uses it. This was indeed often the history of the newly independent countries; many have descended into infernal cycles of violence: civil wars in Algeria, Nigeria, Ivory Coast, Sudan; permanent wars in Congo, numerous *coups d'état*.

New man. In chapter 2 especially, but throughout the book as well, Fanon insists on Africa rejecting (1) colonizers, (2) capitalism, (3) domestic small bourgeoisie often allied with the colonizers, and (4) a return to a romanticized African past. He believes that the objective of the national struggle should be the creation of a "new man" or a new society. This was a common belief of all revolutionary movements throughout most of the twentieth century. They have not achieved much. "The new man" has remained elusive. Often the quest has led to tyrannies. And, indeed, Fanon gives us almost no guidance about how this "new man" and new society are to be created, other than identifying (like Mao before him) peasantry as the truly revolutionary class. But, while Marx explains, at least in theory, why the proletariat might produce the "new man"—because the condition for its own liberation is the liberation of the entire society—Fanon does not explain much at all.

Economics. Fanon does not spend much time on economics (a common feature among Marxisant authors of the 1960s). He obviously rejects capitalism, but rejects also state ownership of the means of production because it would simply lead to state officials taking positions of authority. He is in favor of the nationalization of the tertiary sector (services). Interestingly, he regards control of trade as crucial: perhaps this is a reflection of Africa's backwardness.

Fanon seems, in two comments that he makes on the matter, to be in favor of democratic ownership of capital, perhaps similar to "self-management" or "market socialism" that existed in Yugoslavia. That sounds good because indeed the internal organization of such enterprises was much more democratic than the organization of similar enterprises under capitalism. But (perhaps unfortunately), history seems to have taught us that people work harder under dictatorship in the workplace, and are content to let democracy exist only in the public (but not work) sphere. Thus worker-controlled enterprises tended to waste capital, make bad investment decisions, prefer to distribute income in wages, never fire anyone and not require

HISTORY

workers to put in much effort. As every Marxist would tell you, if you are economically inefficient, you are "toast."

So, Fanon's preferred economic formula would also have failed and, indeed, it failed, not only in Yugoslavia, but also elsewhere it was tried: in Zambia, Tanzania, and Algeria. Countries that kept state ownership but also allowed for a large role of the private sector like Vietnam and China did better. Fanon perhaps did not know the comment attributed to Bela Kun during the 1919 Hungarian Soviet revolution that "workers will die for the revolution, but will not work for it."

Fanon is ferocious in his critique of the inability of the local Third World bourgeoisies to save, innovate, create any value, and go beyond their role of "cocktail party organizers for the Western bourgeoisie." He writes: "national bourgeoisie will take the role of foreman of European companies and will practically convert the country into a brothel." These pages in his chapter 3 ("The problems of national consciousness") are very powerful, and could have been written today. The problem, however, is that when you start with low income and have little education and knowledge, and little or nothing to offer to the rest of the world, you really cannot be more than "a foreman," or a "brothel." Regardless of what you would like to be.

Thus, melancholically, I have to conclude that Fanon was often wrong on all three (important) topics. But, being wrong is not a good reason for not being read. Fanon remains, I think, one of the best sources for the period of decolonization. This is a period which is (self-satisfactorily) ignored today, so much so that Obama, US president, whose own father fought for independence of Kenya, and whose grandfather was jailed and tortured by the British, could, in his long and wide-ranging speech on world history in the twentieth century last year in Brussels, avoid mentioning any names or countries linked with the struggle for independence, except for a few anodyne comments on Nelson Mandela. Thus, no Vietnam, no Algeria, no Zambia, no Ghana, no Indonesia, no Kenya, no Tanzania, no Egypt. No ... Well, if you are satisfied with such a truncated history of the past half century, then you should ignore Fanon too.

(Published April 7, 2015)

COMMUNISM

14.11 The book of the dead: Victor Serge's *Notebooks 1936–1947*

Born to the Russian anti-Czarist emigrés in Belgium in 1890 => engaged in revolutionary anarchist activity as a teenager in France => condemned to five years in jail at 17 => expelled to Spain => exchanged for French soldiers held by the Bolsheviks in 1919 => joined the Bolsheviks => participated in the Civil War and worked for the Comintern => joined the Left Opposition after the Kronstadt rebellion => arrested, imprisoned in Lublianka in 1928 => released => member of the Trotskyist opposition => arrested again in 1933 and exiled to Siberia => released after international protests and sent to France in 1936 => joined POUM and fought in Spain => fled to France after Franco's victory => left France on a refugee boat to Mexico in 1941 => engaged in Trotskyist activities in Mexico=> died in 1947.

How does that look for a biography? Incredible, one could say. But not an unusual one for the people among whom Serge moved and lived. His *Notebooks*, not written for publication and discovered only in the twenty-first century, are a compelling mixture of historical reminiscences, reflections on Marxism and psychoanalysis, attacks on Stalinist totalitarianism (the term is often used), defense of democratic socialism, descriptions of Mexico, literary criticism, and art history. Most entries are mid-size, between one and three pages. They can be read separately, although the chronology is important, as we see how Serge's own thinking evolves with the war that he is observing from faraway, in Mexico.

The entire "Who's Who" of the art and revolutionary world of continental Europe is included in these notes. There is, it seems, no significant revolutionary or writer or painter whom Serge has not met during the forty years of febrile activity. Of the leaders of the Russian revolution, Serge was the closest to Trotsky. Not all of the time though. He joined the Left Opposition after Kronstadt—but the attack on rebellious sailors was led by none other than Trotsky. Nor did Serge later agree with the formation of the Fourth International. Still in the Soviet Union, he was jailed as a Trotskyist and in Spain he worked with POUM, the Trotskyist militia. He arrived in Mexico after Trotsky's assassination. Serge's descriptions of the "tomb" of Coyoácan, the compound where Trotsky lived and was murdered, the utter desolation of the house, which still had armed guards and gun turrets, with Natalia, Trotsky's widow, emaciated, forlorn,

369

HISTORY

children killed, utterly alone, are among the most poignant parts of the *Notebooks*.

The swirling activity around Trotsky, even after his death, is described. Serge (we do not know how) managed to meet in jail—where he is given royal treatment—Trotsky's assassin. Here is a part of Ramón Mercader's (whose identity was then not known) descriptions: "Tall, well-built, vigorous, supple, even athletic. Thick-necked ... a strong, well-formed head. A man with animal vigor. A fleeting gaze, sometimes hard and revealing. His features are sharp, fleshy, vigorous. Very well dressed; coffee-colored leather jacket; expensive. Under it a silk sport shirt, fashionable, khaki. Khaki gabardine slacks with a sharp crease; yellow shoes; good soles."

The *frères ennemis*, Alfaro Siqueiros and Diego Rivera, are present throughout the book: the first, the co-organizer of the unsuccessful assassination of Trotsky who then fled to Chile thanks to Pablo Neruda; the second, Trotsky's inconsistent defender; both "reunited" in the Mexican Communist Party that Diego Rivera joined after the war on the wave of pro-Stalinist enthusiasm, which swept the world after the Soviet victory over Nazi Germany.

The Comintern's "Who's Who" (Willi Münzenberg, Franz Mehring, Otto Rühle, Anton Pannekoek) is accompanied by the Russian and continental European intellectual elite: Ossip Mandelstam, Anna Akhmatova, Maxim Gorky, Boris Pasternak, Andrei Tolstoy, André Breton, André Gide, Antoine de Saint Exupéry, Romain Rolland, Stefan Zweig, Pablo Picasso. Each of them is, often in passing, sketched in a few paragraphs: Andrei Tolstoy, the kindly count who gives fabulous parties while famine rages, and is chauffeured in Stalin's private car; Anna Akhmatova "her enormous brown eyes in the face of an emaciated child"; André Gide in search of popularity, complaining of Malraux trying to upstage him, yet with sufficient intellectual honesty to write *Le retour de l'URSS*; Romain Rolland, to whom Serge owed his release from Siberian exile but who gradually moves to a pro-Stalinist position and refuses to condemn the Moscow Trials; the sky-high vanity of André Breton, "a personality that is nothing but a pose"; the petty-bourgeois Stefan Zweig; Picasso painting for "art galleries catering to bourgeois collectors fed on intellectual refuse."

It is a book of the dead. In an orgy of ideologically inspired killings that engulfed Europe, those who were not killed by Stalin, were killed by Hitler, and those who survived both, were either killed in wars or committed suicide. Almost no one died in his or her bed.

How about politics? Serge does not present a coherent view of it, nor can one expect this in a diary. He sees the world as composed

370

COMMUNISM

of four political forces: conservative capitalist, Stalinist, democratic socialist and fascist. The defeat in the War seems to have eliminated fascism. The fate of Europe and the world depends on the interaction of the remaining three. Capitalism is ideologically bankrupt and the development of technology requires planning. So, it is doomed. Stalinism is ascendant. It destroys human freedom and the human soul and has besmirched all the communist ideals. It needs to be opposed at all costs; intransigently. Democratic socialism is, Serge believes, the only humane alternative, but can it win, as Stalin is poised to conquer half of Europe? (Serge was right on that, even if he was often wrong on a number of predictions made while the war was going on.) Like with every contemporary observer and participant in this struggle, we are left with possibilities. No one knows which one will turn out to be right.

The essential dilemmas and the main forces that shaped the post-War are nevertheless described with remarkable prescience. If we consider the period from 1945 to 1990, it can indeed be described as the struggle between these three ideologies that have each evolved over time: capitalism toward a more liberal state, democratic socialism toward a more pro-capitalist position than Serge could have imagined, and Stalinism toward a much softer variant of Brezhnev-like sovietism.

However, there are forces that Serge underestimated. Mostly because of his historical background. As the very partial list of people mentioned here should make clear, the ideological world within which Serge moved was that of continental Europe, of five great nations: Russia, Germany, France, Spain, and Italy. The Anglo-Saxon world is hardly present at all—especially absent is Britain. The Third World is non-existent. In a few dispersed remarks, Serge strangely failed to see the enormous revolutionary potential of Africa, India, China, Indonesia. These countries are non-existent for Serge. His descriptions of Mexico, as he travels through the country, are worth reading for their glimpses of rural and urban life in the 1940s—pyramids and lost civilizations, but they are observations of a tourist. While his engagement with Europe is close and passionate, his engagement with Mexico is refracted only through the role that Mexico plays in European conflicts, and particularly in the Spanish Civil War. There is a total dearth of political or social observations on Mexico herself.

I would like to finish with Serge's observations on two fascists whom he knew personally at the time when they were communists: Jacques Doriot ("Zinoviev liked him") and Nicola Bombacci. They were both killed in retribution at the end of the War. Bombacci was

371

HISTORY

one of the fifteen executed together with Mussolini. Their transition from communism to fascism is explained by the need for restless activity, great organizational skills, and ambition. But there is one interesting, small ideological detail: both, Serge thinks, might have seen fascism within the Marxist scheme as a ruse of history, where decrepit capitalism adopts fascism as a way of saving itself; yet fascism, by imposing a strong state rule over the private sector, gradually transforms it, and creates an economy that can, in a future evolution, be readily taken over by workers. In such a bizarre way, fascism was, he believes, seen by the former communists as a way of ending capitalism.

P.S. The editing of the book is close to catastrophic. Dozens of people mentioned by Serge are unidentified; those who are, are so in minimalistic endnotes; many events alluded to in the *Notebooks* are left unexplained; the introduction is brief and not very helpful. The publisher was clearly saving on money.

(Published January 6, 2023)

COMMUNISM

14.12 Did socialism keep capitalism equal?

This is an interesting idea and I think that it will gradually become more popular. The idea is simple: the presence of the ideology of socialism (abolition of private property) and its embodiment in the Soviet Union and other communist states made capitalists careful: they knew that if they tried to push workers too hard, the workers might retaliate and capitalists might end up by losing all.

Now, this idea comes from the fact that rich capitalist countries experienced an extraordinary period of decreasing inequality from around the 1920s to the 1980s, and then, since the 1980s, contradicting what a simple Kuznets curve would imply, inequality went up. It so happens that the turning point in the 1980s coincides with (1) the acceleration of the skill-biased technological progress, (2) increased globalization and entry of Chinese workers into the global labor market, (3) pro-rich policy changes (lower taxes), (4) decline of the trade unions, and (5) the end of communism as an ideology. So, each of these five factors can be used to explain the increase in inequality in rich capitalist countries.

The socialist story recently received a boost from two papers. Both argue that the demonstration effect of the Soviet Union internationally (or differently, the threat of communist revolution nationally) produced low inequality in the West. K. S. Jomo and Vladimir Popov write "an alternative view is ... that the reversal of growing inequality followed [happened because of] the 1917 Bolshevik revolution in Russia, the emergence of the USSR and other socialist countries ..." André Albuquerque Sant'Anna does more: an empirical analysis, where the top one percent income share of eighteen OECD countries over the period 1960–2010 is explained by the usual variables (financial openness, union density, top marginal tax rate), *plus* the variable created by Sant'Anna, relative military power. It is equal to military expenditure spending of a country as a share of USSR/Russian military spending (all annual data), interacted with the distance from Moscow. If, say, your spending is one-tenth of Soviet spending, and you are close by (say, in Finland), then the threat of Soviet Union (aka communism) will be greater, and presumably you would depress the top income share of your capitalists more than if you have the same relative spending but are in Portugal.

To put some additional order into that story, let us consider three channels through which socialism could have "disciplined" income inequality under capitalism. The first was strictly ideological or

373

HISTORY

political and is reflected in the electoral importance of communist and some socialist parties (Italy and France come to mind). The second is through trade unions (which many people have indeed included in their work). The trade unions themselves were often affiliated with communist parties (like CGT in France) or were close to Labor parties, as in Sweden and the Nordic countries. And then, you had the "policing" device of the Soviet military power.

I think that one should keep these three channels separate. Ideally, one should treat them empirically as different, although we should note that Albuquerque Sant'Anna does adjust for trade-union density. Since the relative power variable still comes out as robustly negative (the greater the relative power of the Soviet Union, the lower the top income share) he is right to conclude that the Soviet Union's influence is separate from the influence of trade unions. Also, one should keep in mind that the period after 1991, that is after the dissolution of the Soviet Union, is fundamentally different. Not only was there a decrease of Russian military spending compared to what it was under the Soviet Union but that spending no longer had the "communist" connotation which is, according to the argument in the paper, what kept capitalist countries "on the straight and narrow" path of equality.

Going back to the three possible channels of communist influence, I do mention them in my forthcoming book (*Global Inequality*) but, unlike Albuquerque Sant'Anna, I do not do an empirical analysis. I also see them as *one* of the contributory factors to the Great Leveling. I do not think that they were the only factor (no more than I see the accelerated technological progress, or globalization, as the sole factors behind the inequality reversal since the 1980s). Actually, I argue that the Great Leveling was driven by the political forces emphasized by Piketty (war destruction, high taxation, hyperinflation) as well as by the "benign" economic and demographic forces emphasized by Kuznets (increase in the education level combined with a reduction in the education premium, aging of the population and thus greater demand for redistribution, and end of the transfer of labor from rural to urban areas).

Here I want, however, to bring to the fore the work that looks at the whole issue somewhat differently, and does this in a sense from a very global perspective. Indeed, communism was a global movement. It does not require much reading of the literature from the 1920s to realize how scared capitalists and those who defended the free market were of socialism. After all, that's why capitalist countries intervened militarily in the Russian Civil War, and then imposed the

374

trade embargo and the cordon sanitaire on the USSR. Not the sort of policies you would employ if you were not ideologically afraid (because militarily the Soviet Union was then very weak). The threat intensified again after the Second World War, when the communist influence through all three channels was at its peak. And then it steadily declined so much that by the mid 1970s, it was definitely small. The communist parties reached their maximum influence in the early 1970s, but Eurocommunism had already expunged from its program any ideas of nationalization of property. It was rapidly transforming itself into social-democracy. The trade unions declined. And both the demonstration effect and the fear of the Soviet Union receded. So, capitalism could go back to what it would be doing anyway, that is to the levels of inequality it achieved at the end of the nineteenth century. *"El periodo especial"* of capitalism was over.

I am not sure that this particular story can alone explain the decline in inequality in the West, and certainly it is a story that one hears less often in the US than in Europe, as the United States believed itself to be sufficiently protected from the communist virus (although when you look at the repression in the 1920s and the McCarthyism in the 1950s, one is not so sure). But even Solow's recent mention of the changing power relations between capitalists and workers (the end of the Detroit treaty) as ushering in the period of rising inequality is not inconsistent with this view. In a recent conversation, and totally unaware of the literature, an Italian high-level diplomat explained to me why inequality in Italy increased recently: "in the 1970s, capitalists were afraid of the Italian Communist Party." So, there is, I think, something in the Albuquerque Sant'Anna and K. S. Jomo and Popov story.

The implication is, of course, rather unpleasant: left to itself, without any countervailing powers, capitalism will keep on generating high inequality and so the US may soon look like South Africa. That's where I think differently: I think there are, in the longer-term, forces that would lead toward reduction in inequality (and that would not be the return of communism).

P.S. In the revised version of the paper, Sant'Anna and Weller introduce other domestic controls like the strength of communist and socialist parties, and their influence on trade unions. The "Soviet effect" still remains statistically significant.

(Published in *Social Europe*, August 26, 2015)

HISTORY

14.13 Gorbachev: A politician who did not want to rule

God has not been kind to Mikhail Gorbachev not to allow him to die before February 24, 2022 and so not witness the senseless destruction of everything he stood for. And perhaps, even to reflect how sometimes the decision not to use force may later lead to a much greater carnage. If Mikhail Gorbachev had maintained the Soviet Union (perhaps without the Baltics), and used force the way that Deng Xiaoping did, we might not be now looking at a senseless internecine war that has already claimed dozens if not hundreds of thousands of lives, and which, in the worst case, might degenerate into a nuclear holocaust. Politicians, even those who are the most humane, must unfortunately make this calculation, where human lives are just numbers.

Gorbachev refused to do so. Nobody did any longer take him seriously, from Baku to Washington, although he sat atop the largest nuclear arsenal in the world, the second largest military in the world, hundreds of thousands of police and domestic security forces and, as the Secretary General of the monopolistic party, disposed of the unquestionable loyalty of twenty million of its members.

By the standards of statecraft, he must be judged harshly, like one of the most extraordinary failures in history. By the standards of humanity, he must be judged much more kindly: he allowed millions to regain freedom, not only proclaimed, but stuck to the principles of non-violence in domestic and foreign affairs, and left his office willingly, when he did not need to do so, simply because he did not want to risk lives in order to keep it. But, being nice and, in fact, anti-political, he left the field open to much worse men.

He was incapable of running a complicated, fraught by too much history, multinational, and vast empire like the Soviet Union. The country was additionally "saddled" by its reluctant satellites, the unwinnable war in Afghanistan, arms race with a much stronger opponent, and a quasi-stagnant economy. The situation that Gorbachev inherited was far from easy. But, it was manageable, and the fact that nobody predicted the precipitous economic, military, and political decline of the Soviet Union confirms it. Gorbachev, by trying to improve things, made them catastrophic. Many people in retrospect, and perhaps out of respect for Gorbachev (which we do owe to him) tried to explain the descent into the chaos by claiming that the system was "unreformable" and that everything was preordained. The role of Gorbachev, the person, in that view of history is almost non-existent. But this is wrong. A more competent

376

COMMUNISM

ruler, a savvier politician, a more ruthless man, would have handled things differently, and might have forestalled the catastrophe.

The most mysterious part is his rise to power. I do not mean it in a conspiratorial way because there was no conspiracy. The part that must puzzle everybody who reflects on it is the following: given how badly skilled Gorbachev was in handling the economy and politics at the central level, how come that these defects have not become apparent much earlier as he climbed the ladders of power? Didn't anyone notice that in Stavropol? Moreover, given how willing he was to reject the rule of bureaucrats who brought him to power and who worked with him for several decades, how is it that they have not seen the red danger lights flashing behind that man with the affable smile? How is it that Andropov, not a person who displayed a huge sense of humanity, nor who, by his job description, could have been fooled easily, did not see the fault-lines in Gorbachev that, once in power, would blow up the entire Empire?

I do not think that there will ever be a good answer to that, especially because Gorbachev did not conceal his opinions or pretend to be a different person from the one he was. The only way to understand how a powerful bureaucracy would let somebody who is going to destroy it climb to power within that same bureaucracy is to believe that Gorbachev's own views had evolved over time. That when he started reforming the system his view were very much within the acceptable reformist camp, of which even Andropov approved, but that as each step of reforms proceeded, his views evolved in the direction of greater freedom, so that by the end he was presiding over a party that was an amalgam of incompatible factions and tendencies, from KGB stalwarts (Kryuchkov), to anti-reformists (Ligachev), to red directors (Chernomyrdin), to corrupt thieves (many Komsomol leaders), to technocrats (Gaidar), to social-democrats (Roy and Zhores Medvedev).

Can we draw some conclusions? Regarding politics, we would need a person of Machiavelli's caliber to describe what happened and why. But, for Russian politics of succession, the lesson seems clearer: Stalin could not have imagined that somebody like Khrushchev (whom he treated like a not very smart country bumpkin) could ever succeed him; neither could have Khrushchev imagined that the "beau Leonid" would engineer an internal coup against him; Andropov made a misjudgment on Gorbachev, who in turn underestimated Yeltsin. Yeltsin picked Putin to do one job, but received something entirely different. It is unlikely that Putin alone would not commit the same error.

(Published August 3, 2022)

HISTORY

14.14 Did post-Marxist theories destroy communist regimes?

The break-up of the Soviet Union was one of the most unusual events in history. Never before had an empire this powerful and vast given up its power and allowed the dissolution of its internal core (the Soviet Union) and its tributary states (Eastern Europe) so quickly and without a fight. The Ottoman Empire went into a process of disintegration that lasted several centuries and was punctuated by numerous wars, both with Western powers and Russia, and numerous struggles for national independence (Greece, Serbia, Bulgaria). The Habsburg Empire dissolved after four years of the hitherto largest conflict in history. The same is true of the Russian Empire and the Hohenzollerns'. But the Soviet Empire gave way almost entirely peacefully and without a fight. How did that happen?

A slender volume by Wisła Suraska (*How the Soviet Union Disappeared*) tries to answer the question. It is important to explain what the book is not. It is not a book about communism and economics. It does not try to answer (at least, not directly) the question about the successes and failures of communism nor does it deal with economics at all. It is remarkable that the book does not contain a single number. It is a book written by a political scientist and it focuses on internal political determinants of the Soviet collapse.

It is a very well and clearly written volume. The key conclusion of Suraska, enounced in italics in the last chapter, is that the break up is due to "the general failure of communist regimes—*their inability to build a modern state*" (p. 134; emphasis in the original). It is "the state weakness, rather than its omnipotence [that] stalled communist project of modernization and, most notably, Gorbachev's perestroika" (p. 134). Lest somebody believe that Suraska is a partisan of state power, let me explain that what she means is that the arbitrary nature of communist state, overseen by the Communist Party, prevented it from ever developing a responsible and impersonal machinery of Weberian bureaucracy. Such a machinery that follows well-known and rational rules cannot be established if the power is arbitrary. And, without such a machinery, the project of modernization is doomed.

But this still does not explain why the country (the USSR) broke up. It broke up, she argues, because of a Breznevite equilibrium that—lacking a functioning centrally controlled state apparatus and forsaking the use of terror—consisted in the creation of territorially based fiefdoms. The power at the center depended on having

378

peripheral supporters and these peripheral supporters gradually took over most of the local (in the USSR case, republican) functions. They could be dislodged only by the application of mass terror as when, under Stalin, the center actively fought the creation of local centers of power, either by "purging" the leaders or by shifting them constantly between the regions in order to prevent the accumulation of power. But Brezhnevite equilibrium consisted precisely in "decentralizing" power to local "barons" who would then support the faction in the center that gave them most power.

When Gorbachev tried to recentralize the decision-making in order to promote his reforms, he was obstructed at all levels and eventually figured out that without the republican support he could accomplish nothing. This is why, as Suraska writes, at the last Party congress in 1991, he outbid his competitor (Yegor Ligachev) by formally bringing all the regional Party bosses into the Politburo and thus effectively confederalizing the Party and the country. But, even that proved too little too late as the largest unit, Russia under Yeltsin, became, together with the Baltic republics, the most secessionist.

Suraska rightly adds to this vertical de-concentration of power the ever-present wariness and competition between the Party, the secret services (KGB) and the Army. The triangular relationship where two actors try to weaken and control the third contributed to the collapse. She sees the beginning of the end of the Army's role in the Politburo's decision, strongly promoted by Andropov (then the head of KGB), not to intervene in Poland in 1980–1981. Andropov's position (according to the transcripts of the Politburo meetings) that "even if Poland falls under the control of "Solidarity" ... [non-intervention] will be" (p. 70) was grounded in the belief that every Soviet foreign intervention (Hungary 1956, Czechoslovakia 1968) reinforced the power of the Army and thus, if KGB were ever to come on top, Army must not be in the driver's seat.

The ultimate weakness of the Party could be, as Suraska writes, seen in the final denouements in the Soviet Union and Poland: in one case, the top party post went to a head of the secret police, in the other case, to the head of the Army.

In perhaps the most original insight, Suraska deals with the ideology of Gorbachev and the first entirely Soviet-raised and bred generation that came to power in the mid 1980s. They were influenced by post-Marxist thinking, where democracy or its absence were simple external (or non-essential) features: democracy was a sham since the "real power" resides elsewhere. "Armed" with this belief and the 1970s ideas of convergence of the two systems plus

HISTORY

(in my opinion) the millenarian Marxist view that communism represents the future of mankind, they began to see no significant contradictions between the two systems and trusted that even the introduction of democracy would not affect their positions. Thus, in an ironic twist, Suraska, who is thoroughly critical of both Marxist and post-Marxist theories, credits the latter (p. 147) for bringing to an end the Marxist-based regimes.

In the penultimate chapter Suraska quickly and very critically reviews different theories that purported to explain the communist state: modernization theory, totalitarianism, bureaucratic theory, are all found wanting. Suraska's conclusion, stated in the beginning of this text, is then expounded in the last chapter revealingly entitled "Despotism and the modern state." There, in a final note worth pointing out, Suraska discusses communist rejection of the state and its rules-bound procedures (which make communists ideological brethrens of anarchists) and compellingly argues for the complementarity of "council ("soviet") democracy and central planning. Both eviscerate the state, take over its functions, impose arbitrary decision-making, and do away with the division of powers. Anarchic and despotic features are thus shown to go together, moreover to be in need of each other.

P.S. Regrettably, I have to point one extremely odd mistake by somebody whose knowledge of the Soviet and East European politics is, by all indications, quite remarkable. Suraska puzzlingly writes of Gheorghiu-Dej (also misspelled), the Romanian leader, as Bulgarian (p. 128). I think she had in mind Chervenkov, but made a mistake, not spotted by herself or the editors.

(Published February 19, 2017)

— 15 —

TRANSITION TO CAPITALISM

15.1 Democracy of convenience, not of choice: Why is Eastern Europe different?

There are, in my opinion, two considerations that are almost never taken into account when the reluctance, or outright refusal, of East European countries to accept African and Asian migrants, many of them Islamic, is discussed. They are the history of these countries over the past two centuries, and the nature of the 1989 revolutions.

When one draws the line from Estonia to Greece, or to be more graphic and to imitate Churchill, from Narva to Nafplion, one notices that all currently existing countries along that axis were, during the past several centuries (and in some cases, the past half-millennium), squeezed by the empires: German (or earlier by Prussia), Russian, Habsburg, and Ottoman. All these countries fought, more-or-less continuously, to free themselves from the imperial pressure, whether it was exerted through cultural assimilation (as in the case of the Czechs, Slovaks, and Slovenians), imperial conquest and partition (Poland), imperial conquest *tout court* (the Baltics and the Balkans), temporary inclusion as a second-tier ruling nation (Hungary) or any other way.

Their histories are practically nothing but unending struggles for national and religious emancipation (when the religion of the conqueror differed from theirs, as in the case of Ottomans and the Orthodox, or as between Catholics and Protestants). National emancipation meant the creation of a nation-state that would ideally include all members of one's community. Of course, none of the nations was averse, when given half a chance, to convert itself into the ruler of other weaker neighboring states—so they had no valid

HISTORY

ethical superiority compared to the empires that ruled, and often oppressed, them. The line between the oppressed and the oppressor was always thin.

Eventually, as the four empires receded, notably in the aftermath of the First World War, and eventually in the early 1990s, when the last such empire, the Soviet Union, collapsed, all countries along the Narva-Nafplion line became independent and almost wholly ethnically homogenous.

Yes, I know that there is an exception, Bosnia and, precisely because it is an oddity and exception, the civil war was fought there. But every other country is now fully, or fairly close to being fully, ethnically homogenous. Consider Poland, whose inhabitants in 1939 consisted of 66 percent Poles, 17 percent Ukrainians and Belorussians, almost 10 percent Jews and 3 percent Germans. As the result of the Second World War and the Holocaust and then the westward movement of Polish borders (combined with the expulsion of the German minority), in 1945 Poland became 99 percent Catholic and Polish. It fell under the sway of the Soviet Union but since 1989 it has been both free and ethnically compact.

In fact, if we define the national ideals as (a) zero ethnic members outside a country's borders and (b) zero members of other ethnic groups within the borders, Poland, Czech Republic, Slovakia, Slovenia, and Greece (total population of almost 70 million) fulfill this criterion almost to perfection. Close by come Hungary, Croatia, Serbia, Albania, and Kosovo (total population of about thirty million) that fulfill almost fully the criterion (b); Baltic countries, Bulgaria, Macedonia and Romania (about thirty million) satisfy (a), but do have relatively important minorities within their borders. The upshot is that most countries that run from the Baltics to the Balkans have today almost entirely homogenous populations within their borders, i.e. they satisfy either both (a) and (b), or (b) alone.

What would migrants do? They would dissolve that homogeneity, thus undermining the key objective for which these countries fought for several centuries. This time, ethnic heterogeneity would not be imposed from the outside by one of the conquering empires but would, insidiously, come from within, in the form of migrants, people of different culture, religion, and most scary in the eyes of the locals, people whose birth rates significantly outstrip the anemic, or even negative, growth rates of the native population. Migration thus appears as a threat to the hard-won national independence.

The second consideration is related to the first. It has to do with the nature of the 1989 revolutions. They were often interpreted

382

as democratic revolution. Thus, the current "backsliding" of East European countries toward overt or covert authoritarianism is seen as a betrayal of democratic ideals, or even, more broadly and extravagantly, of the ideals of the Enlightenment. The refusal to accept migrants is regarded as contradicting the nature of the revolutions. This is, however, based on a misreading of the 1989 revolutions. If they are, as I believe they should be, seen as revolutions of national emancipation, simply as a latest unfolding of centuries-long struggle for freedom, and not as democratic revolutions per se, the attitudes toward migration and the so-called European values become fully intelligible. These values, in Eastern eyes, never included ethnic heterogeneity within their borders. For Westerners this may be an obvious implication of democracy and liberalism, but not for the Easterners, who are asked to risk their key accomplishment in order to satisfy some abstract principles.

Now, when the revolution of 1989 happened, it was easy to fuse the two principles: nationalist and democratic. Even hard-core nationalists liked to talk the language of democracy because it gave them greater credibility internationally, as they appeared to be fighting for an ideal, rather than for narrow ethnic interests.

But it was a democracy of convenience, not a democracy of choice. It was similar, to give an out-of-Europe example, to the Algerian revolution, which was also viewed by their protagonists not as a national but fundamentally as a democratic revolution. And, indeed, when you have an overwhelming majority in favor, the two objectives, national and democratic, can run together and be easily confounded. It is only when tough choices, like now, have to be made that we can much more clearly see which one of the two was really a driving factor. And, when we see that, we cannot be surprised by the apparent obduracy of Orbáns, Kaczyńskis, Zemans, and many others. It is an inability to see them in the right context that has blinded both Eastern and Western elites to the reality.

(Published June 2, 2021)

HISTORY

15.2 Secessionism and the collapse of communist federations

Vladislav Zubok's splendid *Collapse* is a chronicle of the break-up of the Soviet Union. It opens with the appointment of Yuri Andropov in 1985 and ends at Christmas in 1991 with the end of the Soviet Union and Mikhail Gorbachev's resignation. In the quality of writing it reminded me of Richard Pipes' *Russian Revolution*. In both books, the reader, of course, knows the final outcome, but the books are so skillfully written that at many key points one is almost left wondering about the path history will take. The author presents the reader with the knowledge that was in front of the actors at the time, not with a 20/20 knowledge of the events that followed. It thus helps the reader see the events as they unfold, and appreciate much better the decisions taken by the main actors.

If I have one critique, it is that Zubok seldom passes judgments on the actors. But, from the few cases when he does, handling at perfection irony and scathing comments, we know that he could do it, and surely well, more often. Perhaps Zubok decided to do it sparingly in order to underline that the book is an unbiased chronological review of the events. But, to give another historic precedent, Tacitus, in a similar chronology of dramatic history, does not shy away from judging actors with the severity they deserve.

Although Zubok does not say so explicitly, the book allows us to see clearly how each of the Soviet republics followed an identical three-step approach to secession. This was not, I must say, novelty for me because I know the Soviet case rather well, having followed it closely and having read quite a lot on the collapse, and also having travelled to the Soviet Union and then Russia. And, in addition, because the three-step approach is exactly the same as that followed by the Yugoslav republics in their (as it was then euphemistically called) "disassociation" from each other.

The first step is the creation of an intellectual climate of national grievances, whether they have to do with language rights, service in the federal army, destruction of environment, or—the preferred approach—economic exploitation by other republics. That first step took years if not decades. It was performed almost exclusively by soft or hard nationalist dissidents. Soft dissidents were those like Valentin Rasputin in Russia, Dobrica Ćosić in Serbia, and Dimitrij Rupnik in Slovenia. They were "soft" because their works were published, they enjoyed celebrity status (often making lots of money in the process), and they had a strong, if not openly declared, following among the

384

Communist Party structures of their republic. The "hard" dissidents were those like Solzhenitsyn, who were jailed or exiled and whose works were not published.

The second step comes when these views from the political margin become accepted by the leaderships of the republican communist parties. This, indeed, is not possible without the simultaneous weakening of the center. In Yugoslavia, the disappearance of the center, the so-called "deconstruction [*demontaža* in Serbian] of the federation" began with the 1974 Constitution. In the Soviet Union, it started with Gorbachev's counter-productive and ill-thought reforms.

Republican party leaders, often clever "political animals," felt the center's power eroding. In a single party system, where they had never run for office, they needed an alternative claim to legitimacy. This is the point when the ideologies of resentment and grievance become useful. If people are unhappy with the current situation—the newly minted nationalist leaders tell them—it is because the republic has been mercilessly exploited for years. The narrative was exactly the same across each of the Soviet Republics. The Baltics were exploited by Russia; Russia was exploited by everybody else because it provided cheap gas and oil; Ukraine was exploited because its food was sold for next to nothing; Kazakhstan was never sufficiently appreciated for its cotton production; Slovenia paid too much in taxes; Serbia's food and electricity were underpriced; Croatia's tourist revenues suffered from the overvaluation of the national currency. In a non-market setting, everyone can assume that what they are producing should be sold at "world market" prices but everything they are buying should rightfully remain subsidized.

The leaders, until the day before all exemplary communists, now turn into nationalist heralds. Boris Yeltsin moves with ease from the party secretary in Sverdlovsk and Moscow to be the champion of free enterprise; Leonid Kravchuk, from a skillful Soviet manipulator to the defender of the Ukrainian language (which he had never spoken before); Heydar Aliev from a top KGB official arresting dissidents to a believer in democracy; Slobodan Milošević, from a Communist Party banker to the champion of Serbian rights; Milan Kučan, from a Communist Party apparatchik to an appreciative reader of dissident literature. The path is almost perfect: everybody follows the same playbook.

The third step is a definitive break. The republican Communist Party, which controls, at times in its entirety, the republican parliament, decides that the republic will no longer observe federal laws when it deems them harmful to the republican interests. It seizes

HISTORY

all federal assets on its territory and either stops paying federal taxes, or arbitrarily decides what it would pay. (Yeltsin negotiates on that with Gorbachev like in an Ottoman bazaar: "I'll pay you 10%, okay, you ask, 15%, I will give you 12.5%, but not a penny more.")

The enormity of such a move is breathtaking. People in the former communist federations had grown used to it in the 1980s and such *pronunciamentos* were seen almost as normal. To understand what they mean, take today's case of Catalonia or Scotland. It would mean that Catalonian/Scottish parliament unilaterally decides what legislations emanating from Madrid or London it will accept and what it will not. It would take control over the army units stationed in Catalonia/Scotland. All federal police forces on its territory will henceforth follow the orders from Barcelona or Edinburgh only. The police and army officers will be reappointed if loyal to the provincial government, or dismissed if otherwise. The provincial parliament would also take control of "public goods" like electricity generation and grids, railroad system, road infrastructure, etc. It would cut taxes it pays to Madrid or London to whatever it deems fair, or to zero. And, if necessary, it would, as the Baltic republics and Serbia have done in 1989, impose tariffs or embargoes on the goods coming from the rest of the country.

The deconstruction of the federation looks so far very neat— except for one thing: territorial disputes. Yeltsin, who was always supportive of Baltic secessionism, and in 90 out of 100 occasions, of Ukrainian independence, nevertheless issued, two days after the failed August 1991 coup and his *de facto* assumption of full powers, a statement that Russia will not accept arbitrary Lenin-drawn borders with Ukraine, saying that the new border should follow the exact line as defined by Putin in his February 2022 war speech, and along which the war had been fought for two past years. Identical conflicts appeared in Azerbaijan/Armenia, Moldova, Georgia, Croatia, Bosnia, and Serbia. There were/are twelve wars on the territories of the former Soviet Union and Yugoslavia since 1989. All but one were wars about the borders.

Zubok's book ends in December 1991 and it covers only a few of these wars. But the writing on the wall was very clear, the descent into war inevitable.

And, one may wonder then: where is democracy in all of it? Democracy is purely ornamental. It is seen in nationalist light, as in a movement for self-determination and the end of exploitation by others. National community is unique and unanimous. If not agreeing with unanimity, then a person cannot truly belong to the

386

TRANSITION TO CAPITALISM

national community. These were, as I argued in the previous post in the East European context, more generally (and not only in the context of ethnic-based communist federations), revolutions of national—whether true or not—liberation, not democratic revolutions, as many observers liked to see them at the time. This lesson is, I believe, increasingly obvious today: wars and autocracies had made it plain.

(Published February 15, 2024)

HISTORY

15.3 Coase theorem and methodological nationalism

When I calculate or read about these astonishing numbers regarding wealth concentration in Russia, I cannot but think about the people who made all of this possible. I was then working on "transition countries" in the World Bank research department, and was able to see almost first-hand what was happening. I travelled to Russia, knew lots of people who worked there and "advised" the government, and had a chance to witness the overall disarray and dissolution of the country. But, leaving aside the economists who found in all this chaos their own financial interests, most were driven by economic ideology, which, when it came to privatization, argued three things.

(1) Be a revolutionary. We need to privatize fast because "the window of opportunity" is now and communists may be back any moment. Do like the French Revolution did with Church lands: give it or sell to anyone because it would be hard to nationalize later.
(2) Coase theorem. It does not matter for efficiency to whom the assets go. Sure, assets will be given for free to the people close to Yeltsin and the "family," who really do not know what to do with them, much less manage them efficiently, but this is a distributional matter. The efficiency will not suffer. The newly rich will sell these assets quickly to the entrepreneurs who know how to manage them. Everything will end in the best possible manner.
(3) Demand for rule of law. Once you do that, there will be immediately demand for rule of law, even if privatization is done in the most lawless and non-transparent fashion. The new millionaires will, like the robber barons in the United Stares, demand the rule of law because they will need to protect their newly acquired wealth.

It is clear that if you hold these three views, you would do exactly as the privatizers did in Russia (and Ukraine) in the mid 1990s. Why did economists hold these views? I think because of a wrong paradigm, which, first, disregarded distributional issues by simply relegating them outside economics, and second, because they failed to take into account globalization. Their views were based on "methodological nationalism." Consider points (2) and (3). They go together. Point (2) says that the distribution is immaterial, and that the market left to itself will ensure efficiency however distribution goes. But, for

388

dynamic efficiency you need point (3): you need people who would, even if originally they stole the assets, turn around and demand the rule of law. And, presumably, who will be politically sufficiently strong to get it.

Point (2) is wrong because once rules are broken in such an egregious and unjust manner, this will for a long time remain a political problem. There would be temptation to break the rules again, and to seize the assets that were once stolen, or to give them to the others. This is exactly what Putin is doing when he simply redistributes assets from the plutocrats he does not like to those he does. And, interestingly, there is not much protest because nobody believes that these assets rightfully belong to the people who have them. So, Putin takes from A and gives to B, and it really does not matter to the public who A or B are. For most people, they are equally corrupt.

Point (3) is wrong because it failed to take into account that, with globalization, you do not need to fight a dubious struggle for the rule of law in your own country. A much easier course of action is to take all the money, and run away to London or New York, where the rule of law already exists and where nobody will ask you how you got that money in the first place. A number of Russian plutocrats, and increasingly Chinese, are taking this route. It makes total sense from the individual point of view. And it also shows how our economic thinking has not caught up with the economic reality. In the nineteenth century, it made sense for the Rockefellers et al. to fight for property rights in the United States because there were few places where they could go and squirrel away their money. Moreover, however much robbery the barons did, they were industrialists, that is engaged in some kind of business. But people who became suddenly rich in Russia were political cronies, who were totality uninterested in running steel mills or nickel "kombinates." They did not even care if they ran them aground, so long as they could cash out, and move to the Riviera.

The lesson: do not think that distribution and efficiency can be neatly compartmentalized, kept as it were in different boxes; and check if your theories work when you have a world where capital movements are almost entirely free and difficult to control, and where the rich can easily move from one "jurisdiction" to another. Our methodological nationalism is getting more obsolete by the day.

(Published December 5, 2014)

HISTORY

15.4 Trump and Gorbachev

The conjunction of these two names in the title may come as a surprise to many readers. What do a social-democrat, who wanted to reform communism, and the billionaire right-wing populist magnate have in common? Indeed, if we focus on their ideologies and individual histories (to the extent that they matter) nothing—not "almost nothing," but "nothing"!

But, if we look at the things from a structuralist perspective, similarities are unmistakable. Neither of them believes in the hierarchical international systems over which they preside. They are part of the ruling elite but they think they are fighting against it.

Gorbachev came to power in 1985, planning to reform Soviet communism so that it could be economically more efficient and provide higher incomes for its people. The system whose head he became was a hierarchical one. Internationally, the countries of the "socialist camp" were organized in such a way that the USSR was their head; the USSR in turn was led by the Communist Party. And the Communist Party was led by its Secretary General. So, whatever the Secretary General decided to do, the USSR did, and whatever the USSR wanted to do had to be acquiesced to, or imitated by the "allies," or the satellite countries. In the words of a Yugoslav ambassador to the USSR in the 1950s, Veljko Mićunović, when the "weather" changes in Moscow, if it becomes metaphorically politically colder, "we would all put on winter coats"; if it gets warmer, as with Khrushchev's "thaw," "we would all wear short-sleeved shirts."

When Gorbachev came to power and began producing the noise that was entirely dissonant from whatever came from the Kremlin before, the Soviet and East European communist elites were totally taken aback and paralyzed. Reforming the economic and political system and letting the Warsaw Pact countries "do it their own way" (the Sinatra song evoked by Gorbachev) were deeply troubling ideas, directly antithetical to the power of the elites and to the ideological legitimation of their rule. But the elites could not imagine attacking the Secretary General's position because the Secretary General, not unlike the Pope, was supposed to be infallible. Torn between an obvious undermining of their rule and inability to mount a defense, they helplessly waited for the outcome, doing nothing. We know by now that the outcome was the dissolution of the Soviet Union, the end of the communist regimes in Eastern Europe, and the end of communism as a way of organizing society.

The Western capitalist world was organized in 1945 in a similarly hierarchical fashion. The countries were "equal" but one was "more equal." In fact, were it not for the United States, and the effort and money it expended in Europe and Japan, it is very unlikely that Europe and Japan would today look the way they do. On the top of the "more equal" country, sits its president. And, while the US presidents have had their own idiosyncrasies (Carter was not Nixon), there were basic rules that they all observed: a close military and political union of culturally similar, US-led democracies, was never questioned. The Western elites, including in the United States, might have liked one president more than another (the Europeans' infatuation with Obama was quite extraordinary), but they felt safe that the essential architecture of the international system, created by the United States, will be defended by the United States.

With Trump, who questions the modus operandi of NATO, the way that Gorbachev wondered about the need for the Warsaw Pact, that assurance is gone (or seems to be gone). The EU is not sacrosanct either, nor is the WTO, nor the entire international architecture that the United States had built from 1945 onwards.

The elites in the West, like the communist elites in the East some thirty years ago, are now at a loss. Aping or accepting the rhetoric emanating from Washington goes against the corpus of beliefs they have created and defended over the past seventy years. Yet, opposing Washington, like opposing the Secretary General, is out of the question because no similar system can be set up by a European power, nor by a combination of European powers. The Western elites treat Trump as they would treat a tiger with whom they are unwillingly locked in a cage: they try to be friendly to the tiger, hoping to avoid being eaten, but they hope that the tiger would soon be taken out of the cage.

Will Trump have a similarly devastating effect on democracies as Gorbachev had on communism? I doubt it, because the Western democratic societies are more resilient and organic. If they are not, to use Nassim Taleb's terminology, "anti-fragile" (i.e. thriving in chaos), they are at least robust. Communist societies, being hierarchical, were extremely brittle. Western societies have technocratic elites in power but these elites are subject to recall and they do have democratic legitimation. Further, capitalism, unlike communism, is economically successful. There are very few people in France who would like to be ruled as China is ruled today; there were millions in Poland who craved to be ruled like France.

Trump will not, I think, destroy some essential structures of the Western system as it was built after the Second World War, but he

HISTORY

might, with his rough, chaotic and unpredictable government, scare the ruling elites in the West, encourage "revisionists," and bring about changes that will alter the world as it was created in Yalta and Potsdam.

Many people (myself included) have regretted that the Clinton administration has failed to seize the moment at the end of the Cold War to create a more just international order, which would follow the rules of law, would not be dichotomic or even a Manichean one with its origin in the Cold War, and would include Russia, rather than leave it out in the cold. Trump is unlikely to create a new structure but he can break parts of the old one. If he does that, he might usher in a post-Cold War era, and close the book on 1945. But note that the Cold War had one good feature: it was "Cold."

(Published January 16, 2017)

— PART V —

REFLECTIONS

— 16 —

REFLECTIONS

16.1 Non-exemplary lives

Recently I read, rather by accident than design, short lives of several contemporary economists. What struck me was their bareness. The lives sounded like CVs. Actually, there was hardly any difference between their CVs and their lives (to the extent that I could tell).

The lives (i.e. CVs) typically went like this. He/she graduated at a very prestigious university as the best in their class; had many offers from equally prestigious universities; became an assistant professor at X, tenured at Y; wrote a seminal paper on Z when he/she was W. Served on one or two government panels. Moved to another prestigious university. Wrote another seminal paper. Then wrote a book. And then ... this went on and on. You could create a single template, and then just input the name of the author, and the titles of the papers, and perhaps only slight differences in age for each of them.

I was wondering: how can people who had lived such boring lives, mostly in one or two countries, with the knowledge of at most two languages, having read only the literature in one language, having travelled from one campus to another, and perhaps from one hiking resort to another, have meaningful things to say about social sciences with all their fights, corruption, struggles, wars, betrayals, and cheating. Had they been physicists or chemists, it would not matter. You do not have to lead an interesting life in order to understand how atoms move, but perhaps you do need it to understand what moves humans (Vico).

Can you have a boring life and be a first-rate social scientist? To some extent, probably yes. You can be very smart and figure out how

REFLECTIONS

people behave under conditions that you have never yourself experienced—nor anyone you know. I cannot say it is impossible. But I think it is unlikely: because it is in the human nature, however smart we may be, to understand certain things or to look at different and new aspects of an issue, only when we face the problem ourselves. I think that we have all experienced that. Faced theoretically with a given problem, we can provide a perfectly reasonable and coherent answer and even explain well the choice. But then, if faced by the same problem in our own lives, we may quickly find out that such a well-reasoned answer was only partially correct. It failed to take into account a number of secondary issues, many conditions and constraints that, in the abstract case, we either ignored, assumed away, or most likely just never thought about. Or never imagined.

Orderly and boring lives are a privilege of rich and orderly societies. We all (perhaps except when we are 25) wish to lead such lives. But they are also very limited lives: the range of emotions and choices that we experience is narrow. We may want to have as our teachers in social science people who had to drink poison to make a point (Socrates), or were jailed and tortured (Machiavelli), or were executed on the orders of a national assembly (Condorcet), or banished and killed by a totalitarian regime (Kondratieff); or those who had to flee their governments and reinvent themselves (Marx), or move into incendiary politics (Weber), or migrate to another language and continent (Schumpeter, Hayek, Kuznets, Leontieff), or experience the thrill of forbidden pleasures (Keynes).

But, if our life is a CV, can we understand human choices and human nature—a precondition for being a great social scientist? By asking that question, are we not asking whether well-behaved individuals in orderly and rich societies can really produce breakthroughs in social sciences? Or will their lessons remain circumscribed to the orderly and rich societies only and to the orderly and boring people, and not carry over to the rest of the world? In other words, to use Plutarch's term, do we need exemplary lives for greatness in social sciences?

(Published June 19, 2019)

REFLECTIONS

16.2 The perverse seductiveness of Fernando Pessoa

It is impossible to spend a few days in Lisbon and to be a compulsive voyeur of bookstores, without noticing almost everywhere the name of Fernando Pessoa. I knew that he was a poet and, vaguely, that his star was on the ascendant because I have seen his name mentioned in a number of publications. But I never read anything written by him. Seeing him now everywhere in Lisbon, in French and English translations, and even in a small bookstore dedicated entirely to his writings, spurred my interest.

I was struck by an eerie similarly between Pessoa and Cavafy: one generation apart (Pessoa 1888–1936, Cavafy 1863–1933), both poets of their own civilizations and cultures, almost entirely ignored during their lifetimes, homosexuals who never left their cities (Alexandria and Lisbon), anglophiles whose poetic fame keeps on rising the further we are from their physical lives (as indeed the glory of all great people does). I have to confess that I am a huge fan of Cavafy's poetry (in beautiful English translations by Avi Sharon), but have not, as I mentioned, read any of Pessoa's. Still, luckily for me, the only work in prose that Pessoa published is a short 1922 novella called *The Anarchist Banker*. And as soon as I opened the book (in French translation, *Le banquier anarchiste*) I knew it was something that I would be interested in; and, indeed, I read it in an hour or so.

It is a Dostoyevsky-like monologue by a rich banker, who was born poor, into a working-class family, and used to be an anarchist. To the question asked by the imaginary narrator in the beginning of the novella, why he betrayed his ideals, the cigar-smoking banker bristles: no, he never stopped being anarchist; moreover, it was he, unlike other "conventional anarchists," who combined the theory and practice of anarchism, and is helping human society along toward the ultimate goal of "natural freedom."

How come, you wonder (together with the narrator)? Here is the answer. Every society is composed of inequalities that are "natural" and others that are a "social fiction." The latter are what John Roemer calls "inequality of circumstances." They are inequalities due to one's birth, wealth of his/her parents, connections, or money they inherit. These are inequalities that, our banker-anarchists tells us, have to be eliminated in order for a society to be just and for people to live freely and "naturally." Other inequalities (of innate intelligence, effort, stature, and strength) cannot be remedied because

397

REFLECTIONS

they are not produced by society. (So, our banker-anarchist is a luck egalitarian.)

Having realized this early in his life, the banker (then anarchist) enrolled in attempts to change society, both through anarchist propaganda and "direct action." But he realized that the attempts to eradicate money-driven "social fictions" quickly led to the rule of a minority that imposed another set of "social fictions"—a military dictatorship (a clear reference to Bolshevism) that, not differently from capitalism, constrained human freedom. Moreover, he discovered that even within small anarchist circles that were struggling for "freedom," hierarchical rules soon emerged: some made decisions, others followed.

He was then faced with a choice: either man is born vicious, in need of imposing hierarchy, and the other part of mankind is desirous of submission ("born slave"), in which case all attempts to change capitalist society are vain; or man is made vicious by "social fictions," which ought to be made irrelevant by individual effort; that is, not through social organizations that inevitably re-impose hierarchies. If man is vicious because of society, and not innately, then the way to extricate himself from "social fictions" and to reach Marx's "realm of freedom," where money does not matter, is to become wealthy enough, so that money becomes irrelevant. This is why our anarchist decides to become a banker, and to use the most sordid means to become rich. But didn't he thus exert tyranny over the lives of many other people, didn't he reinforce the "social fictions" against which he was fighting? No, the banker says, because "social fictions" can be destroyed only by wholesale revolutions and, to bring such revolutions about, we need to free ourselves from "social fictions" individually, one by one, by growing rich and extracting ourselves from the vulgar rule of scarcity ("[by getting rich] and overcoming the force of money, by liberating myself from its rule, I become free").

The story is to some extent (but only to some extent) absurd. It has a kind of perverse logic, which we also find in some Marxist literature, where the achievement of a society without scarcity requires the utmost development of the productive forces—using the most capitalistic, selfish, and destructive means possible. For the achievement of happiness (says Pessoa) can be realized in only two ways: either we reduce our needs and live like animals, or we create an abundance of material goods to such an extent that they do not matter anymore.

To reach the state of freedom we need to go through the "valley of tears": the Industrial Revolution, Stalinist industrialization,

398

"trickle-down economics," or Maoist Great Leap Forward. All of them are attempts to increase production, reduce or eliminate scarcity, and do away with "social fictions."

Does it make sense? Perhaps only to the extent that scarcity is scarcity of material goods. Many such scarcities for many people in the world today have been eliminated (food, water, electricity, housing). But other scarcities, of positional goods, will, by definition, always be with us: they cannot be eliminated, no matter how many television sets, iPhones, water melons, and potatoes we produce. So, post-scarcity Utopia seems to be indeed a "none place" that may never exist, and the rationale that unscrupulous exploitation of others is a short-cut to the world free-from-want is indeed perverse.

(Published September 25, 2021)

REFLECTIONS

16.3 Henry and Kant: Outsourcing morality

Many might remember the way in which France qualified for the 2010 World Cup (in which they eventually became vice-champions). The equalizing goal (which was enough for France to qualify) was scored because Thierry Henry, perhaps the most famous player on the French national team, by hand kept the ball from going off the pitch, brought it back and it was then easily tapped (by foot) into the net. The reactions were fierce: from protests of the Irish players in the field, to the disagreements between the Irish and French politicians and requests for a replay. In the end, the Irish Football Association applied that, exceptionally, Ireland be included in the World Cup. Of course, it all ended, as such things usually end: the goal stood and Ireland stayed home.

But, what I found interesting in this story is not soccer but the role of morality and the institutions. The common defense of Henry's act was as follows: sure, handball is a violation of soccer rules, but it is no different from a professional foul, or simulations to force a penalty kick. In every soccer game, players try to use these tricks in order to win. To quote a famous Mourinho quip: to win is my job. So, the defense of Henry went on: it is the task of the referee, that is of institutions, to catch him, prevent him from breaking the rules and eventually to punish him. Hence Henry's handball is not his problem (everybody would do the same), but the problem of inefficient institutions. Either the referees were not up to their task, or soccer should improve its institutions, for example by introducing more referees, or by the use of video recordings.

Now, I would like the reader to forget that we are talking about soccer. Consider the point more generally. Henry's defense implies that in life everything is allowed in order to achieve one's objective, and one should not feel at all bad or dishonest for doing it. Institutions ought to prevent the achievement of such goals by illegal means. If I am a trader on Wall Street, my objective is to make money, by whatever means I can. It is the role of institutions to stop me. If they failed and the financial crisis happened, it is because they were badly designed. The entire moral order of society is outsourced, away from individuals and their internal controls to institutions. We do not expect ourselves or others to be moral and behave fairly. It is not our duty: it is the duty of society to provide good institutions, which would punish those who steal and lie, and to create a good system of incentives, which would reward

400

those who contribute to society through their work, capital, or inventiveness.

This position is close to the heart of many economists. If the institutions and the system of incentives are well "calibrated," the society will move forward because misconduct will be punished and good behavior rewarded. This will come about because each of us is a rational and profit-seeking individual and will follow our own interests. The institutions will ideally "channel" our passions and interests so well that we shall, as "if led by an invisible hand," be doing the things that are in both our own and social interest.

But is the improvement of institution, that is, purely external control of human behavior with an implicit assumption that human nature obeys no rules unless it is punished, really enough to force people to behave morally? Returning to Henry's handball, should our objective be only to improve the quality of refereeing or to introduce cameras, or should our objective be that the rules are "internalized," so that people act in accordance with moral requirements, regardless of whether they are expedient or not? Even if all other players are playing by hand and thus stealing goals, we know that such behavior is immoral, and we shall not resort to it, regardless of consequences. But, how can one convince people to apply internal breaks in a hyper-competitive capitalist society that rewards only success? Even when they start by behaving morally, would not the behavior of those who behave otherwise and who, behaving thus, become rich and successful, lead the first group also to lose their scruples?

It seems to me that with ever greater commercialization, global-ization, and the use of money as the sole criterion of success, we have gone further and further away from any attempt to impose internal control, and have entirely outsourced it to institutions. Perhaps it is inevitable because all previous attempts to do it internally, through religion or secular religion (as in socialism) have failed, either because they led to endless wars ("my religion is better than yours"), or were incompatible with human nature (fall of socialism). So, I have no answer to the "outsourcing" of morality. I see it as inevitable, although I cannot say that I enjoy that prospect. Being an economist, I cannot even see exactly why I should not enjoy it, but I still do not.

After all, Thierry might have done the right thing. We shall get cameras and another handball will not happen. But something else will.

(Published May 22, 2015)

REFLECTIONS

16.4 The mistake of using the Kantian criterion in ordinary economic life

In the last section of his justly celebrated *On Economic Inequality* Amartya Sen discusses the role of incentives in work motivation in socialist societies. He goes over Marx's distinction between the role that material incentives would play in socialism ("a society ... still stamped with the birthmarks of the old society from whose womb it emerges"), and where such incentives would remain important, and communism, where material incentives would not matter and where everybody would contribute according to their abilities and would be rewarded according to their needs.

Sen then discusses the Chinese attempt to move toward the communistic reward structure during the Great Leap Forward. Sen notices that it proved to be a fiasco, even if "it is difficult to disso-ciate the difficulties generated by the use of non-material incentives from those caused by other features of the Leap Forward" (p. 96). The fiasco was due, among other things, to the idea that individuals would not follow their self-interest, namely that they will be indif-ferent to the relationship between their effort and reward. Since reward was independent of effort, people minimized their own effort, which, when done by everybody, led to the reduction of output and eventually to famines and disaster.

Sen however considers a situation where the behavior of individuals would be different, as would the outcome. He assumes a Prisoner's Dilemma two-person game. As is well known, the dominant strategy for each person is to defect, i.e. in the example when rewards are dissociated from effort, to work as little as possible. When everybody follows self-interest only, the collective outcome is low output. This is what, according to Sen, happened during the Great Leap Forward.

But, assume now, Sen writes, that the value system of individuals changes, that they do what is best for community, assuming or being assured that the others would do likewise. When all do so, the outcome of the Prisoner's Dilemma is socially optimal (high output), and is even individually preferred in terms of people's prefer-ences, which might have remained individualistic. Thus, people had to act as if they held an altruistic value system, even if their true preferences were individualistic. The Chinese perhaps were right: *if* self-abnegation, altruism and reciprocity, and not self-interest, could be inculcated or *if* people could be made to behave as if they had these values.

402

REFLECTIONS

The requirement is indeed that people do not behave in a self-interested way, but in, what John Roemer recently introduced (see Section 13.7 above), follow Kantian categorical imperative: that they behave in the way that they would like everybody else to behave. The same idea is present in Plato, who in *Gorgias* and *The Republic* argues that the just man never competes against others but does what he believes to be the best thing to do. Competition (*pleonexia*) is a vice. While this nicely solves the Prisoner's Dilemma, the requirement is so remote from the way people behave in ordinary life that it does violence to any usual and real norms of behavior.

This does not mean that under exceptional circumstances people may not behave without much regard for the balance between rewards and effort: if a ship is sinking, everybody will probably work as much as they can, without looking around to check whether others are also pulling in their weight. There are many other exceptional situations where the same principle might hold. Even in elections, like the ones in today's United States, such a behavior can be seen in people's willingness to stand in long lines in order to cast the vote—the value of which is close to nil. (And is even less so in states that are overwhelmingly Republican or Democratic.)

People might behave altruistically in their interactions with family and close friends. There again, the balance of gain and loss is often overlooked. But, in what Alfred Marshall called "the ordinary business of life" our usual and correct assumption is that of self-interested behavior. Moreover, that assumption has never been as justified as it is nowadays, when significant areas of our ordinary life (the ones where altruism might have obtained in the past) are "invaded" by commercialization. What commercialization or commodification do is to place shadow prices on many activities that in the past were subtracted from the rule of the market. Once such shadow prices exist, it is only a matter of time before more people, including those who never thought of selling and buying certain activities, begin to participate. The mass participation introduces normalcy and converts hitherto non-market goods and activities into objects of market transactions, not different in any way from the usual areas where market reigns, from purchase of food and cars, to the supply of labor or investment of capital.

The expansion of commodification into our leisure time, where insensibly our pleasure in playing computer games or browsing the Internet becomes a potentially lucrative activity (hosting ads on one's website or becoming an influencer), or into our family life (pre-nuptial agreements), or the rest of our lives, as in willingness to forgo the right to free speech for money (non-disclosure agreements), implies that the sphere of self-interest has expanded and the sphere of altruism has receded.

The realization that this is so has important implications for at least two types of discussions that are conducted today. One is the extension of what Sen wrote fifty years ago and John Roemer recently: the idea that socialism can be introduced through a change in people's system of values. This, from all that we have seen in the past, and that we see now, is entirely unrealistic.

The same ideas are also present in discussions regarding the climate change. Here, too, some authors invoke miraculous changes in our behavior, whereby we would no longer care for own income and wealth but would be willing to sacrifice them for the global reduction of CO_2 emissions. The argument is exactly the same as what Sen used in his Prisoner's Dilemma: if everyone were to start behaving in the way he or she would like others to behave, climate change may indeed be controlled.

The problem is here, like elsewhere, that this type of behavior is incompatible with the system of values propagated by capitalism (and necessary for its survival), which we have accepted and which we affirm in our ordinary lives: from the moment when we argue about our wage to the time when we draft pre-nuptial agreements. Thus, here too such assumptions of altruism may be useful in modeling various games, but are entirely useless in dealing with the real world and deciding on actual policies, which, if they are to lead to change, must be based on incentives and punishments.

The assumptions about one's behavior in ordinary life (and far away from lab conditions where they are often investigated) are crucial if we want to make things better. By assuming altruism and selfless reciprocity in economic life, we are led astray and the results cannot be different from those that similar attempts have produced in the past. In fact, they have given free rein to the worst human instincts, as those very far from being naive have draped themselves in the sheepskin of altruism, to better exploit those who either believed in such fictions or were forced to believe them.

It is only by building "on the granite of self-interest" (as George Stigler said regarding *The Wealth of Nations*) that we can make a change.

REFLECTIONS

Addendum

The text needs two clarifications.

(1) When we assume self-interested behavior we are at the same time assuming that our interests clash with the interests of everybody else. But that does not mean that we do not cooperate with people. We cooperate whenever our interest can be enhanced by cooperation, compared to not cooperating. This is why we work in factories with others and not alone at home: output is much greater when we collaborate, and hence our self-interest is better served.

(2) In the Kantian model, we also assume that people are self-interested. But they adjust their behavior to do what they think everybody should be doing. So, behavior is, in some sense, delinked from the underlying individualistic motivation. But, in addition, the beliefs about how everybody should behave may differ. One person may believe that the socially proper behavior is A; another person may believe it is B. Thus, an additional requirement is to be imposed: that through education or socialization these beliefs should be made the same or similar.

Take the following example. My self-interest may be not to pick up after my dog. But, in a Kantian fashion, I might pick up the dog's poop because I think that everybody should do that. But another person might believe that not picking up the poop is actually good for the nature, plants, etc. Thus, although we both follow the Kantian precept we end up by doing two very different things. Hence some cultural "equalization" is necessary. Religion or ethics are supposed to do so—although one may be doubtful as to how well they could do it.

(Published January 3, 2021)

REFLECTIONS

16.5 Is liberal democracy part of human development?

After two and a half years of enforced zooming, that is of living or attending lectures online, I listened today, at UNDP in New York, to an excellent book talk (*Human Development and the Path to Freedom: 1870 to the Present*) given by Leandro Prados de la Escosura, Professor of Economics and of Economic History at the University Carlos III in Madrid.

Prados has just completed a seminal book that extends the Human Development Index (HDI), originally "invented" by Amartya Sen and now for several decades produced by the UN Development Program, in time all the way back to the early nineteenth century, and in scope. The index, as the aficionados of development know, includes three dimensions of welfare: income (proxied by the GDP per capita), education (number of years of schooling) and health (life expectancy). The HDI has generated a huge literature: does adding up or multiplication of such components make sense, how to introduce inequality in each of the components, should some components be included at all. (Last summer, Nuno Palma argued at a conference, rather vociferously, but not unreasonably, that education should be dropped: it is a means toward achieving income, not a good in itself. I have to admit that I thought so for a long time but was reluctant to enter into that discussion). Leandro Prados' book is extremely rich and powerful, as it charts the evolution in human welfare across countries and regions over two centuries, but it is also provocative because Prados uses a somewhat different metric for the three original components and, importantly, introduces the fourth component or dimension (human freedom). The new Prados' "augmented" HDI is possibly the most important development since HDI was first defined. (Another candidate for this title is taking into account the inequality which the three components are distributed.)

It is the proposed inclusion of the political component that I wish to discuss here. Prados' view is well-grounded in the theory of "development as freedom" popularized by Sen. Political rights are seen as an inseparable part of human freedom because they give individuals agency to exercise their choices in general, and even their choice over the three key dimensions in particular (perhaps that people would prefer better health to higher income). The fourth, political, components consists, as Prados explains, of two parts: negative freedoms (that is, absence of coercion and control over one's ability to express opinions and participate in public life) and the way that such negative

406

freedoms are politically "bundled," namely existence of democracy and of political checks and balances.

Now, the agency or voice part of the political variable can be associated with "development as freedom"; the "democracy" part is, in my opinion, much more problematic. Increasing individual's agency, provided that it does not limit the agency of others, is indeed an improvement in one's condition, the same as greater longevity. Being able to access information, to express one's opinions, to participate in political life are valuable *in themselves*. The exercise of individual agency must not come at the expense of others exercising the same agency. This is of course the well-known rule that our freedom is limited only by the same freedom for others. Agency therefore already includes a notion of equality. A country where ninety percent of the population have full agency and voice but ten percent are slaves is abhorrent, even if a statistic of 0.9 may not be too different from that of an alternative country, where everybody has one-tenth of their maximum freedoms abrogated. This implicit egalitarian bias in agency is something that I would leave at this point, but that can be developed further.

Another argument in favor of introducing agency is to check empirically if it tends to be associated with increases in other dimensions of human welfare. It seems so at first. But it is also possible that more agency, more freedom to voice opinions leads to political polarization, even to anarchy, and then to lower income growth and higher mortality. Whether one or other direction is more likely is something we should discover empirically, and this is why adding agency/voice is, in my opinion, very useful.

My concern is with the inclusion of a particular way of aggregating the opinions of the public: democracy. Democracy is just one way of such aggregation of preferences: other ways are not only possible but have existed, and continue to exist. Preferences can be aggregated through corporatist or representative bodies; a single party system via intra-party debate; by consultative monarchy; by theocracy, etc. The best way to rule a society is a topic, in the West, at least 4,500 years old. Plato, who was among the first to think about it, was not a great friend of the specifically democratic way of rule. We are very unlikely ever to agree on the best way to rule, and the introduction of liberal democracy as implicitly being the ideal toward which humankind strives, brings in a very specific political view of the world into an index that at least in its other components is free from excessive politicization. (I do not mean here only the direct politicization that such a component would bring into an international organization,

REFLECTIONS

composed of governments whose legitimacies are widely different—this is obvious—but even the politicization that it would introduce among the academic practitioners or users of the new augmented HDI.)

While agency proper can be measured, however imperfectly, democracy cannot. Regarding the former, one could look at countries that allow full access to the sources of information, those that do not, and others in-between. (China would score low on that, so would today's Russia, which blocked Facebook, but the European Union would also lose points through its censorship of Russian and Chinese media.) One could also look at the freedom to express one's opinion: how many people are fined or jailed for that? Finally, one could look at the freedom to participate in protests and marches and petitions. While agency may never be measured as well as the other three components of the HDI, it is susceptible of at least imperfect measurement.

But this is not the case with democracy. As I mentioned, it is just a particular way to "bundle" people's preferences; its measurement depends intrinsically on our subjective estimates. This is obvious from almost all currently existing indexes of democracy: what the checks are on the executive power cannot be adequately reduced to a number, nor can inequality in real political power readily be measured. How do we account for the fact that the rich "buy" policies they like by supporting electoral campaigns of these who would do their bidding? How do we account for the creation of "the correct" opinion by the media owned by the rich? All of these factors often decisively influence the translation of preferences into actionable policies, and yet they are difficult or impossible to measure.

My point here is threefold. First, I think that the introduction of agency proper in the HDI should be applauded. It is clear what it means, it is measurable, and it is a good in itself. Second, the introduction of democracy as currently defined would represent the introduction of one particular way of doing a political process, which is both geographically and historically limited. This is a conceptual reason for dropping it out. But, in addition (my third point), it is impossible to measure "democracy": even if we could agree on what it is and, even more, if we could agree that it should be introduced into the HDI, it will remain to be measured by subjective "expert opinions," it will remain heavily politicized, and hence would never reach the acceptability of measures such as health or income outcomes.

(Published October 14, 2022)

REFLECTIONS

16.6 Living in own ideology ... until it falls apart

In the summer of 1975, I worked as a tourist guide in Dubrovnik (I started working very young). Dubrovnik is, as many people know, a beautiful city in the Adriatic, on the Croatian coast, which throughout the Middle Ages was a very active port, with contacts throughout the then known world. Venice was its competitor and eventually dominated it; in the end, however, both the Venetian and the Ragusan (Dubrovnik) republics were abolished by Napoleon in 1797–1806. The existence of Dubrovnik as an independent republic, surrounded on all sides by the powerful Ottoman Empire, was somewhat of a miracle. Ottomans might have regarded it as a useful Hong Kong of the time and never mustered the will to conquer it. Dubrovnik always remained proud of its freedom. In its red flag it emblazoned the golden letters of "Libertas."

A couple of times that summer, I went, in the warm and sweet lavender-smell-filled evenings, to watch plays performed at breathtaking spots at the fort overlooking the harbour. The plays were part of a summer-long Dubrovnik festival. The opening of the festival was always accompanied by the raising of the "Libertas" flag. I did not think much of it then, but the flag ceremony with the appropriately rousing music was taken by me to hail back to Dubrovnik's steadfast resistance to foreign invaders. Since Yugoslavia in 1975 was a free country, not ruled by foreigners, or as, it was said then, beholden neither to the "imperialists" (the United States), nor to "hegemonists" (the Soviet Union), I thought it only normal that the flag of "Libertas" be hoisted and cheered.

About ten years later, in a conversation with a friend who watched the same festival, and with communist rule already crumbling, he mentioned how excited he was at seeing the fluttering flag of freedom every year; to him it presaged the end of communism and the return of democracy. I never thought of that then, and, without telling him, I believed that he either made up that feeling ex post (1985 was very different from 1975) or that he simply imputed to others what might have been the thoughts of a tiny minority.

Then, a few years ago, when I visited Zagreb for the first time after the civil wars, I met for dinner a Croatian friend, whom I have not seen for more than twenty years and with whom I worked in 1975. Somehow during the conversation, she mentioned how the flag of "Libertas" always made her think of Croatian independence and freedom, and how she thought that feeling was shared by everyone who was there and saw the flag being raised.

409

REFLECTIONS

That thought, I had to acknowledge, never crossed my mind. But that third interpretation of the very same event made me think, like in Kurosawa's movie, that we all live in our ideological worlds and imagine that everybody else inhabits the same world too.

Until things change.

Something similar is happening now in the United States, with the ideological impact of the Black Lives Matter (BLM) movement. Many people thought that racial inequality was indeed an issue in the United States. But it was seen as an ancillary issue, in need of a solution, but not in itself detracting from the view of America as a land of equal opportunity and progress for all. Under the impact of the movement, racial injustice, and many other forms of injustice, are now seen, by many people who never thought so before, as systemic problems. They cannot be made aright by, as Cornell West dismissively and well said, "putting Black faces in high places." They require a thorough rethinking of the essential features of capitalist societies. Moreover, the BLM movement, by bringing into focus the entire colonial history and Black oppression, has directed our attention to the things that were thought long gone and "solved": King Leopold's rule of the Congo, British use of, and complicity in, the slave trade, American and Brazilian slaveries that extended late into the second half of the nineteenth century. It is very likely that similar issues will be raised soon in other countries: France, the Netherlands, Portugal, Spain, Russia. As we have just seen, the statues of Christopher Columbus are tumbling down.

This is a huge ideological change. We were, until a few weeks ago, witnessing the same events as now—racial discrimination and police brutality are not exactly new—but the ideological lenses through which we were seeing them were entirely different. As in the example of the Libertas flag, the event, the fact, was the same: the understandings entirely different.

Ideologies we live are like the air we breathe. We take them as obvious. We are not aware of them, as I was not aware of my own in 1975. Or as my friends were not aware of the ideology that pervaded the World Bank and the IMF in the last two decades of the twentieth century. Neoliberalism (which did not use that name then) was so obvious, its lessons and recommendations so clear and commonsensical that it fulfilled the requirements of the best possible ideology: the one that a person defends and implements without ever realizing they are doing so. But it, too, is now falling apart.

When people ask me how it was to have worked in the World Bank at the time of high neoliberalism, they often believe that we

410

were somehow compelled to believe in the nostrums of neoliberalism. Nothing is further from the truth. Ideology was light and invisible for many; they never felt its weight. Even today, I am sure that many friends who implemented it are unaware they ever did. In the early 1990s, an influential person, who would never consider him/herself "neoliberal," strongly objected to any work on inequality: the issue was not inequality—on the contrary, we needed to create more inequality so that growth can pick up. Another influential person (Larry Summers in this case) became infamous by writing a memo that argued that pollutants should be shipped to Africa because the value of human life there is much lower than in rich countries. Although Summers later claimed that the memo was written in jest, it did capture well the spirit of the times. Yet another person who strenuously even now defends him/herself against the neoliberalist tag produced a new approach to a problem that, he proudly claimed, solves it by creating a new market—never having heard that commodification of everything is the basic characteristic of neoliberalism.

Alike to religious believers, neoliberalism seemed to many economists a quintessence of reasonable, common-sensical ideas. John Williamson wrote, when he defined the Washington consensus, that it is "the common core of wisdom embraced by all serious economists." Now that neoliberalism, under the shocks of 2007–2008 and 2020, is all but dead, it is easy to see how wrong they were. But, while it lasted, people lived in their own ideological world, "embraced by all serious economists," and it seemed to them that everybody else did too. And that it would last forever. As it seemed to me—in 1975.

(Published March 19, 2023)

REFLECTIONS

16.7 Freedom to be "wrong": The greatest advantage of democracy

Several things came together. A friend sent me a post by N. S. Lyons. Then, independently, a short conversation on Twitter [X] followed upon the statistics showing that today's young people get almost all their information from the social media, while old people rely (as they did in the past) on television. And, finally, and perhaps for this post most importantly, my own recent thinking on the following questions: What do you see as the main gain from democracy, as opposed to dictatorship?

Let me start with Number 3. When I thought of that, my answer was: the freedom to read and listen to whatever I want, and to *say* whatever I want. And I think this is all. I do not believe that democracy leads to higher growth, less corruption, or less inequality. There is no evidence for any of these things. To put it perhaps too strongly, I think democracy has no effect on any real social phenomena, but it does allow people, on a purely personal level, to feel better by accessing more diverse information, and to express any option they have. (Note that this freedom applies only to the political sphere, not to one's place of work, which in capitalist democracies is ruled dictatorially.)

But that definition of the advantage of democracy has recently been under attack by the people who think that social media lead to "fake news," fragmentations of public opinion, polarization of politics, and all kinds of noxious phenomena. And then they paint the picture of some fantasy-world where everybody agrees on all issues and espouses the liberal values in which they believe. For me, this is precisely the undermining, or the destruction of the most (or the only) valuable part of democracy.

N. S. Lyons quotes *in extenso* Polish political philosopher Ryszard Legutko, who equates the modern liberal project with the communist project. And, indeed, the similarities are strong. In both cases, a certain view of the world is supposed to be based on scientific understanding of the way the world works, and everybody who does not see it in such a way must either be "re-educated," or, if stubbornly clinging to the wrong views, considered morally flawed. Thus, the disagreement is with the people who are cognitively or ethically deficient.

I write this as somebody who believes in Enlightenment and economic growth. But I do not believe that people will ever have

412

the same opinion on key matters that relate to the organization of societies. There will always be important differences in values and backgrounds. Any attempt to impose one's views, other than through discussion (while not seriously thinking that one will be successful), or to hold others as "morally challenged" if they do not agree, is not only bound to fail. It is wrong. The segmentation of the space for public discourse is not just inevitable; it is, on balance, a good thing. Between a uniformity of opinion that is imposed through the control of the media (epitomized by television) and plurality, or even an endless multitude, of views afforded by the echo-chambers of the social media, one should choose the latter.

We should not be afraid of polarization and disagreements. They are much better than unanimity. Now, I am not addressing here only an enforced unanimity that comes from having one newspaper and one TV channel, but uniformity which comes from the current liberal project.

I remember that in the 1990s, a Dutch friend pointed out to me, the heathen, the advantages of Dutch democracy, and called it "vibrant" (as opposed to enforced unanimity). But, when Geert Wilders and people like him appeared on the scene, she no longer thought it was so "vibrant." The same, only more so, is true in France: somehow Islamists, Mélenchon, Le Pen, and *les gilets jaunes*, although all coming from very different ideological sides, were not compatible with this "vibrancy." It turns out that "vibrant" meant that everybody would agree with my friend's fundamental beliefs and that the dispute should center on purely peripheral matters. She represented the pensée unique that followed upon the fall of communism, when the liberal view of the world and neoliberal economics were taken to be "normal" and "common sense," not an ideology.

This was rudely challenged by Islam (which, understandably, on many issues has an entirely different take), by the financial crisis of 2007–2008, by China's *Sonderweg*, the rise of illiberal democracies, Trump's presidency and then 75 million votes, Russia's move to Euro-asianism. It clearly does not reflect today's realities.

The expansive liberal ideology creates unnecessary conflict by insisting that on all important political and social issues people *must* share the same opinion, and by denigrating those who do not. Very often they dream, especially if older, of the return of a world of three American TV channels, and two weeklies that always had the same news and the same cover page. This, allegedly, created a consensus of sensible people. But it did so only because others had no say. That world, I think fortunately, will never return, because the Internet

REFLECTIONS

has made it impossible. But, rather than thinking that this is a bad development, we should embrace the freedom to think whatever we want, and to say whatever we want (however strange it might seem to others). For this is probably the only real advantage of democracy.

(Published February 18, 2024)

REFLECTIONS

16.8 99 percent Utopia and money

My friend Leif Wenar asked this question: "Friends, a Utopia query. Keep human nature fixed. Imagine the best possible world Does money exist?" I could not sleep last night so I decided to give it a thought.

Let's start with money. What is its central function? To coordinate plans of individuals and companies and to pull resources in the "right" direction. When I go to Starbucks to buy coffee, and have money to pay for it, I know that there will be a person willing to make that coffee for me, and there will be companies delivering coffee grains because they all expect to get money from me. So, money enables us to make our plans consistent, starting from the coffee growers all the way to the final consumer.

Who is then going to do the coordination in Utopia if there is no money? But, before we answer that question, let's go back and look at what is Utopia. I will use Marx's definition given in the *Critique of the Gotha Program:* Communism is the situation where "the productive forces have increased with the all-around development of the individual, and all the springs of co-operative wealth flow ... abundantly—[so that] ... the narrow horizon of bourgeois right [can] be crossed in its entirety and society inscribe on its banners: From each according to his ability, to each according to his needs!" Utopia is thus a situation where goods and services are absolutely plentiful, there is no scarcity, and we can take as much of them as we like.

Now, some may stop me right there: this will never happen, they will say. But let's not go that fast. Notice that when I go to my local Starbucks I have already entered a bit the "coast of Utopia." I can get there an unlimited quantity of water, ice cubes, water cups, paper napkins, honey, and milk, all for free. They are all laid out for all customers (and even for those who are not customers but just walk in) to take in unlimited quantities. There are other goods that have almost entered this cornucopia in our lifetimes: water, electricity. When I need to refill my laptop I can count on getting free electricity from practically every store, airplane, or airport. There are of course other services like museums and open-air concerts that one can enjoy for free.

So, there is, I think, already now a limited, but growing, number of goods and services, whose marginal cost of production is so low that they are practically free. (The average cost of production is not

415

REFLECTIONS

zero, but to an individual consumer these goods appear as free.) Consider now the behavior of people. Do they go to Starbucks stores and fill their pockets with free paper napkins or grab free ice cubes? No. Do they go to free open-air concerts day after day and fight for the spots? No. Once you know that such goods will be plentiful and free, you do not keep an unreasonable stock of them, nor do you fight to get them. You know they will be around when you need them.

So far, we have, I think, come to two important conclusions: there are goods that fall into the category of "Utopian goods"; and behavior that people exhibit toward these goods does not include hoarding, wanton destruction, or wastefulness.

Can we imagine that with economic progress more and more goods begin to fulfil this condition of Utopian goods? I think we can. Surely forty or fifty years ago, you had to pay for the smallest piece of paper or paper napkin, not get it for free as now. (There is still difference between the US and Europe in this.) You even had to pay for a cup of water in an inn on a dirt road. Not today. So, perhaps one day we shall walk into a Starbucks store and be given as much coffee for free as we like, in the expectation that we shall buy some other, new fanciful product. But, notice when this happens, coffee will have joined paper napkins and ice cubes in our list of Utopian goods. So, the list will be growing.

Extend this many years forward and assume that lots of the goods that we consume today eventually become Utopian. But who is going to produce them? Will not people have to be given some money-like coupons showing how many hours of work they did, coupons that would entitle them to some goods? This does not make sense, however, because all goods, in any quantity, will be free to all, so coupon or no coupon you can get as much as you like. This, then, means that labor has to be entirely voluntary and free, not "paid" in any form. That, too, is not impossible to imagine. I am writing this blog for free. Of course, I hope to enhance my reputation (or to drive it into the ground) but there is not a single good or service that I will get from this writing. You will also read it out of interest, not for any pecuniary reason. Many activities can be done for free, simply because people like to do them. Other, boring, or repetitive, or hard, jobs that people do today will be done by robots. Controlling robots will require a minimum of work—perhaps writing a software code about how they (the robots) should do certain tasks; a thing, which I am sure, thousands of smart young people will compete to do for free.

416

REFLECTIONS

When I go to a restaurant, who is going to make the food or serve me? Partly robots, and partly people who like to be chefs, or to provide good service. Actually, the quality of some goods and services may go up compared to what it is today, simply because people do a better job at something that they like, rather than at something they are (merely) paid to do.

But, here too, I think we run into our first problem. There will always be better and worse restaurants, simply because the chefs will not be the same. But, since the price paid at every restaurant is the same (zero), there will be no mechanism to distribute customers between better and worse restaurants, except through queues. So, we shall have shortages of certain goods and services. The shortages will be, as in a centrally planned economy, "solved" through queueing.

The second problem appears at the level of jobs. We may be able to fill ninety percent of jobs by robots, nine percent of jobs by people who simply like to do these jobs; but one percent of jobs that are hard or done under unpleasant conditions and cannot be mechanized will be always difficult to fill. So, we shall have to give something to people who do these jobs: we shall have to attract them to do them. But, how to attract them if everything is anyway free? So, money, under the guise of some special coupons, would reappear. Perhaps we could give these new Stakhanovites coupons that would allow them to jump the queue in the restaurants. Perhaps something else. But, whatever we do, a rationing mechanism, implied by money, will be back in that segment of the system.

Finally, technological progress. If we assume that technological progress has stopped, I think the idea of moneyless Utopia is ultimately, at least conceptually, almost possible. But, if technological progress continues, with people inventing new things simply out of curiosity, that is without any material interest, these new goods, always scarce in the beginning, will have to be rationed. So, to ration them, we shall need money too.

In a stationary economy, the range of goods that are available for free and in unlimited quantities, and the range of jobs that are performed for free, can be very high. We may have a 99 percent Utopia. But not a one hundred percent Utopia.

However, in a growing economy, Utopia becomes much less realistic. The faster we grow, the greater the number of Utopian goods, and the closer we seem to be to approaching Utopia; but, also, the faster we grow, the more we invent new goods that are necessarily in short supply and, simultaneously, the further we get from

REFLECTIONS

Utopia. Thus, the fundamental nature of economic progress reveals itself in Leif's question: economic progress is making us richer daily, but leaves us equally unsatisfied. For full happiness is possible only in stagnation.

(Published September 25, 2015)

REFLECTIONS

16.9 On the general futility of political discussions with people

Over the years I have had political and ideological discussions with at least three groups of people and have concluded that these discussions are, almost entirely, futile in making people either see things differently, or acknowledging that others may see things differently, or—God forbid—change their opinions, however slightly. That, of course, opens the question of how people come to hold certain political and ideological positions—since at some level they must be influenced by the views of others: their parents, family, and even random interlocuters. I do not have a good explanation for that. I think that reading, watching, listening, and thinking, does lead people to form and then to change opinions but I am very sceptical that direct discussion does it. The former methods are indirect: one reads an author and finds him convincing; but, if one has a discussion with somebody, acknowledging that that person has produced valid arguments appears to diminish him compared to the other person, and one's intellectual vanity does not wish to accept that. Hence, I think, discussions almost never lead toward any genuinely felt greater similarity of opinions. They just leave the participants where they were before. Or worse, lead them further apart.

For the participants who are more passionate or involved in the discussion, such an outcome is more frustrating. They therefore dispense a much greater amount of intellectual, mental, and ultimately, physical energy in trying to convince the other side—without success. They thus spend hours reviewing the arguments made, look for possibly better ways they should have presented their case, explore the weaknesses of the opponents, as if any of that would make any difference. They waste their time and energy.

The three groups of people with whom I had chance (or misfortune) to have discussions and found impossible to move, even a millimeter away from their held beliefs, were Stalinists, nationalists, and liberals. But their way of discussing things was different from each other. They were all equally unyielding in their views, but adopted somewhat different tactics.

Stalinists with whom I had the "privilege" to discuss politics, chronologically the first, introduced me to the type of discussion tactics that were also used by the other two groups. To any strong argument from the interlocutor they would produce either a denial (such and such event never occurred; there is no evidence; it was somebody else's propaganda, etc.), or they would accept that the

419

REFLECTIONS

uncomfortable fact occurred, but will justify it by an even greater perfidy of the other side. As I mentioned, I would see exactly the same arguments used by both nationalists and liberals. One advantage that Stalinists had compared to the other two groups (and that is the advantage of which I became aware much later on) is that they respected the knowledge of communist history. So, if you attacked them, they would produce the denial and petrify arguments, but would respect your knowledge. They might even ask you about a fact they did not know. Communism thus functioned entirely like a religion. Christians have been at each others' throats since the religion was founded: but the knowledge of finer theological or historical points was respected by the different sects, even when they disagreed on almost everything else.

Political discussions with nationalists can, I think, best be described as throwing pebbles against an immense rock. You can throw as many pebbles as you wish, the rock will not be hurt nor moved. Like Stalinists they commonly use denial and perfidy of others, but perfidy of others now spreads to everybody under the sun, except their favored nationality. In that sense, perfidy was much more widespread than for Stalinists, since perfidy included n-1 national groups in the world. Moreover, if you bring two opposite nationalists together, since they both believe that n-1 groups are all equally at fault, the conclusion is that it suffices to have only two of them to prove that the entire world is evil. Thus, one quickly establishes the conclusion that in the nationalists' worldview it is ultimately human nature that is evil, since no nation can be exempt from it, and the individual characteristics do not matter as they are determined by one's ethnicity or race.

The third immovable group are liberals. They tend to be more sophisticated and more knowledgeable but this does not make them more intellectually honest. Actually, one could say the reverse because they handle sophistry with exquisite skills. The Greek rhetorician Aelius Aristide's comment from 1,900 years ago regarding Cynics applies to them: "They deceive like flatterers, handle insults like superior men, combining the two most opposite and repugnant vices: vileness and insolence" (quoted in Benko's *Pagan Rome and the Early Christians*, p. 47). They also use denial and perfidy of others as arguments, but they find them "served alone" to be too crude. That's where sophistry kicks in. To any incontrovertible uncomfortable fact, they do not produce just a denial, but shift the discussion on secondary or tertiary matters of marginal relevance to the topic discussed. That produces huge frustration in the interlocutor. It is

420

akin to playing a soccer game, which one is winning 3–0, but the other side refuses to acknowledge the defeat, arguing that what really counts is the number of shots on goal, or free kicks or any other marginal statistic that is in their favor. All attempts to drive the discussion back to the original topic, and to the argument to which they have no valid counterpoint, fail in the face of this intransigent tactic, which consistently shifts the realm of the discussion elsewhere. Since liberals are more sophisticated than the other two groups they also use "rope-a-dope" tactics where, faced with uncomfortable truth, they do not reply to the argument but just shrug it off as irrelevant: "everyone knows that things are like that." This again has a very negative effect on the interlocutor, as it seems to treat him as a very naive person who takes the ideological stance of the liberals seriously. In reality, they say, even if not loudly and clearly, flexibility is all: we may do things one way one day, and entirely differently the next day, but ideologically we shall always claim to be unswervingly loyal to our beliefs.

I have not had much occasion to discuss issues with the true conservatives (who may not be vulgar nationalists) nor with the new generation of woke liberals, so I cannot tell how their tactics may differ from the ones that I mentioned.

I have thus come to the conclusion that if one believes in a certain point of view and yet has a limited amount of mental energy, it is entirely wasteful to use it in trying to convince others in direct discussions. It is much more effective to write and read and listen than to have Socratic or any other dialogues. They, I think, lead nowhere.

(Published October 1, 2023)

REFLECTIONS

16.10 The many in one: A review of Amartya Sen's *Home in the World: A Memoir*

No contemporary famous economist has as broad interests and knowledge, nor as diverse life experience as Amartya Sen. It is not surprising that many have been looking forward to reading the first volume of his memoirs. It covers the period from his birth in 1933 to the beginnings of his academic career in the United States in the early 1960s. That very term "the beginning," I realized as I wrote it, is misleading. Not for 99 percent of ordinary economists, who at thirty-one we might consider the academic beginners. But for Sen who got his first professorial position at 23, the age of thirty was that of an already "seasoned" academic!

The precociousness of the young Amartya is one of the two most striking things that every reader will notice. At the age of eight, Amartya is engaged in historical discussions with his father and grandfather. At twelve or thirteen, he is into the study of Sanskrit (his first language being Bengali) and the foundational basis of mathematics. I do not think that I have read a memoir where such level of interest for very abstract topics is evinced by such a young person. Perhaps John Stuart Mill may be the only contestant.

The second striking thing is Sen's passion for the intellectual history of India (as a subcontinent), and his disdain for ethnic and religious exclusivism. The first three parts of the book, about 250 pages, which deal with India, are written with an extraordinary passion and, for many readers (including this one), they are full of new things that one can learn from even the shortest discussions about the Indian Buddhist heritage, diverse interpretations of Ramayana and Mahabharata, the elegance of the Sanskrit. The discussions are brief—by necessity, since it is a book of memories, not a philosophic treatise—but, coming from somebody as knowledgeable as Sen, these short one- or two-page commentaries inspire confidence, and may perhaps lead some readers to try to learn more. For we know that they are supported by much more evidence than can be produced in this book.

The relationship between Amartya and his grandfather K. Mohan, a scholar and compiler of Hindu rural poetry, provides the backbone of the early—up to the university years—life of Amartya. Another influential person was Rabindranath Tagore, a close family friend. Amartya did his middle and high school in a school organized according to Tagore's principles. In a chapter entitled "School

422

Without Walls," Sen describes the exhilarating atmosphere of a place where students are motivated not by a combination of incentives and punishments, but by being allowed to follow their inclinations, while being helped by committed professors. The idea is quite extraordinary, even if one doubts that it can be expanded to a larger scale. But for students like Amartya, it was, as he writes, the best possible fit, much better than the more orthodox and competitive St. Gregory in Dhaka, which Amartya attended only briefly, and gladly left, being ranked the 33rd of 36 students!

We are then taken, in several beautiful chapters, to the tumultuous life of Calcutta of the early 1940s, with the beginning of the Second World War, Japanese invasion of Burma, formation of Bose's Indian National Army, pro-independence effervescence among Calcutta's youth and Sen's own family (with several members kept in British jails), and the momentous split between the Hindus and the Muslims. The political excitement, the fear of war (the Japanese having bombed Calcutta's harbor) and the looming intra-communal conflict are the background—and perhaps an indispensable condition—for the exciting intellectual life carried on in innumerable Calcutta's cafés and bookstores. One almost wishes to have been there and then— obviously in the knowledge that he or she would have survived all the upheavals.

While reading that part of Sen's memoirs, I thought of the two autobiographical books written by Sen's Bengali compatriot Nirad Chaudhuri, *The Autobiography of an Unknown Indian* and *Thy Hand, Great Anarch!*, perhaps among the most beautiful books of political reminiscences ever. They, only in part, touch the same period (Nirad being much older), but convey to the reader the same intellectual fervour of Calcutta. Chaudhuri, not always liked by all Indians, was the proponent of the view that the mixture of European, i.e. British, and Indian and Asian, i.e. Bengali, cultures produced a unique Euro-Asian fusion. I thought that, in a brief chapter where Sen assesses the contributions of British colonialism—and the damages it wrought (not least the Bengali famine of 1942)—he tacitly endorses, or comes close to agreeing with, some of Chaudhuri's vision.

The book is written in a simple, engaging style. It is a different style from that used by Sen in his economic and philosophical writings. I find the latter, to the extent that I understand them, written in, at times, unnecessarily obscure style. But here I had the opposite impression: I wanted to read more and wished that Sen's recollections and discussions of political and ideological issues were more extensive. There is, for example, a story of the difference in the perceptions of Tagore in India and in Europe. For Sen, Tagore was a rationalistic thinker, while in Europe he was praised and promoted by Yeats and Ezra Pound as a mystic. Yeats and Pound seemed to have seen in Tagore whatever they wanted to see and Tagore became a prisoner of that false image created in the West.

The last third of the book, when Sen moves, temporarily, to the West, first to Cambridge, England, and then (mentioned very briefly at the end of the book) to MIT in Boston, is much more "problematic." While Sen's youth is convincingly and absorbingly described in both its political and personal aspects (e.g. Sen's bout with cancer), the European part takes place in a social vacuum. There is almost nothing that Sen tells us about the political and social milieu of Europe in the 1950s and 1960s. Even more surprisingly, there are hardly any observations, other than trivial ones, about the encounter of the East and the West that must have impressed such a brilliant and precocious mind like Sen's. Even Sen's European travel reads like a travelogue of places he has visited with not many insights offered: yes, we all know that Michelangelo's David is impressive: is this worth repeating in a memoir? The only memory of Warsaw in 1956 is a one-sentence mention of a political conversation in a bathroom.

The life in Europe seems to take place on campuses and among the multitude of students, teachers, and philosophers. Now, this would be interesting in itself, since Sen had a chance to study with, discuss, and observe some of the most brilliant minds of the time: Piero Sraffa, Dennis Robertson, Joan Robinson, Maurice Dobb, James Meade. Unfortunately for many of them, as for the cities in Europe he visited, Sen lists the names with a sentence or two of generic praise. (The only exceptions are Sraffa and perhaps Maurice Dobb; see below.) It seems that the ubiquitous mention of everyone who has crossed paths with Sen may have been done so that no one could feel slighted or excluded. Glowing adjectives are abundantly assigned ("most original," "delightful," "close friend," "splendid economist," "superb mathematician," "astoundingly talented"). This somewhat skeptical reader cannot believe that several hundred people whom Sen had met had all invariably been extraordinary scholars and the kindest human beings.

Trying to be nice to everybody is a wrong approach in a memoir by one of the foremost intellectuals of our time. A memoir is not a letter of recommendation that one writes for his friends. Neither we, nor future readers, will be interested in the names of the multitudes who have met Sen. We, and they, are interested in Sen's comments on the times and important people. There are, as I mentioned, indeed some, alas too short, vignettes: on Dennis Robertson, Joan Robinson, Sraffa, and Dobb. By his own reckoning, Sen had spent hours and hours conversing with Sraffa and Dobb. But we are given much less of their personalities than is the case with Tagore and people from Amartya's youth.

Rather unexpectedly, among the few persons who are openly criticized (even if mildly) is Joan Robinson for her "dogmatism" and unwillingness to listen to contrary opinions. Samuel Huntington is twice, very indirectly, criticized for his "clash of civilization" thesis that Sen quite convincingly debunks through describing his own experience. Aung San Suu Kyi, the Burmese president, who was Sen's friend, and whose reversal from a pro-democracy martyr to *de facto* supporter of ethnic cleansing, is censured, and her transformation is found both disturbing and incomprehensible.

The non-Indian part of the book seems rather flat, offering less original thinking than we get from Sen's reflections on India and his life there. Perhaps Sen himself, by being not just an economist, but a historian and a philosopher, is "guilty" of having made us expect a uniformly high level of insight. But, even with these minor flaws, *Home in the World* is an extraordinary book written by an extra-ordinary person.

(Published May 19, 2022)

REFLECTIONS

16.11 *Du passé faisons table rase*

I prepared dinner for myself tonight. I am now alone, in a house in Washington, which is about five times as large as the apartment in Belgrade where I grew up. At one point, we were five persons in that apartment. It means, I thought, that my living area had increased by 25 times. How did it happen?

Socially, I was born in what was called the "red bourgeoisie." It has been a while since I wanted to write a post about how communism, at least in the Yugoslav variant, reproduced the class structure of capitalism, even if with a twist (less inequality). An important role in that discussion would have been played by a domestic help lady that my family employed from approximately 1960 to 1968. She was then, when she started working for us ("for us," in communism!), about 25 years old. I cannot remember the names of people I met yesterday but I remember her name very clearly. I will never forget it. But, I realized, as I thought of writing about it, that it is not only the social issues that her memories brought to me, it was something else as well.

She was a Serbian girl, who had escaped from the Nazi-installed Croatian government's genocide during the Second World War. I do not know how she survived or what happened to her parents or siblings, nor even if she had any brothers and sisters. (As you will see in a few paragraphs this is not surprising.) I would not have even known, so indifferent and willfully ignorant I was of her stories, that she was a Serbian genocide survivor, had I not remembered a short story she told us. The Ustašas would give little kids a small candy, and then, before they could put the candy in their mouth, they would strike their hands with whips so that the starved little children would both suffer from not having had the candy and would have their hands bloodied. This is the only thing that I remember. And most likely the only story she told us.

But why did we not know more? I think it was because my father, with his whole family murdered in most brutal way by Serbian Nazi collaborators because they were communists, did not want to think about the past. He had had enough of killings after his family was murdered and he spent four years in German captivity. My mother, from a Serbian bourgeois family, was not particularly interested in the history of the poor people from Croatia, who barely escaped a genocide. But there was yet a deeper reason. We all wanted to forget about the past. We wanted to believe that the world had been created anew and whatever injustices and murders had been committed before would not be repeated. Everyone will get a fair chance. No one will be killed. In a traumatized country like Yugoslavia, where brother turned on brother, neighbor on neighbor, this was the greatest contribution of communists. Every nationality was guilty in one way or another, everyone at some point supported Hitler, so let us draw a thick line and not repeat the past.

This is what I think my parents and millions of others wanted to believe.

But other people did not want to draw a big thick line under the past. They wanted to find out who killed whom and when. And, while this was a worthy project, imbued—in some cases—with the idea that it would bring justice, I wonder if it had not encouraged another round of ethnic slaughter that began in 1990s. In order to straighten our history, we, it seemed, had to relive it: perhaps with murderers and victims now reversed, but with killings still going on.

So, do people in America need now, when they drag statues down, new truth and justice commissions? Would truth and justice commissions bring justice or new bloodshed? I really do not know. A part of me believes that calling out past injustices is right and should be done. But another part of me believes that by never letting sleeping dogs lie, we may repeat history, even if with different people playing different roles. We may take Santayana's advice upside down.

Some ten years ago I went to watch, on the opening day, Quentin Tarantino's *Django Unchained*. It was a Christmas afternoon, a day for families, and for people to take their kids to the movies. In front of my family, in a Washington cinema, sat a Black family. The movie opens with a most frightful scene of slave torture: cutting limbs, beating, whipping. The poor mother and father in front of us precipitously grabbed their children and left the theater. Do you want your kids to grow up feeling that they are equal to everybody else, or do you want them to believe they are the offspring of people who were considered inferior and treated horribly? The family made the right choice. And I was overwhelmed with a wave of sympathy for them.

As Plato said, sometimes we have to have beautiful myths. Or otherwise we may have to relive our history. Which was not pretty.

(Published August 20, 2020)

REFLECTIONS

16.12 English language and American solipsism

Several months ago, Simon Kuper published what seemed to me a bizarre piece in the weekend edition *of The Financial Times*, arguing that native English speakers are handicapped by the fact that the entire world (or to be more realistic, the global middle and ruling classes) are able to read or speak English. This gave to the latter the advantage of fully understanding English speakers, their opinions, prejudices, and motivations, while taking away all incentive for the native English speakers to learn foreign languages (why bother, if everyone speaks your language) and thus to understand and influence other cultures that still conduct most of their bread-and-butter business using national languages.

What struck me as odd in Kuper's piece was that it reversed the normal and long-standing view that having foreigners learn your language was always a mark of cultural or technological superiority, that it entrenched that superiority, and was therefore a very desirable thing. Greece influenced Romans through their love and awe of the Greek language (what Gibbon called "the perfect idiom"), and thus transmitted its culture and way of thinking. It is not for nothing that such diverse emperors as Hadrian, Marcus Aurelius, and Julian were Hellenophiles, often more at ease in Greek than in the rather coarse Latin. (I am writing this some 200 meters from the Hadrian's Gate in Athens.)

The advantage of having others speak your language was always taken as a fact: it helps your culture, religion, or trade, as we see among the French-speaking elites in the Middle East, English-speaking elites in the Indian subcontinent, or most of Africa. World-wide expansions of Christianity and Islam are unthinkable without cosmopolitanism of, at first, Greek language, and then Latin, English, and French, and for Islam, Arabic. The US gains from foreigners speaking English are immense: domination in the popular culture, media, and book worlds, easy propagation of American ideas in politics, philosophy, sciences, or economics. Such advantages have led the philosopher Philippe van Parijs to claim that, as a matter of justice, native English speakers should compensate non-native English speakers for the "unearned" advantage they (the speakers) enjoy.

So, how can such obvious advantages become a handicap? While disagreeing with Kuper, there was, in my mind even then, a slight doubt, that perhaps in some cases he might be right. And, I think that an argument can be made for it. "Cultural solipsism" of

428

REFLECTIONS

native English speakers is exacerbated by everybody's speaking their language, tolerably well (as I do here). This then reinforces a very human tendency toward intellectual laziness, where one communicates only with the people who speak English and learns everything about the country one travels to, or more seriously, on which one works or writes about from English-language sources or English-speaking natives. This is bound to give a very truncated view of reality.

I was struck by observing native English speakers, who actually do speak foreign languages, being entirely indifferent to native-language media sources in the countries where they live. Some of them might have spent a decade or more living in X, speaking its language, without bothering much to read the news in the local language or engaging in a more demanding intellectual intercourse in that language.

It was brought to me again when, a couple of days ago, I watched, in my hotel room, a Russian political talk show where a clearly smart and somewhat insolent host discussed with a number of guests the current US–Russia relations. The loquacious host dictated the structure of the show and, to represent the US point of view, he invited an American journalist working in Moscow. His Russian was passable and I even think that he could conduct a real conversation in Russian in a one-on-one setting. But, in a fast-paced talk show, where he did not control other speakers, and people were interrupting each other, his attempts to make a point were nothing short of pathetic. (I vaguely thought that he might have been deliberately brought here for that reason.) Showing that he lived, even in Moscow, in an entirely Anglo world, he referred to Montenegro (in the context of NATO expansion) as "Montenegro," not as "Cherna Gora," as it is called in Russian. That indicated to me that he was not reading or watching Russian media discussing NATO, but was probably learning about Russia from the reading of American papers and a few conversations with local English-speaking Russians. Exactly the thing that a foreign correspondent should not do.

I could go on with such examples for a long time, since in my travels I have seen them aplenty. As, for example, the discussion of the Russian revolution in Moscow, where some of the most famous Western historians did not feel confident enough to speak in Russian in front of a 99 percent Russian audience (some of whom had to resort to listening to translation). I thought that it would be rather odd if a Frenchman who wrote a book on US Revolutionary War decided, at a conference on the topic held in the United States,

429

REFLECTIONS

to speak in … French. Or I remember a famous medieval Greek and Byzantine historian who asked for even ordinary information in Athens only in English. Or a Western ambassador who, in the middle of the Bosnian civil war, kept on pronouncing the name of a city where the battle the raged as it was (wrongly) pronounced in Washington, not in Sarajevo. And I do not need to expand on people who know not a bit of the language of the country on which they write but nonetheless bravely pen compendia of common places, which proceed to win prizes in the Anglo world.

Thus, Kuper's piece, while in some respects extreme, did contain some truth. The ubiquitousness of English language has stimulated human intellectual laziness by making native English speakers less likely to make an effort to learn foreign languages. And, even when they do learn them, to use them mostly to hire taxis and read restaurant menus, and not to engage with the language and culture of the country they are supposed to know and to write about. It has led them to live, even in places thousands of miles away from the United States, and culturally entirely different, in a bubble of the ideas generated by the Anglo-American media, to believe only in such ideas, and to reinforce the solipsism that has always been strong in well integrated, big, and geographically isolated nations like the United States.

(Published August 5, 2017)

REFLECTIONS

16.13 The problems of authenticity under capitalism

In the last chapter of *Capitalism, Alone*, I discussed a number of changes in private life that are introduced by greater wealth (and thus ability to procure commercially services that were in the past procured within family) and the "invasion" of capitalistic relations into our private lives. One of the issues discussed there is the diminished usefulness of family in highly commercialized societies and an obvious decline in family size (or rather expressed preference for solitary living) in more affluent societies.

Here, I want to discuss another issue in which we face a fundamental contradiction between the principles according to which hyper-capitalist societies are organized and what may be considered desirable outcomes. The topic is authenticity in arts and, to a lesser degree, in social sciences. When we deal with reproducible goods, the advantage of capitalism is that profit can be made only if somebody else's needs are satisfied. Thus, two objectives, personal needs of a buyer and the profit goal of the producer, are aligned.

But this is not the case in arts. The reason is that arts thrive on, or require, individualism, uniqueness, and authenticity. When you try to guess the public's preferences in shoes, and produce such shoes, this is good and useful. But when you try to guess public's preference in literature, films, or paintings, it may, if you guess them correctly, make you rich, but from the point of view of artistic creation, it could very easily be fake and ephemeral. In arts, we are interested in an individual's view of the world, not in an individual's ability to ape public preferences or prejudices.

I will illustrate it with some extreme examples. When we read Kafka's *Diaries*, we are sure that they represent his own true and unvarnished take on the world: he wrote them for himself, never thought they would be published, and explicitly asked that they be burned. The same is true, for example, of Marx's 1848 manuscripts, which were saved largely by accident and were published more than a century after they were written. Whether one likes them or not is a matter of taste and interest. But there is no doubt that they are the authentic works of these two people.

But, when we watch a film whose ending was tested on different audiences to produce the ending that most people would like to see, and pay for, there is—likewise—no doubt that the author's role in such an enterprise is diminished, and in some cases totally obliterated. The same is true for works of fiction. If they are written with

431

the main objective of money-making, they have to play on popular preferences and to present as little of an author's personal opinions (which may be unpopular) as possible. Why should one then, if in search of new or challenging ideas, read such novels?

We thus face a very peculiar inversion of roles. Authors try to lose their authenticity in order to please the audience, so that they can maximize income. And the only value of such an oeuvre resides in that it allows us to gauge public preferences—not in any own (inherent) value.

This problem exists in most artistic creations under capitalism. Everyone can give many examples, going perhaps from Steven Spielberg to the writers of innumerable (and readily forgotten) bestseller books.

It can be argued, however, that artists were always producing for *i potenti*. Their works were commissioned and expressed little of their own personality, except in the part which had to do with skills (most obviously in painting and sculpture where the topic would be given to the artist, and he may be distinguished only by his skill in executing it). This is a good point, except that art producers themselves had not then fully mastered commercialization to nearly the same extent as they have today. It was then an "artisanal" commercialization, compared to today's mass commercialization.

Topics are now chosen by professionals in function of what they believe will sell: I conversed only once with a book agent and, when he began telling me what I should be writing, it was enough to dissuade me from ever talking to another. The texts are edited and reedited to please the audience and to avoid lawsuits. Most extraordinary, authors of works of fiction attend workshops where their voice is additionally muted as they are taught how to write like everybody else.

This all makes sense if the objective is solely profit. In fact, one of the reasons I was told it is good to have an agent is because he can extract the best deal for the author from the publisher. But, here is the hitch: he can extract the best deal only by stifling the authenticity of the author.

These are some areas of human endeavor where excessive commercialization is not likely to produce the best results. The problem has no solution because it derives from the fundamental contradiction between a system where profit is to be made by pleasing buyers, and a system that puts the premium on individualism, which, by definition, is not shared by many.

(Published April 30, 2021)

REFLECTIONS

16.14 The abolition of paper and the
pompous rule of the present

China is considered to have been the first country (civilization) to have created the modern version of paper. Paper is listed as one among the four big Chinese inventions (the other three are compass, gunpowder, and printing). Perhaps it will be the first country to desinvent paper too.

What is striking in today's China, compared to even as recently as five years ago, is a complete disappearance of paper. I mean paper as a means of conveying information, not paper as in paper napkins in cafés. Some of that disappearance is perhaps justifiably celebrated: instead of metro cards that can be easily misplaced, there are electronic tickets on cell phones; instead of plastic credit cards, there are Alipay and similar systems available within your phone; instead of crumpled banknotes, there are touchless screens that pay your bills.

It would be wrong to take this as an ideological feature linked to the current system of electronic surveillance in China. Very similar developments are observable elsewhere, in all modern societies: China is just slightly ahead of the rest of the world. Further, even very ideological propaganda is affected by this. In the past, museums linked with various CPC events had on display a variety of officially approved publications: speeches, resolutions, biographies. Almost nothing of that remains. In the excellent Shanghai museum dedicated to the founding congress of the Chinese Communist Party, there is just one book that can be bought in the museum store. The store sells pens, badges, umbrellas, toys, bags, pandas, but no written documents. One would search in vain for such elementary publications as the Founding Act of the CPC, its first resolutions, etc. Moreover, looking at the rich exhibits that deal with the New Culture movement of the 1920s and numerous publications that are displayed in the museum, one wonders what could in the future be shown from similar cultural movements of today. Copies of emails? Laptops where the texts are stored?

Such dematerialization of information can be celebrated, perhaps at times excessively, given the relatively modest gains in efficiency that are achieved compared to the older system, but the paeans disregard one important feature.

People's interactions are not solely based on the present. Our interactions and opinions are so many "bottles thrown into the sea"

REFLECTIONS

in the hope of explaining our current thinking and conveying to the future what we feel and what we have learned. This is the advantage of a written system compared to the oral. The oral system could neither transmit information over time, nor do it accurately. We have Homer's verses today because somebody eventually was able to write them down.

Things would not have come to us had they not been preserved on scripts made of papyrus. Or, even better, as the Egyptians, Greeks, and Romans did, preservation of certain facts was entrusted to the stone: it was more durable than paper, but it was hard to carve and carry longer and more complex messages.

In the three weeks I spent in China, I have seen, in a Beijing hotel, two desultory copies of a Chinese-language newspaper and *China Daily* displayed in a bar and not touched by anyone; one person reading what appeared to be a newspaper in a Shanghai museum; and a father reading to his kid a comic book on a train—and no other piece of information recorded on paper. In three weeks. Surely, I went to a big bookstore in Shanghai with six floors of books; or have seen a beautiful new library at the Zhejiang university. There are plenty of books there. So, paper as a means of conveyance or storage of information has not completely disappeared. But its function to convey today's information into the future has apparently ceased.

This is not a trivial issue. Whether information about a subway trip is encrusted on a piece of paper or stored within your cell phone does not matter to the future generations. But, placing the entire modern knowledge in the electronic format is dangerous. We can already see the first effects of it. The electronic system of storage is old enough for us to have noticed that many websites, links, blogs, where information was stored are already by now broken, deleted, or have been moved elsewhere. Information on household income or people's characteristics that was collected in the past is in many cases lost because the software systems used to read and process such information have changed. Ironically, but not at all surprisingly, all the information that we can get regarding some past surveys of population (and I am not talking here about ancient data, but information that is twenty years old) comes from the *printed* summaries of such sources. I have seen this very clearly with Soviet household surveys, whose data have all been irretrievably lost because, already by the early 1990s, the technology had entirely changed and, short of enormous and expensive effort, the Soviet-made computer cards could no longer be read. But the problem is the same everywhere. US

REFLECTIONS

micro data from the 1950s and early 1960s are impossible to access any more.

With full transfer to electronic-only information, we are moving to an ever-ruling "presentism." Information can be seemingly efficiently and costlessly transmitted today or over a very short time period, but is afterwards lost forever. When our civilization vanishes, the new researchers, perhaps thousands of years away, will be faced by a conundrum: did literacy disappear? How to explain that a civilization from which there are millions of written records (that would be saved the way that the Dead Sea Scrolls were saved) had suddenly abandoned literacy and gone back to oral communication and barbarism?

In fact this very post will be forever gone as soon as the website you read it on folds and another format of dissemination takes over. Until then, try to carve it in stone ...

(Published January 2, 2024)

REFLECTIONS

16.15 Who are we?

Today a friend (unprompted) told me that he enjoys my blog posts. This is happening relatively frequently nowadays and I am of course every time delighted. I do write to be read. I am happy that my writings find resonance in other people's minds.

But it also gives me pause. I am somewhat fearful of getting too many accolades from the people whose opinions I value: I am afraid that they might disagree with my next post or find it disappointing. But, if I start thinking about what they like or do not like, I am no longer writing what I like or what I think. I am then writing what I think other people think I should write.

Now, this may be seen as a simple catch-22 problem that had always plagued the relationship between writers and readers. But it is, I think, made worse by the commercialization of all opinion. Pleasing others is a necessary condition for being successful and for making money. Adam Smith was entirely right when, among the virtues of the market economy, he listed (perhaps ahead of any other virtue) that the baker, in order to sell us bread, has to consult his own self-interests, which, unless he pleases us, will remain unfulfilled. (This is just the other side of the equation that we do not expect bread from the baker's benevolence but from his self-interest.) Yet this, which is an advantage in most of human interest-driven interactions, may be a disadvantage in some of the more intellectual pursuits.

If our subsistence as writers depends on writing things that please the greatest number of people, it is not only that we do not express ourselves and our opinions any more, it is also that we do not advance the debate. We are centered around what the received ideas, the common-places of the time are, and about what the majority believes. In order to go forward though, as we know from history, we need active minorities. But, if nobody dares express opinions of an active minority for fear that his own livelihood would be affected—not because he or she would be jailed for dissension—but because he would be a failed writer or opinion-maker, not likely to be hired by anyone, is not the outcome the same?

Perhaps the most important reason I like Kafka (although I admit that I would not, right now, reread most of his books, but do definitely suggest reading his *Diaries*) is that we know that he was not writing for others. He was doing it all for himself. When we read him we are indeed in direct contact with what he believed—whether we agree with it or not. But, when art and opinion-making

REFLECTIONS

are fully commercialized, only those who are rich or indifferent to wealth (the latter category is tiny) can afford Kafkaian luxury. This is why no Hollywood movie can be really thought of as genuine: the authors have to redesign the plot, the heroes, the actors, to please the audience. Why would a studio otherwise finance a movie that upsets the audience and that no one cares to see?

In our writing or any other creative work (say, even when writing a very technical paper in economics) we always have—some of us more, others, perhaps, less—to keep in the back of our minds the work's usefulness, or, more exactly, its "pleasantness" and thus ultimately its commercial value. I found this out with my own blog posts that, when they were not carried over integrally *tel-quel,* caused some media outlets to request that some parts be expanded and others shortened: not because they were in the business of censorship but because they wanted to please their readership and to second-guess what their readers want to hear. They believe that their audience would like to hear from me, more on X, and less on Y. But what happens when I really want to write about Y and not about X? Who am I then? Am I the person who cares about Y, or am I the person who wants to make you believe that I care about X?

When I was recently in Buenos Aires, I came, by chance, to a square in Palermo that carries the name of Julio Cortazar. I suppose that he either lived, or was born there. I loved his writings from the very first time I discovered them in a literary periodical published in Belgrade in the 1970s. A couple of decades later I wrote down (in my own translation) those lines from one of his short stories. And, I often think that they apply to everything that we, the engineers of human souls, do:

"Y *después de hacer todo lo que hacen se levantan, se bañan, se entalcan, se perfuman, se visten, y así progresivamente van volviendo a ser lo que no son.*" ("And after they did all that they usually do, they get up, take a shower, put a cream on their faces, perfume their bodies, get dressed, and thus slowly become again what they really are not.")

(Published December 14, 2019)

REFERENCES

1 Growth and Climate Change

1.5 And does growth in the North by itself make Africa poorer?
Noah S. Diffenbaugh and Michael Burke, "Global Warming has Increased Global Economic Inequality," *Proceedings of the National Academy of Sciences*, 2019. https://www.pnas.org/doi/epdf/10.1073/pnas.1816020116

1.6 Kate Raworth's economics of miracles
Kate Raworth, *Doughnut Economics: Seven Ways to Think like the Twenty-First-Century Economist*. Chelsea Green Publishing, 2017.

1.7 Abundance, capitalism, and climate change
Karl Marx, *Critique of the Gotha Program*, part I (1875), in Karl Marx and Friedrich Engels, *Selected Works*, vol. 3. Moscow: Progress, 1970, pp. 13–30. https://www.marxists.org/archive/marx/works/download/Marx_Critque_of_the_Gotha_Programme.pdf
Kohei Saito, *Slow Down: The Degrowth Manifesto*. Astra House, 2024. Originally published in Japanese in 2021.

2 Migration

2.1 Should some countries cease to exist?
Paul Collier, *Exodus: How Migration is Changing Our World*. Oxford University Press, 2015.
Neli Esipova, Julie Ray, and Anita Pugliese, "The Many Faces of Global Migration," Gallup World Poll No. 43, International Organization for Migration and Gallup, 2011. https://news.gallup.com/poll/152660/Faces-Global-Migration.aspx

REFERENCES

2.3 Migration's economic positives and negatives

Paul Collier, *Exodus: How Migration is Changing Our World.* Oxford University Press, 2015.

Bill Easterly and Ross Levine, "Africa's Growth Tragedy: Policies and Ethnic Divisions," *Quarterly Journal of Economics*, 112 (4), November 1997: 1203–1250. https://doi.org/10.1162/003355300555466

Herbert Frankel, "The Presidential Address: World Economic Solidarity," *South African Journal of Economics*, 10 (3), September 1942. https://onlinelibrary.wiley.com/doi/abs/10.1111/j.1813-6982.1942.tb02798.x

Paul Krugman, "History versus Expectations," *Quarterly Journal of Economics*, 110, May 1995: 61.

Assar Lindbeck, "Welfare State Disincentives with Endogeneous Habits and Norms," *Scandinavian Journal of Economics*, 97 (4), 1995: 477–494. https://www.jstor.org/stable/3440539

Branko Milanovic, *Global Inequality: A New Approach for the Age of Globalization.* Harvard University Press, 2016.

Lant Pritchett, "Let Their People Come: Breaking the Gridlock on Global Labor Mobility, Breaking the Gridlock on International Labor Mobility," Washington D.C.: Center for Global Development, 2006. https://www.cgdev.org/sites/default/files/9781933286105-Pritchett-let-their-people-come.pdf

2.4 Trade and migration: Substitutes or complements?

Robert Schiller, "Next Revolution Will Seek to Overthrow Privileges of Nationhood," *Guardian*, September 19, 2016. https://www.theguardian.com/business/2016/sep/19/the-looming-anti-national-revolution

2.5 Habermas and pimps: The world of the day and the world of the night

Dragan Lakićević Lakas, *Portret političara u mladosti.* Belgrade: Arhipelag, 2018.

V. S. Naipaul, "The Crocodiles of Yamoussoukro," *New Yorker*, May 5, 1984. Reprinted in *The Writer and the World: Essays.* Vintage Books, 2003.

2.6 The simplicity of views regarding civil conflicts

Alberto Alesina and Enrico Spolaore, "On the Size and Number of Nations," *Quarterly Journal of Economics*, 112 (4), November, 1997: 1027–1056.

Branko Milanovic, "Nations, Conglomerates, and Empires: The Trade-off between Income and Sovereignty," in Dominick Salvatore, Marijan Svetličič, and Jože Damijan (eds.), *Small Countries in a Global Economy: New Challenges and Opportunities.* Palgrave, 2000, pp. 25–70. Earlier version as World Bank PRE Working Papers Series, No. 1675, October 1996. https://stonecenter.gc.cuny.edu/research/nations-conglomerates-empires-the-trade-off-between-income-and-sovereignty/

REFERENCES

3 Politics

3.1 What is a paleo-left agenda?
Branko Milanovic with Alex Hochuli and Philip Cunliffe, "What was Communism?" Tuesday September 6, 2022. podcast. https://bungacast .podbean.com/e/286-what-was-communism-ft-branko-milanovic/

3.4 How is the world ruled?
Nirad Chaudhuri, *Thy Hand, Great Anarch: India 1921–1952*. Addison-Wesley Publishing Company, 1987.

3.5 Multi-party kleptocracies rather than illiberal democracies
Michela Wrong, *In the Footsteps of Mr. Kurtz: Living on the Brink of Disaster in Mobutu's Congo*. Harper Perennial, 2002.

3.7 There is no exit for dictators
Kaushik Basu, "The Morphing of Dictators: Why Dictators Get Worse Over Time," *Oxford Open Economics*, vol. 2, 2023. https://academic.oup.com /ooec/article/doi/10.1093/ooec/odad002/7036634

3.8 Trump as the ultimate triumph of neoliberalism
Mancur Olson, *Power and Prosperity: Outgrowing Communist and Capitalist Dictatorships*. Basic Books, 2020.

3.9 What we owe to Donald Trump: A different angle
Dino Buzzati, *The Tartar Steppe*. Verba Mundi 2005. Originally published in Italian in 1940.

3.10 The comprador intelligentsia
Aidan Coville, Sebastian Galiani, and Paul Gertler, "A Comment on the Ethical Issues," Twitter Discussion in "Enforcing Payment for Water and Sanitation Services in Nairobi's Slums," August 8, 2020. https://drive .google.com/file/d/1nVGR4qlhWt2EcNiy6d02By3e4kptVSer/view
Angus Deaton and Nancy Cartwright, "Understanding and Misunderstanding Randomized Controlled Trials," *Social Science and Medicine*, 210, August 2018: 2–21. https://www.sciencedirect.com/science/article/pii /S0277953617307359
Andrew Green, "A New Research Experiment in Kenya Raises Questions about Ethics," *Devex*, September 8, 2020. https://www.devex.com/news /a-new-research-experiment-in-kenya-raises-questions-about-ethics-98039
Martin Ravallion, "Should the Randomistas (Continue to) Rule?," National Bureau of Economic Research, Working Paper No. 27554, July 2020. https://www.nber.org/papers/w27554
Sanjay Reddy, "Randomize This: On Poor Economics," *Review of Agrarian Studies*, 2 (2), 2012. https://ras.org.in/randomise_this_on_poor_economics

440

REFERENCES

Edward Said, *Orientalism*. Vintage Books, 2014. Originally published in 1978.

4 Inequality Within Nations

4.1 Why inequality matters
John Maynard Keynes, *The Economic Consequences of the Peace*. Olive Garden Books, 2013. Originally published in 1919.
Branko Milanovic, "Why We All Care About Inequality (But Some of Us Are Loathe to Admit It)," *Challenge*, 50 (6), November–December 2007: 109–120. https://www.jstor.org/stable/40722484.
Roy van der Weide and Branko Milanovic, "Inequality is Bad for the Growth of the Poor (but not for that of the Rich)," *World Bank Economic Review*, 32 (3), 2018: 507–530. https://documents1.worldbank.org/curated/en /888731468331207447/pdf/WPS6963.pdf

4.2 In defence of equality (without welfare economics)
Miles Corak. "Income Inequality, Equality of Opportunity, and Intergenerational Mobility," *Journal of Economic* Perspectives, 27 (3), 2013: 79–102.
Martin Gilens, *Affluence and Influence: Economic Inequality and Political Power in America*, Princeton University Press, 2012.
Gustavo Marrero and Juan-Gabriel Rodriguez, "Inequality of Opportunity and Growth," *Journal of Development Economics*, 104(C), 2013: 107–122.
John Rawls, *A Theory of Justice*. Harvard University Press, 1971.
Sarah Voitchovsky, "Does the Profile of Income Inequality Matter for Economic Growth?," *Journal of Economic Growth*, 10, 2005: 273–296.
Roy van der Weide and Branko Milanovic, "Inequality is Bad for the Growth of the Poor (but not for that of the Rich)," *World Bank Economic Review*, 32 (3), 2018: 507–530. https://documents1.worldbank.org/curated/en /888731468331207447/pdf/WPS6963.pdf

4.3 Why twentieth-century tools cannot be used to address twenty-first-century income inequality
Tony Atkinson, *Inequality: What Can be Done?* Harvard University Press, 2015.

4.4 The welfare state in the age of globalization
Atossa Araxia Abrahamian, "An Economist's Case for Open Borders," *Dissent*, Winter 2017. https://www.dissentmagazine.org/article/branko -milanovic-economist-proposal-open-borders-migration-citizenship/
Peter Lindert, "Private Welfare and the Welfare State," in Larry Neal and Jeffrey G. Williamson (eds.), *The Cambridge History of Capitalism*, vol. 2: *The Spread of Capitalism: From 1848 to the Present*. Cambridge University Press, 2014, pp. 464–500.

REFERENCES

Branko Milanovic, *Global Inequality: A New Approach for the Age of Globalization*. Harvard University Press, 2016.
Branko Milanovic, "There is a Trade-off Between Citizenship and Migration," *Financial Times*, April 20, 2016. https://www.ft.com/content/2e3c93fa-06d2-11e6-9b51-0fb5e65703ce
Avner Offer and Daniel Söderberg, *The Nobel Factor: The Prize in Economics, Social Democracy and the Market Turn*. Princeton University Press, 2016.

4.5 All our needs are social
Harry G. Frankfurt, *On Inequality*. Princeton University Press, 2015.
Branko Milanovic, "Why We All Do Care about Inequality (but are Loath to Admit it)," *Challenge Magazine*, 50 (6), November–December 2007: 109–120.

4.6 Why the focus on horizontal inequality undermines efforts to reduce overall inequality
Göran Therborn, *The Killing Fields of Inequality*. Polity, 2013.

4.7 Basic difference between wage inequality and income inequality studies
Anthony B. Atkinson, *The Economics of Inequality*. Clarendon Press, 1975.
Claudia Goldin and Lawrence Katz, *The Race between Education and Technology*. Harvard University Press, 2010.
Branko Milanovic, *Visions of Inequality: From the French Revolution to the End of the Cold War*. Harvard University Press, 2023.

4.8 Distinguishing incomes from capital and labor
Matthew Smith, Danny Yagan, Owen Zidar and Erick Zwick, "Rise of Pass-Through Understates Labor's Share of Income," National Bureau of Economic Research Working Paper No. 29400, January 3, 2022. https://www.nber.org/digest/202201/rise-pass-throughs-understates-labors-share-income

4.9 Why "Make America Denmark Again" will not happen
Gerald Davis and J. Adam Cobb, "Corporations and Economic Inequality Around the World: The Paradox of Hierarchy," *Research in Organizational Behavior*, 30 (1), May 2010.
Francisco F. Ferreira, "Kuznets Waves and the Great Epistemological Challenge to Inequality Analysis," World Bank Blogs, April 27, 2016. https://blogs.worldbank.org/en/impactevaluations/kuznets-waves-and-great-epistemological-challenge-inequality-analysis
Branko Milanovic, *Global Inequality: A New Approach for the Age of Globalization*. Harvard University Press, 2016.

REFERENCES

4.10 *À la recherche* of the roots of US inequality "exceptionalism"

Janet Gornick, Branko Milanovic, and Nathaniel Johnson, "American Exceptionalism in Market Income Inequality: An Analysis Based on Microdata from the Luxembourg Income Study (LIS) Database," in Raj Chetty, John Friedman, Janet Gornick, Barry Johnson, and Arthur Kennickell (eds.), *Measuring and Understanding the Distribution and Intra/Inter-Generational Mobility of Income and Wealth.* National Bureau of Economic Research, October 2020.

Branko Milanovic, "The Median Voter Hypothesis, Income Inequality and Income Redistribution: An Empirical Test with the Required Data," *European Journal of Political Economy*, 16 (3), September 2000: 367–410.

4.11 What are the limits of Europe?

Branko Milanovic, "Nations, Conglomerates, and Empires: The Trade-off between Income and Sovereignty," in D. Salvatore, M. Svetličić, and J. Damijan (eds.), *Small Countries in a Global Economy: New Challenges and Opportunities.* Palgrave, 2000, pp. 25–70. Earlier version as World Bank PRE Working Papers Series, No. 1675, October 1996. https://stonecenter.gc.cuny.edu/research/nations-conglomerates-empires-the-trade-off-between-income-and-sovereignty/

5 Global Inequality

5.1 The history of global inequality studies

Montek Ahluwalia, "Inequality, Poverty and Development," *Journal of Development Economics*, 3 (4), December 1976: 307–342.

Montek Ahluwalia, "Income Distribution and Development: Some Stylized Facts," *American Economic Review*, 66 (2), 1976: 128–135.

Christian Olaf Christiansen and Steven L. B. Jensen (eds.), *Histories of Global Inequality.* Palgrave, 2020.

Shail Jain, "Size Distribution of Income: Compilation of Data," World Bank Staff Working Paper No. 190, 1974. https://documents.worldbank.org/en/publication/documents-reports/documentdetail/637191468740412077/size-distribution-of-income-compilation-of-data

Mick McLean and Mike Hopkins, "Problems of World Food and Agriculture: Projections, Models and Possible Approaches," *Futures*.

Branko Milanovic, "True World Income Distribution, 1988 and 1993: First Calculations Based on Household Surveys Alone," *Economic Journal*, 112 (476), January 2002: 51–92. Earlier version as World Bank Policy Research Working Paper No. 2244, November 1999.

Branko Milanovic, *The Haves and the Have-Nots: A Brief and Idiosyncratic History of Global Inequality.* Basic Books, 2011.

Samuel Moyn, *Not Enough: Human Rights in an Unequal World.* Harvard University Press, 2018.

REFERENCES

Quinn Slobodian, *The Globalists: The End of Empire and the Birth of Neoliberalism*. Harvard University Press, 2018.

5.2 Athenian dialogues on global income inequality

Paul Collier, *Exodus: How Migration is Changing Our World*. Oxford University Press, 2015.

Paul Collier, *The Future of Capitalism*. Penguin, 2019.

5.3 How much of your income is due to your citizenship?

Branko Milanovic, "Global Inequality of Opportunity: How Much of our Income is Determined by Where we Live?" *Review of Economics and Statistics*, 97 (2), May 2015: 452–460.

Branko Milanovic, *Global Inequality: A New Approach for the Age of Globalization*. Harvard University Press, 2016.

Branko Milanovic, "The Three Eras of Global Inequality, 1820–2020 with the Focus on the Past Thirty Years," *World Development*, 177, May 2024.

Thomas Pogge, *World Poverty and Human Rights*. Polity, 2008.

John Rawls, *The Law of Peoples*. Harvard University Press, 2001.

John Roemer, *Equality of Opportunity*. Harvard University Press, 2000.

Ayalet Shachar, *The Birthright Lottery: Citizenship and Global Inequality*. Polity, 2008.

5.4 Is citizenship just a rent?

Branko Milanovic, "Global Inequality of Opportunity: How Much of our Income is Determined by Where we Live?" *Review of Economics and Statistics*, 97 (2), May 2015: 452–460.

Branko Milanovic, *Capitalism, Alone*. Harvard University Press, 2019.

5.5 Why foreign aid cannot be regressive

Peter T. Bauer, *Dissent on Development*. Harvard University Press, 1972.

Angus Deaton, *The Great Escape: Health, Wealth, and the Origins of Inequality*. Princeton University Press, 2013.

William Easterly, *The White Man's Burden: Why the West's Efforts to Aid the Rest Have Done So Much Ill And So Little Good*. Oxford University Press, 2007.

Dembisa Mayo, *Dead Aid*. Farrar, Straus and Giroux, 2010.

Ludwig von Mises, *Human Action: A Treatise on Economics*. Martino Fine Book, 2012. Originally published in 1949.

5.6 Formal and actual similarities between climate change and global inequality, and suboptimality of the nation-state

Branko Milanovic, *Global Inequality: A New Approach for the Age of Globalization*. Harvard University Press, 2016.

Branko Milanovic, *Capitalism, Alone*. Harvard University Press, 2019.

REFERENCES

6 Wealth Inequality

6.1 What is wealth?
Branko Milanovic, *The Haves and the Have-Nots: A Brief and Idiosyncratic History of Global Inequality*. Basic Books, 2011.
Vladimir Nevezhin, Застолья Иосифа Сталина (*At Stalin's Dining Table*). Seria Airo-Monografiya, Moscow, 2019.

6.2 Historical wealth: How to compare Croesus and Bezos
Angus Maddison, *Contours of the World Economy, 1–2030 AD: Essays in Macro-Economic History*. Oxford University Press, 2007.
William D. Nordhaus, "Do Real-Output and Real-Wage Measures Capture Reality? The History of Lighting Suggests Not," in Timothy N. Breshanan and Robert Gordon (eds.), *Economics of New Goods*. University of Chicago Press 1996.

6.3 My wealth and the lives of others
World Economic Forum Annual Meeting, January 21–24, Davos-Klosters, Switzerland. https://www.weforum.org/events/world-economic-forum -annual-meeting-2015/sessions/bbc-world-debate-richer-world-whom
Helen Epstein, "Colossal Corruption in Africa," *New York Review of Books*, December 4, 2014. https://www.nybooks.com/articles/2014/12/04 /colossal-corruption-africa/

6.5 On luxury
John Maynard Keynes, *The Economic Consequences of the Peace*. Skyhorse, 2007. Originally published in 1919.
Dennis C. Rasmussen, *Fears of a Setting Sun: The Disillusionment of America's Founders*. Princeton University Press, 2021.
Barton Swain, "'Fears of a Setting Sun' Review: Factions at America's Founding," *Wall Street Journal*, July 2, 2021. https://www.wsj.com /articles/fears-of-a-setting-sun-review-factions-at-americas-founding -11625237515
Max Weber, *The Protestant Ethic and the Spirit of Capitalism*, translated by Talcott Parsons. Routledge, 1992. Originally published in German in 1904.

6.6 Absurdity of World Bank wealth accounting
World Bank, *The Changing Wealth of Nations*. Washington, 2021. https:// www.worldbank.org/en/publication/changing-wealth-of-nations

6.7 Repeat after me: Wealth is not income and income is not consumption
James B. Davies, Susanna Sandström, Anthony Shorrocks, and Edward N. Wolff, "The Level and Distribution of Global Household Wealth," *Economic Journal*, 121 (551), March 2011: 223–254.

445

REFERENCES

Markus M. Grabka and Christian Westermeier, "Persistently High Wealth Inequality in Germany," DIW Berlin Working Paper, 4 (6), June 2014. https://www.diw.de/documents/publikationen/73/diw_01.c.466668.de /diw_econ_bull_2014-06-1.pdf

Oxfam, "Wealth: Having it All and Wanting More," Oxfam Policy and Practice, January 19, 2015. https://policy-practice.oxfam.org/resources /wealth-having-it-all-and-wanting-more-338125/

Felix Salmon, "Oxfam Misleading Wealth Statistic." https://www.felixsalmon .com/2015/01/oxfams-misleading-wealth-statistics/

Edward Wolff, *A Century of Wealth in America*. Harvard University Press, 2017.

Edward Wolff, "Recent Trends in Household Wealth in the United States: Rising Debt and the Middle-Class Squeeze—an Update to 2007," Levy Economics Institute of Bard College, Working Paper 589, March 2010. https://www.levyinstitute.org/pubs/wp_589.pdf

"The Wrong Yardstick: Oxfam Causes a Stir with a Statistic," *Economist*, January 22, 2015.

6.8 Was everybody under socialism a millionaire?

Oxfam, "Wealth: Having it All and Wanting More," Oxfam Policy and Practice, January 19, 2015. https://policy-practice.oxfam.org/resources /wealth-having-it-all-and-wanting-more-338125/

Thomas Piketty, *Capital in the Twenty-first Century*. Harvard University Press, 2014.

Edward Wolff, "The Asset Price Meltdown and the Wealth of the Middle Class," *Discover America in a New Century,* May 2013. https://s4.ad .brown.edu/Projects/Diversity/Data/Report/report05012013.pdf

7 Inequality and Literature

7.1 Literature and inequality

Branko Milanovic, *The Haves and the Have-Nots: A Brief and Idiosyncratic History of Global Inequality*, Basic Books, 2011.

Branko Milanovic, Peter Lindert and Jeffrey Williamson, "Pre-industrial Inequality," *Economic Journal*, March 2011: 255–272.

S. S. Prawer, *Karl Marx and World Literature*. Verso, 2014. First published in 1976.

Daniel Shaviro, *Literature and Inequality: Nine Perspectives from the Napoleonic Era through the First Gilded Age*. Anthem Press, 2020.

7.2 Was the novel born and did it die with bourgeois society?

John Lukacs, *The Future of History*. Yale University Press, 2012.

Daniel Shaviro, *Literature and Inequality: Nine Perspectives from the Napoleonic Era through the First Gilded Age*. Anthem Press, 2020.

446

REFERENCES

8 Globalization

8.2 Disarticulation goes North
Wojciech Kopczuk, Joel Slemrod, and Shlomo Yitzhaki, "The Limitations of Decentralized World Redistribution: An Optimal Taxation Approach," *European Economic Review*, 49, 2005: 1051–1079.

Annie Lowrey, "No, Depressed American Towns Do Not Look Like Zimbabwe," *Intelligencer*, October 5, 2015. https://nymag.com /intelligencer/2015/10/free-trade-didnt-turn-america-into-zimbabwe.html

Branko Milanovic, *Global Inequality*. Harvard University Press, 2016.

Paul Theroux, "The Hypocrisy of 'Helping' the Poor," *New York Times*, October 4, 2015. https://www.nytimes.com/2015/10/04/opinion/sunday /the-hypocrisy-of-helping-the-poor.html?_r=0

8.3 Let's go back to mercantilism and trade blocs!
Rana Faroohar, *Homecoming: The Path to Prosperity in a Post-Global World*. Penguin Random House, 2022.

Rana Faroohar, "Free Trade Has not Made us Free," *Financial Times*, October 17, 2022.

Christoph Lakner and Branko Milanovic, "Global Income Distribution: From the Fall of the Berlin Wall to the Great Recession," *World Bank Economic Review*, 30 (2), July 2016: 203–232.

8.6 No one would be unemployed and no one would hold a job
Steven Hill, *Raw Deal: How the 'Uber Economy' and Runaway Capitalism Are Screwing American Workers*. St. Martin's Griffin, 2017.

Thomas Piketty, *Capital in the 21st Century*. Harvard University Press, 2014.

9 China

9.1 Socialism with Chinese characteristics for the young person: A review of the book of Xi Jinping's sayings
Anecdotes and Sayings of Xi Jinping. People's Publishing House, 2017. http://www.china.org.cn/m/english/china_key_words/2017-06/19/content _41055520.html

9.2 The long NEP, China, and Xi
Giovanni Arrighi, *Adam Smith in Beijing: Lineages of the 21st Century*. Verso, 2009.

Jacques Gernet, *Daily Life in China on the Eve of the Mongol Invasion, 1250–1276*. Stanford University Press, 1962.

Ho-fung Hung, *The China Boom: Why China Will not Rule the World*. Columbia University Press, 2017.

447

REFERENCES

Martin Jacques, *When China Rules the World: The End of the Western World and the Birth of a New Global Order*. Penguin Press, 2009.

Branko Milanovic, *Capitalism, Alone*. Harvard University Press, 2019.

Kenneth Pomeranz, *The Great Divergence, China, Europe, and the Making of the Modern World Economy*. Princeton University Press, 2021. Originally published in 2001.

Edward Wolff, *A Century of Wealth in America*. Harvard University Press, 2017.

Li Yang, Filip Novokmet and Branko Milanovic, "From Workers to Capitalists in Less than Two Generations: A Study of Chinese Urban Elite Transformation between 1988 and 2013," *British Journal of Sociology*, 72 (3), June 2021: 478–513. https://onlinelibrary.wiley.com/doi/abs/10.1111/1468-4446.12850

9.3 Hayekian communism

Pablo Neruda, *Memoirs*. Farrar, Straus and Giroux, 2001.

"Peking University Threatens to Close Down Marxism Society," *Financial Times*, September 23, 2018.

9.4 *The World Turned Upside Down*: A critical review

Yang Jisheng, *The World Turned Upside Down: A History of the Chinese Cultural Revolution*. Farrar, Straus and Giroux, 2021.

9.5 License to kill: *The World Turned Upside Down*: A laudatory review

Yang Jisheng, *The World Turned Upside Down: A History of the Chinese Cultural Revolution*. Farrar, Straus and Giroux, 2021.

Roy Medvedev, *Let History Judge*. Columbia University Press, 1989. Originally published in 1972.

9.6 Interpreting or misinterpreting China's success

Yuen Yuen Ang, *China's Gilded Age: The Paradox of Economic Boom and Vast Corruption*. Cambridge University Press, 2020.

Loren Brandt and Barbara Sands, "Beyond Malthus and Ricardo: Economic Growth, Land Concentration, and Income Distribution in Early Twentieth-Century Rural China," *Journal of Economic History*, December 1990: 807–827.

Loren Brandt and Thomas G. Rawski, "China's Great Boom as a Historic Process," IZA Institute of Labor Economics, Discussion Paper, December 2020.

Lin Chen, *Revolution and Counterrevolution in China*. Verso, 2021.

Julian Gewirtz, *Unlikely Partners: Chinese Reformers, Western Economists, and the Making of Global China*. Harvard University Press, 2017.

Chang-Tai Hsieh and Zheng (Michael) Song, "Grasp the Large, Let Go of the Small: The Transformation of the State Sector in China," *Brooking Papers on Economic Activity*, 2015.

REFERENCES

Debin Ma and Richard von Glahn (eds.), *The Cambridge Economic History of China*, vol. 2. Cambridge University Press, 2022.

Branko Milanovic, *Capitalism, Alone*. Harvard University Press, 2019.

Thomas G. Rawski, *Economic Growth in Prewar China*. University of California, 1989.

Isabella Weber, *How China Escaped Shock Therapy: The Market Reform Debate*, Studies on the Chinese Economy. Routledge, 2021.

Li Yang, Branko Milanovic, and Filip Novokmet, "From Workers to Capitalists in Less than Two Generations: A Study of Chinese Urban Elite Transformation between 1988 and 2013," *British Journal of Sociology*, 72 (3), June 2021: 478–513.

Shunlin Zhang, "How Much Do State-Owned Enterprises Contribute to China's GDP and Employment?," World Bank, July 15, 2019. https://openknowledge.worldbank.org/server/api/core/bitstreams/23b90089-290e-5afc-a1e8-6a56d41cb96f/content

10 Russia

10.3 The novelty of technologically regressive import substitution

"Стадия окрыления" ("The fledgling state"), *Kommersant*, April 28, 2022. https://www.kommersant.ru/doc/5329222

10.4 Russia's economic prospects: The short-run

Branko Milanovic, *Income, Inequality, and Poverty during the Transition from Planned to Market Economy*. Washington, D.C.: World Bank, 1998.

10.5 Long term: Difficulties of import substitution and delocalization

"Ничего не конфисковано, но все арестовано" ("Nothing confiscated, but everything frozen"), *Novaya Gazeta*, 26, March 14, 2022. https://novayagazeta.ru/articles/2022/03/11/nichego-ne-konfiskovano-no-vse-arestovano

"Embraer: Brazil's Pioneering Aviation Giant," WIPO Magazine, December 2017. https://www.wipo.int/wipo_magazine/en/2017/06/article_0003.html

Branko Milanovic, "Preface to the Russian edition of *Global Inequality*," Глобальное неравенство. Instutut Gaidara, 2019. https://glineq.blogspot.com/2016/12/preface-to-russian-edition-of-global.html

10.6 What if Putin's true goals are different?

Branko Milanovic, "Nations, Conglomerates, and Empires: The Trade-off between Income and Sovereignty," in Dominick Salvatore, Marijan Svetličič, and Jože Damijan (eds.), *Small Countries in a Global Economy: New Challenges and Opportunities*. Palgrave, 2000, pp. 25–70. Earlier version as World Bank PRE Working Papers Series, No. 1675, October

REFERENCES

1996. https://stonecenter.gc.cuny.edu/research/nations-conglomerates
-empires-the-trade-off-between-income-and-sovereignty/

11 Economic History

11.1 Byzantium: Economic reflections on the Fall of Constantinople
David Landes, *The Wealth and Poverty of Nations.* W. W. Norton, 1988.
Michael Rostovtzeff, *The Social and Economic History of the Roman Empire.* Oxford University Press. Originally published in 1926.
Peer Vries, *Escaping Poverty: The Origins of Modern Economic Growth.* Vienna University Press, 2013.
Leif Wenar and Branko Milanovic, "Are Liberal Peoples Peaceful?," *Journal of Political Philosophy,* 17 (4), July 2009: 462–486.

11.2 Global poverty over the long term: Legitimate issues
Robert Allen, "Absolute Poverty: When Necessity Displaces Desire," *American Economic Review,* 107 (12), December 2017: 3690–3721.
François Bourguignon and Christian Morrisson, "Inequality among World Citizens: 1820–1992," *American Economic Review,* 92 (4), September 2002: 727–744.
Jerry Coyne, "Is the World Really Getting Poorer? A Response by Steve Pinker." https://whyevolutionistrue.com/2019/01/31/is-the-world-really -getting-poorer-a-response-to-that-claim-by-steve-pinker/
Angus Deaton, "Measuring Poverty in a Growing World (or Measuring Growth in a Poor World)," *Review of Economics and Statistics,* 87 (1), February 2005.
Joe Hassell and Max Rosen, "How do we Know the History of Extreme Poverty?" https://ourworldindata.org/extreme-history-methods
Jason Hickel, "A Letter to Steven Pinker about Global Poverty." https:// www.resilience.org/stories/2019-02-04/a-letter-to-steven-pinker-about -global-poverty/
The Maddison Project, Groningen Growth and Development Centre, Faculty of Economics and Business. https://www.rug.nl/ggdc/historicaldevelopment /maddison/?lang=en
Branko Milanovic, "A Short History of Global Inequality: The Past Two Centuries," *Explorations in Economic History,* 48, November 2011: 494–506.
Steve Pinker, "A Response from Steve Pinker to Salon's Hit Piece on *Enlightenment Now.*" https://whyevolutionistrue.com/2019/01/29 /a-response-from-steve-pinker-to-salons-hit-piece-on-enlightenment-now/
Thomas Pogge and Sanjay Reddy, "How Not to Count the Poor," SSRN Paper October 29, 2005. https://papers.ssrn.com/sol3/papers.cfm?abstract _id=893159
Jan-Luiten van Zanden, Joerg Baten, Peter Foldvari, and Bas van Leeuwen

REFERENCES

(2014), "The Changing Shape of Global Inequality, 1820–2000: Exploring the New Dataset," *Review of Income and Wealth*, 60 (2), June: 279–297.

11.3 On Eurocentrism in economics

Daron Acemoglu and James Robinson, *Why Nations Fail: The Origins of Power, Prosperity, and Poverty*. Crown, 2013.

Robert Allen, *Global Economic History: A Very Short Introduction*. Oxford University Press, 2011.

Paul Bairoch, *Victoires et déboires, Histoire économique et sociale du monde du XVe siècle à nos jours*, vols. 1 and 2. Gallimard, 1997.

Colin Clark, *The Conditions of Economic Progress*. Macmillan, 1940.

Sebastian Conrad, *What Is Global History?* Princeton University Press, 2017.

David Landes, *Wealth and Poverty of Nations, Why Some Are So Rich and Some So Poor*. W.W. Norton, 1999.

Angus Maddison, *Contours of the World Economy, 1–2030 AD: Essays in Macro-Economic History*. Oxford University Press, 2007.

Pankaj Mishra, *From the Ruins of Empire: The Revolt Against the West and the Remaking of Asia*. Picador. 2013.

Peer Vries, *Escaping Poverty: The Origins of Modern Economic Growth*. Vienna University Press, 2013.

11.4 Net economic output in history: Why we work

Diane Coyle, *GDP: A Brief but Affectionate History*. Princeton University Press, 2015.

Moshe Syrquin, "A Review Essay on *GDP: A Brief but Affectionate History* by Diane Coyle," *Journal of Economic Literature*, 54 (2), June 2016: 573–588.

Some suggested readings on Physiocrats:

Marguerite Kuczynski and Ronald L. Meek (edited with new material, translations and notes), *Quesnay's "Tableau économique."* Macmillan for the Royal Economic Society and the American Economic Association, 1972. (*Le Tableau* in all its grandeur and complexity with the commentary.)

Ronald L. Meek (ed.), *Economics of Physiocracy*. Routledge, 1962. (A standard reference text with translation of selected writings, including *Le Tableau économique* and brilliant introduction by the editor.)

Gianni Vaggi, *The Economics of François Quesnay*. Duke University Press, 1987. (Excellent and sophisticated analysis of the physiocracy enlightened by Sraffianism.)

Georges Weulersse, *Le movement physiocratique en France, de 1750 à 1770*. Maison des Sciences de Homme, Editions Mouton, 1910. http://archive.org/details/lemouvementphysi01weuluoft (A monumental two-volume discussion of the intellectual milieu before the Revolution, within which Physiocrats grew, their rise and fall, and their ideology.)

451

REFERENCES

11.5 Capital as a historical concept
Mauricio de Rosa, "Essays on Capital and Inequality in Latin America," Ph.D. dissertation presented at the Paris School of Economics, December 2022.

11.6 The plight of late industrializers: What if peasants do not want to move to cities?
Francis Fukuyama, *Political Order and Political Decay: From the Industrial Revolution to the Globalization of Democracy*. Farrar, Straus and Giroux, 2014.
Boško Mijatović and Branko Milanovic, "Real Urban Wage in an Agricultural Economy Without Landless Farmers: Serbia, 1862–1910," *Economic History Review*, 74 (2), 2021: 424–448.

11.7 Can Black Death explain the Industrial Revolution?
Daron Acemoglu and James Robinson, *Why Nations Fail The Origins of Power, Prosperity, and Poverty*. Crown, 2013.
Robert Allen, "The Great Divergence in European Wages and Prices from the Middle Ages to the First World War," *Explorations in Economic History*, 38, 2001: 411–447.
Robert Allen, "Progress and Poverty in Early Modern Europe," *Economic History Review*, 56 (3), August 2003: 403–443.
Robert Allen, "Real Wages in Europe and Asia: A First Look at the Long-Term Patterns," in Robert C. Allen, Tommy Bengtsson, and Martin Dribe (eds.), *Living Standards in the Past: New Perspectives on Well-Being in Asia and Europe*. Oxford University Press, 2005.
Mattia Fochesato, "Origins of Europe's North–South Divide: Population Changes, Real Wages and the 'Little Divergence' in Early Modern Europe," *Explorations in Economic History*, October 2018: 91–131.
David Landes, *Wealth and Poverty of Nations, Why Some Are So Rich and Some So Poor*. W.W. Norton, 1999.
Orhan Pamuk, "The Black Death and the of the 'Great Divergence' across Europe, 1300–1600," *European Review of Economic History*, 11 (3), December 2007: 289–317.
Kenneth Pomeranz, *The Great Divergence: China, Europe, and the Making of the Modern World Economy*. Princeton University Press, 2001.

11.8 Why were the Balkans underdeveloped? A geographical hypothesis
Angus Maddison, *Contours of the World Economy, 1–2030 AD: Essays in Macro-Economic History*. Oxford University Press, 2007.
Branko Milanovic, "Income Level and Income Inequality in the Euro-Mediterranean Region, *c.* 14–700," *Review of Income and Wealth*, March 2019: 1–20.
Andrew Wilson, "City Sizes and Urbanization in the Roman Empire," in

REFERENCES

Adam Bowman and Andrew Wilson (eds.), *Settlement, Urbanization, and Population*. Oxford University Press, 2018, pp. 160–195.

Ludger Woessmann and Sascha O. Becker, "How the Long-Gone Habsburg Empire is still Visible in Eastern European Bureaucracies Today," EUVox, May 31, 2011. https://cepr.org/voxeu/columns/how-long-gone-habsburg-empire-still-visible-eastern-european-bureaucracies-today

12 Adam Smith

12.1 Through the glass, darkly: Trying to figure out Adam Smith, the person

Branko Milanovic, *Visions of Inequality: From the French Revolution to the End of the Cold War*. Harvard University Press, 2023.

Dennis C. Rasmussen, *The Infidel and the Professor: David Hume, Adam Smith, and the Friendship that Shaped Modern Thought*. Princeton University Press, 2017.

12.2 America's Adam Smith: A review of Glory M. Liu's *Adam Smith's America*

Glory Liu, *Adam Smith's America: How a Scottish Philosopher Became an Icon of American Capitalism*. Princeton University Press, 2022.

12.3 People, associations, and government policy in Adam Smith

Adam Smith [1776], *The Wealth of Nations*, edited with notes and marginal summary by Edwin Cannan; preface by Alan B. Krueger. Bantam Classics, 2003.

Adam Smith, *Lectures on Jurisprudence*, Part II, University of Life Library, Carlile Media, 2017. From the first edition Clarendon Press, Oxford 1896 (first publication). Lectures were delivered in 1762–1763.

Adam Smith [1759], *The Theory of Moral Sentiments*, printout.

12.4 Is democracy always better for the poor?

Thomas Hauner, Branko Milanovic, and Suresh Naidu, "Inequality, Foreign Investment and Imperialism," Munich Personal RePEc Archive (MPRA) Working Paper 83068, November 2017. https://papers.ssrn.com/sol3/papers.cfm?abstract_id=3089701

Adam Smith [1776], *The Wealth of Nations*, edited with notes and marginal summary by Edwin Cannan; preface by Alan B. Krueger. Bantam Classics, 2003.

12.5 Why slave-owners never willingly emancipated their slaves

Adam Smith, *Lectures on Jurisprudence*, edited by R. L. Meek, D. D. Raphael and P. G, Stein, Liberty Fund; reproduction of the Oxford University Press edition from 1978. (Includes notes of lectures given at University of Glasgow in 1762–1763: LoJ(A) and LoJ(B).)

453

REFERENCES

Barry Weingast, "Persistent Inefficiency: Adam Smith's Theory of Slavery and Its Abolition in Western Europe," December 2016. https://papers.ssrn .com/sol3/papers.cfm?abstract_id=2635917

12.6 How Adam Smith proposed to have his cake and eat it too
Adam Smith, *The Theory of Moral Sentiments*, printout. Originally published in 1759.
David Wootton, *Power, Pleasure and Profit: Insatiable Appetites from Machiavelli to Madison*. Harvard University Press, 2018.

13 Ricardo and Marx

13.1 Ricardo, Marx, and interpersonal inequality
Robert Allen, "Capital Accumulation, Technological Change and the Distribution of Income during the British Industrial Revolution," Economics Series Working Papers 239. University of Oxford, Department of Economics, 2005.
Peter Lindert and Jeffrey Williamson, "Reinterpreting Britain's Social Tables 1688–1913," *Explorations in Economic History*, 20, 1983: 94–109.
Karl Marx, *Capital*, vol. I, translated by Ben Fowkes; Introduction by Ernest Mandel. Penguin Books, 1978.
Karl Marx, *Theories of Surplus Value*, vol. 32 of the *Collected Works*.
David Ricardo, *The Principles of Political Economy and Taxation*. Dover Publications, 2004.
Roman Rosdolsky, *The Making of Marx's 'Capital'*, translated by Pete Burgess. Pluto Press, 1977. Originally published in German in 1968.

13.2 Reading David Ricardo's letters
David Ricardo, *The Works and Correspondence of David Ricardo*, edited by Pierro Sraffa with the collaboration of M. H. Dobb, vol. VII, *Letters, 1816–1818*. Cambridge University Press, 1952, p. 78.
David Ricardo, *Letters of David Ricardo to Hutches Trower and others, 1811–1823*. Elibron Classics, 2006; facsimile reprint of the 1899 edition by Clarendon Press, Oxford.

13.3 The Ricardian windfall: David Ricardo and the absence of the equity-efficiency trade-off
Robert Allen, *The Industrial Revolution: A Very Short Introduction*. Oxford University Press, 2017.
David Ricardo, *The Principles of Political Economy and Taxation*. Dover Publications, 2004.

13.4 The influence of Karl Marx—a counterfactual
Leszek Kolakowski, *Main Currents of Marxism: The Founders*, translated

REFERENCES

by P. S. Falla. Oxford University Press, 1978. Originally published in Polish in 1976.

Peter Singer, "Is Marx Still Relevant?," Project Syndicate, May 1, 2018. https://www.project-syndicate.org/commentary/karl-marx-200th-birthday -by-peter-singer-2018-05

"The Young Karl Marx" ("Le jeune Karl Marx"), a film directed by Raoul Peck, 2017. Trailer at https://www.imdb.com/title/tt1699518/

13.5 Marx for me (and hopefully for others too)

Moses Finley, *Ancient Slavery and Modern Ideology*. Viking Press, 1980.

Branko Milanovic, *Capitalism, Alone*. Harvard University Press, 2019.

Thomas Piketty, *Top Incomes in France in the Twentieth Century: Inequality and Redistribution, 1901–1998*, translated by Seth Ackerman. Harvard University Press, 2018. Originally published in French in 2001.

Javier Rodriguez Weber, *Desarrollo y desigualdad en Chile (1850–2009): Historia de su economía política*. Centro de Investigaciones Diego Barros Araña, 2018.

13.6 Marx on income inequality under capitalism

Shlomo Avineri, *The Social and Political Thought of Karl Marx*. Cambridge University Press, 1968.

Leszek Kolakowski, *Main Currents of Marxism: The Founders*, translated by P. S. Falla. Oxford University Press, 1978. Originally published in Polish in 1976.

Karl Marx, *Critique of the Gotha Program*, part I (1875), in Karl Marx and Friedrich Engels, *Selected Works*, vol. 3. Progress, 1970, pp. 13–30. https://www.marxists.org/archive/marx/works/download/Marx_Critque _of_the_Gotha_Programme.pdf

Allen W. Wood, "Marx on Equality," in *The Free Development of Each: Studies on Freedom, Right, and Ethics in Classical German Philosophy*. Oxford University Press, 2014. https://oxford.universitypressscholarship .com/view/10.1093/acprof:oso/9780199685530.001.0001/acprof -9780199685530-chapter-11

13.7 Transcending capitalism: Three different ways?

Branko Milanovic, "The 'Crisis of Capitalism' is not the one Europeans think it is," *Guardian*, November 27, 2019. https://www.theguardian .com/commentisfree/2019/nov/27/crisis-of-capitalism-europeans-gig -economy

Branko Milanovic, *Capitalism, Alone*. Harvard University Press, 2018.

Thomas Piketty, *Capital and Ideology*, translated by Arthur Goldhammer. Harvard University Press, 2018. Originally published in French in 2017.

John Roemer, "What is Socialism Today?: Conceptions of a Cooperative Economy," March 2, 2020. https://politicalscience.yale.edu/sites/default /files/2020-03-03-what.is_.socialism.pdf

REFERENCES

The debate: Thomas Piketty vs. Frédéric Lordon. *Journal l'Humanité*, 2019. https://www.youtube.com/watch?v=dDY3aczWOd0

13.8 On unproductive labor
"How Venezuela Fell into a Crisis and What Could Happen Next," *New York Times,* May 27, 2016.
Jagdish Bhagwati, *Why Growth Matters*, Public Affairs, 2014.

13.9 When Tocqueville and Marx agreed
Karl Marx, *The Eighteenth Brumaire of Louis Napoleon*, translated by D. L., September 1897. Originally published in 1852.
Karl Marx (no date), *Class Struggles in France 1848–1850*. New World Publishers. Originally published in 1850; recollected and republished by Engels in 1895.
Alexis de Tocqueville, *Souvenirs*. Gallimard, 1978. Originally published in French in 1893.

13.10 A short essay on the differences between Marx and Keynes
Carolina Alves, "Joan Robinson on Karl Marx: 'His Sense of Reality Is Far Stronger'," *Journal of Economic Literature*, 36 (2), Spring 2022: 247–264.
John Maynard Keynes, *The General Theory of Employment, Interest and Money*. Houghton Mifflin Harcourt, 2016. Originally published in 1936.
Karl Marx, *Capital,* vol. III, translated by David Fernbach; Introduction by Ernest Mandel. Penguin Books, reprinted 1991.
Joan Robinson, *Essai sur l'économie de Marx,* Preface et traduction de Ulysse Lojkine, Editions Sociales, 2022. Originally published in English in 1942.

13.11 Marx in Amerika
Daniel Markovits, *The Meritocracy Trap*. Penguin Press, 2019.
Bhashkar Mazumdar, "Intergenerational Mobility in the United States: What We Have Learned from the PSID," *The Annals of The American Academy of Political and Social Science*, 690 (1), 2018. https://journals.sagepub.com/doi/full/10.1177/0002716218794129
Stefan Zweig, *The World of Yesterday*. University of Nebraska Press, 1964.

14 Communism

14.1 A secular religion that lasted one century
Daron Acemoglu and James Robinson, *Economic Origins of Dictatorship and Democracy*. Cambridge University Press, 2009.

REFERENCES

14.2 State capitalism one hundred years ago and today
Vladimir Ilych Lenin, *Lenin's Final Fight: Speeches and Writings, 1922–1923*. Pathfinder Press, 2010.
Branko Milanovic, *Visions of Inequality*. Harvard University Press, 2023.
Li Yang, Filip Novokmet, and Branko Milanovic, "From Workers to Capitalists in Less than Two Generations: A Study of Chinese Urban Elite Transformation between 1988 and 2013," *British Journal of Sociology*, 72 (3), June 2021: 478–513. https://onlinelibrary.wiley.com/doi/abs/10.1111/1468-4446.12850

14.3 Milton Friedman and labor-managed enterprises
Milton Friedman, Report on Yugoslavia and Italy, April 13, 1973. Hoover Institution Library Archives. https://miltonfriedman.hoover.org/objects/52216/report-on-yugoslavia-and-italy
Susan Woodward, *Balkan Tragedy: Chaos and Dissolution after the Cold War*. Brookings Institution Press, 1995.

Here is selection, in my opinion, of some important books and papers on labor-managed enterprise and labor-managed economy. It is provided as a background to this and several other pieces in this chapter. Most of the readings do not deal with specifically Yugoslav issues but with general theoretical features of a labor-managed market economy.
Abram Bergson, "Market Socialism Revisited," *Journal of Political Economy*, 75 (5), October 1967: 655–673.
Michael Conte, "On the Economic Theory of the Labor-Managed Firm in the Short Run," *Journal of Comparative Economics*, 4 (2), June 1980: 173–183.
Dinko Dubravčić, "Labor as an Entrepreneurial Input: An Essay in the Theory of the Producer Co-operative Economy," *Economica*, 37, August 1970: 297–310.
Eirik Furubotn, "The Long-Run Analysis of the Labor-Managed Firm: An Alternative Interpretation," *American Economic Review*, 66 (1), March 1976: 104–123.
Branko Horvat, *The Political Economy of Socialism: A Marxist Social Theory*. Routledge, 1983.
Branko Horvat, "Critical Notes on the Theory of the Labor-Managed Firm and Some Macro-Economic Implications," *Economic Analysis*, 1972.
James Meade, "The Theory of Labor-Managed Firms and Profit Sharing," *Economic Journal*, 82, March 1972: 402–428.
Branko Milanovic, "The Austrian Theory of the Labor Managed Firm," *Journal of Comparative Economics*, 6, 1982: 379–395.
Jaroslav Vanek, *The General Theory of Labor-Managed Market Economies*. Cornell University Press, 1970.
Benjamin Ward, "The Firm in Illyria: Market Syndicalism," *American Economic Review*, 48 (4), September 1958: 556–589.

REFERENCES

14.5 Disciplining workers in a workers' state
Fritz Bartel, *The Triumph of Broken Promises: The End of the Cold War and the Rise of Neoliberalism*. Harvard University Press, 2022.

14.7 The red bourgeoisie
Milomir Marić, *Deca komunizma I – Magle sa istoka*. Laguna, 2004. Originally published in Serbian in 1987.
Yuri Slezkine, *The House of Government: A Saga of the Russian Revolution*. Princeton University Press, 2017.
Tereza Torańska, *"Them": Stalin's Polish Puppets*. Harper and Row, 1987. Originally published in Polish in 1986.

14.8 On charisma and greyness under communism
David Halberstam, *The Best and the Brightest*. Ballantine Books, anniversary edition, 1993. Originally published in 1963.

14.9 Trotsky after Kolakowski
Leszek Kolakowski, *Main Currents of Marxism: The Founders*, translated by P. S. Falla. Oxford University Press, 1978. Originally published in Polish in 1976.
Junya Takiguchi, "Projecting Bolshevik Unity, Ritualizing Party Debate: The Thirteenth Party Congress, 1924," *Acta Slavica Iaponica*, 31, 2012: 55–76.

14.10 Notes on Fanon
Frantz Fanon, *The Wretched of the Earth*, translated by Constance Farrington. Penguin Classics, 2001. Originally published in French in 1961.
Branko Milanovic, *Global Inequality: A New Approach for the Age of Globalization*. Harvard University Press, 2018.
Barack Obama, "President Obama Gives Speech Addressing Europe, Russia," *Washington Post*, March 26, 2014. https://www.washingtonpost.com /world/transcript-president-obama-gives-speech-addressing-europe-russia -on-march-26/2014/03/26/07ae80ae-b503-11e3-b899-20667de76985 _story.html

14.11 The book of the dead: Victor Serge's *Notebooks 1936–1947*
André Gide, *Le retour de l'URSS*. Gallimard Education, 2009. Originally published in 1936.
Victor Serge, *Notebooks: 1936–1947*, *New York Review of Books: Classics*, 2019.

14.12 Did socialism keep capitalism equal?
André Albuquerque Sant'Anna, "A Spectre Has Haunted the West: Did Socialism Discipline Income Inequality?," Munich Personal RePEc Archive, April 20, 2015. https://mpra.ub.uni-muenchen.de/64756/1/MPRA_paper _64756.pdf

REFERENCES

André Albuquerque Sant'Anna and Leonardo Weller, "The Threat of Communism during Cold War: A Constraint to Income Inequality," *Anais do XLIV Encontro Nacional de Economia* [Proceedings of the 44th Brazilian Economics Meeting), 2018.

Branko Milanovic, *Global Inequality: A New Approach for the Age of Globalization*. Harvard University Press, 2018.

Jomo Kwame Sundaram and Vladimir Popov, "Income Inequalities in Perspective," Initiative for Policy Dialogue, International Labour Office, ESS Document No. 46, 2015. https://www.networkideas.org/featart/may2015/pdf/Income_Inequalities.pdf

14.14 Did post-Marxist theories destroy communist regimes?
Wisła Suraska, *How the Soviet Union Disappeared*. Duke University Press, 1998.

15 Transition to Capitalism

15.2 Secessionism and the collapse of communist federations
Richard Pipes, *The Russian Revolution*. Vintage, 1991.
Vladislav Zubok, *Collapse: The Fall of the Soviet Union*. Yale University Press, 2022.

15.4 Trump and Gorbachev
Veljko Mićunović, *Moskovske godine*. Liber, 1978.

16 Reflections

16.2 The perverse seductiveness of Fernando Pessoa
Constantine Cavafy, *Selected Poems*, translated by Ari Sharon. Penguin Classics, 2008.
Fernando Pessoa, *Le banquier anarchiste*, translated by Joaquim Vital. Difference, 2017.

16.4 The mistake of using the Kantian criterion in ordinary economic life
John Roemer, *How We Cooperate: A Theory of Kantian Optimization*. Yale University Press, 2019.
Amartya Sen, *On Economic Inequality* (Radcliffe Lectures). Clarendon Press, 1997. Originally published in 1972.

16.5 Is liberal democracy part of human development?
Leandro Prados de la Escosura, *Human Development and the Path to Freedom: 1870 to the Present* (New Approaches to Economic and Social History). Cambridge University Press, 2022.

REFERENCES

16.6 Living in own ideology ... until it falls apart
John Williamson, "A Short History of the Washington Consensus," Peterson Institute for International Economics, September 24, 2004. https:// www.piie.com/commentary/speeches-papers/short-history-washington -consensus

16.7 Freedom to be "wrong": The greatest advantage of democracy
N. S. Lyons, "Poland and the Demon in Democracy: Liberal Authoritarianism's Tusks have been Bared across the West." https://theupheaval.substack .com/p/poland-and-the-demon-in-democracy?r=7ihg4&utm_medium=ios &utm_campaign=post

16.9 On the general futility of political discussions with people
Stephen Benko, *Pagan Rome and the Early Christians*. Indiana University Press, 1984.

16.10 The many in one: A review of Amartya Sen's *Home in the World: A Memoir*
Nirad Chaudhuri, *The Autobiography of an Unknown Indian, New York Review of Books: Classics*, 2001. Originally published in 1951.
Nirad Chaudhuri, *Thy Hand, Great Anarch!: India 1921–1952*. Addison-Wesley Publishing Company, 1987.
Amartya Sen, *Home in the World: A Memoir*. Allen Lane, 2021.

16.12 English language and American solipsism
Simon Kuper, "The Problem with English," *Financial Times*, January 11, 2017.
Philippe Van Parijs, *Linguistic Justice for Europe and for the World*. Oxford University Press, 2011.

16.13 The problems of authenticity under capitalism
Franz Kafka, *The Diaries of Franz Kafka*. Schocken Kafka Library, 2023.
Branko Milanovic, *Capitalism, Alone*. Harvard University Press, 2019.

16.15 Who are we?
Franz Kafka, *The Diaries of Franz Kafka*. Schocken Kafka Library, 2023.
Julio Cortazar, Amor 77 in *Un tal Lucas*, 1979. https://ciudadseva.com/texto /amor-77/.
Yonatan Berman and Branko Milanovic, "Homoploutia: Top Labor and Capital Incomes in the United States, 1950–2020," *Review of Income and Wealth*, August 2023.

INDEX

Page numbers in *italics* refer to figures.

Abrahamian, A. 91
abundance
  and climate change 22–24
  of goods and services 415–418
accidents of birth 279–280
Acemoglu, D. and Robinson, J.
  264, 339
Adams, J. 153, 154
Aelius Aristides 420
Africa 14
  clientelism 58
  decolonization 367, 368
  foreign aid 134–137
  global inequality 117–118,
    120–121, 125, 128, 131
  growth and climate change
    16–18
  migration 26–27, 28, 30
  population growth 35, 86,
    117–118
  research 74–75, 120–121
  trade 247–248
  US domestic poverty and
    183–184
Africans: day and night worlds
  38–39
agency, freedom and democracy
  407–408

agriculture vs. manufacturing
  255–256, 261–263
air transportation 11–12
aircraft industry, Russia 228–229,
  236
Akhmatova, A. 370
Alesina, A. and Spolaore, E.
  40–41
Alhuwalia, M. 120
alienation 320
Allen, B. 251, 264, 265, 301,
  308–309
Allen, R. 252–253
Alliluyeva, S. 65
altruism and self-interest 402–404,
  405
America
  and Marx 335–337
  and Smith 274–277
  see also US
America First policy 70–71
American-English colonialism
  288–290
Amin, S. 117, 183
The Anarchist Banker (Pessoa)
  397–398
Andropov, Y. 377, 379, 384
"animal spirits" 334

INDEX

Anna Karenina (Tolstoy) 167–168, 171
Aristotle 184
arts and literature: authenticity problem 431–432, 436–437
Asian countries, economic rise of 117, 188
asset seizure 225–227, 388, 389
association, freedoms of speech and 45
associations, skepticism towards 278, 280–284
Athenian dialogues on global income inequality 123–126
Atkinson, T. 88, 100, 316
Aung San Suu Kyi 425
Austen, J. 166–167, 171, 172, 174, 175, 176
Austria 28, 311
Austria-Hungary 311
authenticity
in arts and literature 431–432, 436–437
of needs 93, 94
autocratic vs. democratic states, slavery in 289–290, 291–292
Avineri, S. 320

Bairoch, P. 17
Balkan underdevelopment: geographical hypothesis 266–269
Balzac, H. de 168, 169, 171, 174
bandits, roving vs. stationary 69
Bartel, F. 351
Basu, K. 64, 65–66
Bauer, P. 134
Becker, G. 97
Belgium and North Korea: sovereignty vs. income 239–240
Berezovsky, B. 225
Berman, Y. and Milanovic, B. 335
Bezos, J. 142

billionaires/millionaires 142, 161, 162, 225–256
China 207, 225
Davos 151–2
luxury consumption 153–155
modes of wealth acquisition 147–150
Russian oligarchs 66, 142, 149, 225–227, 388–389
Black Death and Industrial Revolution 264–265
Black Lives Matter 7, 410
Blair, T. 62
Bombacci, N. 371–372
Bosnia 382
bourgeoisie *see* middle class/ bourgeoisie
Bourguignon, F. and Morrison, C. (B–M) 250, 251
Brandt, L. 217
and Rawski, T. (B–R) 217–221
Braudel, F. and Mayer, J.P. 328–329
Brazil 128, 156, 236
Brest–Litovsk treaty, new 241–242
Breton, A. 370
Brexit 112–113
Brezhnevite period, USSR 223, 378–379
Bulgaria 28, 113, 261
Byzantium: Fall of Constantinople 245–457

cabal, world rule by 54–55
Cambridge Controversy 258
Cannan, E. 31
"capabilities approach" 319
capital, as historical concept 258–260
capital and labor
in advanced economies 335–336
distinguishing incomes from 101–103
economic crises 332–333
"human capital wealth" accounting 156–157

462

INDEX

impact of globalization 317
inequality 86, 87–88
relative scarcities of 323–234
capitalist groups 281–282
influence on government policies
284–286
capitalists, workers and landlords
299–300, 304, 308–309
cash vs. non-cash incentives 20
Castro, F. 338
Cavafy, C. 397
Ceauşescu, N. 360
Chaudhuri, N. 54, 423
Chicago school 275–276
China
abolition of paper and rule of
present 433–435
covid-related deaths 232
Cultural Revolution 209,
210–112, 213–216
"culture of withdrawal" 306
and East India Company 13,
247–248
and Eastern Roman Empire
246–247
economics, role and definitions of
116–117
global inequality 118, 121, 123,
125
globalization 179, 180
and global labor market 373
Great Leap Forward 209, 212,
251, 402
Hayekian communism 207–209
interpreting or misinterpreting
success 217–221
knowledge creation 73
labor-managed enterprises 350
long New Economic Policy (NEP)
203–206, 343
poverty elimination by "dirty"
growth 21
re-integration into world
economy 86
and Russia 238

technocratic political capitalism
52
and US
GDP per capita, compared 35
share of global GDP 187
Trump 71, 240
see also specific leaders
China Cotton Mill Owners'
Association (1930s) 218
Christiansen, C. 119–120, 121
citizenship and income 127–130,
131–133
premium and penalty 34, 127,
129, 131
civil conflicts and migration 40–42
civil servants 281
class
abolition of 318
analysis 315–316
and "location" inequality 127
revolution 60–1
struggles 117, 328
see also elite/ruling class; middle
class/bourgeoisie
classical definition of economics
115–116
clientelism 58
climate change
abundance, capitalism and 22–24
and behavior change 404
critique of degrowth 3–5, 6–9,
10, 24
doughnut economics 19–21
and global inequality 10–12
North-South effects 16–18
similarities between 138–140
global progressive (GP)
perspective 47–48
globalization thesis 181
Norway as new East India
Company 13–15
Clinton, B. 61, 62, 392
Coase theorem and methodological
nationalism 388–389
Cold War, end of 354, 392

INDEX

Collier, P. 26, 33, 124
colonialism
  Balkans 266–267
  and BLM movement 410
  British 336, 368
  British-American 288–290
  Marx and anti-imperialist
    struggle in Third World
    312–313
  national liberation movements
    and violence 366–367
  post-colonial studies 119,
    253–254
Colquhoun, P. 166, 308–309
commodification/commercialization
  194, 323, 401, 403–404,
  431–432, 436–437
communism 312–313
  charisma and greyness under
    360–362
  and liberal projects 412
  Notebooks (1936–1947) (Serge)
    369–372
  red bourgeoisie 357–359, 426
  as secular religion 338–340
  and state capitalism, past and
    present 341–343
  Trotsky after Kolakowski
    363–365
  and US, comparative wealth
    measurement 163–165
  welfare policies 164–165
  see also China; Eastern Europe;
    labor-managed/self-managed
    enterprises (SMEs); Marx,
    K./Marxism; transition to
    capitalism; USSR/Soviet
    Union; *specific countries and
    individuals*
companies
  environmentally-friendly 19
  structural and technological
    change 104–107
  wealth acquisition 148, 149, 151,
    326

comprador intelligentsia 73–75, 183
conditional convergence 25
Confucius 201
Conrad, S. 252, 253–254
Constantinople, Fall of (1453)
  245–247
consumption
  and emissions 5, 10
  and income measures 158–162
  inequality in communist society
    318–319
  luxury 153–155
  production and 317, 318–320
convergence economics 25, 26, 35,
  123–124, 125–126, 134
  China and India 180
Corbyn, J. 62
Corn Laws 308, 309–310
corruption 71–72, 134, 152, 201,
  221, 232
Cortazar, J. 437
covid pandemic 12, 71, 232
Coyle, D. 256
Coyne, J. 249
Credit Suisse report on global
  distribution of wealth *see*
  Oxfam report
Croatia 113, 247, 267
  flag of "Libertas" 409–410
crony capitalism 286–287
Crusaders 246, 247
Cultural Revolution
  China 210–212, 213–216
  East and West 60–63
  "cultural solipsism" 428–429
cultural/religious heterogeneity,
  effects of 32–33
"culture of withdrawal", China
  306
cultures
  languages and religions,
    disappearance of 26–27
  other 305
Czechoslovakia/Czech Republic 60,
  61, 66, 112

464

INDEX

data-gathering: global inequality
    studies 120–121
Davis, G. 104–106
    and Cobb, J. A. 104
Davos 147, 150, 151–152, 158
day and night worlds 37–39
de Rosa, M 258
Deaton, A. 134, 251
deception and inequality 296–298
decolonization period 366–368
degrowth, critique of 3–5, 6–9, 10,
    24
democracy
    and collapse of Soviet Union
        386–387
        Eastern Europe 381–383
    colonialism and slavery 288–290
    freedom to be "wrong"
        412–414
    illiberal, vs. multi-party
        kleptocracies 57–59
    negative effect of equality on
        83–84
    and neoliberalism 45, 69
    and non-democratic settings 131
    as part of human development
        406–408
    post-Marxist view 379–380
    Russia: counterfactual alternative
        to revolution 262
    social democracy/democratic
        socialism 89, 205, 311, 312,
        318, 371, 374
    vs. autocratic states, slavery in
        289–290, 291–292
    vs. dictatorship 51–53
    workplace 346
Deng Xiaoping 208, 209, 217, 219
dependency theories 17–18
Dickens, C. 169, 174
dictatorship
    no exit 64–66
    vs. democracy 51–53
Diffenbaugh, N. and Burke, M.
    16–17

disappointments and gains of
    globalization 180–181
division of labor 283
Djindjić, Z. 37–8
Djukanović, M. 58, 66
Dobb, M. 303, 424–245
Doriot, J. 371–372
doughnut economics 19–21
Dreiser, T. 174, 175, 176
Dylan, B. 62

East Asia and Russia 237–238
East India Company 247–248
    Dutch and English 288
    Norway as new 13–15
Easterly, B. 134
Eastern Europe 10
    Communist Youth Movement
        61
    EU enlargement 112–114
    "Gorbachevization" 205
    history and nature of 1989
        revolutions 381–383
    immigration 381, 382–383
    negative effect of emigration 33
    productive-unproductive labor
        dichotomy 326
    red bourgeoisie 358
    welfare state 131
Eastern Roman Empire 245–247
economic crises, causes of 332–333
economic growth
    benefits of 278–279
    global progressive (GP)
        perspective 47
    and inequality within nations
        79–81, 83, 84
economic history
    Balkan underdevelopment:
        geographical hypothesis
        266–269
    Black Death and Industrial
        Revolution 264–265
    Byzantium: Fall of
        Constantinople 245–248

INDEX

economic history (*cont.*)
  capital as historical concept
    258–260
  Eurocentrism 252–254
  global poverty 249–251
  Marxist interpretation 312
  net output and net income
    255–257
  plight of late industrializers
    261–263
economic positives and negatives of
  migration 31–33
economics, definitions and role of
  115–118
economists, non-exemplary lives of
  395–396
education
  equalizing quality of schools 88
  graduate 37
  in HDI 406
  influence of Marx 313
  mass 86–87
  and self-awareness 278
  and training: skilled wage 301
  wage inequality and income
    inequality studies 98, 99
election of directors: labor-managed
  enterprises 348–349
elections 57, 58–59, 83–84
  EU parliament 132
  US 45, 132, 402
  voter turnout 132
electronic currencies 19
electronic information 433–435
"elephant graph" 187
elite/ruling class
  China 343
  comprador intelligentsia 73–75,
    183
  red bourgeoisie, Yugoslavia
    357–359, 426
  US 185, 335–337
  and Russia 390–392
Ellul, J. 194–195
emigration, negative effect of 33

emissions 5, 6, 10, 11–12
  see also climate change
empathy/sympathy vs. self-interest
  274, 275–276, 279
employers *see* capitalists
Engels, F. 311, 318
English language speakers 428–430
English literature 167–168, 169,
  171
English/welfarist vs. Italian schools
  measurement of income
  inequality 82–85
entrepreneurs 101, 103, 220–221,
  255
equality between countries: global
  progressive (GP) principle 49
equalization of endowments 87–88,
  91
  vs. redistribution of income 19
equity-efficiency trade-offs, absence
  of 308–310
Erdoğan, R. T. 57, 66
Eurocentrism
  in economics 252–254
  to anti-imperialist struggle in
    Third World 312–313
Europe, post-war 190–191
Europe/EU
  foreign aid to Africa 134
  immigration 28–30
  and India 422–425
  limits of 112–114
  parliament elections 133
  and USSR: view of civil conflict
    40–41
  see also specific countries
exclusion 80–81
"existential" inequality 95–97
exogenous changes 306
"expatriates" 132

fairness/justice and inequality
  within nations 81
famines 251, 262, 402
Fanon, F. 117, 366–368

466

INDEX

Faroohar, R. 187
fascism 371–372
fashion/preferences as exogenous
  change 306
feminist perspective on prostitution
  96–97
Ferreira, F. 104
financial crisis
  global (2007–2008) 313, 321
  Russia (1988–1999) 231–232
financial and industrial capitalism
  101
financial sector
  political lobbying and wealth
  148
  as unproductive labor 325
financialization and amorality:
  globalization thesis 181
financing research 73–75
Finley, M. 317
Fischer, J. 62
Fochesato, M. 264–265
food see Corn Laws; rationing
foreign aid 48
  regressive and progressive
  transfer 134–137
foreign donors/financing research
  73–75
foreign languages 429–430
formal/legal equality 95, 96, 97
Forster, E. M. 169, 175
France 28, 30, 413
  and Germany 40–41
  Gilets Jaunes movement 14, 413
  and Mali 131
  revolution (1789) 331
  revolution (1848) 328–330, 331
  Smith in 271–272
  and Hume in 270
Frankfurt, H. G. 92–94
free trade see trade/free trade
freedom
  augmentation of HDI 406–407
  and democracy 407–408
  from scarcity 397–399

reaching 398–399
  of speech and association 45
  to be "wrong" 412–414
Freeland, C. 187
Friedman, M. 181, 276, 344–346
"friend-shoring" 187, 188
Fukuyama, F. 190, 191–192, 261
functional and interpersonal income
  distribution 299–302,
  308–309

Gates, B. 142, 148, 149, 249
GDP
  estimations/measurement 7, 249,
  250, 256
  per capita
  comparisons 35, 266
  in HDI 406
  Russia 222, 224, 231
  see also global GDP
gender inequality
  prostitution 96–97
  and racial inequality 95–96
Germany 30, 37–38, 62, 66
  East and West 355
  and France 40–41
  social democrats 312
  and sub-Saharan Africa 35
  and US, welfare policies 109–111
  zero net wealth households 159
Gertler, P. 74
Gibbons, E. 267, 428
Gide, A. 370
Gini, C. 82
Gini coefficient 80, 108, 113, 114,
  299–300
  global 4–5
global GDP
  illusion of "degrowth" 3–5, 6
  increasing 19, 26, 181
global governance of climate change
  139
global inequality 117–118
  Athenian dialogues 123–126
  foreign aid 134–137

467

INDEX

global inequality (*cont.*)
history of studies 119–122
see also citizenship and income;
climate change; global
poverty
global influence of Marx 312–313
global neoliberalism 119
global poverty 18, 47–48, 49, 138
economic history 249–251
globalization thesis 179
US domestic and 183–185
see also degrowth, critique of
global progressiveness (GPs)
47–50
globalization 336
dining alone in hyper-competitive
world 193–195
eleven theses on 179–182
and global labor market, China
373
hidden dangers of Fukuyama-like
triumphalism 190–192
impact of technology on labor
196–198
North disarticulation 183–186
return to mercantilism and trade
blocs 187–189
Goldin, C. and Katz, L. 98
goods, buyers and resellers of
subsidized 325–326
goods and services, abundance of
415–416
Gorbachev, M. 223, 359
anti-Gorbachev coup 204
and Clinton 61
collapse of Soviet Union 384,
385, 386
reforms 376–377, 379, 385
and Trump 390–392
"Gorbachevization" 205
Gornick, J. et al. 108
governance, Xi Jinping's theory of
200–201
government
and organized religion 282–283

role and tax-and-transfer policies
87
skeptical approach to role of
281–282
government policies, capitalists'
influence on 284–286
government transfers, post-Second
World War 86
graduate education 37
Gramsci, A. 364
Great Convergence 180
Great Leveling 374
Great War 312
Greece
Athenian dialogues on global
income inequality 123–126
and Balkans 266, 267, 269
and EU 30
late industrialization 261
Greek language 428
greyness under communism 360–362
groundedness, political participation
and 131, 132–133
growth and climate change *see*
climate change
growth incidence curve 309

Habermas, J. 37, 39
Halberstam, D. 360–361
Hamilton, A. 228, 275
happiness 296–298, 326, 398
Hassel, J. and Roser, M. 249
Hauner, T. et al. 289
Hausmann, R. 325–326
Havel, V. 66
"Hayekian communism" 207–209
health in HDI 406
Henry, T. 400, 401
Hickel, J. 10, 249–251
Hill, S. 196, 197–198
Hitler, A. 65
Hochuli, A. and Cunliffe, P. 43
Hong Kong 13
horizontal inequality 95–97
household size 194

INDEX

household surveys 98, 99, 100, 120–121, 127–128
electronic-only data 434–435
Howard's End (Forster) 174, 175
"human capital" approach 301
"human capital wealth" accounting 156–157
human development, democracy as 406–408
Human Development Index (HDI) 406, 407–409
Hume, D.
and Smith 270–271, 272–273
and Rousseau 272
Hungary 28, 61
Huntington, S. 425
hyper-competitiveness and being alone 193–195

identity politics 95, 96, 97
ideology
and change 409–411
global inequality studies 120, 121
neoliberal 413–414
vs. "scientific" perspectives on capitalism 333
illiberal democracies vs. multi-party kleptocracies 57–59
import substitution, Russia 228–230, 235–238
income
Balkan underdevelopment: geographical hypothesis 266, 267
and citizenship *see* citizenship and income
from capital and labor, distinguishing 101–103
vs. sovereignty 239–240
wealth and consumption measurement 158–162
income inequality/distribution
functional and interpersonal/personal 299–302, 308–309
and immigration 90–91

Marx 318–320
Smith 284–286
US 80–81, 104–105, 108–111
and wage inequality studies, difference between 98–100
see also global inequality; global poverty; mean incomes
India 248
and Europe 422–425
globalization 180
Indignados' demonstrations, Spain 38–39
individual and collective values 25, 26–27
individual utility function 82–83
individualism *see* self-interest
industrial and financial capitalism 101
Industrial Revolution 249–250, 251, 252, 253
and Black Death 264–265
Eastern Roman Empire and China 245–247
and rise of Asian countries 117
vs. modernized "putting out" system 106
industrializers, late 261–263
inequality
forms of 397–398
and poverty: globalization thesis 179
within and between countries 127, 138
see also global inequality; global poverty; income inequality/distribution; literature and inequality; wealth inequality
inequality of opportunity 49–50, 84, 129
see also citizenship and income
inequality within nations
distinguishing incomes from capital and labor 101–3
focus on horizontal inequality 95–97

469

INDEX

inequality within nations (*cont.*)
importance of 79–81
limits of Europe 112–114
limits of twentieth-century tools
86–88
role of economics 115–118
social needs 92–94
wage inequality and income
inequality studies, difference
between 98–100
welfare state in age of
globalization 89–91
welfarist vs. Italian measurement
of 82–85
see also US
inflation, Russia 232–233
inheritance of wealth 143–144,
147
marriage and swindle 174–176
tax 88
institutions 317
"background institutions" 318,
320
role of morality in 400–401
intellectual property rights 49
inter-generational mobility 81, 336
international aid *see* foreign aid
International Monetary Fund (IMF)
49, 188, 344, 410
internationalism 45–46
interpersonal and functional
inequality of income
299–302, 308–309
intrinsic vs. extrinsic motivation 20
investment
and labor 101–103
and profit 334
"invisible girlfriend" 196–197
invisible hand 276, 296, 297
Iron Curtain, new 240–241
isolationism, Russia 240
Italian vs. English schools
measurement of income
inequality 82–85
Italy 28, 54–55, 375

Jagger, M. 62
Jain, S. 120
Japan 157, 194, 228, 306
Jaruzelski, W. 360
Jensen, S. 119
Jisheng, Y. 210–212, 213–216
job-automatization and robotics
196–198
Jomo, K. S. and Popov, V. 373, 375
Judt, T. 354

Kafka, F.: *Diaries* 431, 436–437
Kant, I. 321–322, 403, 405
Kenya 74–75, 368
Keynes, J. M. 79, 80, 153, 154–155
and Marx 332–334
Khodorkovsky, M. 142
Khrushchev, N. 377, 390
Klaus, V. 62
kleptocracies vs. illiberal
democracies 57–59
Knight, F. 276
knowledge creation, domestic and
international 73–75
Kolakowski, L. 154, 312, 320, 363,
364
Kornai, J. 347
Kristol, I. and Himmelfarb, G. 276
Krueger, A. 120, 326
Krugman, P. 33
Kun, B. 368
Kuper, S. 428, 430
Kuznets, S. 256, 374

labor
and capital *see* capital and labor
and definition of wealth
141–142, 145, 146
division of 283
forced 251
"guard labor" 327
"human capital wealth"
accounting 156–157
and import substitution, Russia
229–230, 236–237

470

INDEX

inegalitarian policies 152
job-automatization and robotics
  196–198
productive and unproductive
  325–327
productivity of 257
"reserve army of labor" 334
temporary migrant 91
see also wages; worker–owners;
  workers
labor-managed/self-managed
  enterprises (SMEs) 344–346,
  367–368
  inefficiency of 349–350,
    351–352
  power structure and soft-budget
    constraint 347–350
lack of affinity and welfare state 90
Lakićević, D. 37–38
Lakner, C. 187
Landes, D. 264
landholding peasants 261, 262
landlords
  capitalists and workers 299–300,
    304, 308–309
  slave-holding 292–294
Latin America 10, 98, 117, 159,
  185, 258
  Brazil 128, 156, 236
  Venezuela 325–326
Le Père Goriot (Balzac) 168, 169,
  174, 175
left
  -right wing relationship 62
  paleo-left agenda 43–46
legal/formal equality 95, 96, 97
Legutko, R. 412
Lenin, V. 209, 212, 341–343, 363,
  364
Lerner, A. 332
"liberal capitalism" /"liberal
  democracy", crisis of
  190–192
liberals, political discussions with
  420–421

life expectancy
  changes in 251
  in HDI 406
Lindbeck, A. 32–33
Lindert, P. 90
  and Williamson, J. 301
List, F. 228, 275
literature: authenticity problem
  431–432, 436–437
literature and inequality 166–170
  bourgeois society 171–173
  forms of wealth acquisition
    174–176
Liu, G. M. 274–276
long-term vs. short-term
  perspectives on capitalism
  333–334
Louis Napoleon 328, 331
Louis-Philippe regime (1830–1848),
  France 329–330
Lowrey, A. 184, 186
Lukács, J. 171–173, 363
Luxembourg Income Study 108
luxury consumption 153–155
Lyons, N. S. 412

Machiavelli, N. 64–65
McLean, M. and Hopkins, M. 119
Maddison, A. 145, 146, 218, 249,
  253, 266, 267
magical thinking
  degrowth as 6–9, 10
  doughnut economics 19–21
Malthus, T. 303–304
Mandeville, B. 154
manufacturing
  agriculture vs. 255–256,
    261–263
  to service sector 86
Mao Zedong 143, 144, 202, 210,
  211–112, 213–214, 217,
  218–219, 361
  Little Red Book 199–200
marginal utility 82–83
Marić, M. 358

471

INDEX

marriage and wealth acquisition 166–168, 171
inheritance and swindle 174–176
Marshall, A. 115, 116, 403
Marx, K./Marxism 61, 252, 367, 398, 431
  in America 335–337
  and Balzac 168, 171
  concept of capital 258–260
  counterfactual approach to influence of 311–314
  definition of capitalism 323, 324
  definition of communism 415
  definition of economics 115, 117
  income inequality under capitalism 318–320
  influence in social sciences 315–317
  and Keynes 332–334
  luxury consumption 154
  material abundance in communist societies 22–23
  material incentives 402
  neo-Marxist perspective on globalization 183, 185
  post-Marist theory and destruction of communist regimes 378–380
  productive and unproductive labor 325–327
  and Smith 275, 282, 283
  surplus value 257
  and Tocqueville 328–331
mass education 86–87
material abundance see abundance
material net product 325–326
Mayo, D. 134
mean incomes
  differences between countries 26, 127, 131–132, 135–137
  global 4, 5
  interpersonal inequality 299, 300
means of production 258, 316–317, 319
media 413

Anglo-American 430
local language 429
Mercader, R. 370
mercantilism 288
  and trade blocs 187–189
merit/meritocracy 55–56, 97, 286
methodological nationalism 388–389
Mexico 369–370, 371
Mićunović, V. 390
middle class/bourgeoisie
  China 205
  comprador intelligentsia 73–75, 183
  France (1830–1848) 329–330
  and globalization 185, 187
  literature and inequality 171–173
  red 357–359, 426
  Third World 368
  US 336
Middle East 120
  Saudi Arabian oil wealth 157
migration 25–27
  and citizenship premium 128–129
  and civil conflicts 40–42
  economic positives and negatives 31–33
  and global inequality 138, 139–140
  and global progressive (GP) perspective 48
  globalization thesis 181
  into Eastern European countries 381, 382–383
  into Europe 28–30
  reduced groundedness and political participation 132–133
  reduction and foreign aid 134
  and trade: substitutes vs. complements 34–36
  and welfare state 32–33, 90–91, 129

472

INDEX

worlds of day and night 37–39
Mijatović, B. 261
military power/spending, USSR 373, 374, 379
Mill, J. 305
Milošević, S. 346, 385
Mishra, P. 254
Mobuto, S. S. 58
"modest" standards of living 8
monopoly and wealth 148
Montenegro 58, 66
Montesquieu 17
morality
financialization and amorality: globalization thesis 181
luxury consumption and wealth inequality 153–155
role in institutions 400–401
Moyn, S. 119

Naipaul, V.S. 38, 223–224
Nash, J. 321–322
nation-state, suboptimality of 138–140
national accounts/system of national accounts (SNA) 256–257, 326
and concept of capital 258, 259
socialist countries 325–326
national grievances, in secession 384–385
national level issues 49–50
nationalism
and collapse of Soviet Union 383, 384–385, 386–387
methodological 388–389
political discussions 420
NATO 239, 240, 391
"natural" inequality 397–398
natural resources and "human capital wealth" accounting 156–157
Navigation Act, England 274, 288
needs
Basic Needs approach 50

satisfaction of 23
social 92–94
neoclassical definition of capitalism 258
neoclassical definition of economics 115, 116
neoliberal plutocracy 45
neoliberalism 410–411, 413–414
Putin 233
Trump 68–69
Netherlands 285, 413
and Mali 134–137
New Economic Policy (NEP)
China 203–206, 343
USSR 341–343
New International Economic Order (NIEO) 50, 119
Nigeria 14, 26
non-exemplary lives 395–396
non-Western thinkers 254
Nordhaus, W. D. and DeLong, B. 145, 146
North Korea and Belgium: sovereignty vs. income 239–240
North–South European wage divergence 264–265
North/Center–South relationship
climate change and global inequality 16–18
disarticulation 183–186
knowledge creation and financial resources 73–75
Norway: climate policy hypocrisy 13–15

Obama, B. 368
October Revolution see Russia
OECD countries 108, 373–374
Offer, A. 89
Olson, M. 69
online work 256
Opium Wars (1840s) 13, 117, 248
optimal currency area/economic policy 112

INDEX

Orbán, V. 57
others
  cultures 305
  needs of self and 92–94
  wealth acquisition through
    activities benefiting 149–150
Ottoman Empire 266–267, 278,
  378, 381
  and Eastern Roman Empire
    245–247
Oxfam report 158–162, 163

paleo-left agenda 43–46
Pareto, V. 173, 302
peasantry
  plight of late industrializers
    261–263
  post-Revolutionary France 331
pensions *see* welfare
Pessoa, F. 397–8
philanthropic activities 149, 150,
  152
philosophical defence of equality 84
physiocrats 255–256, 286
Picasso, P. 370
Piketty, T. 163, 168, 171, 316,
  322–323, 324, 374
Pinker, S. 249
Plato 403, 407, 427
plutocracy 45, 83–84
Pogge, T. 129, 250–251
Poland 61, 164, 379, 382
political capitalism 286–287
political connections and wealth
  147–148
political discussions, futility of
  419–421
political economy, role of 306
political effects of inequality within
  nations 81, 83–84
political equality 44–45
political lobbying and wealth 148,
  326
  influence of capitalist groups
    284–286

political participation and
  groundedness 131, 132–133
political parties 261
political position and wealth 147
political role of capitalists 282
politics
  comprador intelligentsia 73–75
  and "existential" equality 97
  global inequality studies
    120–121
  global progressiveness 47–50
  how the world is ruled 54–56
  paleo-left agenda 43–46
  Revolutions: East and West
    60–63
  see also communism; democracy;
    dictatorship
Pomeranz, K. 264
Poor Laws 303–304
populist protests 336
poverty, global *see* global poverty
poverty and income redistribution,
  US 108–111
poverty line/PPP 3, 6, 94, 160,
  250–251
poverty studies 120
power
  USSR 378–379
  and wealth 142–143, 144,
    147–148, 162
Prados de la Escosura, L. 406
"presentism" 435
Prichett, L. 31–32
Pride and Prejudice (Austen)
  166–167, 171, 174, 175
"primitive accumulation" 282
Prisoner's dilemma 402, 403, 404
private life, changes in 431
private property *see* property
private and public schools 88
private sector, China 220–221,
  343
privatization
  China 221
  Russia 226, 232, 388–389

474

INDEX

pro-growth/pro-equality and
  paleo-left agenda 43–45
production and consumption 317,
  318–320
productive and unproductive labor
  325–327
profit
  and investment 334
  rate of 285
  and wages 300, 308, 310, 317
property 322, 330, 331, 335, 340
  intellectual property rights 49
  limiting power of property
    owners 322–323
  and slavery 289–290
Protestantism 153
Putin, V. 57, 58, 66, 389
  neoliberalism 233
  possible goals 239–242
  and Yeltsin 223, 225, 226,
    231–232, 234, 377

Quesnay, F. 255, 270
quota system of immigration 30

randomized controlled trials (RCTs)
  74–75
Rasmussen, D. 270–273
rationing 8, 10, 11
  USSR/Russia 232–233
Ravallion, M. 249
Rawls, J. 84, 97, 129
Raworth, K. 10, 19–21
Rawski, T. 217
real and relative income differences
  124–125
real and relative needs 92–93
real wage 300
red bourgeoisie 357–359, 426
religion
  communism as secular 338–340
  Protestant ethic 153
  Smith 282–383
    and Hume 272–273
  see also magical thinking

rent
  agricultural ground 255–256
  see also citizenship and income
Renzi, M. 28
representative agent, role of 316
Republican communist parties, in
  secession 385–386
Revolutions: East and West 60–63
Ricardo, D. 79
  absence of equity-efficiency
    trade-off 308–310
  letters 303–307
Rivera, D. 370
Robbins, L. 116
Robinson, J. 332, 333, 334, 424,
  425
robotics 196–8
Rockefeller, J. D. 142
Roemer, J. 321–322, 324, 403,
  404
Rolland, R. 370
Roman Empire 267, 268, 269, 317,
  428
  Eastern 245–247
Romania 113, 120
Rosenvallon, P. 153
Roser, M. 249
Rostovtzeff, M. 245, 246, 264
Rousseau, J.-J. 93, 272
rule of law, demand for 388–389
Russia 57, 58–59, 65, 66
  circular economic history
    222–224, 231–232
  covid-related deaths 232
  economic prospects, short term
    231–234
  import substitution 228–230,
    235–238
  October Revolution 312, 313
    counterfactual alternative 262
  oligarchs 66, 142, 149, 225–227,
    388–389
  sanctions 228, 229, 232,
    233–234, 235, 242
  and US 225, 235, 429

475

INDEX

Russia (*cont.*)
  and West, possible objectives
    239–42
  see also Ukraine; USSR/Soviet
    Union; *specific leaders*

Saito, K. 24
Salmon, F. 158
sameness of people and accidents of
    birth 278–280
Sant'Anna, A. A. 373–374
  and Weller, L. 375
Sarkozy, F. 28
Saudi Arabian oil wealth 157
scarcity
  between capital and labor,
    relative 323–324
  freedom from 398–9
  "scarcity = ends" definition of
    economics 115, 116
Schengen visas 28
Schumpeter, J. 23–24, 79
"scientific" vs. "ideological"
    perspectives on capitalism
    333
Scott Fitzgerald, F. 169, 175
secessionism and collapse of
    federations 384–387
security personnel 327
self and other, needs of 92–94
self-awareness 278
self-deception and inequality
    296–298
self-interest 436
  vs. altruism 402–404, 405
  vs. sympathy/empathy 274,
    275–276, 279
self-managed (SME) enterprises *see*
    labor-managed/self-managed
    enterprises (SMEs)
Sen, A. 83, 319, 402, 404, 406,
    422–425
Serbia 58, 261
Serge, V. 369–372
Shachar, A. 129

shareholders and tax policies 88
shareholding workers 322,
    347–348
Shaviro, D. 168–169, 171, 174, 176
Shiller, R. 34–35
Simeon the Stylite 8
Simon, H. and Mayer, T. 104
Siqueiros, A. 370
Sismondi, J. C. L. de 304–305
skills
  higher education gap 86
  and migrant selection of countries
    90–91
  and wages 301
slavery
  in autocratic vs. democratic states
    289–290, 291–292
  day and night worlds 38
  Django Unchained (Tarantino)
    427
  and serfdom 253–254
  slave-owners and emancipation
    282, 291–295
  vs. abolitionism 275
Slezkine, Y. 358
Slim, C. 142, 148
Slobodian, Q. 119
Smith, A. 270–273
  colonialism 288–290
  definition of wealth 141–142,
    145, 146
  East India Company 13
  having cake and eating it too
    296–298
  and Hume 270–271, 272–273
  and Marx 275, 282, 283
  people, associations, and
    government policy 278–287
  reception in America 274–277
  self-interest 436
    vs. sympathy/empathy 274,
    275–276, 279
  slave-owners and emancipation
    282, 291–295
  socially acceptable needs 92

476

INDEX

stadial theory of development
115, 275
social activism 320
social class *see* class
social conditions and accidents of
birth 279–280
social democracy/democratic
socialism 89, 205, 311, 312,
318, 371, 374
"social fictions", inequality as
397–399
social insurance 89
social media 412, 413
social mobility 124, 129
in communist societies 339
social needs 92–94
social security *see entries beginning*
welfare
"social separatism" 90
social tables 301, 308–309
social transfers and taxation
108–111
socialism vs. communism, income
distribution under 318–319
solidaristic ethos 321–322
Solzhenitsyn, A. 385
sovereignty vs. income 239–240
Soviet Union *see* USSR/Soviet Union
Spain 41
Indignados' demonstrations and
Africans 38–39
Sraffa, P. and Dobb, M. 303,
424–425
stadial theory of development 115,
275
Stalin, J./Stalinism 65, 142–143,
208, 209, 211, 213, 226,
262, 361, 364, 370, 371,
377, 379
Stalinists, political discussions with
419–420
state, redistributive role of 319–320
state capitalism
China 203–206, 343
USSR 341–343

state-owned enterprises (SOEs),
China 219, 220
stationary society 23–24
Stendahl 169, 174
stock markets 203–204
Summers, L. 410
Suraska, W. 378–380
surplus value 257, 326
surrogate mothers 198
Swaim, B. 153
Sweden 108, 128, 129
sympathy/empathy vs. self-interest
274, 275–276, 279
Syrquin, M. 256
system of material balance 256–257
system of national accounts (SNA)
see national accounts

Tagore, R. 422–424, 425
tax 10, 11, 12, 44
agriculture vs. manufacturing
255
climate change reduction 139
and equalization of endowments
91
evasion and wealth acquisition
148
global progressive (GP)
perspective 49
high 86, 87
inheritance 88
luxury goods 155
pro-rich 373
reducing capital concentration 88
regressive transfer and
progressive transfer, foreign
aid 134–137
social transfers and 108–111
wealth 88, 154
technocratic political capitalism
52–53
technology
electronic currencies 19
electronic information 433–435
as exogenous shock 306

477

INDEX

technology (*cont.*)
global progressive (GP)
perspective 49
and globalization 105–106
historical comparisons of wealth
145–146
Industrial Revolution 264
job-automatization and robotics
196–198
and needs 23
and rise of inequality 373
Russia/USSR 228–230, 235–236
term limits 66
theft 326–327
Therborn, G. 95
Theroux, P. 183–184
Tinbergen, J. 86, 98
Tito, J. B. 355, 358, 360, 361
Tocqueville, A. de 141, 283
and Marx 328–331
Tolstoy, A. 370
Tolstoy, L. 167–168, 171, 172
Torańska, T. 358
trade blocs
globalization thesis 180
and mercantilism 187–189
trade unions
activism 320
affiliations 374
decline of 86, 106, 373, 375
labor-managed enterprises 348
Yugoslavia and France 352
see also workers' associations
trade/free trade
and migration 31–32, 34–36
vs. protectionism 274, 275
and war 247–248
"tragedy of the commons" 321–322
transcending capitalism 321–324
transition to capitalism
Coase theorem and
methodological nationalism
388–389
democracy of convenience not
choice 381–383

secessionism and collapse of
federations 384–387
Trump and Gorbachev 390–392
transportation 256
air 11–12
Trollope, A. 169, 174
Trotsky, L. 363–365, 369–370
Trower, H. 303, 304–305, 306
Trump, D. 152, 187, 315, 336
different angle on 70–72
and Gorbachev 390–392
stock market 203
as ultimate triumph of
neoliberalism 68–69
Turkey 28, 57, 66, 120
and EU 114
Tymoshenko, Y. 30

Ukraine 30, 386
Russian war 225, 231, 233, 306,
239
unemployment 198
cyclical 334
Yugoslavia 344

United Nations (UN) 46, 49, 406
unproductive labor 325–327
US
African American and white
populations 90
Black Lives Matter 7, 410
and China 117, 118, 203,
208–209, 210–211, 240
citizenship premium 128, 129
communist threat 375
companies, structural and
technological change in
104–107
democracy vs. dictatorship
51–52
domestic and global poverty
183–185
English language and American
solipsism 428–430
and EU28 compared 113

478

INDEX

Gilded Age writers 169, 171,
174–175
inequality "exceptionalism"
108–111
inequality and growth 80–81
migration 26, 132
per capita income growth 335
across income distribution *44*
"robber barons" 226, 388
and Russia 225, 235, 429
sovereignty vs. income 240
wealth measurement issues 142,
162, 163–165
zero net wealth households 158,
160, 165
see also America/American;
specific individuals
US dollar
poverty line 3, 6, 94, 160,
250–251
World Bank wealth accounting
156
USSR/Soviet Union
bureaucracy 360–361, 377, 378
collectivization 251, 261
dissolution of 374, 378–380,
382–383, 384–387, 388–389
industrialization 235–236,
262–263
international influence of
373–375
and liberal capitalism 190, 191
New Economic Policy (NEP) and
state capitalism 341–343
see also Russia; *specific countries
and individuals*
Utopia and money 415–418

values system, change in 402, 404
van der Weide, R. and Milanovic,
B. 80–81
van Parijs, P. 428
van Zanden, J.-L.
et al. 250
and Milanovic, B. 250

Vanek, J. 345
Venezuela 325–326
Vidal, G. 70
violence, national liberation
movements and 366–367
Vries, P. 252

wages 259, 261, 264–265,
300–301, 308, 309, 336
equalization/equal country
incomes 34–35
inequality and income inequality
studies 98–100
Ward, B. 345
wars
globalization thesis 180
and trade 247–248
Yugoslavia 426–427
Washington consensus 410
wealth accounting 156–157
wealth inequality
Davos 147, 150, 151–152, 158
and luxury consumption 153–155
measurement issues 163–165
historical comparisons
141–144, 145–146
income and consumption
158–162
World Bank wealth accounting
156–157
modes of wealth acquisition and
147–150
Weber, M. 150, 153, 323, 324
Weber, R. 316
Weber, S. 222
Weingast, B. 292
welfare policies
in communist/socialist countries
164–165
Poor Laws 303–304
Russia 232
Sweden, US and Germany
108–111
welfare state
in age of globalization 89–91

479

INDEX

welfare state (*cont.*)
  and citizenship 131
  and migration 32–33, 90–91, 129
Wenar, L. 415
West
  Cultural Revolution 60–63
  globalization thesis 179–180
  influence of USSR on 373–375
  relations with Russia 239–242
  return to mercantilism and trade
    blocs 187–189
West, C. 410
Weulersse, G. 255
Wilde, O. 51, 52
Williamson, J. 411
Wolff, E. 158, 163, 164, 203
Wooton, D. 297–298
worker–owners/self-employed 258,
    259–260, 301
workers
  alienation 320
  capitalists and landlords
    299–300, 304, 308–309
  shareholding 322, 347–348
  see also labor
workers' associations 320
  skepticism towards 283–284
  see also trade unions
World Bank 49, 55–6, 120–121,
    160, 239, 388
  neoliberalism 410–411
  wealth accounting 156–157
world population 5
World Trade Organization 49
world-systems theory 252

The World Turned Upside Down
    (Jisheng) 210–212, 213–216
Wrong, M. 58

Xi Jinping 199–202, 217–218, 220,
    343

Yang, L. et al. 205, 220–221, 343
Yeltsin, B. 223, 225, 226, 231–232,
    234, 377, 385, 386
Yugoslavia 54–55, 112, 120, 208,
    352, 385
  civil war 354
  labor-managed enterprises/SMEs
    344–346, 347, 367–368
  red bourgeoisie 357–359, 426
  reminiscences 354–356, 426–427
  Tito 355, 358, 360, 361
  trade unions 352
  and US
    democracy vs. dictatorship
      51–52
    wealth data 164–165
  see also specific countries
Yumatle, C. 93

Zaire 58
Zakaria, F. 57
"zero growth"/"no-growth" 19, 20
zero net wealth households
    158–160, 161, 164, 165
"Zhang Zeminism" 205–6
Zubarevich, N. 222–223
Zubok, V. 384
Zweig, S. 335–336, 370